Phillip Pappas

Word 97 One Step at a Time

Word 97 One Step at a Time

Trudi Reisner

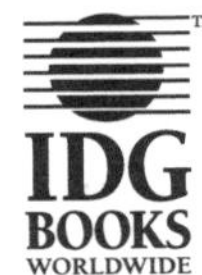

IDG Books Worldwide, Inc.

An International Data Group Company

FOSTER CITY, CA · CHICAGO, IL · INDIANAPOLIS, IN · SOUTHLAKE, TX

Word 97 One Step at a Time

Published by
IDG Books Worldwide, Inc.
An International Data Group Company
919 E. Hillsdale Blvd., Suite 400
Foster City, CA 94404
`http://www.idgbooks.com` (IDG Books Worldwide Web site)

Library of Congress Catalog Card No.: 97-76686

ISBN: 0-7645-3129-8

Printed in the United States of America

10 9 8 7 6 5 4 3

1E/QR/QU/ZY/IN

Distributed in the United States by IDG Books Worldwide, Inc.

Distributed by Macmillan Canada for Canada; by Transworld Publishers Limited in the United Kingdom; by IDG Norge Books for Norway; by IDG Sweden Books for Sweden; by Woodslane Pty. Ltd. for Australia; by Woodslane Enterprises Ltd. for New Zealand; by Longman Singapore Publishers Ltd. for Singapore, Malaysia, Thailand, and Indonesia; by Simron Pty. Ltd. for South Africa; by Toppan Company Ltd. for Japan; by Distribuidora Cuspide for Argentina; by Livraria Cultura for Brazil; by Ediciencia S.A. for Ecuador; by Addison-Wesley Publishing Company for Korea; by Ediciones ZETA S.C.R. Ltda. for Peru; by WS Computer Publishing Corporation, Inc., for the Philippines; by Unalis Corporation for Taiwan; by Contemporanea de Ediciones for Venezuela; by Computer Book & Magazine Store for Puerto Rico; by Express Computer Distributors for the Caribbean and West Indies. Authorized Sales Agent: Anthony Rudkin Associates for the Middle East and North Africa.

For general information on IDG Books Worldwide's books in the U.S., please call our Consumer Customer Service department at 800-762-2974. For reseller information, including discounts and premium sales, please call our Reseller Customer Service department at 800-434-3422.

For information on where to purchase IDG Books Worldwide's books outside the U.S., please contact our International Sales department at 650-655-3200 or fax 650-655-3295.

For information on foreign language translations, please contact our Foreign & Subsidiary Rights department at 650-655-3021 or fax 650-655-3281.

For sales inquiries and special prices for bulk quantities, please contact our Sales department at 650-655-3200 or write to the address above.

For information on using IDG Books Worldwide's books in the classroom or for ordering examination copies, please contact our Educational Sales department at 800-434-2086 or fax 817-251-8174.

For press review copies, author interviews, or other publicity information, please contact our Public Relations department at 650-655-3000 or fax 650-655-3299.

For authorization to photocopy items for corporate, personal, or educational use, please contact Copyright Clearance Center,
222 Rosewood Drive, Danvers, MA 01923, or fax 978-750-4470.

PREFACE

Welcome to *Word 97 One Step at a Time*. This book is part of a unique new series from IDG Books Worldwide, Inc. Our goal with this series is to give you a personal training book to help you with every step of learning the many features of software such as Word 97.

Your *One Step at a Time* book has been designed to support your learning in the following ways:

- Lessons are paced to present small, manageable chunks of information so you never feel you're in over your head. You are always prepared for each step you're asked to take.
- You learn Word 97 by doing; every lesson is packed with hands-on examples and procedures.
- You are told at the start of each lesson what materials you'll need to do the lesson, and how much time to set aside to complete it.
- A CD-ROM with sample files accompanies this book, so you can begin working with typical business and personal documents right from the first page.

WHAT IS MICROSOFT WORD?

Microsoft Word is the top-selling word processing program in the world. You could create your documents on a typewriter, but Word makes writing, editing, and printing easier. You can use it to prepare professional-looking letters, reports, tables, memos, flyers, and much more. You can use Word to create almost anything that involves text.

In addition to processing text, Microsoft Word includes easy methods to customize character and paragraph formats and to incorporate graphic elements into a document. You can check grammar and spelling, and add graphic images, lines, boxes, and shading to text to create professional-looking documents. You can also combine text, pictures, graphics, spreadsheet tables, and charts in the same document, and then see onscreen how the page will look when it is printed.

You can buy Word 97 as a stand-alone product or as part of a suite of programs called Microsoft Office. Office contains Word and several other programs that complement one another, such as a spreadsheet (Excel), presentation (PowerPoint), and personal information manager program (Outlook).

Before you can start Word, you must install it on your hard disk. If Word is installed, it appears in your Windows Programs menu. The exact procedure for installation depends on whether you purchased the CD-ROM or diskette version of the program, and whether you bought it as part of the Microsoft Office suite or as a separate program. For installation instructions, refer to Appendix A.

WHO SHOULD READ THIS BOOK?

Word 97 One Step at a Time is for people who have only a basic knowledge of computers and have never used Word 97. We assume that you understand rudimentary computer skills, such as turning on a computer, using a mouse and keyboard, and the like. However, we have provided detailed steps for each procedure covered so even readers with minimal knowledge will be comfortable working through these lessons.

If you are new to Windows itself, we have provided some Windows basics in Lesson 1 to help you. If you are already comfortable with Windows, you can skip over the Windows basics in that lesson and move on to the sections that teach you the various parts of Word 97.

If you have used Word, you can read only those sections that relate to the features you want to learn. Or you can start from Lesson 1 and proceed in a linear fashion through the entire book (recommended if you consider yourself a rank beginner).

SPECIAL ELEMENTS TO HELP YOU LEARN

The designers of this series thought long and hard about how people learn. They came up with some features that are designed to help you feel in control of your learning, yet challenged in a way that keeps you interested. Every lesson has a consistent structure so you can quickly become comfortable using all the following elements:

- **Stopwatch** Because the best way to learn is to complete each lesson without interruption, we've provided a Stopwatch symbol at the beginning of each lesson. This stopwatch tells you approximately how much time to set aside to work through the lesson.
- **Goals** The goals of each lesson are provided at the beginning, so you can anticipate what skills will be practiced.
- **Get Ready** This section explains what you will need to complete the steps in the lesson, and shows you an illustration of the document you will create in completing the exercises.
- **Visual Bonus** This is a one- or two-page collection of illustrations with callouts that help you understand a process, procedure, or element of a program more clearly.
- **Skills Challenge** Every lesson ends with a long exercise that incorporates all the skills you've learned in the individual exercises. The Skills Challenge is a little less explicit about the steps to take, so you are challenged to remember some of the details you've learned. This reinforces your learning and significantly improves your retention.
- **Bonus Questions** Sprinkled throughout the Skills Challenge section are Bonus Questions. If you want to push yourself a little harder, you can answer these questions and check Appendix C to see if you got them right.
- **Troubleshooting** This section appears near the end of each lesson and contains a table of troubleshooting questions and answers that address common mistakes or confusions that new users of Word often encounter.
- **Wrap Up** This section provides you with an overview of the skills you learned, as well as a suggested practice project you might try to get more experience with these skills.

Appendix B contains suggestions of real-world projects for you to work on to get further practice with Word. Projects, such as creating an up-to-date résumé or fax cover sheet, help you take that all-important step from learning to doing.

Finally, there are two elements you'll see sprinkled throughout the book, **Notes** and **Tips**.

Notes provide some background or detail that is helpful for you to know about the feature being discussed.

Tips offer reassurances or solutions to common problems.

HOW THIS BOOK IS ORGANIZED

Word 97 One Step at a Time has a simple structure.

The **Jump Start** gives you a brief introduction to Word by having you run through some typical features and tools of the Word program, and giving you your first glimpse of the Word product.

Part I: Basic Training introduces you to the concepts of a Windows word processing product and the Word environment. You learn Word skills; how to create your first document; how to navigate around a document; and how to change the view of a document.

Part II: Getting Your Document in Shape teaches you how to edit, proofread, and format your Word documents. You learn all the basic editing commands you need to know; all about Word's proofing tools; how to enhance the appearance of your text; how to create lists, insert page numbering, and work with headers and footers; and how to use some Word formatting shortcuts.

Part III: Enhancing What You've Got shows you how to add pictures and organize information in your documents. The lessons walk you through inserting objects and WordArt, and creating a simple drawing; how to create columns; and how to create a table and an outline.

Part IV: Outputting Your Results covers how to print your documents, use mail merge, and make use of Word and the World Wide Web. You learn how to print documents, envelopes, and labels; how to set up mail merge to create form letters; how to work with Word and the World Wide Web; and how to use Word in conjunction with other Microsoft Office programs.

Finally, the four appendixes include information on installing Microsoft Word 97, practice projects, answers to bonus questions, and information about the CD-ROM's contents. You'll also find a glossary of terms, and a CD-ROM with sample files and the exclusive One Step at a Time On Demand software. See Appendix D for more information about the software.

CONVENTIONS USED IN THIS BOOK

It will help you use this book if you understand how we've dealt with a few, simple conventions:

- All exercises are based on default settings for all options. If you or someone else has changed the settings, you may get slightly different results.
- All illustrations in the book occur just after the relevant step or comment in the text. There is no need to search around for figure numbers, the visual reinforcement you need is always right where you need it.
- When we say "click" we mean the left mouse button unless stated otherwise.
- In numbered steps, actual text that you are to type is in **boldface**. Text that you are to select is in *italics*.
- You will be asked from time to time to open files located in the One Step folder. (In Lesson 1 you will learn how to install the folder from your CD-ROM drive to your computer). You will work in these files as you step through the exercises in a lesson. Simply locate the folder that corresponds to the lesson you're working on, and open the file from there. Each lesson folder also contains saved versions of these same files after all the exercises have been completed; these files start with the word "Result" to indicate final versions.

That's it! Sit back, relax, and enjoy your sessions with *Word 97 One Step at a Time.*

ACKNOWLEDGMENTS

My warmest thanks to one of the most talented and professional teams I've worked with. Special thanks to Ellen Camm, Acquisitions Editor, who gave me the opportunity to write this book; Cindy Putnam, my developmental editor, who tirelessly got the entire project into shape and kept her great sense of humor as she developed the content and gave excellent suggestions; and Maryann Brown, who technically reviewed the manuscript with great efficiency, thereby preventing any embarrassment. Also, many thanks to Tracy Brown, my copy editor, and the production staff for proofreading and producing the entire book.

Special thanks to Tom McCaffey, Marilyn Russell, and everyone at Real Help Communications, Inc. (http://www.realhelpcom.com) for creating the several thousand sound files required for the CD-ROMs in this series, under very aggressive deadlines.

CONTENTS AT A GLANCE

Preface ix

Acknowledgments xii

Jump Start 1

Part I: Basic Training 7

- Lesson 1: Meet Microsoft Word 9
- Lesson 2: Creating and Saving Documents 25
- Lesson 3: Moving Around a Document 47
- Lesson 4: Changing Views 57

Part II: Getting Your Document in Shape 69

- Lesson 5: Revising Text 71
- Lesson 6: Proofreading Text 87
- Lesson 7: Formatting Fonts and Paragraphs 99
- Lesson 8: Creating Lists, Headers, and Footers 121
- Lesson 9: Taking Shortcuts 135

Part III: Enhancing What You've Got 151

- Lesson 10: Shaping Up with Graphics 153
- Lesson 11: Creating Columns 171
- Lesson 12: Organizing Information with Tables, Outlines, and Organization Charts 185

Part IV: Outputting Your Results 211

- Lesson 13: Printing Your Word Document 213
- Lesson 14: Working with Mail Merge 227
- Lesson 15: Using Word to Create a Web Page 243
- Lesson 16: Integrating Other Microsoft Office Applications 261

Appendixes

- Appendix A: Installing Microsoft Word 97 279
- Appendix B: Practice Projects 285
- Appendix C: Answers to Bonus Questions 293
- Appendix D: What's on the CD-ROM 303

Glossary 309

Index 313

CONTENTS

Preface ix

Acknowledgments xii

Part I: Basic Training 7

Jump Start 1

- Get Ready 2
- Opening Microsoft Word 2
- Entering text 3
- Editing text 3
- Formatting Text 4
- Printing a Document 5
- Saving a Document 5
- Wrap Up 6

Lesson 1: Meet Microsoft Word 9

- Get Ready 10
  - Creating folders 10
- The Basics 11
  - Opening Microsoft Word 11
- Using Menus 13
  - Working with the menu bar 14
  - Exploring shortcut menus 14
- Using Toolbars 15
  - Using toolbars 17
- Help! 18
  - Getting help 19
- Exiting the Program 20
  - Exiting Microsoft Word 20
- Skills Challenge: Exploring the Word Program 21
- Troubleshooting 22
- Wrap Up 23

Lesson 2: Creating and Saving Documents 25

- Get Ready 26
- Creating Your First Document 26
  - Entering the current date 27
  - Entering text 28
  - Separating paragraphs 30
  - Combining paragraphs 31
  - Inserting text 31
  - Overwriting text 32
- Saving, Closing, and Opening Word Documents 34
  - Saving a Word document 35
  - Closing a Word document 37
  - Opening a Word document 38
- Using a Wizard to Create a Document 40
  - Creating a Word document 40
- Skills Challenge: Creating a Word Document 43
- Troubleshooting 44
- Wrap Up 45

Lesson 3: Moving Around a Document 47

- Get Ready 48
- Getting from Here to There 48
  - Moving around your document 49
- Working with More than One Page 50

Inserting page breaks 51

Jumping to a specific page 52

Deleting page breaks 52

Skills Challenge: Navigating a Document 54

Troubleshooting 55

Wrap Up 56

Lesson 4: Changing Views 57

Get Ready 58

Changing Word Views 58

Switching to Page Layout view 59

Zooming the document 60

Displaying Online Layout view 61

Checking out Outline view 62

Skills Challenge: Switching Word Views 64

Skills Challenge: Switching Word Views 65

Troubleshooting 66

Wrap Up 67

Part II: Getting Your Document in Shape 69

Lesson 5: Revising Text 71

Get Ready 72

Making Changes to Text 72

Selecting text 73

Deleting text 75

Cutting and pasting text 76

Copying and pasting text 77

Using the Undo/Redo command 78

Dragging and dropping text 79

Finding and replacing text 80

Skills Challenge: Editing a Memo 83

Troubleshooting 84

Wrap Up 85

Lesson 6: Proofreading Text 87

Get Ready 88

Checking Your Document 88

Checking spelling 90

Checking grammar 92

Finding synonyms with the thesaurus 93

Skills Challenge: Proofing It All 95

Skills Challenge: Proofing It All 96

Troubleshooting 97

Wrap Up 98

Lesson 7: Formatting Fonts and Paragraphs 99

Get Ready 100

Changing Character Formatting 100

Adding bold, italics, and underline 101

Changing the font 102

Changing the font size 104

Setting Tabs and Margins 106

Setting tabs 106

Setting margins 109

Indenting, Aligning, and Spacing Text 111

Indenting text 112

Aligning text 113

Adjusting line spacing 114

Skills Challenge: Formatting a Memo 116

Troubleshooting 118

Wrap Up 119

Lesson 8: Creating Lists, Headers, and Footers 121

Get Ready 122

Creating Bulleted and Numbered Lists 122

Creating a bulleted list 122

Creating a numbered list 124

Numbering Pages 126

Numbering your pages 126

Creating Headers and Footers 127

Creating headers and footers 127

Formatting headers and footers 129

Skills Challenge: Creating a Laundry List 131

Troubleshooting 133

Wrap Up 134

Lesson 9: Taking Shortcuts 135

Get Ready 136

What Is a Style? 136

Applying a style 137

Viewing the contents of a style 138

Creating a style 139

Fast Formatting 141

Using the Repeat command 142

Copying formats 142

Templates and AutoText 143

Using a template 143

Creating AutoText 144

Applying AutoText 145

Skills Challenge: Taking Formatting Shortcuts 146

Troubleshooting 148

Wrap Up 149

Part III: Enhancing What You've Got 151

Lesson 10: Shaping Up with Graphics 153

Get Ready 154

Adding Objects 154

Inserting clip art 155

Adding WordArt 156

Drawing shapes and lines 157

Creating and modifying a 3-D shape 161

Working with Objects 162

Selecting objects 162

Moving objects 163

Resizing objects 164

Formatting Objects 165

Changing line styles 165

Changing colors and patterns 166

Skills Challenge: Creating a Simple Drawing 167

Troubleshooting 169

Wrap Up 170

Lesson 11: Creating Columns 171

Get Ready 172

Creating Columns 172

Creating columns 173

Editing columns 174

Adding section breaks 174

Adding Borders and Shading 177

Adding a border to a paragraph 177
Shading a paragraph 179
Skills Challenge: Creating a Simple Newsletter 180
Troubleshooting 182
Wrap Up 183
Lesson 12: Organizing Information with Tables, Outlines, and Organization Charts 185
Get Ready 186
Creating a Table 186
Inserting a table 186
Entering text in a cell 188
Selecting and aligning text 189
Changing fonts for text in a table 190
Rotating text in a table 190
Inserting and deleting rows and columns 191
Adjusting column width 194
Formatting a Table 194
Displaying gridlines 195
Using Table AutoFormat 195
Creating and Modifying an Outline 196
Creating an outline 198
Modifying an outline 200
Viewing outline headings 201
Numbering an outline 202
Creating an Organization Chart 203
Creating an organization chart 203
Changing an organization chart 205
Skills Challenge: Building an Order Form 206
Troubleshooting 209
Wrap Up 210
Part IV: Outputting Your Results 211
Lesson 13: Printing Your Word Document 213
Get Ready 214
Preparing to Print 214
Centering a page vertically 215
Previewing a document 216
Printing Your Document 218
Printing from the Print dialog box 218
Printing Envelopes and Labels 222
Printing an envelope 222
Printing a label 223
Skills Challenge: Printing a Report 224
Troubleshooting 225
Wrap Up 226
Lesson 14: Working with Mail Merge 227
Get Ready 228
What Is Mail Merge? 228
Setting Up Mail Merge 228
Creating the main document 229
Creating a data source 230
Entering names and addresses 232
Placing merge fields in your document 234
Merging the Document and Data 236
Viewing and checking a mail merge 236
Printing to a printer or document 237
Skills Challenge: Producing Form Letters 238

Troubleshooting 240

Wrap Up 242

Lesson 15: Using Word to Create a Web Page 243

Get Ready 244

Word and the Web 244

Converting a Word document in a Web page 245

Adding audio to your Web document 246

Adding video to your Web document 248

Viewing a Web page with Online Layout view 250

Sending a Web page to an FTP site 251

Browsing the Web 254

Creating Hyperlinks 255

Creating a hyperlink 255

Browsing through files that contain a hyperlink 257

Skills Challenge: Publishing a Word Document As a Web Page 257

Troubleshooting 259

Wrap Up 260

Lesson 16: Integrating Other Microsoft Office Applications 261

Get Ready 262

Sharing Microsoft Office Applications 262

Creating a hyperlink to move between Office documents 263

Copying and pasting between Office documents 264

Linking Office documents 265

Embedding Office documents 267

Inserting an Excel worksheet into a Word document 270

Inserting an Excel worksheet into a Word document 271

Inserting an Excel chart into a Word document 272

Opening Word files in Outlook 273

Skills Challenge: Sharing Information in Office Documents 275

Troubleshooting 277

Wrap Up 278

Appendix A: Installing Microsoft Word 97 279

Get Ready 280

Appendix B: Practice Projects 285

Project 1 286

Project 2 286

Project 3 287

Project 4 287

Project 5 288

Project 6 288

Project 7 289

Project 8 289

Project 9 290

Project 10 290

Project 11 291

Project 12 291

Appendix C: Answers to Bonus Questions 293

Lesson 1: Meet Microsoft Word 294

Lesson 2: Creating and Saving Documents 294

Lesson 3: Moving Around a Document 295

Lesson 4: Changing Views 295

Lesson 5: Revising Text 296

Lesson 6: Proofreading Text 297

Lesson 7: Formatting Fonts and Paragraphs 297

Lesson 8: Creating Lists, Headers, and Footers 298

Lesson 9: Taking Shortcuts 298

Lesson 10: Shaping Up with Graphics 299

Lesson 11: Creating Columns 299

Lesson 12: Organizing Information with Tables and Outlines 300

Lesson 13: Printing Your Word Document 300

Lesson 14: Working with Mail Merge 301

Lesson 15: Using Word to Create a Web Page 301

Lesson 16 302

Appendix D: What's on the CD-ROM 303

Using the One Step at a Time on-demand Interactive Software 304

Stopping the Program 307

Exiting the Program 307

Glossary 309

Index 313

Jump Start

GOALS

In this Jump Start, you learn the following skills:

- Opening Microsoft Word
- Entering text
- Editing text
- Formatting text
- Printing a document
- Saving a document

Get ready

GET READY

You're about to learn one of the most robust and popular word processing products on the market today—Microsoft Word 97. Your challenge is to learn how to use the key features of this program. To help you prepare for this challenge, we've included this Jump Start. Working through this section will familiarize you with the step-by-step structure of this book and give you a glimpse at key functions in Word 97.

Don't be concerned about remembering all the procedures or features you're about to see. You'll revisit each of them in more detail within the lessons that follow. Just work your way through these steps to get comfortable with the Word environment and the look and feel of the program.

For this Jump Start, you'll need to turn on your computer and have the Windows desktop on your screen (this usually appears automatically when you turn on your computer). Also, be sure that no other programs are open and running.

When you finish this tour, you'll have produced the document in the accompanying illustration.

My First Word Masterpiece

OPENING MICROSOFT WORD

The first step in working with Word is opening the program.

1. Click the Start button on the Windows taskbar.
2. Choose Programs from the Start menu.
3. Choose Microsoft Word from the Programs menu.

   Microsoft Word is now open.

ENTERING TEXT

In Word, you enter text to build a document such as a letter, memo, or report. Let's type some text in the document.

1. Type **My Word Masterpiece**.
2. Press Enter.

The accompanying illustration shows the text you typed in your document.

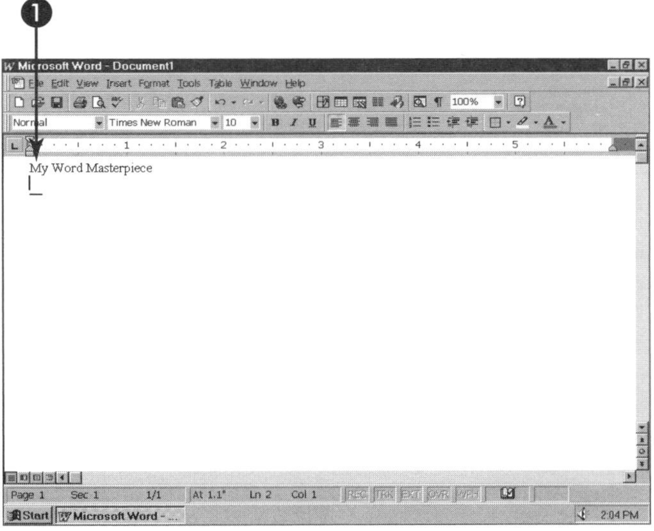

If you make a mistake when typing, you can delete text to make minor corrections. Use the Backspace key to delete text to the left of the insertion point. (The insertion point is the blinking vertical bar that marks where you last typed or edited text.) Use the Delete key to delete text to the right of the insertion point.

EDITING TEXT

After you enter text, you may want to change and correct what you've typed. Let's add text to the document and then delete text.

1. Click after the *y* in *My*.

You can place the insertion point by clicking the mouse pointer over the location you want to insert text or by using the arrow keys.

2. Press the spacebar.
3. Type **First Creative**.

By default, Word is in Insert mode. When Word is in Insert mode and you type text at the insertion point, the existing text moves to the right to make room for the new text.

Formatting text

4. Double-click the word *Creative*.
5. Press Delete.

The text is deleted. The remaining text moves up (or over) to fill in the gap. The edited text on your screen should look like the text in the accompanying illustration.

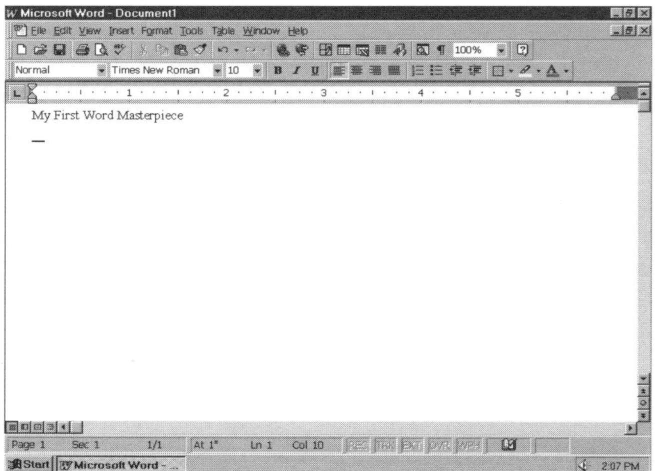

FORMATTING TEXT

You can polish your document by formatting the text. Word offers many formatting features, such as the capability to change the font, font size, or font style. Let's try them.

1. Click in the left margin next to *My First Word Masterpiece* to select the phrase.
2. Click the Format menu.
3. Choose Font. The Font dialog box opens.
4. In the Font list, use the scroll bar to find the font named Impact and click it.
5. In the Font Style list, click Bold.
6. In the Size list, use the scroll bar to locate 24 and click it.
7. In the Effects section, click in the Shadow checkbox.
8. Click OK.

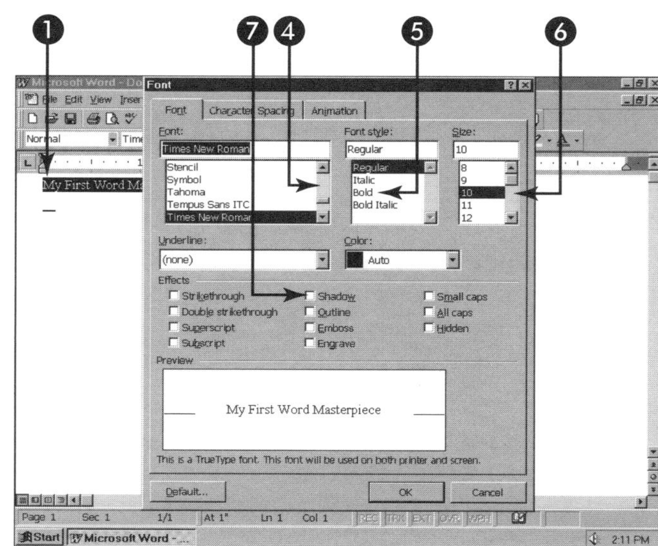

You'll frequently see dialog boxes in Word; you use them to choose options and settings for your documents. Typically, dialog boxes contain lists with scroll bars, lists that drop down when you click the arrow next to them (such as the Underline and Color choices in the Font dialog box), and checkboxes (such as the ones shown in the Effects section of the Font dialog box). Often, you'll see a preview. The preview shows you what would happen if you were to apply all the choices you've made. You can usually leave a dialog box without applying your choices by clicking Cancel.

9 Click anywhere in the document to deselect the text.

Your Word document should now look like the accompanying illustration.

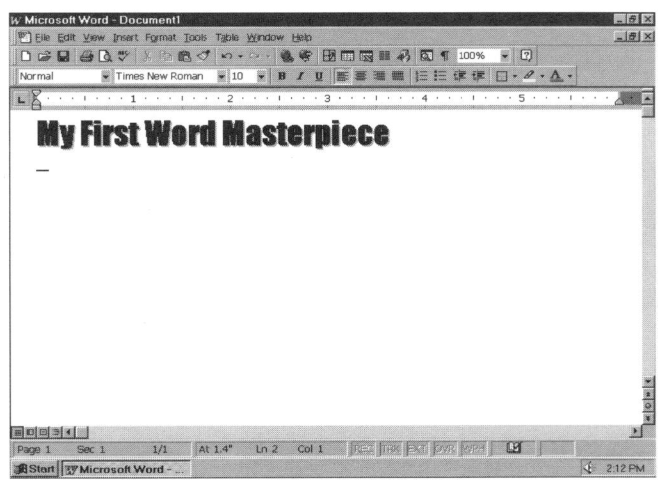

PRINTING A DOCUMENT

If you use the default print settings, you can print a Word document with one click of the mouse. You can also adjust the default settings easily to do more specific tasks, such as print a range of pages within your document, print multiple copies, or print in color.

Follow these easy steps to print your Word document. Also, be sure to put this masterpiece on your refrigerator door.

1 Choose the File menu.

2 Click Print. The Print dialog box opens.

3 Check the Name drop-down list to make sure your current printer is selected.

If your printer is not shown in the Name text box, click the Name drop-down arrow to see the available printers. If your printer is not listed there, refer to Lesson 13 or get some help from someone in your office or at home. Your Windows and printer documentation can also be helpful with this process.

4 Click the Number of Copies up arrow to specify two copies.

5 Click OK.

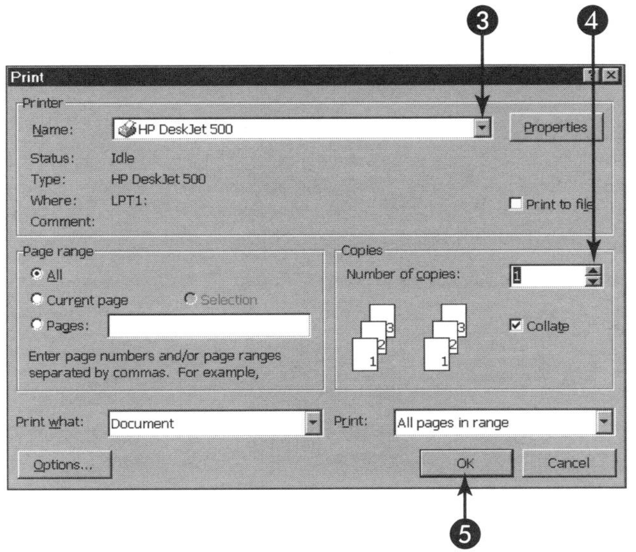

SAVING A DOCUMENT

Now that you've created your first Word masterpiece, why throw away all that hard work? Saving a document is a simple task, so let's try it.

1 Choose the File menu.

Wrap up

2. Click Save. The Save As dialog box opens.

   Word automatically creates a filename based on the first line of text in the document. We're going to replace this name.
3. In the File Name text box, type **Masterpc**.
4. Click the Save In drop-down arrow.
5. Click the (C:) drive.
6. Click the Create New Folder button (the third button over from the Save In text box).
7. In the New Folder Name text box, type your own name.
8. Click OK. The Save As dialog box reappears.
9. Click the Save button.
10. Choose the File menu.
11. Click Exit to close Word.

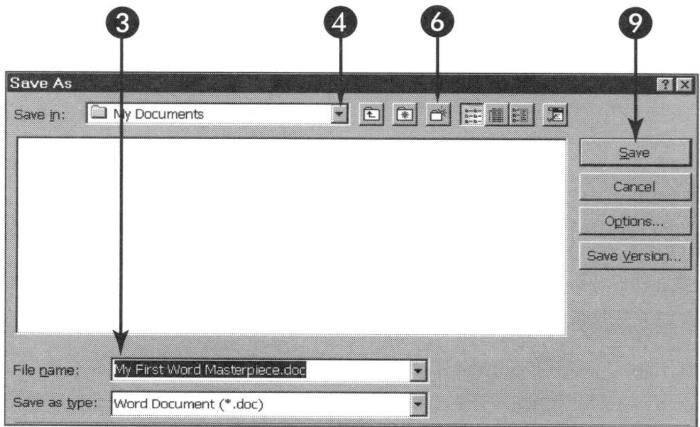

WRAP UP

You've now gone through several key operations used in Word, including the following tasks:

- Opening Word
- Entering text
- Editing text
- Formatting text
- Printing and saving files

While you were examining some of the tools and menus in Word, you got a sneak preview of the program. Now you know that performing tasks in Word is a simple matter of learning to use the tools, menus, and dialog boxes.

The lessons in this book give you a working knowledge of these features and much more so you can master the basic skills of Word 97.

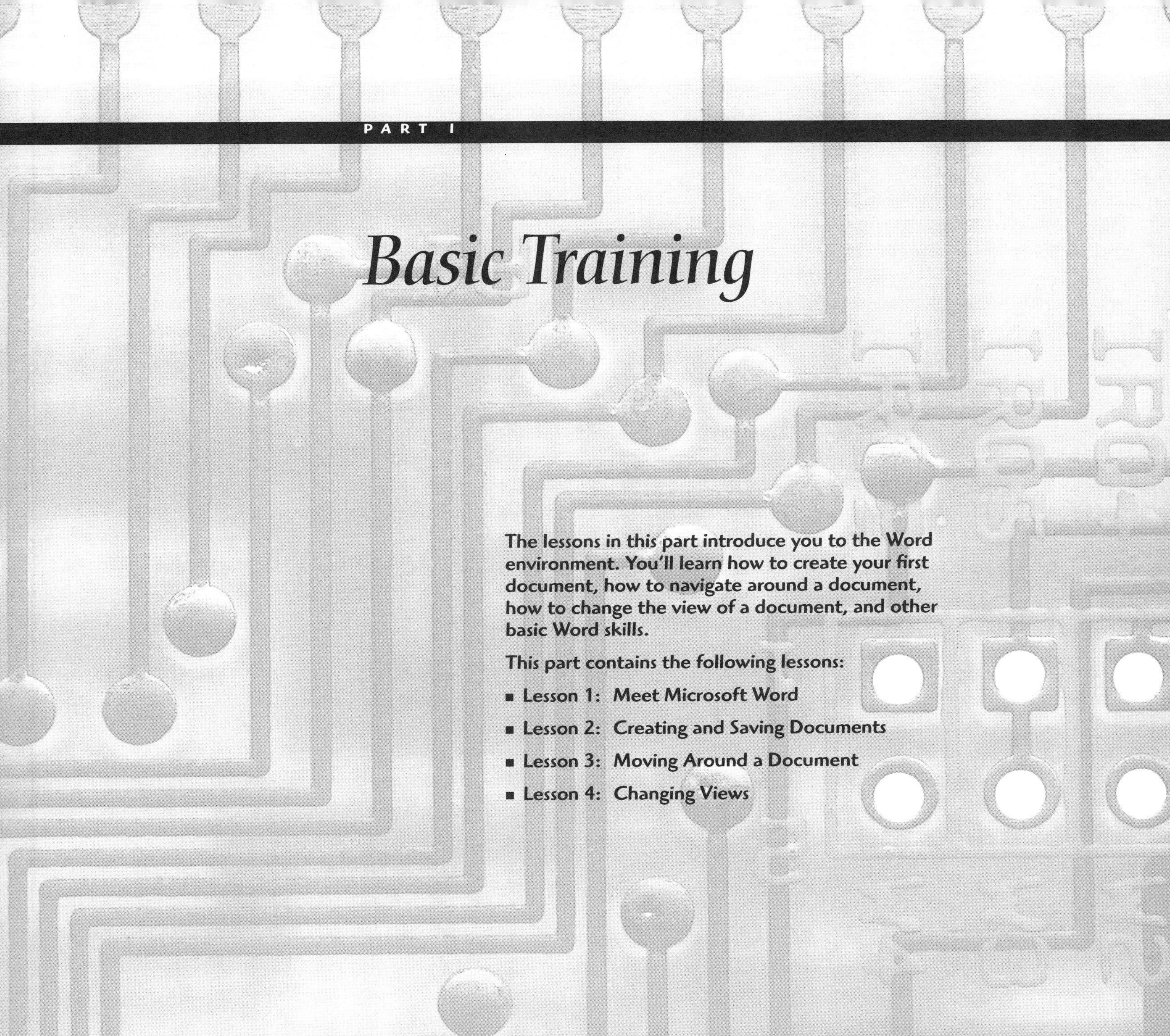

PART I

Basic Training

The lessons in this part introduce you to the Word environment. You'll learn how to create your first document, how to navigate around a document, how to change the view of a document, and other basic Word skills.

This part contains the following lessons:

- Lesson 1: Meet Microsoft Word
- Lesson 2: Creating and Saving Documents
- Lesson 3: Moving Around a Document
- Lesson 4: Changing Views

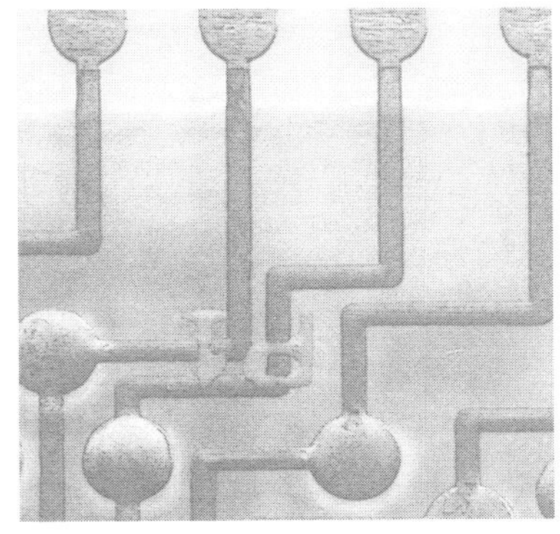

Meet Microsoft Word

GOALS

In this lesson, you learn the following skills:

- Creating folders
- Opening Microsoft Word
- Working with the menu bar
- Using shortcut menus
- Using toolbars
- Getting help
- Exiting Microsoft Word

Creating folders

GET READY

To complete this lesson's exercises, you need the accompanying CD-ROM, so you can create the One Step folder.

You will use the files EX01-1.DOC and EX02-2.DOC from the One Step folder.

When you've finished these exercises, you will be familiar with the elements of the Word window.

Creating folders

Generally, your computer works more efficiently with files located on the hard drive, rather than a floppy disk or CD-ROM drive. To make your work in this book easier, you will copy the exercise files from the accompanying CD-ROM into a folder on your hard drive. Then you can open and use the files from that folder as instructed in the exercises.

1. Double-click the My Computer icon on your desktop.
2. In the My Computer window, double-click the hard drive (C:).
3. Select the File menu.
4. Click New.
5. Choose Folder from the submenu.

   A new folder appears at the end of the list, with the name New Folder.
6. Type **One Step** to name the folder.
7. Press Enter.
8. Place the CD-ROM disc that accompanies this book into the CD-ROM drive.
9. In the My Computer window, double-click the CD-ROM icon to open the drive where you inserted the disc.
10. In the CD-ROM window, click the folder named *Exercise.*

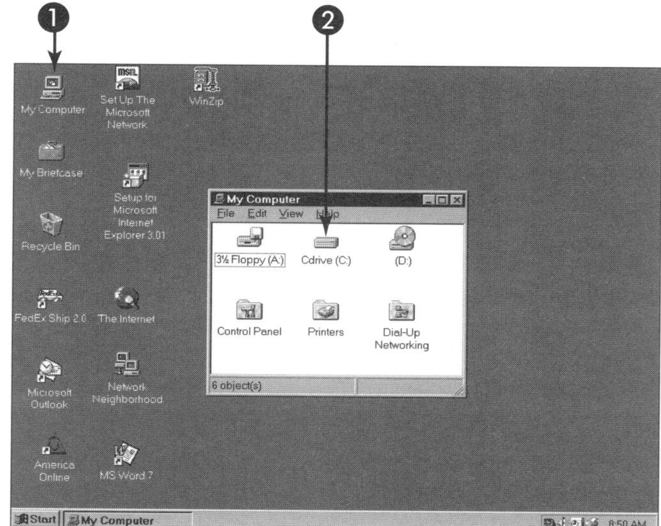

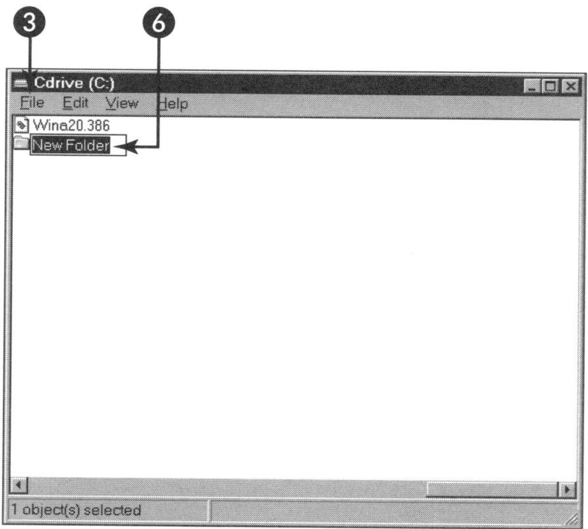

⓫ Point to the Exercise folder, hold down the left mouse button, and drag the folder from the CD-ROM window to the One Step folder you just created.

The One Step folder is highlighted while you hold the other folder over it, letting you know that if you release the mouse button, the item you're dragging will drop into the folder.

⓬ Release the mouse button.

⓭ Double-click the One Step folder.

All the exercise files are now located within this folder, and you can work with them from here.

⓮ Click the Close (X) button in the upper right corner of each window to close all the open windows on your desktop.

TRY OUT THE
INTERACTIVE TUTORIALS
ON YOUR CD!

THE BASICS

Starting Word is simple. When you turn on your computer and monitor, the Windows 95 desktop appears on your screen. You start Word from the Windows desktop.

In this book, we would like you to imagine you work for Whole Food, Inc., a fictional company that develops, manufactures, and markets whole foods for natural food supermarkets. Whole Food, Inc. has grown rapidly in recent years, and is now a medium-sized company with several departments including research and development, marketing, manufacturing, personnel, sales, and accounting.

As a member of Whole Food, Inc.'s marketing communications staff, you have just had your computer upgraded to run Windows 95, with a copy of Word 97 installed. Your first assignment is to become familiar with the basic control and help features of the program.

Opening Microsoft Word

In this exercise you learn how to start Microsoft Word. You can start Word as you would any Windows application by selecting it from the Start menu. Let's get started now by opening Microsoft Word.

Opening Microsoft Word

1. Click the Start button on the Windows taskbar.
2. Select Programs from the Start menu.

If you installed Microsoft Word as a standalone program, you will see Microsoft Word on the Programs menu. If you installed Microsoft Word as part of the Microsoft Office suite, you will see Microsoft Office on the Programs menu. Select Microsoft Office, and then select Microsoft Word.

3. Select Microsoft Word from the Programs menu.

   After a brief introductory screen, the Word window appears, as shown in the accompanying illustration.

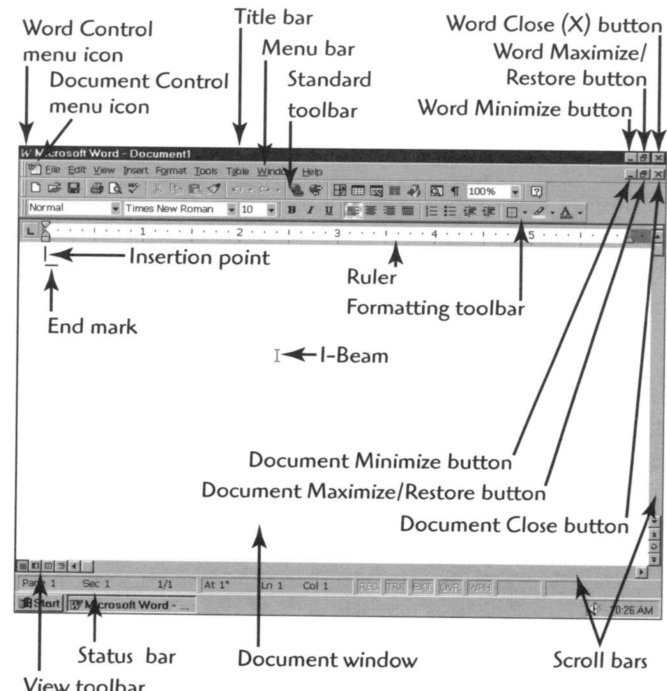

The document window contains a blank document, much like a blank piece of paper. You store your data in this document, or *file*. The title bar displays the file's name. Word calls the file Document1 until you save the file and give it a new name. Word increases the number in the Document1 title by one for each document you create during a session.

The insertion point is a flashing vertical bar that appears in the document window. Text that you type appears at the insertion point. A horizontal line at the end of the text area is called the *end mark*. When you move the mouse pointer inside the text area to the left of or above the end mark, the mouse pointer appears as an I-beam, a thin vertical icon in the shape of the letter I. You click the mouse pointer to position your insertion point.

The View toolbar at the bottom of the screen enables you to change views for a document. The Status bar contains the current page number, section number, page number and total page count, vertical and horizontal position of the insertion point, and other indicators that are dimmed until you perform certain tasks in Word.

The Document buttons are at the far right of the menu bar: Minimize, Maximize/Restore, and Close. To minimize the document window, click the Document Minimize button on the menu bar. The document shrinks to an icon with a title bar and Document buttons at the bottom of the Word window (just above the Status bar).

To maximize the document window, click the Document Maximize button in the document's title bar. The document window reopens.

A quick way to close a document is to click the Close (X) button. Another way to close a document is to double-click the Document Control menu icon.

The Word screen that you start out with in this book is set up with the default settings. These settings include the Standard toolbar, Formatting toolbar, ruler, and Normal view. If your screen doesn't look like the figure in this exercise, perform the following steps to change your settings: To display the Standard toolbar, right-click the toolbar that appears beneath the Menu bar. From the Toolbar shortcut menu, choose Standard. To display the Formatting toolbar, choose Formatting from the Toolbar shortcut menu. To display the ruler, select View ➢ Ruler. To switch to Normal view, select View ➢ Normal.

USING MENUS

The menu bar contains main menu commands. You select a menu command to perform operations such as saving a file, formatting text, or printing a document. The menu bar contains drop-down menus that are similar to a list of items on a restaurant menu. When you click a menu name, a list of commands drops down

When you select a command followed by an ellipsis (...), Word displays a dialog box. Some dialog boxes have more than one set of options, indicated by tabs at the top of the dialog box. You can display a different set of options by clicking a tab.

When you point to text or a graphic in Word and then click the right mouse button, you see a shortcut menu. This menu appears next to the text or graphic. Shortcut menus apply to the current situation and contain fewer commands than a menu in the menu bar. The commands on the shortcut menus vary, depending on the text or object you select in the document. You might find it quicker and easier to use a shortcut menu than to select commands from the menu bar and the drop-down menus.

Working with the menu bar

Word's menu bar is directly below the Word title bar. This menu bar gives you pull-down menus with Word commands. In this exercise you practice selecting menu commands.

1. To open the File menu, select File from the menu bar.

   The File menu opens and you see a list of commands.

2. Select the Open command from the File menu.

   Word opens the Open dialog box.

3. Click Cancel to close the dialog box.

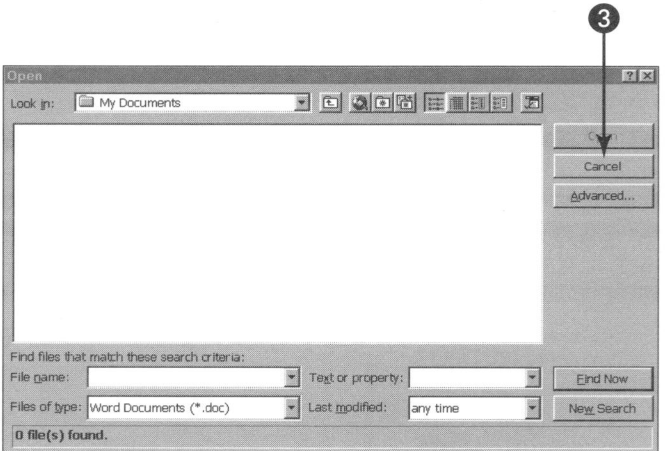

To close a menu without making a selection, press Esc or click anywhere outside of the menu.

You will learn and use many different menu commands during subsequent exercises in this book.

Exploring shortcut menus

Word's shortcut menus pop up when you point to text, a cell(s), or a graphic and click the right mouse button. A shortcut menu contains only those commands that pertain to the text, cell(s), or graphic you clicked. You might want to use a shortcut menu to quickly edit or format text, cells, or a picture. For this exercise, you will open the file EX01-1.DOC from the accompanying CD-ROM. Let's look at a shortcut menu for editing and formatting text.

1. Select the File menu.
2. Click Open.

Exploring shortcut menus

3. Double-click the One Step folder to select it.
4. Double-click EX01-1.DOC to open the file.
5. In the first sentence, double-click the word *most*.
6. Right-click the selected word.

   A shortcut menu with a list of commands for editing and formatting text appears.
7. Select Cut.

   The word *most* is cut from the document. Now let's close the document.
8. Click the document's Close (X) button to close the document.
9. Click No in the dialog box that appears.

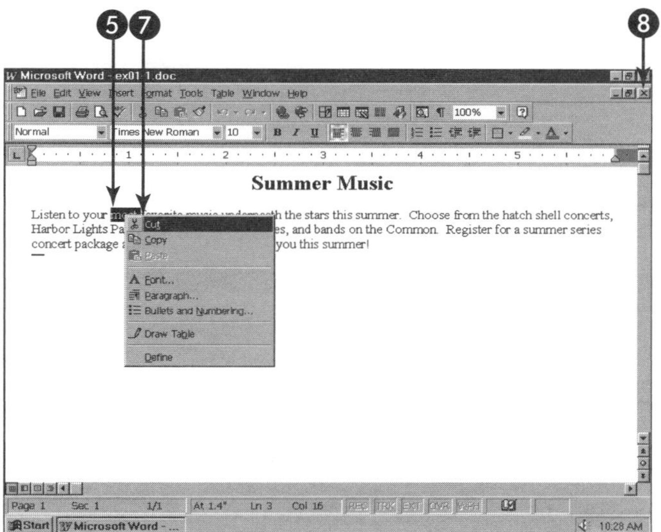

1

Meet Microsoft Word

USING TOOLBARS

A toolbar contains buttons that provide quick access to commands you use frequently. To perform some tasks, you can select a toolbar button instead of selecting a menu command. The Standard and Formatting toolbars are at the top of the document window. The View and Status toolbars are at the bottom of the screen to the left of the horizontal scroll bar.

Word ships with many different toolbars that appear automatically when you select various commands, or that you can customize to meet your particular requirements. You use these tools for drawing graphics, lines and borders, working with outlines, creating macros, and performing many other operations.

As you get more comfortable with Word, you will find that using the tools on the toolbar is a lot more efficient than selecting commands from the menus. Even though you will work with the default toolbars in this book, you can customize the toolbars to contain buttons for the features you use most frequently.

Exploring shortcut menus

VISUAL BONUS: THE WORD TOOLBARS AND THE STATUS BAR

The Standard and Formatting toolbars are two of the most important toolbars you use in Word. The Status bar is a visual aid you can use while working in Word. Checking the information about your document in the Status bar is just like looking in the rearview mirror of your car to check for other cars on the road.

The Standard toolbar

The Standard toolbar contains buttons for the most common Word commands. It is located at the top of the screen, just below the menu bar. If this toolbar doesn't appear on your screen, right-click the menu bar and select Standard from the Toolbar shortcut menu.

The Formatting toolbar

The Formatting toolbar contains tools for the most common formatting commands. It is located at the top of the screen, just below the Standard toolbar. If this toolbar doesn't appear

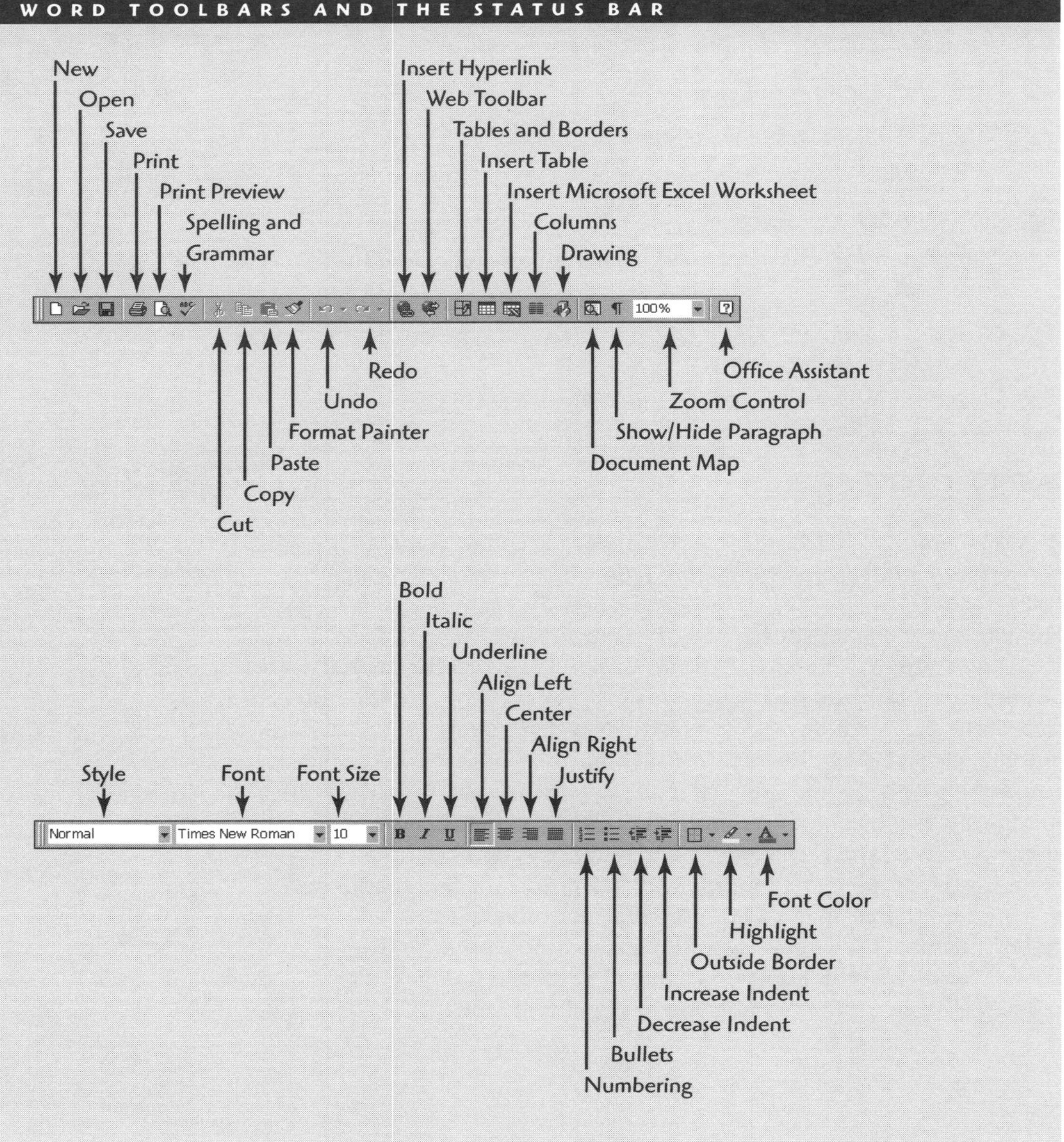

on your screen, right-click the menu bar and select Formatting from the Toolbar shortcut menu.

The Status bar

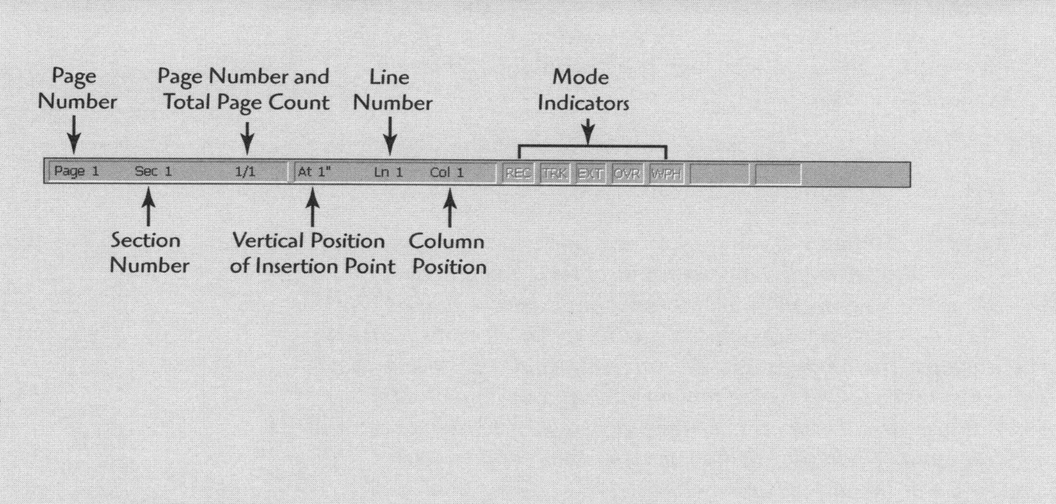

The Status bar shows you the current position of the insertion point in the document. It also indicates whether other tools (for example, overtype) are being used. It is located below the View toolbar and horizontal scroll bar.

Using toolbars

A toolbar enables you to select the most frequently used commands quickly. Word provides two default toolbars, the Standard and Formatting toolbars, in addition to several other toolbars. You click the buttons on a toolbar as shortcuts for executing commands. The Standard toolbar gives you the most common editing buttons and the Formatting toolbar offers buttons that help you format text quickly. This exercise shows you how to use buttons on a toolbar.

1. Point to the New button on the Standard toolbar.

   You see the button's name, New, in a yellow box near the button. This is called the ScreenTip feature. If you're unsure what a toolbar button does, leave the mouse pointer on the button for a second or two. Word will display the button name.

2. Click the New button.

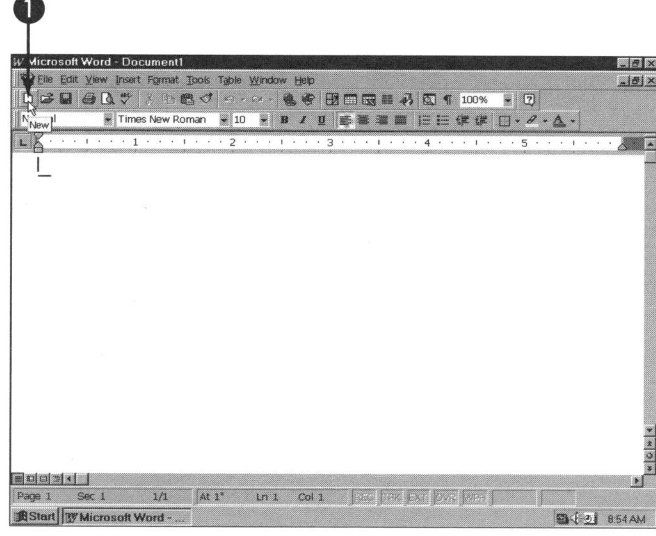

Using toolbars

Word opens a new document and displays Document2 in the title bar. This document covers (and hides) the preceding document. Each time you create a new document, Word gives it a generic name until you save the document and give it a name of your own.

3. Click the document's Close (X) button to close the document.

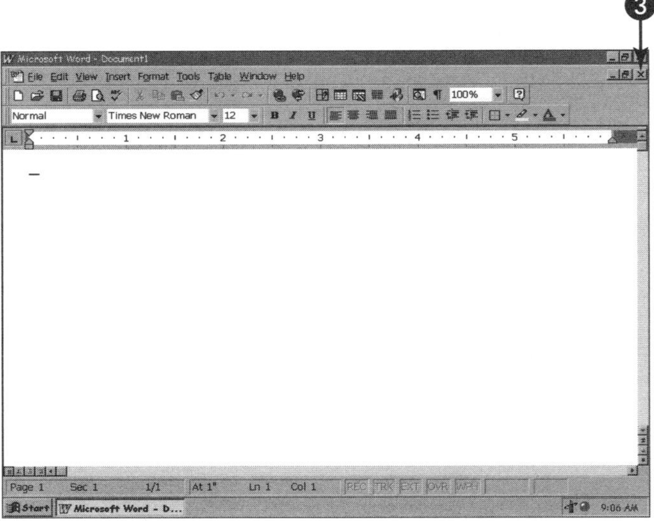

Sometimes you may want a tidier screen or you may want to display more rows of text. You can hide the toolbars to make more room onscreen. To hide a toolbar, right-click the toolbar. The Toolbar shortcut menu appears. The toolbars that are currently displayed have a check mark next to them. Choose the toolbar you want to hide and the toolbar disappears. To display a toolbar, right-click the menu bar or another toolbar. When the Toolbar shortcut menu appears, select the toolbar you want to display onscreen.

HELP!

Word makes sure that help is always there when you need it by giving you as much of it as you can handle. There are several ways of getting help:

- **Help menu with Help Contents and Index** At the right-end of the menu bar is the Help menu. Through the Help Contents and Index command, you can access extensive online documentation about various commands and procedures.
- **F1 key** (context-sensitive help) A more direct way to get help on a specific topic is through the F1 key, which opens the Help window in a context-sensitive way. *Context-sensitive* means that the help message applies to the current operation. Word displays relevant information about the most recently activated command, procedure, or window.
- **Shift+F1** (Help pointer) Another way to get context-sensitive help is to press Shift+F1, and then select a command. Instead of

executing the command, the program will display the Help window with the appropriate information.

- **Office Assistant** This is a quick way to search for help on a particular topic and find shortcuts in Word.

Getting help

When you run into trouble with a task you're performing, or you need more information on how to perform a task, you can get help from Word. There are many ways to get help; we will focus on Word's newest Help feature, the Office Assistant. This Help feature gives you step-by-step instructions and demonstrations while you work. Let's get some help on moving text.

1. Click the Office Assistant button on the Standard toolbar.

   The Office Assistant balloon appears. The Office Assistant enables you to search for help, get tips, and change Office Assistant options.

2. Type **move text** in the text box.
3. Click the Search button.

   The Office Assistant displays a list of help topics for moving text.

4. Click *See more.*
5. Click the topic called *Move or copy text and graphics.*

   A dialog box with a list of subtopics for moving text appears.

6. Click the topic *Move or copy text and graphics a short distance within a window.*

   A dialog box appears, containing steps for you to follow to move text.

7. Click the Close (X) button in the dialog box's title bar to close the Help dialog box.
8. Click the yellow light bulb in the Office Assistant window.

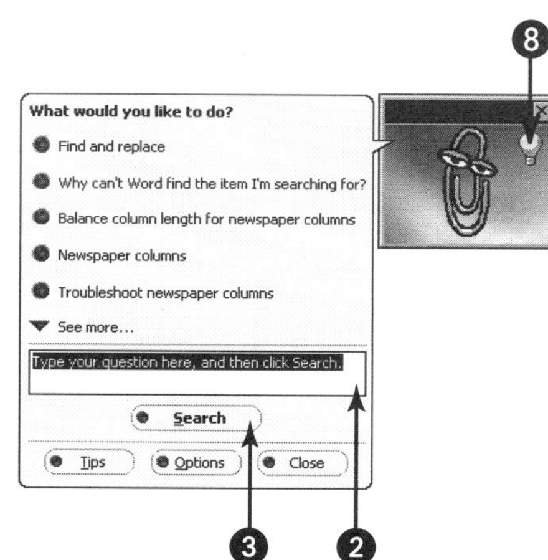

Exiting Microsoft Word

Keep in mind that the yellow light bulb only appears in the Office Assistant window when there is a tip to match the actions you perform.

The Office Assistant Tips balloon appears. You see one of Word's shortcuts, which is called Shortcut, F.Y.I, Try This, or Tip of the Day, depending on the type of tip.

If the Office Assistant balloon is displayed, you can click the Tips button to display F.Y.I and Tip of the Day information.

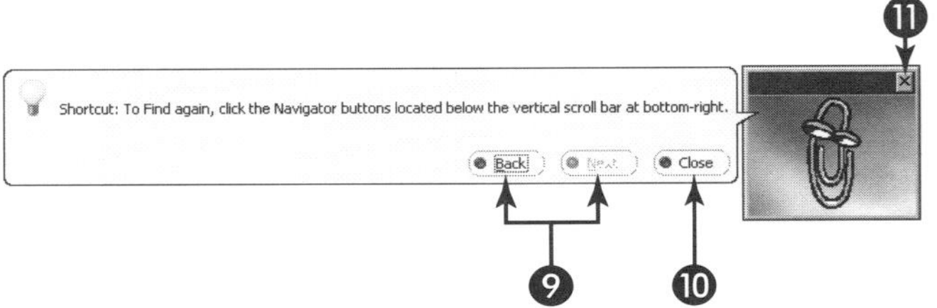

9. Click the Back or Next button to display the preceding or the next shortcut.
10. Click the Close button to close the Tips balloon.
11. Finally, click the Close (X) button to close the Office Assistant window.

EXITING THE PROGRAM

When you're finished using Microsoft Word, you can exit Word and return to the Windows desktop.

Exiting Microsoft Word

In this exercise you exit Microsoft Word. In the Skills Challenge coming up, you will open the Word program.

To close Word, follow these steps:

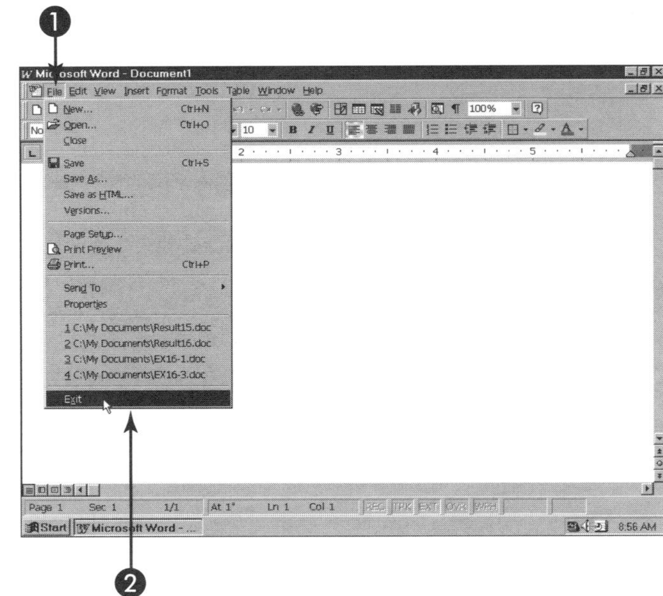

1. Open the File menu.
2. Click Exit.

Word closes, and you return to the Windows desktop.

To exit Word, you can also double-click the Control menu icon or click the Close (X) button in the upper right corner of the Word window.

SKILLS CHALLENGE: EXPLORING THE WORD PROGRAM

This exercise gives you the opportunity to apply the skills you learned in this lesson. Answer the bonus questions to review the lesson and help you determine your understanding of the topics covered. The answers to these bonus questions are in Appendix C.

1. Open Microsoft Word.

Can you name the three Document Control buttons on the document window?

2. Open the File menu.
3. Choose the Open command.

What does an ellipsis next to a menu command indicate?

4. Select the file EX01-2.DOC.
5. In the first sentence, double-click the word *neon*.
6. Open a shortcut menu.
7. Select the Cut command.
8. Use the Standard toolbar to create a new document.

If you're unsure of what a toolbar button does, how do you find out the button's name?

9. Use the Office Assistant to search for help on the Status bar.
10. Take a look at Word's shortcuts by opening the Tips balloon.
11. Close the Tips balloon.
12. Close the Office Assistant window.

TRY OUT THE INTERACTIVE TUTORIALS ON YOUR CD!

13. Close both documents without saving changes.
14. Exit Microsoft Word.

What is one of the two shortcuts for exiting Word?

TROUBLESHOOTING

You've learned a lot of the basics of getting around Word. The following table answers some questions that might have come up during this lesson.

Problem	Solution
My document window shrunk to an icon at the bottom of the screen.	Click the Maximize button on the document icon's title bar to maximize the document window.
When I clicked the mouse button to execute a command, nothing happened.	Be sure you point to the correct command and click the left mouse button. If nothing happens, or if a strange menu appears, check the location of the mouse pointer and try clicking again.
I accidentally opened a menu.	Press Esc or click anywhere outside the menu.
I accidentally opened a dialog box.	Click the Cancel button or the Close (X) button in the dialog box to close it.
I tried to view a toolbar button's name, but the ScreenTip didn't appear.	Try moving the mouse pointer again and pause a few seconds longer.

WRAP UP

Let's go over some of the things you learned in this lesson:

- Opening and exiting Microsoft Word
- Understanding the elements of the Word screen, such as menus and toolbars
- Selecting menu commands and using shortcut menus and the toolbars
- Using the Office Assistant to get help and learn shortcuts

For more practice, review the Word screen elements in this lesson and the Visual Bonus. Explore all the menus and view the ScreenTips for the buttons on all the toolbars.

In the next lesson, you'll learn how to create your own Word documents and save them.

LESSON 2

Creating and Saving Documents

GOALS

In this lesson, you'll learn the following skills:

- Entering the current date
- Entering text
- Separating paragraphs
- Combining paragraphs
- Inserting text
- Overwriting text
- Saving a Word document
- Closing a Word document
- Opening a Word document
- Using a wizard to create a document

Get ready

GET READY

For this lesson, you will not use any exercise files from the One Step folder.

When you've finished these exercises, you will have created a business letter that looks like the letter in the accompanying illustration.

TRY OUT THE INTERACTIVE TUTORIALS ON YOUR CD!

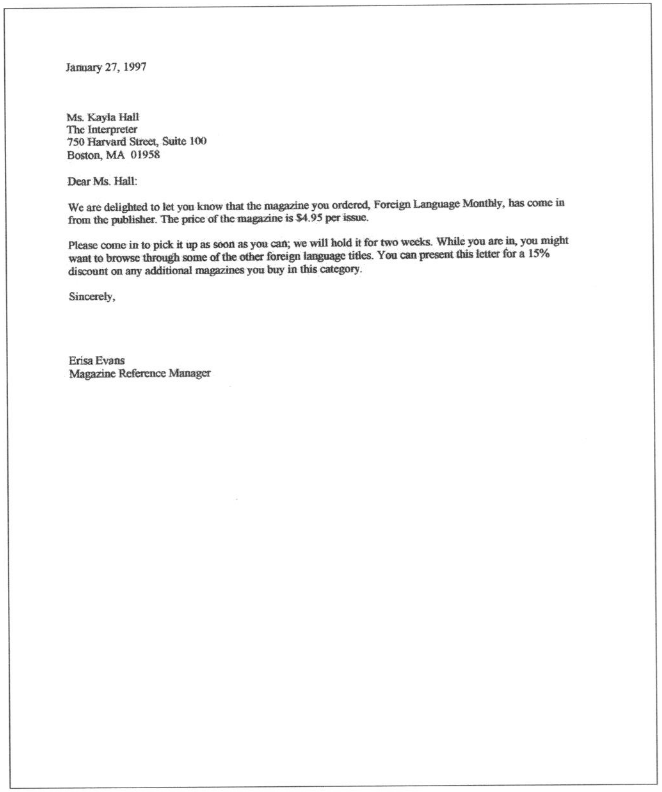

January 27, 1997

Ms. Kayla Hall
The Interpreter
750 Harvard Street, Suite 100
Boston, MA 01958

Dear Ms. Hall:

We are delighted to let you know that the magazine you ordered, Foreign Language Monthly, has come in from the publisher. The price of the magazine is $4.95 per issue.

Please come in to pick it up as soon as you can; we will hold it for two weeks. While you are in, you might want to browse through some of the other foreign language titles. You can present this letter for a 15% discount on any additional magazines you buy in this category.

Sincerely,

Erisa Evans
Magazine Reference Manager

CREATING YOUR FIRST DOCUMENT

There are two methods for starting a new document in Word. You can choose the File ➢ New command, or click the New button on the Standard toolbar. Each method has its own merits and you can pick the one that makes you most comfortable. In fact, you'll probably use both methods, depending on the type of document you create.

When you choose the File ➢ New command to create a new document, Word offers a choice of templates or wizards to use in creating the document. A *template* provides a pattern for shaping a document. It contains boilerplate text, styles, glossary items, macros, a menu, key, and toolbar assignments. A template enables you to create a new document based on the special text and formatting elements the template provides. You could create these elements yourself, but it would take quite some time.

Word provides several categories of templates: General, Publications, Other Documents, Letters & Faxes, Memos, and Reports. You can use a template at any time to standardize documents that you use frequently.

Word has another helpful feature called a *wizard*. You can use a wizard to quickly create almost any kind of document such as a letter, memo, report, and fax cover sheet.

In this lesson, a colleague of yours, Meryl, needs a favor. You've agreed to develop a business letter for her. After you create this letter and save it, you will use it in exercises in the lessons ahead.

Entering the current date

The Date and Time command inserts the date and/or time into a document automatically. Word inserts the date and time using your computer's clock. Having dates in a document can help you keep track of the last time your document was modified, and it keeps you from having to manually add this information. Let's start by inserting today's date automatically.

1. Start Word, if you haven't already.

   When you first start Word, a blank document appears. This document is named Document1 until you save it and give it a new name. By default, when you start a new document on this blank page, Words uses the NORMAL.DOT template, which contains the standard document settings. Notice that the Formatting toolbar contains the settings for font (Times New Roman), font size (10 points), and text alignment (left aligned).

The New button assigns the NORMAL.DOC template to your document by default, as does the blank document that appears on your screen when you first open Word. If you want to base your document on a different template, you must use the File ➢ New command, which displays the dialog box containing the template names.

2. Select the Insert menu.
3. Click Date and Time.

   The Date and Time dialog box appears, listing the available date and time formats. (Notice that the dialog box on your screen displays the current date and time.)

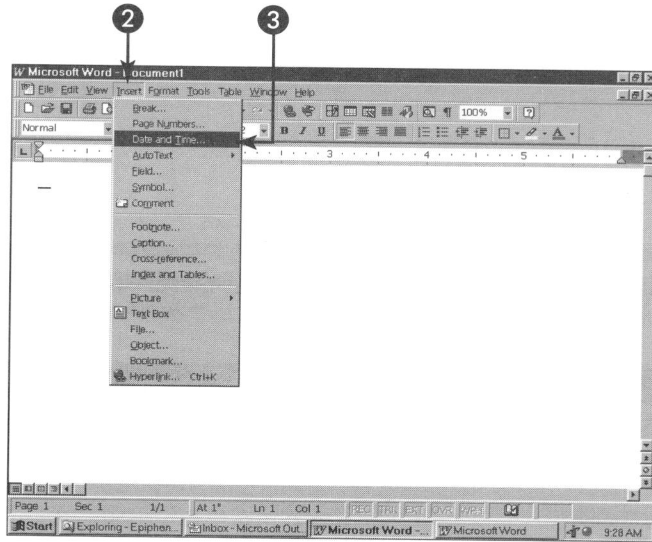

Entering text

A quick way to insert the date is to press Alt+Shift+D. The date format appears as numbers separated by slashes (/), such as 12/15/98. To insert the time quickly, press Alt+Shift+T. The time format appears as hours and minutes with the time of day separated by a colon (:), such as 9:42 AM.

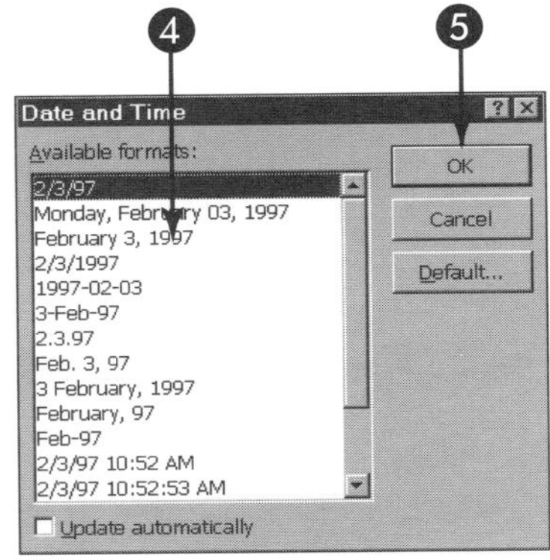

4. Select the third date format from the top of the list.
5. Click OK.

   Word inserts the date in the document, as shown in the accompanying figure.

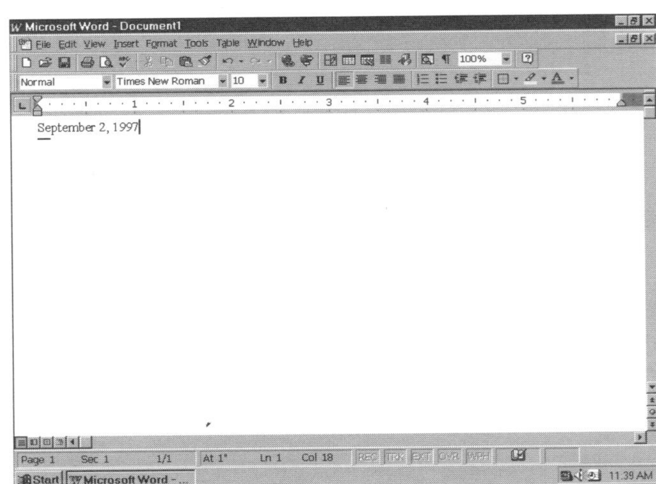

6. If you want to remove the date, select the date by holding down the mouse button and dragging the mouse over the date to highlight it. Then press Delete.

If you choose the Update automatically option in the Date and Time dialog box, Word updates the date and time according to the computer's clock when you print the document. This way, you don't have to update this information manually.

Because Microsoft Word uses your computer's clock to insert the current date and time, you must be sure to set the computer's clock to the correct date and time. If the wrong date or time appears, use the Date/Time program in the Windows Control Panel to reset the date and time.

Entering text

Entering text inserts new text at the insertion point. The text you type moves to the right, and then wraps to the next line when the current line is full. This is called "word wrap." In this exercise, we'll enter the address, salutation, body of the letter, and letter closing.

1. Press Enter four times.
2. Type **Ms. Kayla Hall**, and press Enter again.

If you make a mistake when typing, you can delete text to make minor corrections. Use the Backspace key to delete text to the left of the insertion point. Use the Delete key to delete text to the right of the insertion point.

3. Type **The Interpreter** and press Enter.
4. Type **750 Harvard Street** and press Enter.
5. Type **Boston, MA 02110** and press Enter twice.
6. Type **Dear Ms. Hall:** and press Enter twice.

   The Office Assistant appears and asks if you would like some help creating the letter.

7. Select *Just type the letter without help*.
8. Type: **We are delighted to let you know that the magazine you ordered, *Foreign Language Monthly*, has arrived from the publisher. The price of the magazine is $4.95. Please come in to pick it up as soon as you can; we will hold it for two weeks**.

   Notice that you don't have to press Enter when you get to the end of a line. Word has a feature called *word wrap*. This automatically breaks a line at the most appropriate place and sends your insertion point to the beginning of the next line. You only need to press Enter when you want to end a short line or begin a new paragraph.

   Also, notice that the word *Monthly* is underlined with a green wavy line, which indicates that there may be a grammatical error. You'll use grammar check in Lesson 6 to remove that green wavy line.

9. Press Enter twice.

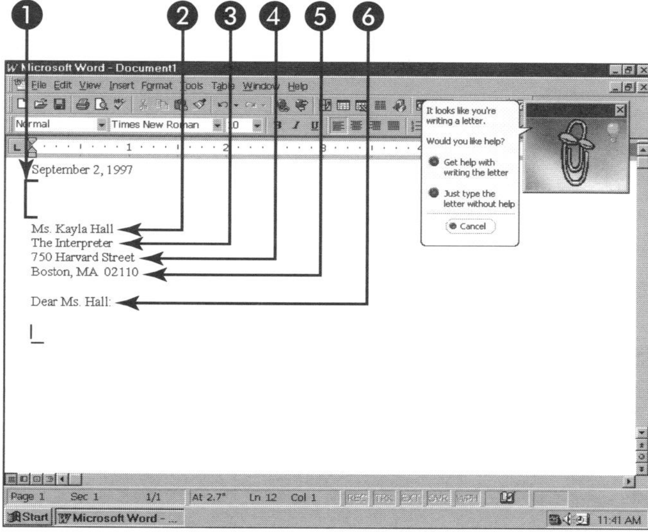

Separating paragraphs

10. Type: **You can present this letter for a 15% discount on any additional magazines you buy in this category.** Press Enter twice.
11. Type **Sincerely,** and press Enter five times.
12. Type **Erisa Evans** and press Enter.
13. Finally, type **Magazine Reference Manager** and press Enter again.

 Notice the name Erisa is underlined with a red wavy line, which indicates that there may be a spelling error. You'll use spell check in Lesson 6 to remove the line.

 Now you have a complete letter with the current date, proper return address, and a closing.

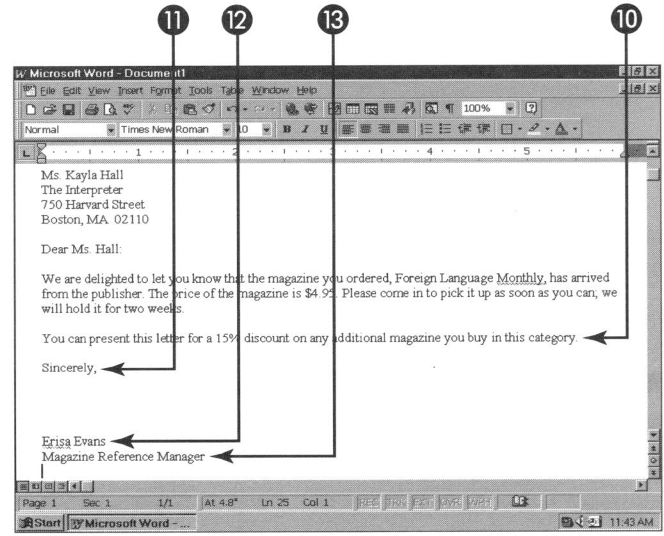

Separating paragraphs

As you saw in the preceding exercise, you don't have to press Enter at the end of each line. Word automatically wraps the text to the next line. Press Enter when you want to insert a hard return at the end of a short line, place a blank line between paragraphs, or end a paragraph. Let's separate the first paragraph into two paragraphs.

1. In the first paragraph, at the end of the second sentence, click after *$4.95*. Be sure the insertion point appears after the period.
2. Press Enter twice.

 You have split the paragraph into two paragraphs by adding a blank line between them. By default, actual paragraph marks (¶) do not appear onscreen or in your printed document, but sometimes it's helpful to see these and other characters as you work.

3. Click the Show/Hide (¶) button on the Standard toolbar.

 A paragraph symbol appears at the end of a short line and a paragraph, and at the beginning of a blank line. A dot represents a space. There are one or two extra spaces before the second paragraph that we need to delete.

4. Click before the space to move the insertion point to the space you want to delete.
5. Press Delete once or twice, depending on the number of spaces you entered originally.

   The accompanying illustration shows you how your document looks after you separate the paragraphs.
6. To hide the symbols, click the Show/Hide button on the Standard toolbar.

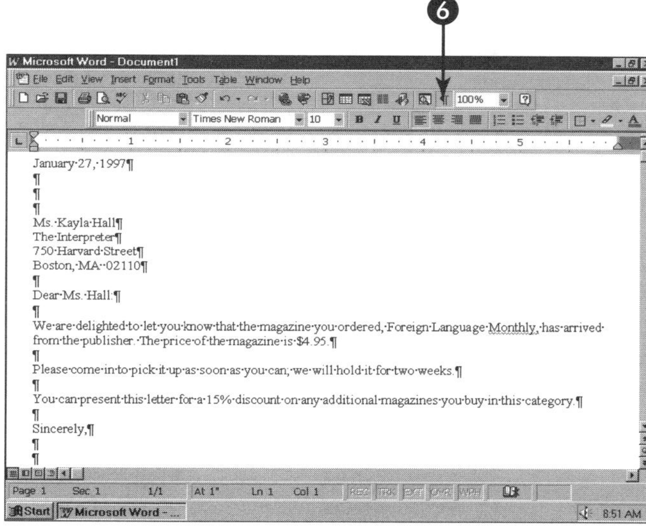

Combining paragraphs

You can combine paragraphs by removing two paragraph marks: the one at the end of a paragraph and the one at the beginning of the blank line between the paragraphs. Let's combine paragraphs two and three into one paragraph.

1. In the second paragraph, click after *weeks* at the end of the sentence. Be sure to click after the period.
2. Press Delete. This removes the paragraph mark at the end of the current paragraph.
3. Press Delete again. This removes the blank line between the paragraphs. The third paragraph moves up next to the second paragraph.
4. Press the spacebar to separate the sentences. Word inserts a space between the two sentences. Your screen should now look like the accompanying figure.

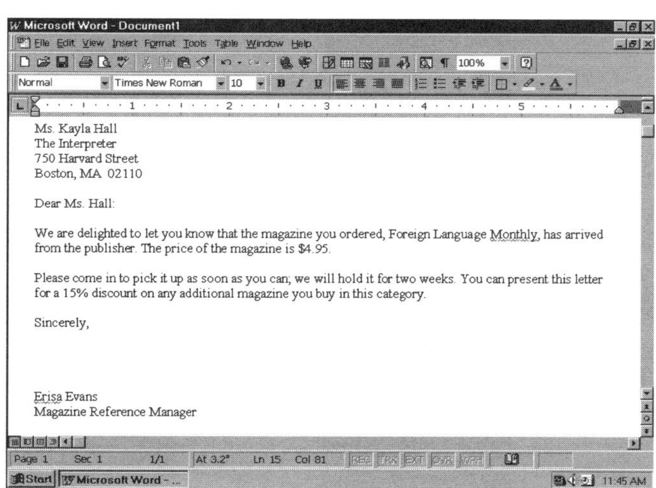

Inserting text

Inserting text adds text to existing text. Insert mode is the default mode. It lets you insert new text at the insertion point. First we'll insert a couple of words at the end of a sentence.

1. In the first paragraph, at the end of the second sentence, click after *$4.95*. Be sure the insertion point appears before the period.

Overwriting text

You can place the insertion point by clicking the mouse pointer where you want to insert text, or by using the arrow keys. For more information on using the arrow keys, see Lesson 3.

2. Press the spacebar.
3. Type **per issue**.

   By default, Word is in Insert mode. When Word is in Insert mode and you type text at the insertion point, the existing text moves to the right to make room for the new text.

   Let's insert a sentence.

4. In the second paragraph, at the end of the first sentence, click after *weeks*. Be sure the insertion point appears after the period.
5. Press the spacebar.
6. Type: **While you are in, you might want to browse through some of the other foreign language titles.**

   The accompanying illustration shows how the letter looks after inserting text.

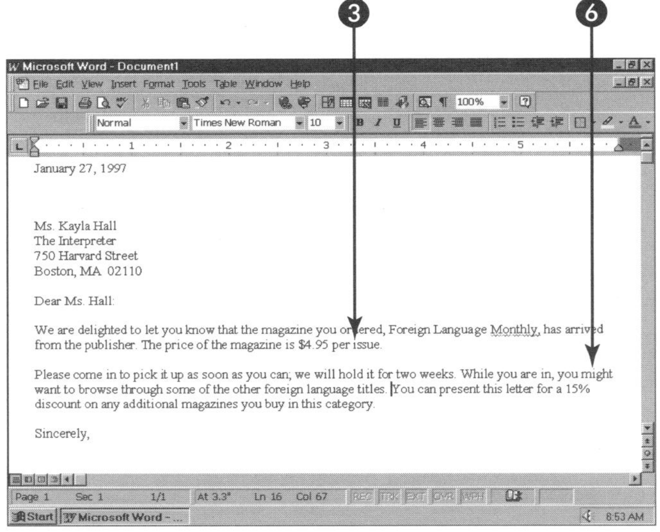

Overwriting text

You can type over existing text in Overtype mode. This mode replaces existing text with the new text. Overwriting text is good for correcting typing errors. Let's correct the ZIP code.

1. In the address, click after the first *0* in the ZIP code *02110*. This places the insertion point where you want to overwrite text.
2. Double-click the OVR indicator in the Status bar.

   This puts Word in Overtype mode and highlights the OVR indicator in the Status bar. Text you type now will overwrite existing text, one character at a time.

The OVR indicator is a toggle. You double-click it to turn on Overtype mode. You double-click it again to turn off Overtype mode and return to Insert mode.

3. Type **1958** to change the ZIP code. Word deletes the original text and replaces it with the new text.

   Let's replace a word.

4. In the first sentence of the first paragraph, click before the *a* in *arrived.*

5. Type **come**, press the spacebar, and type **in**. Word deletes the original word and replaces it with two new words, as shown in the accompanying illustration.

6. To turn off Overtype mode, double-click the OVR indicator in the Status bar. The OVR indicator appears dimmed on the Status bar.

You can also replace a block of text by selecting it, and then typing over it. The new text replaces all the selected text. For more information on selecting text, see Lesson 5, "Revising Text".

In previous versions of Word, the Insert key was a toggle for turning Overtype mode on and off. To use it in Word 97, you need to change the Overtype setting. Select Tools ➢ Options, and click the Edit tab. Click in the Overtype mode checkbox and click OK. Now you can use the Insert key for Overtype mode in Word 97.

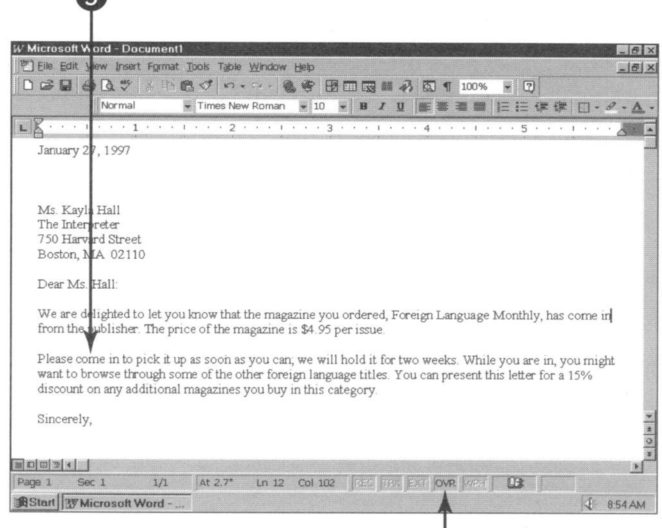

Saving, closing, and opening in Word

SAVING, CLOSING, AND OPENING WORD DOCUMENTS

Whether or not you've finished working in your document, you may want to leave your computer eventually and do something else, such as eat or sleep. Or perhaps you need to use a different software application on your computer. You have to save your document before exiting Word.

By default, Word saves your work to a backup file every ten minutes. However, it is a good idea to save your file often by using the File ➢ Save command. If you don't save your work, you could lose it. Suppose you've been working on a document for a few hours and your power goes off unexpectedly—an air-conditioner repairman at your office shorts out the power, a thunderstorm hits, or something else causes a power loss. If you haven't saved your files to disk, you lose all your work. You should also back up your files on floppy disks from time to time, just in case your hard disk crashes.

A document contains the work you do onscreen and is only in your computer's memory, which is temporary. When you save your document, the Word program copies the information from memory to a file on disk (hard disk or floppy disk).

Saving a file does not remove it from the screen. To remove a file from the screen, you must close the file. Regardless of whether you saved a file, you can close it using the File ➢ Close command. But if you close a file without saving it, you lose any work you did.

After you save a file and close it, you can open it later to view it or make changes to it. The maximum number of files you can open at one time depends on your system memory, but it's a good idea to keep the number of open windows to a minimum.

Word gives a document the title Document1 (or Document2, Document3, and so on) until you save and name the file. The number represents the number of new, unsaved documents you have created since you started Word.

In the next set of exercises, you will save, close, and open the document that contains the letter you created.

Saving a Word document

If your computer gives you any technical problems and your documents get damaged, you can avoid a lot of extra work if you have saved the document recently. You won't have to retype an entire document because Word will automatically recover the most recent version that was saved with the File Save command. After you save a document for the first time and give it a name, you should save your document about every ten minutes with the File Save command. This command replaces the original copy of a document (the file on your drive) with the document onscreen. If you try to close a document without saving it, Word asks whether you want to save the document. Let's save our document now.

1. Click the Save button on the Standard toolbar.

   The first time you save the file, Word displays the Save As dialog box, shown in the accompanying illustration. This dialog box lists the current folders and drive and shows a suggested filename, which is based on the document's first line of text.

   You can use the Save In drop-down list and the buttons on the Save toolbar to browse around your hard drive, CD-ROM drive, floppy drives, or any network drives to which your computer may be connected.

The Up One Level button on the Save toolbar saves your files in a different folder. In the Save In box, you double-click the folder in which you want to save the file.

The first time you open the Save As dialog box after you start Word, you will see the My Documents folder in the Save In box. We'll create a new folder in the My Documents folder and save this file there.

2. Click the Create New Folder button. The Create New Folder dialog box appears. It enables you to assign a name to the new folder.

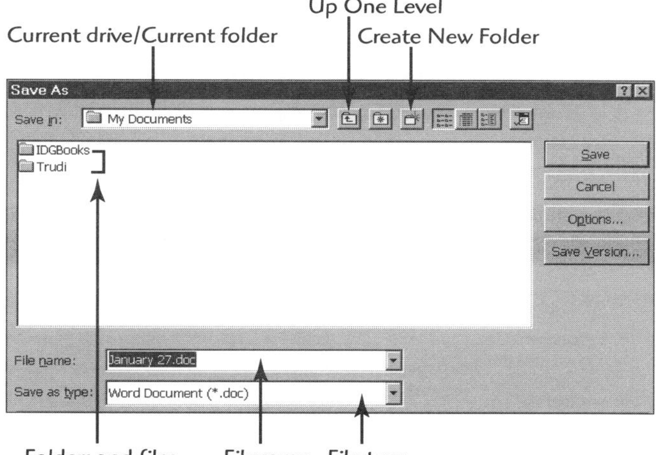

Saving a Word document

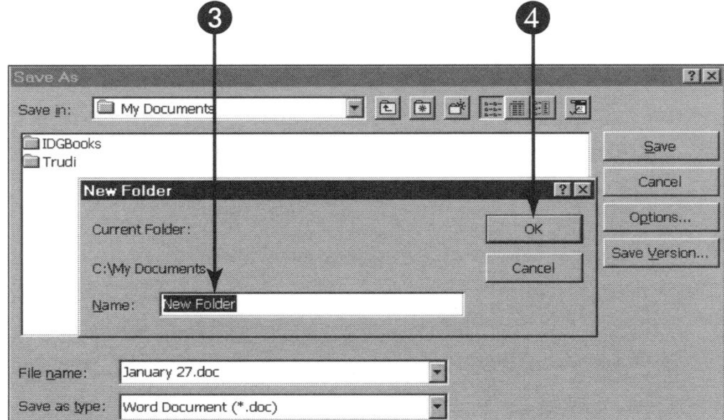

3. In the Name box, type **My Work** for the folder name. This replaces the words *New Folder*.
4. Click OK to return to the Save As dialog box. The new folder name is now listed along with the other folders in the My Documents folder.
5. Double-click the My Work folder to open it.
6. In the File Name box, click and drag your mouse across the suggested file name to highlight it. Then release the mouse button.
7. In the File Name box, type **Magazine Arrival**.

   The new name replaces the suggested filename. Your filenames can be as long as you want, and they can contain upper- or lowercase letters. You can use spaces or commas, but not periods.

   The default file type is Word Document, which is typically the file type you would want. If, however, you are saving the file for someone who uses a different word processor, such as WordPerfect, or as a new Word template that you can base future documents on, you can use the Save As Type drop-down list to change the file type. Also, if you want to save the file as a Word 6.0 document, you select the Word 6.0/95 file type.

If you type a filename that already exists, Word asks, Do you want to replace the existing file? If you replace the file, you lose its contents. If you do not want to replace that file, click Cancel and then type a new name.

8. Click the Save button or press Enter.

Word saves the file in the location you've specified and with the name you've assigned. The filename, Magazine Arrival.doc, appears in the title bar of the file.

Closing a Word document

Now that you have given the file a name, you have two options for saving this document in the future:

- You can save the file with the same filename. To do so, you can either click the Save button on the Standard toolbar, or select File ➢ Save. Any changes you've made to the document will be saved.
- You can save the file with a different name. This gives you two copies of the same document. The first file contains the last saved version, and the new file contains current changes. Creating a copy of the document in this way is useful for saving various drafts of a document for future reference or comparison. To save a file with a new name, select File ➢ Save As. The Save As dialog box appears, and you can use the settings described above to save the file with a new filename. You can also save the file in a different directory or drive.

Closing a Word document

When you no longer want to work with a document, you can close the document and clear the screen. If you close a document without saving it, Word asks whether you want to save any changes you made. If you didn't make any changes to the document, Word just closes the document. Now you can close the saved file.

❶ Select the File menu.

❷ Click Close.

Word closes the active document. Only the menu bar, toolbars, and a blank window (if no other documents are currently open) remain on the screen. From here, you can close and/or save any other documents that are open, open a file, create a new document or template, or access Word Help.

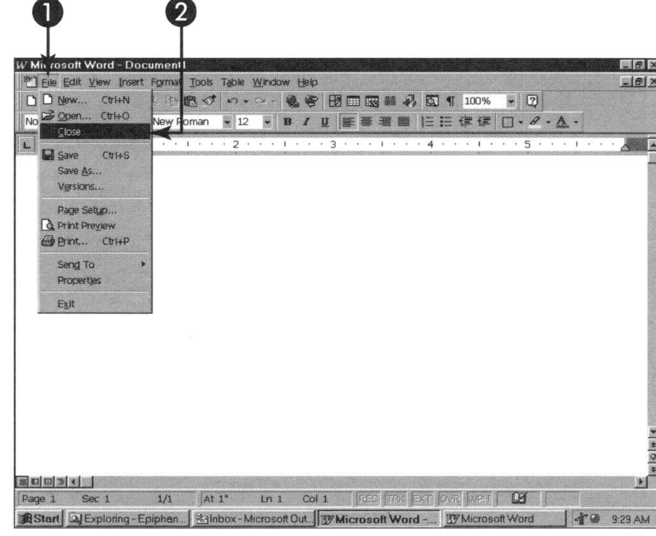

Closing a Word document

A quick way to close a document is to click the Close (X) button in the upper right corner of the document window (on the right end of the menu bar).

If you haven't saved your most recent changes, Word gives you the chance to do it before you close the document. Let's open the Magazine Arrival document using the File menu. The last four files you worked on are listed at the bottom of the File menu for quick access to them. We'll make a change to the document and then close it.

3. Select File from the Menu bar.
4. Then, select *Magazine Arrival* from the list of recently opened files at the bottom of the File menu.
5. In the address, click after the second *t* in *Street.*
6. Type a comma (,) and then type **Suite 100**.
7. Select File.
8. Click Close.

A message appears asking if you want to save changes to the file. (The same message also appears in an Office Assistant balloon if Office Assistant is active when you go to close the file.)

9. Click Yes to save the changes and close the document.

If you want to discard all the work you've done since the last time you saved the file, select No. The changes will be ignored and Word will close the file. If you decide that you need to make more changes before closing, select Cancel. Word will abort your attempt to close the file and take you back to the document window.

Microsoft Word

Do you want to save the changes you made to "Magazine Arrival.doc"?

Yes No Cancel

9

Opening a Word document

If you want to work with the file again, you have to open it again. The File Open command opens a file in a document window. Let's open a document.

Opening a Word document

1. Click the Open button on the Standard toolbar. You see the Open dialog box, as shown in the accompanying illustration. This dialog box lists the current folders and drive.

   You can use the Look In drop-down list and the buttons on the Open toolbar to browse around your hard drive, CD-ROM drive, floppy drives, or network drives to which your computer may be connected.

The Up One Level button on the Open toolbar enables you to open the folder that is one level above the active folder. This is handy when your files are stored in a different folder than the one that appears in the Look In text box. In the Look In box, click the folder that contains the file you want to open.

The first time you open the Open dialog box after you start Word, you see the My Documents folder in the Look In box. But in your dialog box, you should see the My Work folder in the Look In box.

Suppose you want to view more information about the files. Let's change the view of the file list.

2. Click the Details button on the Open toolbar.

   Word displays the file size and type, and the date and time of the most recent file modification, as shown in the accompanying illustration.

   Now let's return to the file list that contains small icons and filenames.

3. Click the List button on the Open toolbar.

   (If you already know the name of the document that you want to open, you can simply type the filename in the File Name text box.)

4. Select the *Magazine Arrival* file.

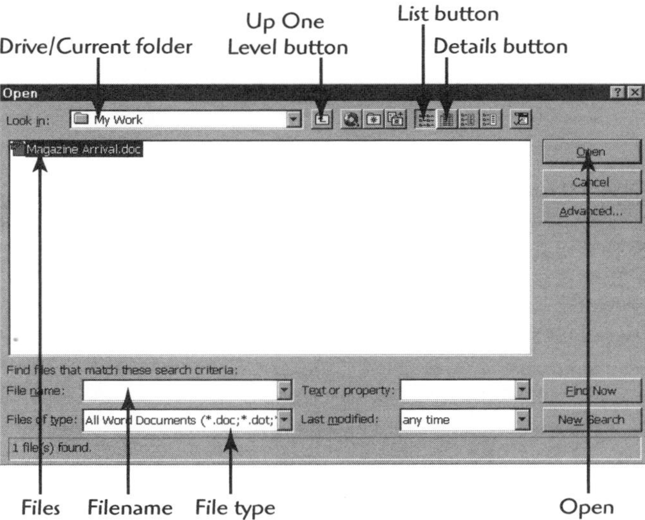

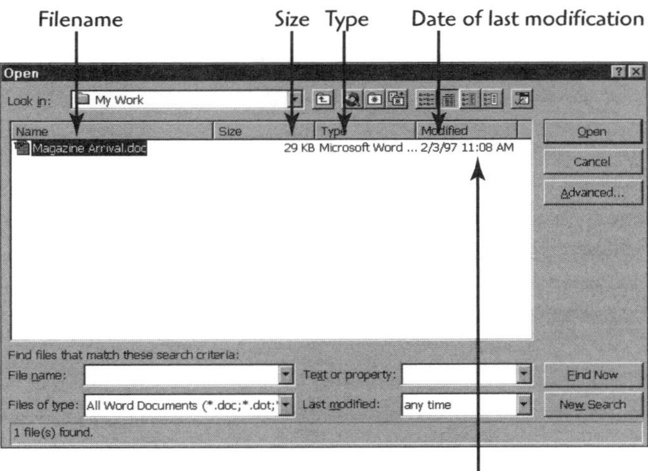

2 Creating and Saving Documents

Creating a Word document

5. Click the Open button.

   The file appears onscreen with its filename in the title bar.

If you have more than one document open and want to switch among them, select Window in the menu bar, and then select an open document from the list at the bottom of the menu.

A fast way to open a document is to double-click the filename of the document you want to open.

USING A WIZARD TO CREATE A DOCUMENT

A *wizard* is a special template that provides a pattern for shaping a document and guides you through the process of creating it. A wizard displays dialog boxes, messages, and graphics that tell you how to fill in a template or create forms. With a wizard you can prepare a résumé, a letter to your attorney, a fax cover sheet to the Mambo King, envelopes for your holiday cards, mailing labels for your invitations, or a memo to a colleague. Also, you can use a wizard to quickly set up agendas, awards, calendars, legal pleading papers, newsletters, and tables. You get to make the design and formatting decisions, but you don't have to do all the design work.

Creating a Word document

A wizard uses dialog boxes to walk you through the process of creating a document. Just choose the wizard you want, and you get a running start on creating a professional-looking letter, memo, report, fax cover sheet, and much more. Let's use a wizard to create a fax cover sheet.

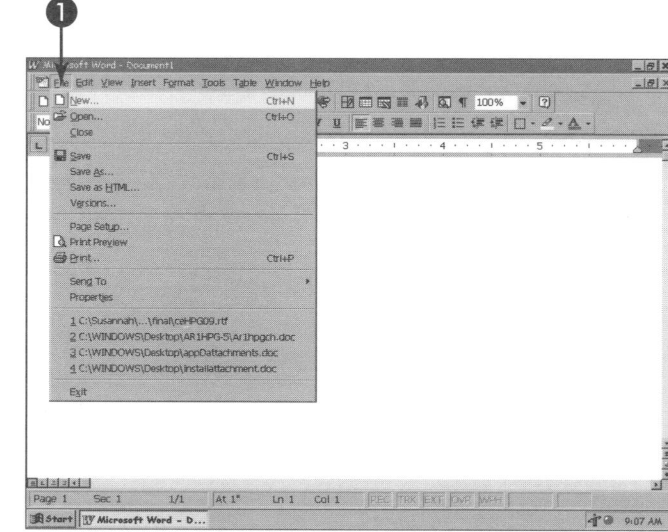

1. Select File on the menu bar.

❷ Click New.

The New dialog box appears with six tabs: General, Letters & Faxes, Memos, Other Documents, Web Pages, and Office 95 Templates.

TIP

If you don't see all the template and wizard tabs in the New dialog box, you need to install the templates and wizards using your Microsoft Word software CD-ROM.

❸ Click the Letters & Faxes tab.

You see template and wizard icons for various letters, faxes, envelopes, and mailing labels.

❹ Click the Fax Wizard icon.

The icon for the wizard you want to start is selected, and it appears in the Preview box on the right side of the dialog box.

❺ Click OK.

❻ Word shows the first wizard dialog box for creating a new document. The steps involved in creating a fax document from start to finish are listed on the left side of the dialog box.

NOTE

If you're already familiar with the Fax Wizard and know exactly which steps you want to perform, click the pertinent option in the Start to Finish list to go directly to the wizard dialog box you want to fill in.

❼ Click the Next button.

The Document to Fax dialog box appears.

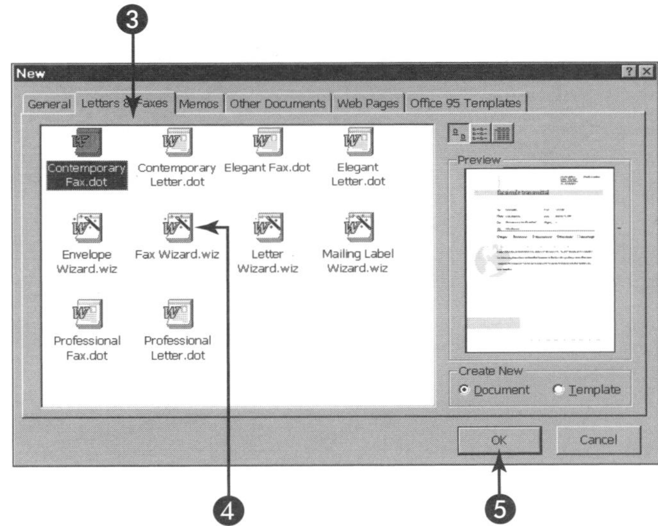

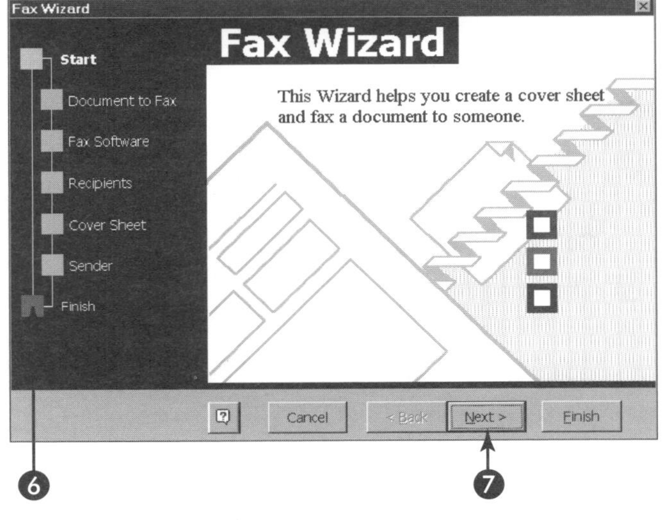

Creating a Word document

8. Choose the document you want to fax from the drop-down list.
9. Choose a fax cover sheet option.
10. Click the Next button.

    The Fax Software dialog box appears.

If you want to return to the preceding wizard dialog box, click the Back button in the current wizard dialog box. If you don't want to create a document using the wizard, abandon it by clicking the Cancel button in a wizard dialog box.

11. Choose the fax software you are going to use to fax the document and click the Next button.

    The Recipients dialog box appears.

12. Enter the names of the recipients to whom you want to send the fax.
13. Click the Next button.

    The Cover Sheet dialog box appears.

14. Choose the fax cover sheet style you want to use and click the Next button.

    The Sender dialog box appears.

15. Fill in the sender information in the text boxes.
16. Click the Finish button to create the fax cover sheet.

    The fax cover sheet appears in the document window. The Office Assistant may also appear.

17. Click the File menu.
18. Select Save As.
19. Name the file **MYFAXCOVER** and press the Enter key to save the fax cover sheet.

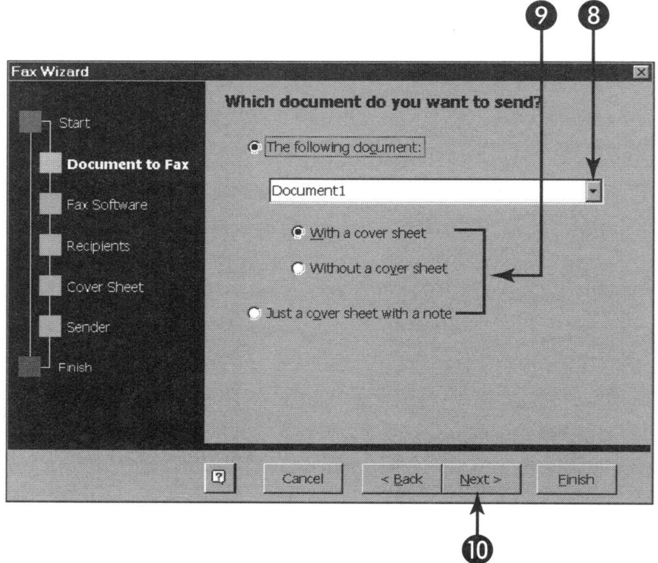

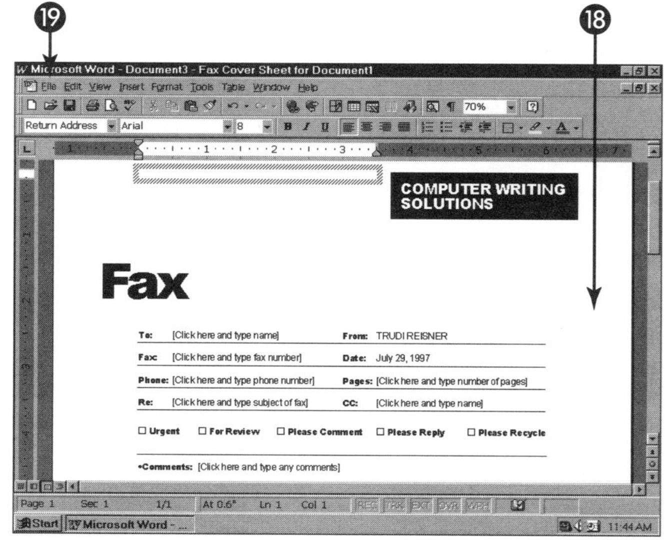

SKILLS CHALLENGE: CREATING A WORD DOCUMENT

TRY OUT THE
INTERACTIVE TUTORIALS
ON YOUR CD!

This exercise brings together all the skills you've learned in this lesson. Answer the bonus questions to review the skills and help you determine your understanding of the topics covered. The answers to these bonus questions are located in Appendix C.

1. Open Microsoft Word.
2. Insert the current date by opening the Insert menu.
3. Choose the Date and Time command.
4. Type an address and salutation.

What is the difference between using the Backspace key and the Delete key?

5. Type two paragraphs for the body of the letter.
6. Type the letter closing.

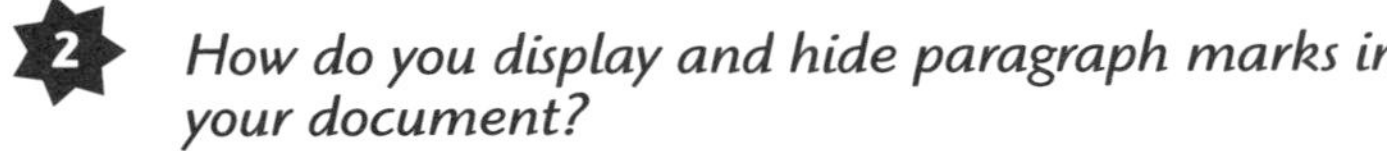

How do you display and hide paragraph marks in your document?

7. Name the file.
8. Save the file.

If you want to save this as a Word 6.0 document, what change do you make in the Save As dialog box?

9. Close the file.

4 *What is the fastest way to close a document?*

10. Open the file.

How do you view file details in the Open dialog box?

11. Insert a sentence at the end of the letter.
12. Overwrite one of the words with a new word.

    6 *How do you know that Word is in Overtype mode?*

13. Save the file.
14. Close the file.
15. Create a fancy fax cover sheet using the Fax Wizard.
16. Exit Microsoft Word.

TROUBLESHOOTING

You've learned a lot of the basics of creating, saving, closing, and opening a document, as well as making minor corrections to the text. The following table answers some questions that might have come up during this lesson.

Problem	Solution
My insertion point jumps down two spaces at the end of a line.	You may have pressed Enter at the end of the line, which causes Word to create a new paragraph. Remember that Word wraps text for you automatically. Delete the paragraph mark at the end of each line.
I inserted the current date, but it doesn't update automatically when I print the document.	You must choose the Update automatically option in the Date and Time dialog box.
I cannot find the file that I saved.	In the Open dialog box, browse through the folders by clicking the Up One Level button to change the current folder in the Look In box, and double-clicking the folders in the file list.

Problem	Solution
I opened the wrong file.	Close the file you don't want, use the File ➢ Open command again, and click the Up One Level button to search for the correct folder and file.

WRAP UP

Before you go to the next lesson, let's go over some of the things you learned in this one:

- Creating a new Word document
- Inserting the current date with the Insert ➢ Date and Time command
- Entering text and making some minor changes to it
- Saving, closing, and opening a document
- Using a wizard to create a document

For more practice, create a cover letter for your résumé

In the next lesson, you'll learn how to move around a document and work with multiple pages in a document.

Moving Around a Document

GOALS

In this lesson, you learn the following skills:

- Moving around your document
- Inserting page breaks
- Jumping to a specific page
- Deleting page breaks

Get ready

GET READY

For this lesson, you need the files EX03-1.DOC and EX03-2.DOC from the One Step folder.

When you finish these exercises, you'll have created the document shown in the accompanying illustrations.

GETTING FROM HERE TO THERE

Sometimes a document is too large to fit on one screen. To place text and edit text in other areas of the document, you must be able to move to the desired locations. Once you've created a document, there are a few easy ways to move around in it rapidly.

The arrow keys enable you to move one character and one line at a time. Key combinations help you zip up, down, left, and right as you move to different parts of a page or through an entire document.

Table 3-1 lists the arrow keys and key combinations you can use to navigate around the document.

TABLE 3-1 NAVIGATION KEYS

To Move	Press
Right one character	→
Left one character	←
Up one line	↑
Down one line	↓
To the previous word	Ctrl+←
To the next word	Ctrl+→
To the beginning of a line	Home
To the end of a line	End
To the beginning of the document	Ctrl+Home
To the end of the document	Ctrl+End
To the previous screen	PgUp
To the next screen	PgDn

Whole Foods, Inc.

Proposal and Marketing Plan

Whole Foods' Best Opportunity for West Region Expansion

Whole Foods Marketing Plan

Whole Foods' Best Opportunity for West Region Expansion

Starting the West Expansion

The first steps toward expanding Whole Foods in the West region are:

1) Confer with Western Commercial Realty Corporation.
2) Discuss expansion plans with company accountant and attorneys.

Real Estate

The Western Commercial Realty Corporation will need to know the following information from our construction department:

Land Parcel

- Building location, building size, and land acreage.
- Accessibility to airport.
- Super-sized cafeteria
- Gym facility
- Day care facility
- Shopping mall

Employee Relocation

Whole Foods employees who would like to transfer to the West location will be accommodated with a packer and mover and any other item and service necessary to make the move as easy as possible.

Warehousing

There are three items on the agenda for warehousing the products for the West region:

1) Warehouse supervisors will be notified with purple routing slips to send products to the West region.
2) A list of products that are not going to be stocked in the West region warehouse will be provided one month before the move.
3) A list of products that will be stocked in the West region warehouse will be provided two months before the move.

Moving around your document

You can use the vertical and horizontal scroll bars to move to other portions of the document. Simply click the mouse on the scroll box within the scroll bar and move the mouse in the direction you want to move in the document.

Scrolling through the document doesn't move the insertion point; it remains in its current position until you click within the document window where you want it to appear.

In this exercise, you learn how to move quickly around the document with the mouse. You also practice using some of the navigation keys listed in the table. These skills are important because they are the foundation for making revisions more easily. In the next section, we'll create more pages and get some practice moving from one page to another.

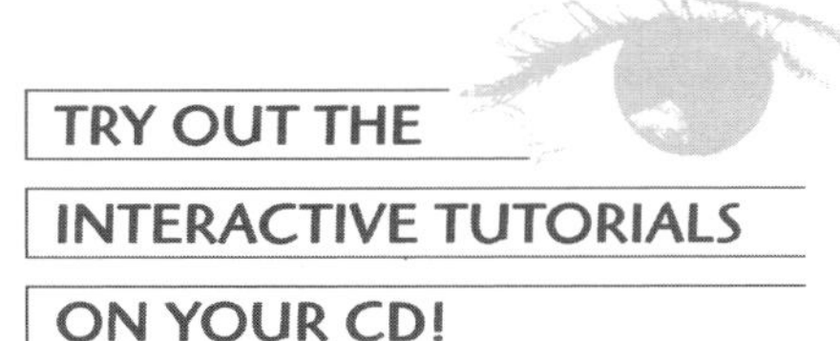

Moving around your document

Using a mouse is often the easiest way to move around a Word document. Simply click a different location onscreen or use the scroll bar to move to another area of the document. For the following exercises, you'll use the file EX03-1.DOC from the One Step folder. This is a report that contains a marketing plan for Whole Foods, Inc. It consists of a title page and two pages with text. We'll use this report to practice using the mouse and the keyboard to navigate around a document.

1. Open the file EX03-1.DOC.
2. Click the down scroll arrow at the bottom of the vertical scroll bar until you reach the second page.

   Word moves down through the document one line at a time.
3. Click the up scroll arrow at the top of the vertical scroll bar twice.

   Word scrolls up the document one line at a time.

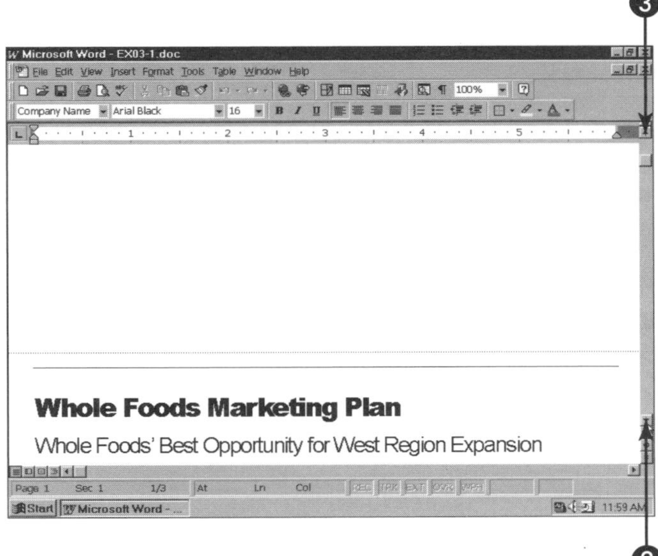

For even faster scrolling, point to the up, down, left, or right scroll bar arrow and hold down the left mouse button.

Moving around your document

4. Click and drag the scroll box to the top of the vertical scroll bar.

   The document moves quickly in the direction you drag the scroll box. Notice that as you drag the scroll box, Word displays a ScreenTip indicating the current page number and heading at the top of that page.

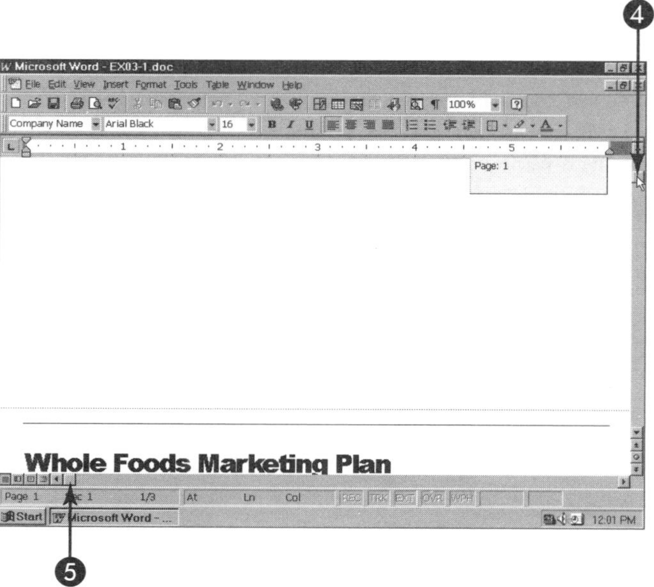

To scroll quickly, click near the scroll bar arrow that's facing the direction in which you want to move. The document will move in large increments—as much as a screen at a time.

5. Click and drag the scroll box to the far right of the horizontal scroll bar.

   Word moves the page across your window to the right and displays a blank portion of the far right side of the document.

If you run out of room to move the mouse on your desktop or mouse pad, just lift the mouse and then put it down in the middle of the mouse pad.

6. Press Ctrl+Home to move to the beginning of the document.
7. Press Ctrl+End to move to the end of the document.

WORKING WITH MORE THAN ONE PAGE

Most documents are longer than one page. As a draft document becomes more polished, you need to consider its final form—the printed page.

What happens if you haven't fit everything you want on the first page? Just keep typing away and don't worry about it. When the text reaches the end of a page, Word inserts a soft (automatic) page break.

Automatic page breaks are based on the top and bottom margin settings. The exact contents of each page may change due to editing or formatting. If you insert text, Word repaginates the document, adjusting the locations of the automatic page breaks.

If you want to end the page at a specific place, you can insert a hard (manual) page break. Manual page breaks override automatic page breaks inserted by Word. Establishing new manual page breaks does not change existing manual page breaks—it just adds to them.

You can recognize a page break because it appears as a dotted line onscreen. The dots are farther apart on an automatic page break than they are on a manual page break. Also the manual page break is labeled with the words *Page Break*, whereas the automatic page break is not labeled.

Page breaks remain in the document until you remove them. You can eliminate page breaks by using the Backspace or Delete key.

When you want to jump to a specific page that is out of view in the current document, use Word's Go To command. For example, perhaps you're working on page 4, and you want to make a change on page 1. You can get there quickly with the Go To command.

The following sections show you how to work with page breaks and use the Go To command.

Inserting page breaks

The Insert Break command allows you to insert page breaks where you want one page to end and another page to begin in documents. By default, Word inserts a soft page break whenever you fill a page of text. If you add or delete text, any soft page breaks move accordingly. To insert a page break in a specific location, you manually insert a hard page break. Hard page breaks remain in the same locations even if you add or delete text. The document on which we're working has three pages. We'll insert a new page at the end of the document. If you are not at the end of the document, press Ctrl+End to move there before beginning this exercise.

1. Select the Insert menu.
2. Click Break.

   Word brings up the Break dialog box. By default, the Page Break option is selected.
3. Click OK.

   This inserts a manual page break and creates a new page after the current page. Word moves the insertion point to page 4.

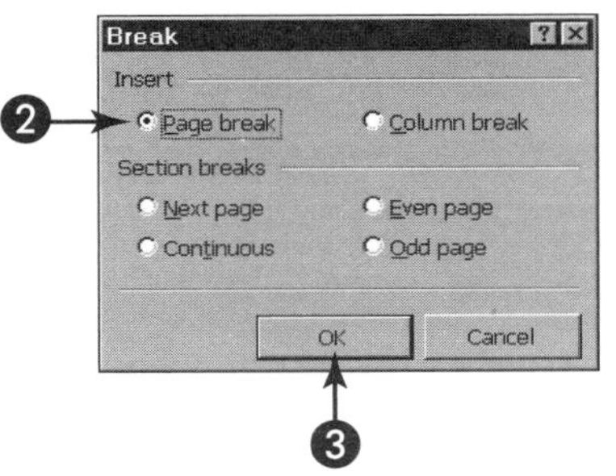

You see a dotted line and the words *Page Break,* as shown in the accompanying illustration.

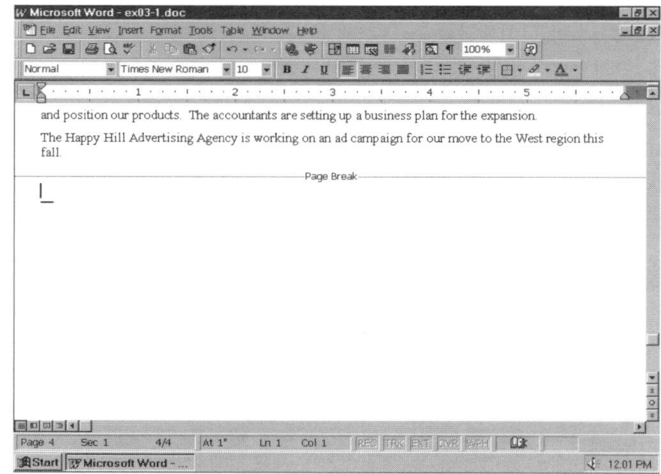

To insert a new page break quickly, press Ctrl+Enter.

Jumping to a specific page

You can select the Edit ➢ Go To command to go to a specific page, but in this exercise, we'll use a shortcut to go back to page 1 in the document.

1. Press F5 (Go To).

   Word opens the Find and Replace dialog box.

   The Go To tab is currently selected, and the default choice in the Go To What list is Page, which takes you to a specific page in the document.

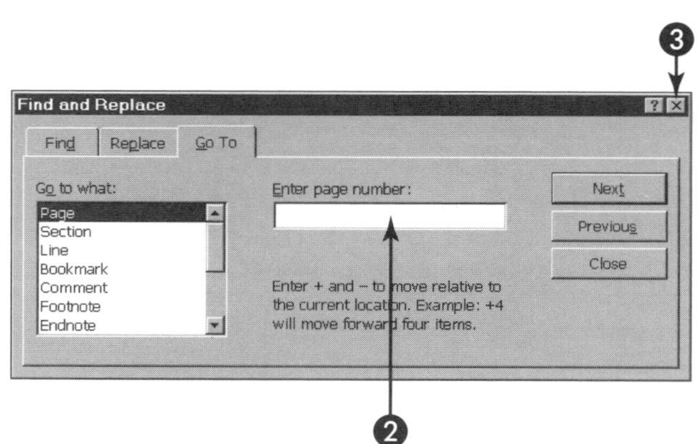

You can also double-click the Page indicator (such as Page 1) at the left end of the Status bar to select the Go To command.

2. In the Enter Page Number text box, type **1** and press Enter.

   Page 1 appears on your screen. The Find and Replace dialog box remains onscreen, so that you can continue searching for pages. If you want to view another page, enter a new page number.

3. Click the Close (X) button to close the dialog box.

Deleting page breaks

You can remove a hard page break at any time to combine pages. Let's delete the page break we inserted earlier.

1. Press Ctrl+End to move to the end of the document.

2. Press Backspace.

The manual page break disappears.

To delete a page break, you can also click anywhere on the page break to select it, and then press Delete.

VISUAL BONUS: SCROLL BARS AND PAGE BREAKS

This visual workout gives you a close-up view of the vertical and horizontal scroll bars. These scroll bars are important because they enable you to use the mouse to quickly scroll up, down, left, and right within a document.

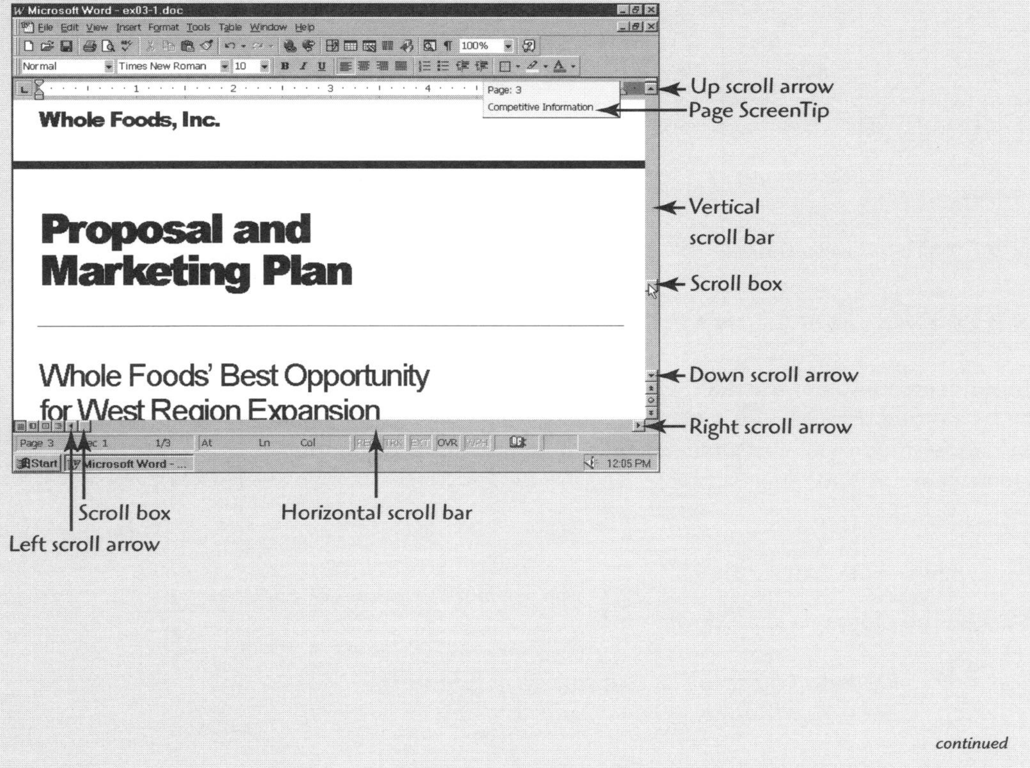

Vertical and horizontal scroll bars

The vertical scroll bar contains arrows, a scroll box, and page arrows to scroll up and down in a document. The horizontal scroll bar contains arrows and a scroll box that enable you to scroll left and right in a document.

continued

VISUAL BONUS: SCROLL BARS AND PAGE BREAKS *(continued)*

An automatic page break is a dotted line entered by Word. A manual page break is entered by pressing Ctrl+Enter; it appears as a dotted line with the words *Page Break.*

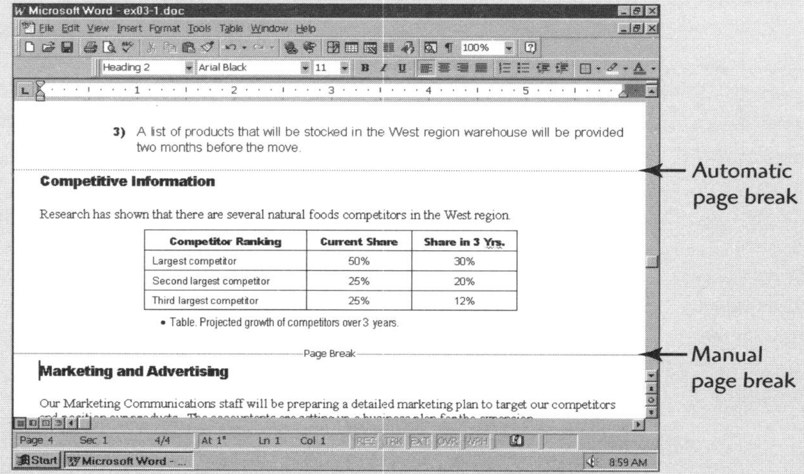

Microsoft Word - ex03-1.doc

3) A list of products that will be stocked in the West region warehouse will be provided two months before the move.

Automatic page break

Competitive Information

Research has shown that there are several natural foods competitors in the West region.

Competitor Ranking	Current Share	Share in 3 Yrs.
Largest competitor	50%	30%
Second largest competitor	25%	20%
Third largest competitor	25%	12%

• Table. Projected growth of competitors over 3 years.

Page Break

Manual page break

Marketing and Advertising

Our Marketing Communications staff will be preparing a detailed marketing plan to target our competitors

Page 4 Sec 1 4/4 At 1" Ln 1 Col 1

Page breaks

SKILLS CHALLENGE: NAVIGATING A DOCUMENT

This exercise reinforces the skills you've learned in this lesson. Answer the bonus questions to review the skills and help you determine your understanding of the topics covered. The answers to the bonus questions are in Appendix C.

1. Open Microsoft Word.
2. Open the file EX03-2.DOC.
3. Use the mouse to scroll down a few lines.

How do you scroll to the far right side of the document?

4. Use the mouse to scroll down one screen.
5. Use the mouse to scroll down to the bottom of the document.

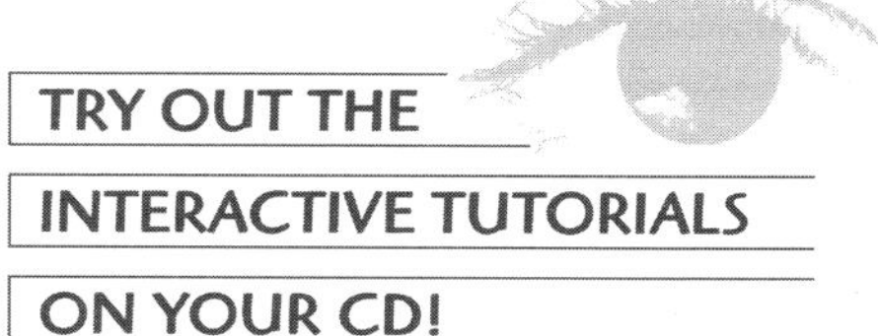

What are the combination keys for moving to the bottom of the document?

6. Insert a page break.

3 *Describe how a manual page break looks.*

7. Go to page 2.

4 *How do you remove the Find and Replace dialog box from the screen?*

8. Delete the new page break.
9. Save the file.
10. Close the file.
11. Exit Microsoft Word.

TROUBLESHOOTING

You've learned about moving around a document and working with page breaks. The following table might answer some questions that have come up during this lesson.

Problem	Solution
When I use the scroll bars to move through the document, the insertion point doesn't move.	Click in the document and use the navigation keys to move the insertion point where you want it.
I need a new page between pages 1 and 2.	Move the insertion point to where you want to end page 1 and press Ctrl+Enter.

Wrap up

Problem	Solution
In a 40-page report, I want to get to page 22.	Press F5, type 22 in the Enter Page Number text box, and then press Enter.
The second page in my document is blank, and I want to delete it.	Move the insertion point just below the page break at the bottom of page 1 and press Backspace.

WRAP UP

Let's go over some of the things you learned in this lesson:

- Using the navigation keys to move around a document
- Scrolling around a document
- Inserting page breaks
- Moving to a specific page
- Deleting page breaks

For more experience, open any document and practice scrolling around the document and working with page breaks.

In the next lesson, we'll change views of a document to see how things look on a page as you're creating it.

LESSON 4

Changing Views

GOALS

In this lesson, you learn the following skills:

- Switching to Page Layout view
- Zooming the document
- Displaying Online Layout view
- Checking Outline view

Get ready

GET READY

For this lesson, you need the file EX04-1.DOC from the One Step folder.

When you've finished working on these exercises, you will have viewed the Whole Foods, Inc. Proposal and Marketing Plan document in various ways. The accompanying illustration shows the report in Page Layout view.

CHANGING WORD VIEWS

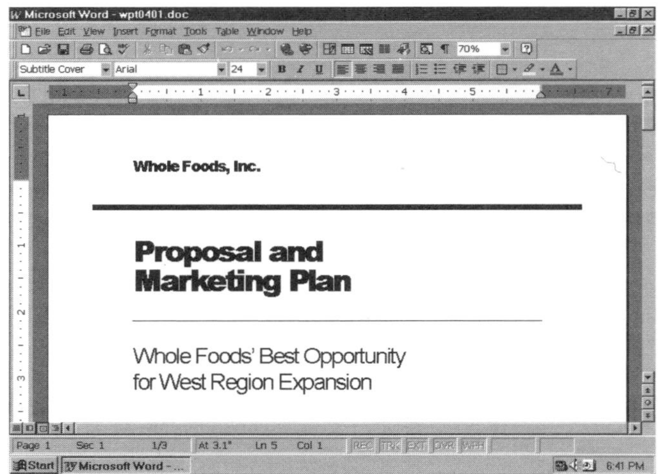

There are many useful tools in your Word window that help you get an accurate view of how the finished product will look. Some views are clearer and more efficient than others, depending on what you're trying to accomplish.

Word provides several views for your document: Normal, Online Layout, Page Layout, Outline, and Zoom. You can change views using the view buttons on the View toolbar in the lower left corner of the screen. The Zoom control is on the Standard toolbar.

Normal view is the default view. This view is best for entering, editing, and formatting your text. In this view, breaks between pages are indicated with a dotted line.

Online Layout view approximates how someone viewing your document on the Internet would see it. You can view any document with Online Layout view. In this view, text wraps to the View window so that you can see the end of every line of text (not the way it wraps for printing, where you might not see some text on the far right of your screen).

Your Web page might look different in a browser such as Netscape, Microsoft Internet Explorer, or America Online than it does in Word, depending on how your browser interprets HTML codes.

Switching to Page Layout view

Page Layout view is similar to Normal view, except that the breaks between pages are represented by gray space around the white area of your document, and a vertical ruler is positioned on the left side of the page. This view displays how your document will look when printed. You can see how text flows from one page to the next, or work with elements on your page, such as text, graphics, charts, tables, columns, headers, and footers. Use Page Layout view when you are making a lot of format changes and need to see the results.

Outline view shows you the contents of your document in a traditional outline format, with text indented beneath headings in a hierarchical structure. This view helps you create outlines from scratch, and write manuscripts and term papers that require an outline structure.

Word makes it easy to work "up close" by providing zoom features. In fact, you can zoom in farther than you'll probably ever need. This feature works with any view. Zooming in and out gives you different perspectives on your page and the text and graphics that it contains. Zooming can make the text on the screen appear smaller or larger; it may show the whole page or a smaller section of it at higher magnification.

Zooming is excellent when you work with small font sizes. When you enter text in a small font size, such as 8 points, you can't always make out the characters. If you zoom in on your text, you can see what you've typed and inspect your text more closely without having to preview or print the document.

In this exercise, you practice switching from Normal view to Page Layout view.

Switching to Page Layout view

By default, the view is set to Normal view, which enables you to type, edit, and format a document. Page Layout view displays multiple columns, headers and footers, and footnotes in a document. For the following exercises, you'll use the file EX04-1.DOC from the One Step folder. You worked with the report in this file in Lesson 3. It consists of a title page and two pages with text. We'll use the report to practice switching views.

Zooming the document

1. Open EX04-1.doc. Click the Page Layout View button (the third button from the left on the View toolbar).

   You see the title page in its actual size.

2. Use the down scroll arrow on the vertical scroll bar to scroll down through the document.

   Notice the whole page on your screen. Word shows you where each page starts and stops. Notice that there is a gray space between pages.

3. Click the Normal View button (the button farthest to the left on the View toolbar). You return to Normal view.

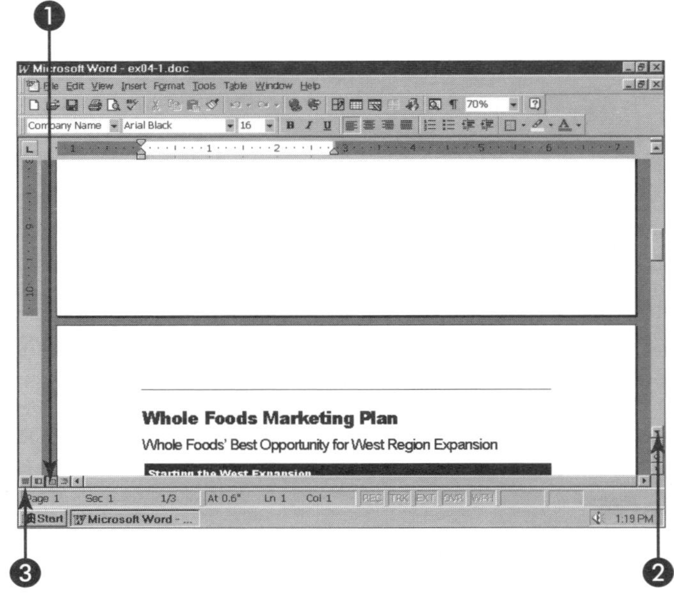

The Page Layout command is not a toggle. To turn off Page Layout view, you must select another view.

Zooming the document

With Zoom, you can enlarge your view of a page to as much as 500 percent, or you can reduce the view down to as little as 10 percent. When you want to zoom in, select a higher percentage of magnification. When you want to zoom out, select a lower percentage. You can edit your document at any zoom setting. We'll zoom in at 200 percent.

1. Click the Zoom drop-down arrow on the Standard toolbar. The Zoom magnification percentages are listed in the Zoom box.

2. Select 200% to zoom in.

   The text enlarges to a magnification of 200 percent. Next, we'll zoom out at 50 percent to see more of the document at a glance.

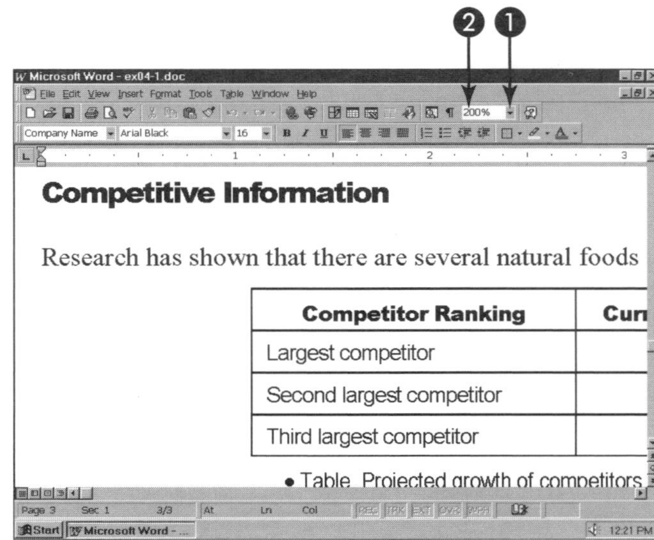

3. Click the Zoom drop-down arrow on the Standard toolbar.
4. Select 50% to zoom out.

   The accompanying figure shows how the document looks in Page Layout view when reduced to 50 percent of its normal size. Now we'll return to 100 percent magnification.

5. Click the Zoom drop-down arrow on the Standard toolbar.
6. Select 100%.

   The 100 percent setting is the percentage of magnification you see on a printed page.

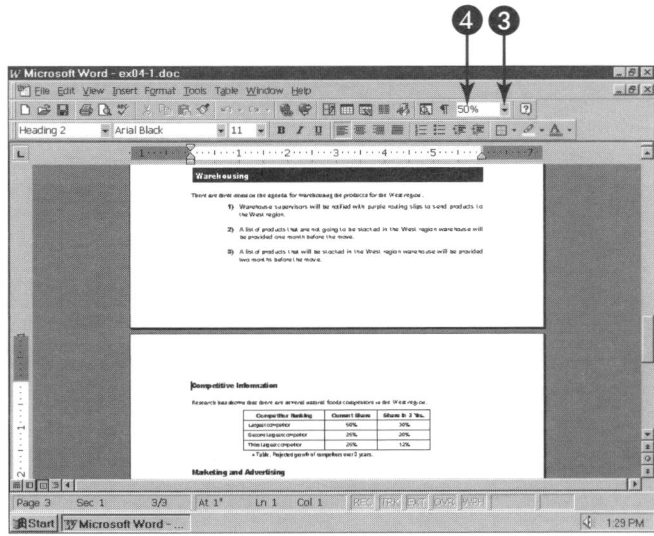

Displaying Online Layout view

In this exercise, we'll take a peek at Online Layout view and see what a Word document will roughly look like as a Web page on the Internet.

1. Click the Online Layout View button (the second button from the left on the View toolbar).

   As you can see, the document contains text that appears taller and bolder compared to Normal view, and wraps to fit in the window so that you can see the end of every line of text. The accompanying illustration shows you the document in Online Layout view.

2. Use the scroll bars to see the rest of the document.

   Notice the Document Map on the left side of the window. It is a separate pane that contains an outline of your document. You can use the Document Map to move around your document and track where you are in the document. We'll return to Normal view by using the menu command.

3. To return to Normal view, select the View menu.
4. Then, click Normal.

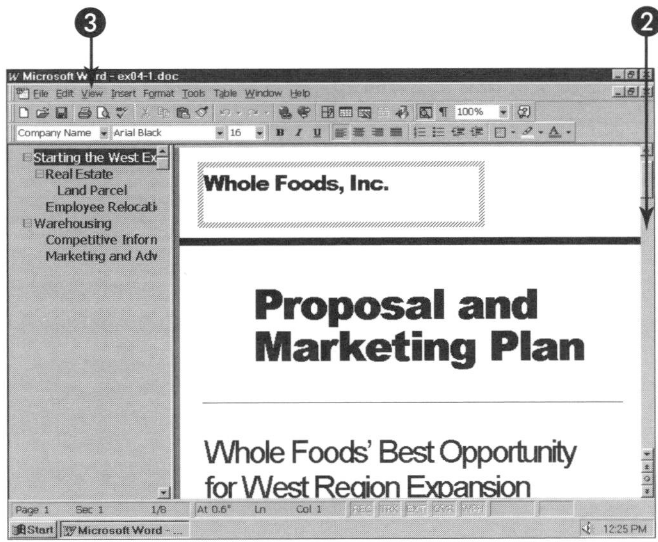

The Online Layout command is not a toggle. To turn off Online Layout view, you must select another view.

To make sure the text that appears in Online Layout view is always legible, you can change the minimum size for the text. While you are in Online Layout view, select Tools ➢ Options and click the View tab. Enter the minimum font size you want in the Enlarge Fonts Less Than box. The default font size is 12 points. See the accompanying figure.

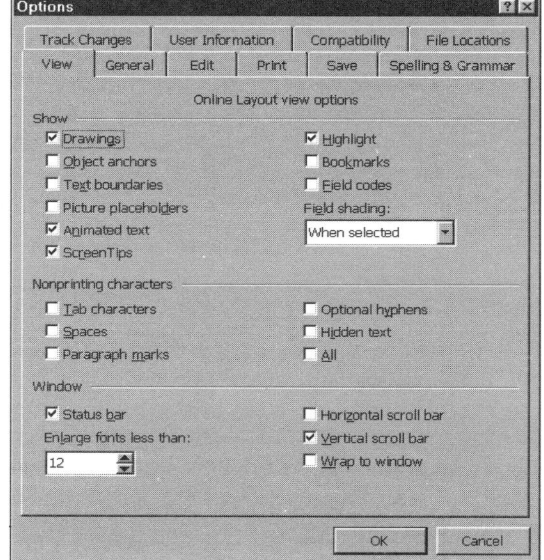

If you would like some more practice with Online Layout view, refer to Lesson 15, the section, "Viewing a Web Page with Online Layout view."

Checking out Outline view

Outline view enables you to view the overall structure of a document. It also lets you move to a different location in the document or to copy and move text more quickly than in Normal view. Now we'll check out Outline view and the Outline toolbar.

Checking out Outline view

❶ Click the Outline View button (the fourth button from the left on the View toolbar).

The accompanying illustration shows you the document in Outline view. The Outline toolbar at the top of the document window gives you tools to expand and collapse headings, promote and demote headings, and change the position of the headings in the outline hierarchy. The toolbar also has buttons with numbers on them, which enable you to display all heading levels (default) or one or more heading levels. We'll display heading levels 1 through 3.

❷ Click the 3 button on the Outline toolbar.

Only heading levels 1 through 3 appear in the document. See Lesson 12 for detailed information on creating and editing outlines.

❸ Click the Normal View button on the View toolbar, and you return to Normal view.

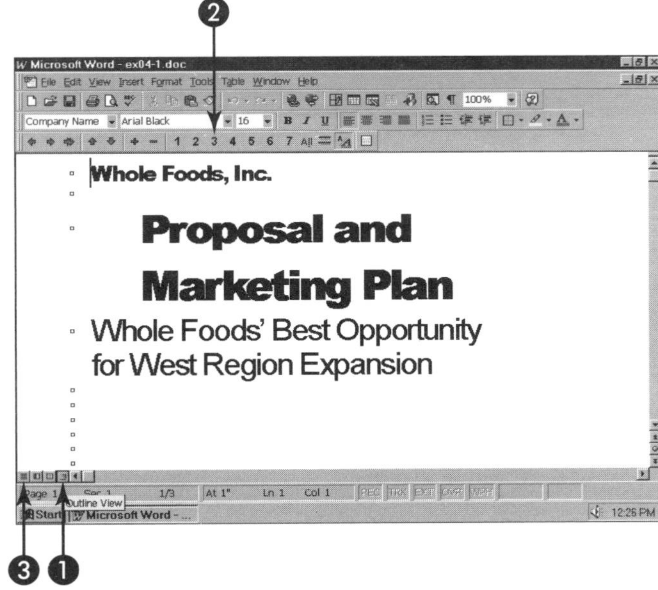

The Outline command is not a toggle. To turn off Outline view, you must select another view.

VISUAL BONUS: VIEW TOOLBAR AND OUTLINE TOOLBAR

The View toolbar contains tools for changing views of a Word document.

View toolbar

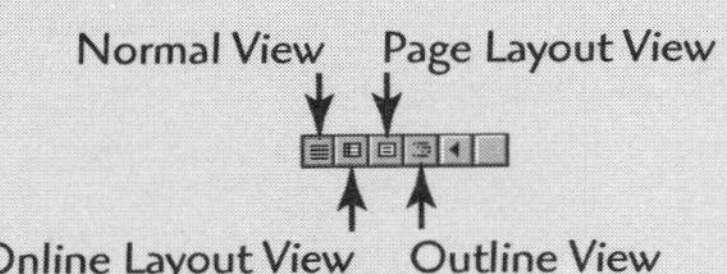

continued

4 Changing Views

Checking out Outline view

VISUAL BONUS: VIEW TOOLBAR AND OUTLINE TOOLBAR *(continued)*

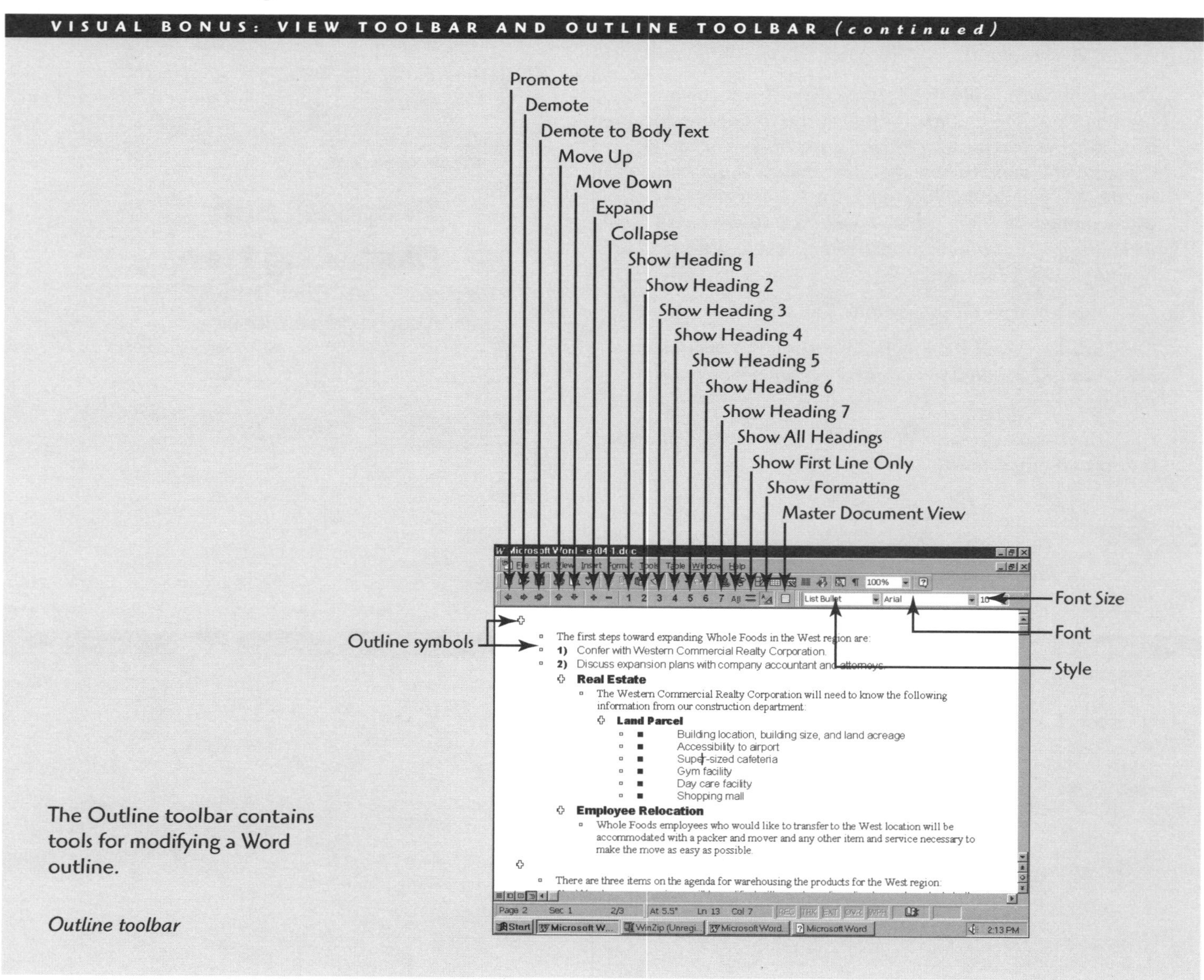

The Outline toolbar contains tools for modifying a Word outline.

Outline toolbar

REORGANIZING HEADINGS AND OUTLINES

You can modify an outline in various ways by using the buttons on the Outline toolbar. To reorganize your outline more easily, you can collapse and expand headings. Select the headings you want to collapse, and then click the Collapse button. Then you can promote, demote, or move the headings up or down. To expand headings, select them, and then click the Expand button.

- To change a heading, click anywhere in the heading.
- To promote a heading to a higher level (closer to the left margin), click the Promote button. To demote a heading to a lower level (indented farther from the left margin), click the Demote button.
- To promote and demote outline levels quickly, drag the outline symbol to the left to promote and to the right to demote.
- To demote a heading to body text, click the Demote to Body Text button.
- To move a heading up, click the Move Up button. To move a heading down, click the Move Down button.

SKILLS CHALLENGE: SWITCHING WORD VIEWS

This exercise recaps the skills you learned in this lesson. Answer the bonus questions to review the skills and help you determine your understanding of the topics covered. The answers to the bonus questions are located in Appendix C.

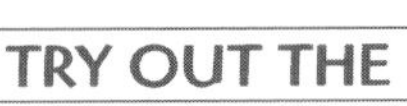

TRY OUT THE INTERACTIVE TUTORIALS ON YOUR CD!

1. Open Microsoft Word.
2. Open the file EX04-2.DOC.

Which view is used as the default view in Word 97?

3. Switch to Page Layout view.

How is the Page Layout view useful?

4. Scroll through the document.
5. Switch to Normal view.
6. Zoom in at 150 percent.
7. Zoom out at 50 percent.

When you want to get a closer look at your document, do you select a higher or lower magnification percentage?

8. Return to 100 percent magnification.

What is the name of the view that shows you what a document looks like as a Web page on the Internet?

9. Save the file.
10. Close the file.
11. Exit Microsoft Word.

TROUBLESHOOTING

Now you know more about changing document views. If you had any questions during this lesson, you might find the answers in the following table.

Problem	Solution
While I was in Page Layout view, I clicked the Page Layout View button to turn off the view and nothing happened.	To turn off Page Layout view, click the View button for the view you want to see.
I've been typing all the text into my document while in Page Layout view, but it seems very inefficient.	Switch to Normal view, which is the most efficient view for typing, editing, and formatting.
The fonts that I use are very small and I would like to see what they look like before I print the document.	Zoom in at a high percentage of magnification.
I selected the wrong magnification percentage when zooming.	Choose the percentage you want in the Zoom drop-down list.

WRAP UP

Before you take a break, let's review what you learned in this lesson:

- Switching to Page Layout view
- Zooming in and out in a document
- Looking at Online Layout view
- Using Outline view

For more practice, open any document and switch to different views of the document.

In the next lesson, we'll use Word's editing tools to make changes to your text and format the text on your page.

PART II

Getting Your Document in Shape

In this part, you'll learn how to edit, proofread, and format your Word documents. The lessons cover basic editing commands, Word's proofing tools, and how to enhance the appearance of your text. You'll also discover how to create lists, insert page numbering, and work with headers and footers.

This part contains the following lessons:

- Lesson 5: Revising Text
- Lesson 6: Proofreading Text
- Lesson 7: Formatting Fonts and Paragraphs
- Lesson 8: Creating Lists, Headers, and Footers
- Lesson 9: Taking Shortcuts

Revising Text

GOALS

In this lesson, you learn the following skills:

- Selecting text
- Deleting text
- Cutting and pasting text
- Cutting and copying text
- Using the Undo/Redo command
- Dragging and dropping text
- Finding and replacing text

Get ready

GET READY

For this lesson, you need the files EX05-1.DOC and EX05-2.DOC from the One Step folder.

When you've finished these exercises, you will have used Word's editing features to make changes to your business letter. The accompanying illustration shows the business letter after it has been edited.

TRY OUT THE INTERACTIVE TUTORIALS ON YOUR CD!

January 27, 1997

Ms. Kayla Hall
The Interpreter
750 Harvard Street, Suite 100
Boston, MA 01958

Dear Ms. Hall:

We are delighted to let you know that the periodical you ordered, Foreign Language Monthly, has come in from the publisher. The price of the periodical is $4.95 per issue. You can present this letter for a 15% discount on any additional foreign language periodicals you buy in this category.

Please come in to pick it up as soon as you can; we will hold it for two weeks. While you are in, you might want to browse through some of the other titles.

Sincerely,

Erisa Evans
Periodical Reference Manager

MAKING CHANGES TO TEXT

When you write letters, reports, memos, or any other kind of document, be prepared to revise and rework the text. As your ideas change and evolve, your original document becomes the first in what may be a series of drafts before you reach the final version.

In order to make changes to text, you have to know about Word's editing functions. You already know how to insert and overwrite text—these skills were introduced in Lesson 2. In Lesson 2 you also used the Backspace and Delete key to delete characters and make minor corrections. Now we'll talk about making some major corrections, such as deleting large amounts of text and copying, moving, and replacing text.

Before you learn how to use Word's editing functions, you need to know how to select or highlight text. You select text to define a portion that you want to type over, delete, move, copy, edit, or enhance. Knowing how to select text is essential because most of the commands and options in Word require that you select text first. For example, to make the text in a title bold or larger, you have to select it. You can select any amount of text with the mouse: a block of text, a word, a line, a sentence, a paragraph, or even the whole document.

You can also use key combinations to select text. Table 5-1 lists these combinations.

TABLE 5-1 USING KEY COMBINATIONS TO SELECT TEXT

To Select	Press
One character to the right of the insertion point	Shift+→
One character to the left of the insertion point	Shift+←
One word to the right of the insertion point	Shift+Ctrl+→
One word to the left of the insertion point	Shift+Ctrl+←
One line above the insertion point	Shift+↑
One line below the insertion point	Shift+↓
From the insertion point to the end of the line	Shift+End
From the insertion point to the beginning of the line	Shift+Home
From the insertion point to the beginning of the document	Shift+Ctrl+Home
From the insertion point to the end of the document	Shift+Ctrl+End
The entire document	Ctrl+A

In this lesson you'll find out how to move text using Cut and Paste and drag-and-drop. You'll also learn how to delete text, copy text from one location to another, search for text, replace text, and use the Undo and Redo commands.

The Whole Foods International Department has reviewed the business letter that you created in Lesson 2. They think the letter is excellent, but there are some changes that have occurred since you created the draft. In order to update the letter, you will need to make some corrections and changes using Word's editing commands.

Selecting text

By selecting text, you define a portion of text you want to type over, delete, move, copy, or enhance. Word highlights the text you select. You can use the mouse or the keyboard to select text. For the following exercises, you will need the file EX05-1.DOC from the One Step folder. This is the business letter you created in Lesson 2. It

Selecting text

consists of one page of text. In this exercise you select text in many different ways.

1. Open the file EX05-1.DOC.
2. Place the mouse pointer at the beginning of the first paragraph, hold down the left mouse button, and drag the mouse pointer across the word *Foreign*. This selects the text and highlights it, as shown in the accompanying illustration.
3. Double-click anywhere in the word *delighted*. Double-clicking a word selects only that word.

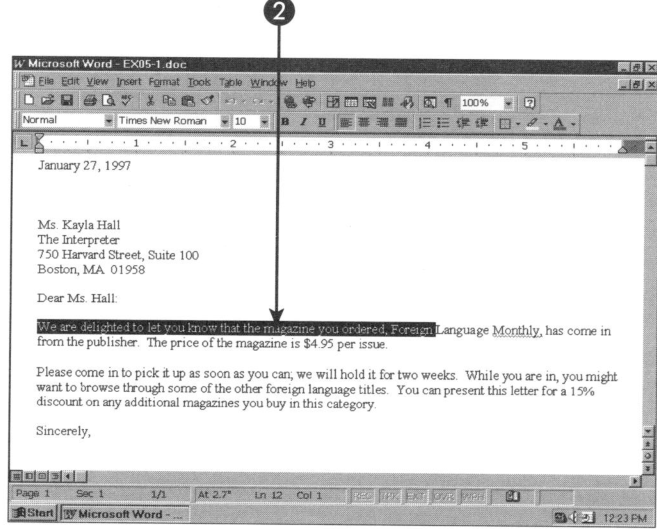

If you double-click a word to select it for dragging and then click (and hold) for the drag operation too quickly, the entire paragraph will be unintentionally selected. To avoid this, pause briefly before you click-and-hold to drag a word.

4. Click in the left margin next to the first line of text.

   Clicking in the left margin next to a line of text selects that line. Before you click, be sure the mouse pointer arrow points up and to the right when you place the mouse pointer in the left margin.

5. Hold down Ctrl and click anywhere in the second sentence in the first paragraph. This technique is called Ctrl-clicking; use it to select a sentence.
6. Double-click in the left margin next to the first paragraph.

   Double-clicking in the left margin next to a paragraph selects that paragraph. Before you click, be sure the mouse pointer arrow points up and to the right when you place the mouse pointer in the left margin.

A quick way to select a paragraph is to triple-click anywhere inside the paragraph.

7 Position the mouse pointer at the beginning of the second paragraph, click the left mouse button, and then hold down Shift as you click after the word *discount*.

This technique is called Shift-clicking; use it to select a block of text.

8 Hold down Ctrl and click anywhere in the left margin.

Ctrl-clicking in the left margin selects the entire document. Now that you've practiced selecting text, you need to know how to deselect highlighted text. We'll deselect the text for the whole document.

9 Point to anywhere on the open page and click the left mouse button.

Clicking the left mouse button anywhere on the page deselects the text.

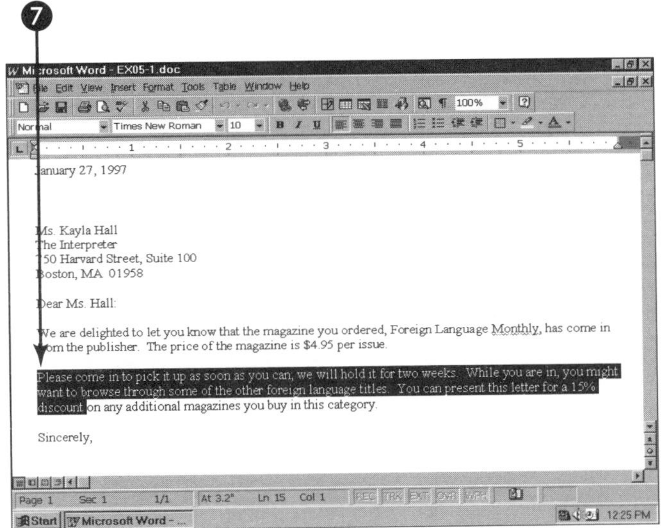

Deleting text

Until now, you've deleted a few characters with Backspace and Delete. Sometimes you may find that large portions of text you initially typed into the document are incorrect and need to be changed. Instead of overwriting the text to remove it, you can select any amount of text and then press Delete. We'll be courageous and delete the last paragraph.

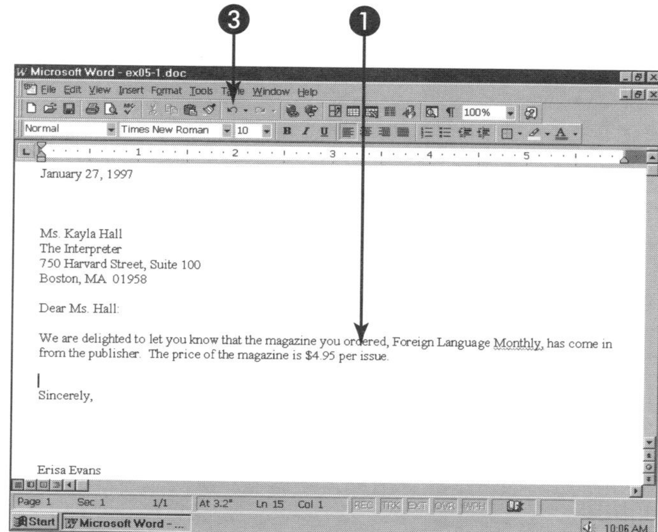

1. Double-click in the left margin next to the second paragraph to select the text you want to delete.
2. Press Delete.

   Word deletes the text. The remaining text moves up (or over) to fill in the gap.

Remember: When you delete text with the Delete or Backspace key, Word doesn't store it on the Clipboard. Therefore, you cannot paste the deleted text anywhere else.

It turns out that we really do need that paragraph we just deleted. Don't fret! We can restore it with the Undo command. When you delete text, Word can be very forgiving—as long as you catch your mistake right away. Let's undo the deletion now.

3. Click the Undo button on the Standard toolbar.

   It's like magic! Word restores the deleted paragraph. As you can see, the document returns to its original form.

4. Click anywhere on the page to deselect the text.

   In the "Using the Undo/Redo command exercise" you get a chance to use the Undo command again.

Cutting and pasting text

Cutting and pasting text is also referred to as moving text. This editing operation enables you to move information from one location to another in the document. For example, you might want to swap the order of paragraphs, or you might want to move text in a document because the layout of the document has changed. You don't have to go to the new location, enter the same text, and then erase the text in the old location. We'll move a couple of words from one location to another to show you how it works.

1. In the second paragraph, second sentence, double-click the word *foreign* hold the mouse button down, and drag across the word *language* to select the words you want to cut.
2. Click the Cut button (the button that shows scissors) on the Standard toolbar. This cuts the text from the document and places it on the Clipboard, a temporary holding area. The text no longer appears in its original location.
3. In the second paragraph, third sentence, click before the *m* in *magazines.*
4. Click the Paste button on the Standard toolbar. This pastes the text in the new location.

   Now let's delete the words *in this category* at the end of the last sentence in the letter.
5. In the second paragraph, third sentence, select *in this category*.
6. Press Delete. Word deletes the text.

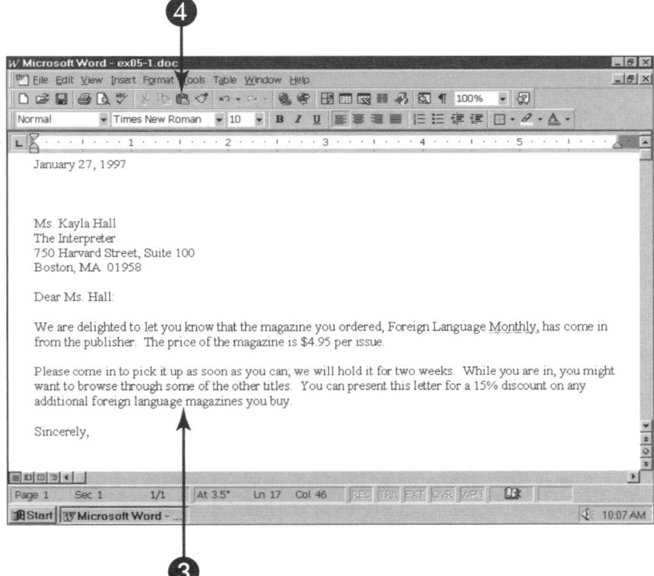

Another way to cut and paste is to use the key combinations Ctrl+X to delete the selected text and Ctrl+V to copy it to a new location.

Copying and pasting text

Suppose you want to copy text instead of moving it. For instance, you might want to use the same paragraph on more than one page. If you copy it, you don't have to type the paragraph over again. Let's create a second page, and then copy the first paragraph to the new page.

1. Press Ctrl+End to move to the bottom of the document.
2. Press Ctrl+Enter to insert a page break.

   The insertion point moves to page 2. Notice the Page 2 indicator at the left end of the Status bar.

3. Scroll up to Page 1.
4. Double-click in the left margin next to the first paragraph to select the text you want to copy.
5. Click the Copy button on the Standard toolbar.

   Clicking the Copy button copies the text to the Clipboard. The Clipboard is a temporary holding area for text and graphics.
6. Scroll down to Page 2 and click at the top of the page.
7. Click the Paste button on the Standard toolbar.

   By clicking the Paste button, you paste a copy of the text in the new location. Notice that the text still remains in the original location. Once the text is on the Clipboard, you can continue to paste that text over and over again, until you copy or cut text again to the Clipboard.

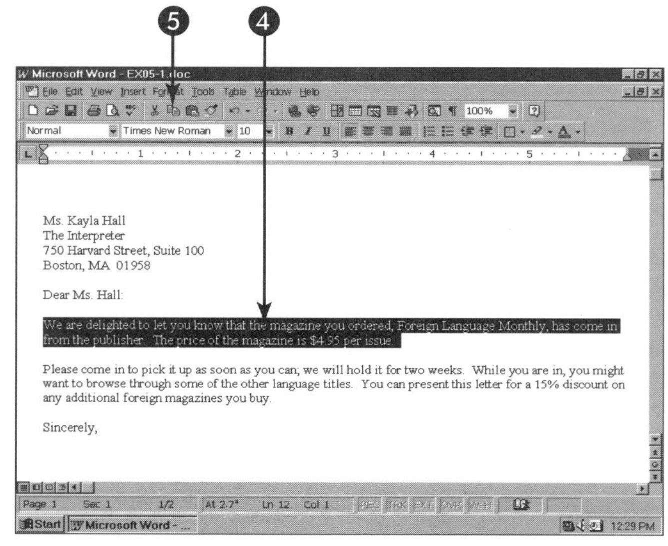

Another way to copy and paste is to use the key combinations Ctrl+C to copy and Ctrl+V to paste the text into a new location. If you're planning to copy text a short distance, you can also use drag-and-drop. See the exercise "Draggging and dropping text" for details.

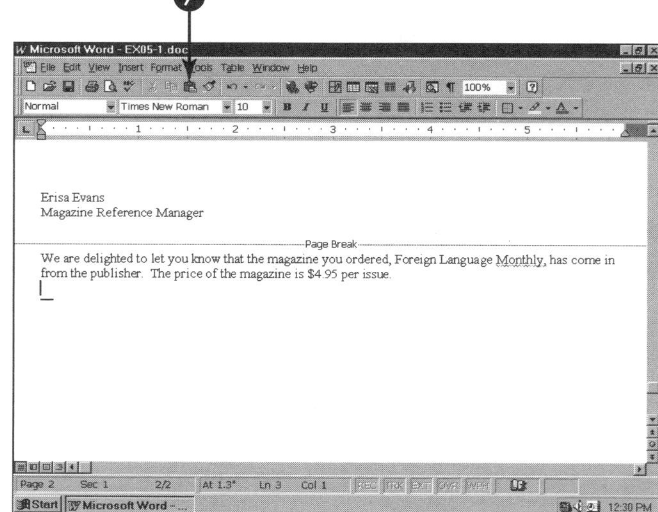

Using the Undo/Redo command

Earlier in this lesson, you used the Undo command to restore deleted text. You can also use the Undo feature to reverse many other types of actions: You can take out added text or remove character formatting, for example. Let's use the Undo command to reverse the Cut command.

1. Double-click in the left margin next to the paragraph on page 2.
2. Click the Cut button on the Standard toolbar to cut the text.
3. Click the Undo button on the Standard toolbar.

   Word restores the text you cut.

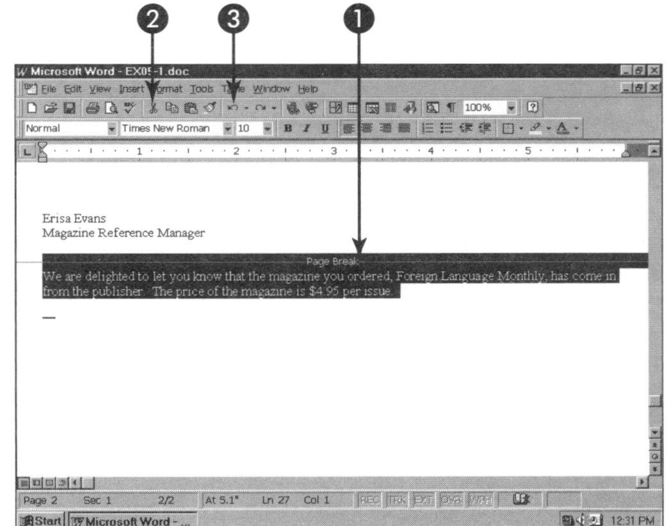

If you want to undo multiple actions, click the Undo drop-down arrow on the Standard toolbar. You'll see a list of your actions, starting with the most recent. You can undo them in this order only. Select the action(s) you want to undo, and Word reverses your action(s).

And just in case you change your mind again, Word provides the Redo feature to "undo" an action you just reversed with Undo. We'll use the Redo command to reverse undoing the Cut command.

4. Click the Redo button (the button that contains an arrow that curves to the right and down) on the Standard toolbar.

   Word undoes the Cut command you just reversed with Undo. The text is cut again.

Dragging and dropping text

In the "Cutting and pasting text" exercise, you moved text with the Cut and Paste commands. If you want to move text a short distance, you can also use the drag-and-drop method. We'll move the last sentence in the second paragraph to the end of the first paragraph.

1. Hold down Ctrl and click in the last sentence in the second paragraph to select the text you want to move.
2. Move the mouse pointer back over the selected text.
3. Click and hold down the left mouse button.

   A small box appears below the mouse pointer and a vertical line appears in the text near the mouse pointer arrow. The vertical line is a temporary insertion point. If you release the mouse button, the text you're dragging will drop where the temporary insertion point is located.

4. Drag the text to the end of the first paragraph, after the period, and then release the mouse button.

5. Click anywhere on the page to deselect the text.

   The sentence appears in the new location.

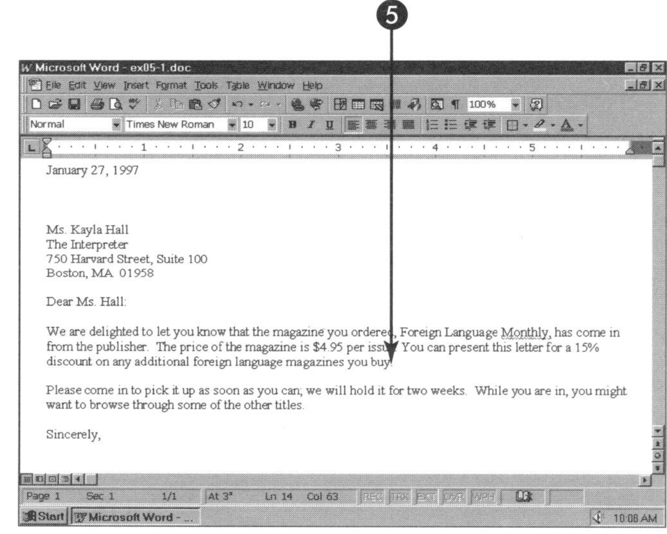

Finding and replacing text

With Word's Find and Replace features, you can locate text, character and paragraph formatting, or special characters and replace the original work with new text or formatting. Suppose you have a word, phrase, formatting characteristic, or special character that you entered incorrectly throughout the document. You can use the Edit ➢ Replace command to have Word search for and replace all occurrences of the incorrect information with the correct information.

Let's search for the word *language* throughout the business letter document.

1. Press Ctrl+Home to move to the beginning of the document.

   When you begin a search, Word starts at the insertion point and moves forward. So if you start the search in the middle of the document, Word searches the entire document—going from the middle to the end, and then to the beginning.

2. Press Ctrl+F.

   Word displays the Find and Replace dialog box with the Find tab selected. The insertion point is in the Find What text box.

3. Type **language** to enter the search string (the text you want to find).

4. Click the Find Next button to start the search.

   You can also press Enter to search. Word finds the first occurrence of the search string and highlights that text. The dialog box remains open onscreen. If you can't see the text that

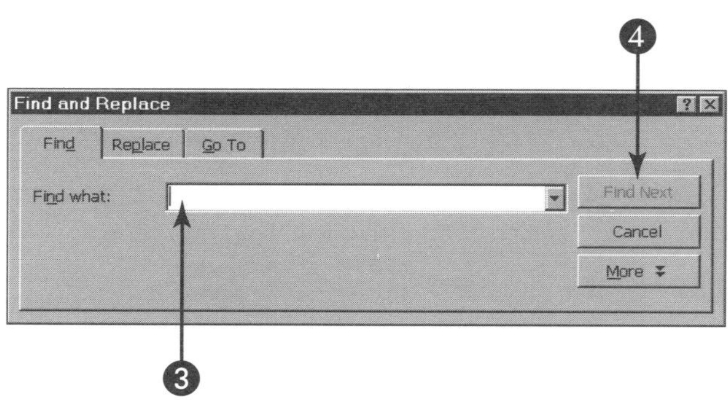

Word finds, drag the Find and Replace dialog box by its title bar to uncover the selected text.

If Word doesn't find any matching text, an alert message appears. Make sure you typed the search string correctly and click OK to try the search again.

5. Click the Find Next button again to find the next occurrence.
6. Click Cancel to stop searching.

While the Find and Replace dialog box is onscreen, you can make corrections to text in the document. Just click in the document and make the necessary changes. Then click anywhere in the dialog box to resume your search. After you close the dialog box, you can press Shift+F4 to repeat the search.

Now let's replace all occurrences of the word *magazine* with *periodical.*

7. Press Ctrl+Home to move to the beginning of the document.
8. Press Ctrl+H.

   Word displays the Find and Replace dialog box with the Replace tab selected. The previous search string appears highlighted in the Find What box.
9. Type **magazine** in the Find What box.
10. Press Tab.
11. Type **periodical** in the Replace With box.
12. Click the Replace All button to replace all occurrences.

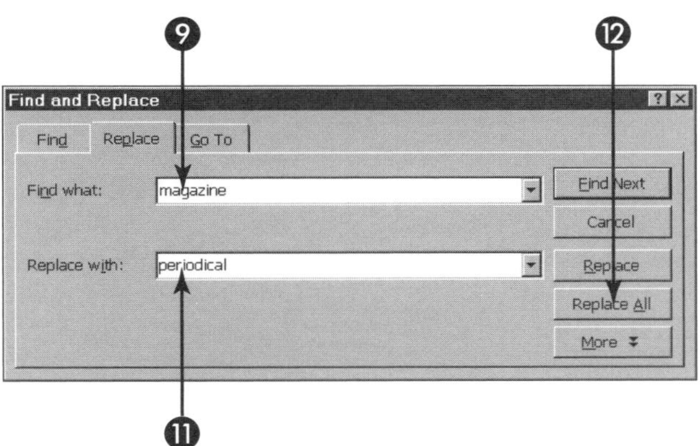

Finding and replacing text

13. Click OK to confirm the replacements.
14. Click Close to close the dialog box.
15. Save the file and close it.

If you replace all occurrences in one shot, be careful. Replace finds words that are parts of larger words and replaces only the matching portion. Make test replacements with Replace before you choose Replace All. If you want to replace text selectively, click Find Next to find the first occurrence. Then, click Replace when you want to replace the text. If you come to text that you don't want to replace, click Find Next to skip it.

Now that you've created and edited a business letter with Word's powerful editing commands, try creating your first memo and then edit it.

VISUAL BONUS: EDITING AND UNDO TOOLS

The Standard toolbar contains several tools for the editing and Undo commands.

Editing and Undo tools

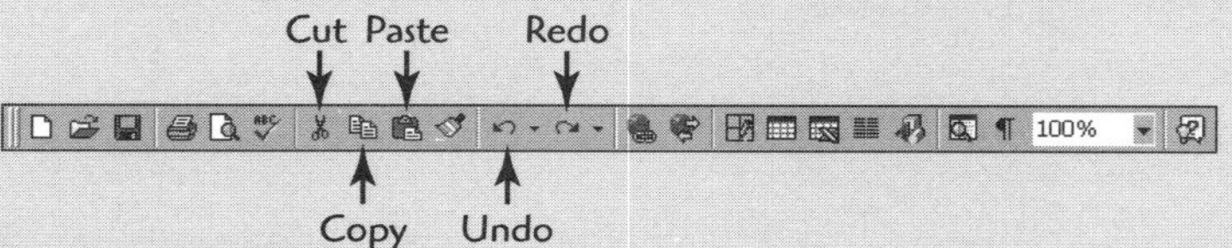

SKILLS CHALLENGE: EDITING A MEMO

In this review exercise, you use all the skills you've learned in this lesson to make some changes to a simple memo. Answer the bonus questions to review the skills and help you determine your understanding of the topics covered. The answers to the bonus questions are located in Appendix C.

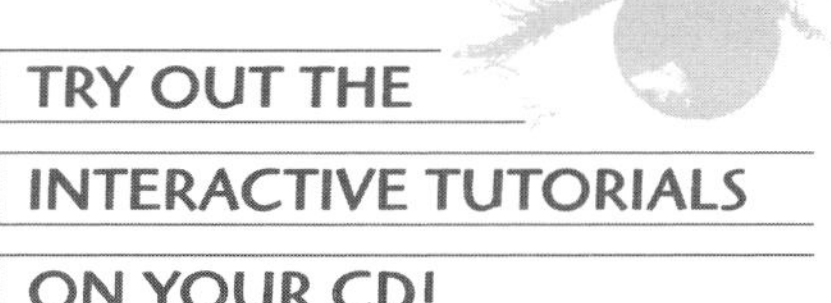

TRY OUT THE INTERACTIVE TUTORIALS ON YOUR CD!

1. Open the file EX05-2.DOC.
2. Delete the words *Marketing and* in the *To* line.

When you delete text, is the text stored on the Clipboard?

3. Cut the Date line and both the following end-of-paragraph marks.
4. Paste the cut items above the *To* line.
5. Copy *Planning* in the *Re* line and paste it before *meeting* in the first sentence.

When you copy or cut text, how long does it remain on the Clipboard?

6. Delete the last sentence in the second paragraph.

How do you undo more than one action?

7. Undo the deletion.
8. Redo the deletion.
9. Use drag-and-drop to swap the order of the first two sentences in the second paragraph.
10. Search for the word *agenda*.
11. Replace all occurrences of the words *Food & Beverage* with the word *product*.

Your document should now look like the accompanying illustration.

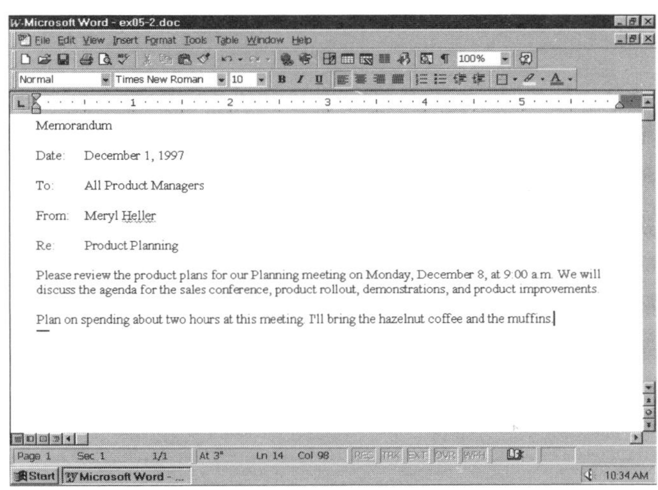

Troubleshooting

 *How can you replace text selectively?*

 Save your changes and close the file.

TROUBLESHOOTING

Finishing this lesson means you've grasped many of the skills needed to edit your documents. The following table offers solutions to some questions or challenges you might have experienced in practicing these skills.

Problem	Solution
I double-clicked a word to select it for dragging, but the entire paragraph was accidentally selected.	After you double-click, pause briefly before you click and hold to drag a word.
I selected too much text in my document.	Click anywhere in the document and then start over.
I copied the wrong text to the wrong location.	Click the Undo button on the Standard toolbar to undo the most recent copy. Or you can just delete the copied text and start over.
I tried to use drag-and-drop to move text a long distance and it's difficult to move the text.	Drag-and-drop should only be used for moving text short distances, within a screen. When you drag text a long distance, you may accidentally drop it in the wrong place. You can use Cut and Paste instead.

WRAP UP

Before you move on to the next chapter, let's review what you've learned:

- Selecting text
- Deleting, cutting, copying, and pasting text
- Using the Undo and Redo commands
- Moving text with drag-and-drop
- Finding and replacing text

If you would like more practice with these skills, try creating an invitation to a dinner party at your house next week.

In Lesson 6, you'll learn about the proofreading tools that will help you improve your documents.

Proofreading Text

GOALS

In this lesson, you learn the following skills:

- Checking spelling
- Checking grammar
- Finding synonyms with the thesaurus

Get ready

GET READY

To complete these exercises, you need the file EX06-1.DOC from the One Step folder.

When you've finished these exercises, you will have proofread a document using Word's proofing tools. The accompanying illustration shows the document after it has been proofed.

January 27, 1997

Ms. Kayla Hall
The Interpreter
750 Harvard Street, Suite 100
Boston, MA 01958

Dear Ms. Hall:

We are delighted to let you know that the magazine you ordered has arrived from the publisher. The price of the magazine is $4.95 per issue.

Please come in to pick it up as soon as you can; we will hold it for two weeks. While you are in, you might want to browse through some of the other foreign language titles. You can present this letter for a 15% discount on any additional magazines that you buy in this category. No coupons are necessary.

Sincerely,

Erisa Evans
Magazine Reference Manager

CHECKING YOUR DOCUMENT

What is more embarrassing than having spelling errors or blatant grammatical mistakes in your documents? The answer: Nothing. Word's three important proofing tools, spelling checker, grammar checker, and the thesaurus, are just what you need to save yourself a lot of embarrassment. These tools will help you correct errors and improve your writing.

By default, Word's AutoCorrect spelling checker finds possibly misspelled words as you type them. It compares each word in your document with words in its dictionary, and flags a word with a wavy red underline each time it cannot find a match. The built-in dictionary contains thousands of words.

AutoCorrect also automatically corrects common typing errors as you type. For instance, if you type two capital letters at the beginning of a word, AutoCorrect changes the second capital letter to a lowercase letter. If you type a lowercase letter at the beginning of a sentence, Word capitalizes the first letter of the first word in the sentence. If you type a lowercase letter at the beginning of the name of a day, Word capitalizes the first letter for you. Finally, if the Caps Lock key is accidentally turned on, in the case of words that should be capitalized, Word reverses the case of those letters and then turns off the Caps Lock key for you.

The spelling checker also alerts you if it finds repeated words (for example, *the the*), uncommon capitalization (*tHe*), or words that should be capitalized but aren't (*boston*). If the word in question is similar to words in spelling checker's dictionary, spelling checker offers alternative spellings that you may use for the correction. You can also add new words to the dictionary so they will not be flagged when encountered again.

Although a spelling checker is not a substitute for careful proofreading, it can often catch errors that the human eye may inadvertently overlook. Keep in mind, however, that a spelling checker cannot catch a word that is out of place in a sentence, grammatically incorrect, or misspelled in a way that makes a different, valid word. For example, the spelling checker will not find the error in the phrase "and then their was light." The word *their* is a correctly spelled pronoun in English, even though it is used incorrectly in this context. The word *there* is the correct choice.

The grammar checker locates possible grammatical, word usage, and punctuation errors, as well as stylistic flaws in your document. It examines each sentence in your document and determines whether the text conforms to a collection of grammatical and stylistic rules. The grammar checker's default setting is for standard writing, though it can be changed to formal, casual, or technical writing. You can also customize the rules to suit your own writing needs.

For each sentence that seems to break one or more of these rules, the grammar checker flags the text with a wavy green underline. In some cases, the grammar checker will suggest specific changes that the program can make directly. In other cases, problems will be identified that may require you to rewrite a sentence. You can choose to ignore a questioned phrase, get further explanation of a problem, or change the grammar checking rules as they apply to your document.

The thesaurus provides lists of synonyms for words you select in your document. It is perhaps the most valuable of Word's proofing tools because it helps you improve the precision, clarity, and style of your writing.

Word's proofing tools leave the actual decisions to you. Only you can decide whether you want to make specific changes in your text. However, these tools can help you see possible weak points in your writing, and offer various options to make your documents look professional and letter perfect.

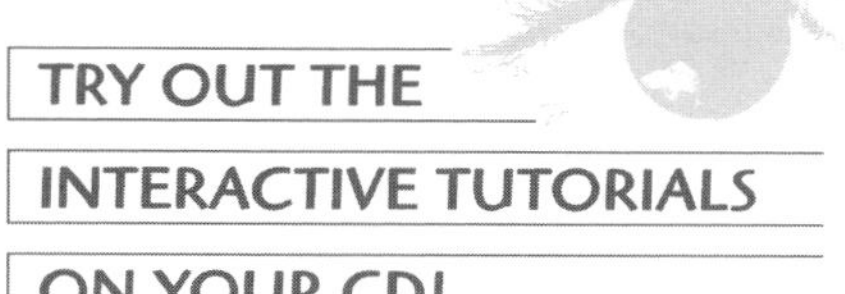

TRY OUT THE
INTERACTIVE TUTORIALS
ON YOUR CD!

Checking spelling

Checking spelling

Word's AutoCorrect spell checker finds misspelled words automatically as you type them. Keep it turned on to prevent misspellings from occurring. To complete the following exercises, you'll need the file EX06-1.DOC from the One Step folder. It's a first draft of the business letter we used in earlier lessons. The first draft has some spelling errors, each flagged with a red wavy line.

1. Open the file EX06-1.DOC.
2. Move the mouse pointer to the first word with a wavy red underline, *harvard*.

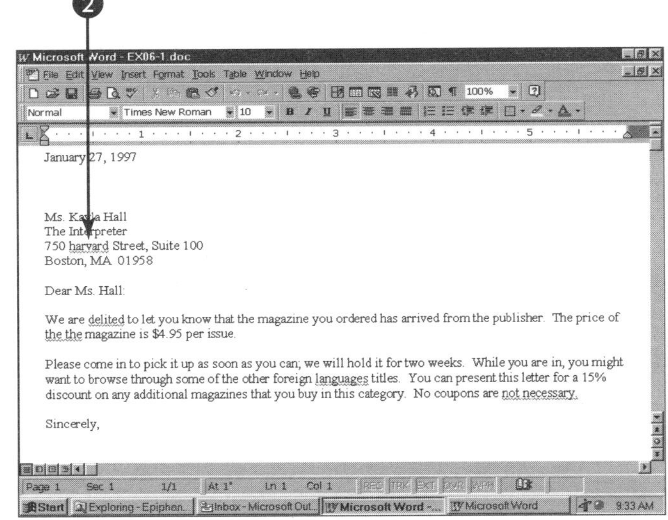

You can change the AutoCorrect settings at any time. To do so, select Tools ➢ AutoCorrect. The AutoCorrect tab in the AutoCorrect dialog box is selected by default. All the AutoCorrect options are turned on, but you can turn any of them off. At the bottom of the dialog box is the Replace Text as You Type list. This list contains commonly misspelled words and their correct replacement words. For example, if you always type chnage instead of change, Word corrects the word automatically because it is in the Replace Text as You Type list. You can add or delete words from the list. When you're satisfied with the AutoCorrect settings, click OK.

❸ Click the right mouse button to open the Spelling shortcut menu.

The Spelling shortcut menu lists a suggested spelling for the word. You can also select from several options to correct the error. If you choose the Spelling option, Word displays the Spelling and Grammar dialog box so you can check spelling using the dialog box instead of the shortcut menu.

You can also check spelling by clicking the Spelling and Grammar button on the Standard toolbar, or by choosing the Tools ➢ Spelling and Grammar command. Both methods display the Spelling and Grammar dialog box. One advantage of the dialog box is that it has an Undo button that enables you to undo the most recent spelling correction. Otherwise, you can click the Undo button on the Standard toolbar immediately after you make a spelling correction with the shortcut menu.

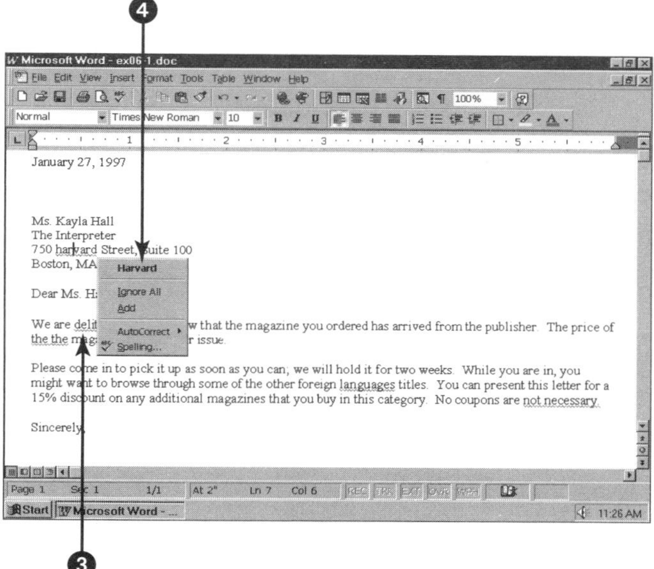

It's a good idea to keep AutoCorrect spelling checker turned on to prevent misspellings. However, if it's annoying to you, you can turn off the feature. To do so, choose Tools ➢ Options, click the Spelling tab, and click the Automatic Spelling Checking checkbox.

❹ Choose the suggested word, *Harvard,* in the menu to correct the capitalization of the word.

❺ Right-click the next wavy red-underlined word, *delited.*

❻ Choose the third suggested word in the list, *delighted,* to correct the misspelled word.

❼ Right-click the next wavy red-underlined word, *the.*

❽ Choose *Delete Repeated Word.*

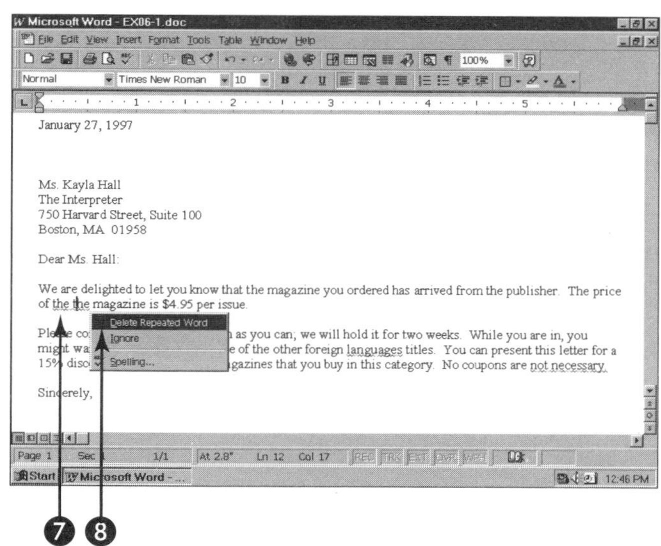

9. Scroll to the bottom of the document.

10. Right-click the last wavy red-underlined word, *Erisa*.

    As you can see, the spelling checker flags proper nouns. Unusual names are not in Word's dictionary, but popular names such as Eric, John, and Robert are in the dictionary and will not be flagged. Names of some countries and common proper nouns such as Hiroshima are also included in Word's dictionary.

11. Choose Ignore All to remove the underline and to tell Word to ignore all occurrences of this word (that is, not to flag this word again).

If you frequently use a word that the spelling checker keeps flagging, you might want to add that word to the dictionary. Simply choose the Add option in the Spelling shortcut menu. Word will then accept the word as a correctly spelled word in all future Word sessions.

Checking grammar

Word's grammar checker proofreads documents for correct grammar and use of language automatically as you type sentences. Grammar checking a document does not eliminate the need for proofreading, but does reduce the amount of proofreading you need to do. We'll use the grammar checker to respond to the possible grammar errors that are flagged in the letter with a wavy green underline.

1. Scroll to the top of the document.

2. Right-click the wavy green-underlined word, *languages*.

   The Grammar shortcut menu lists a suggested correction for the phrase. You can also select other grammar options: Ignore Sentence or Grammar. If you choose the Grammar option, Word displays the Grammar dialog box so that you can check grammar using the dialog box instead of the shortcut menu. To find out the grammatical reason for the flagging, click the button with the question mark in the lower left-hand corner of the dialog box.

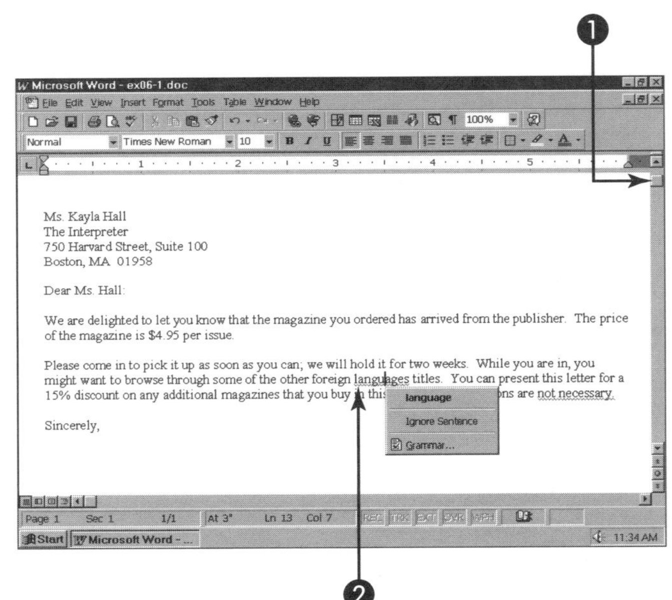

You can also check grammar by clicking the Spelling and Grammar button on the Standard toolbar or choosing the Tools ➢ Spelling and Grammar command. Both of these methods display the Spelling and Grammar dialog box. One advantage of the dialog box is that it has an Undo button that enables you to undo the most recent grammar correction. Otherwise you can click the Undo button on the Standard toolbar immediately after you make a grammar correction with the shortcut menu.

3. Choose *language* to change the word from plural to singular.
4. Right-click the last wavy green-underlined phrase, *not necessary*.
5. Choose *necessary* to correct the double negative.

Finding synonyms with the thesaurus

Word's built-in thesaurus looks up synonyms and antonyms and replaces a word with the word of your choice. Let's explore some alternatives for a particular word in the letter. First we'll locate the word *magazine*, and then we'll use the thesaurus to replace that word with a synonym.

1. Press Ctrl+Home to jump to the top of the document.
2. Press Ctrl+F to select the Edit ➢ Find command.
3. Type **magazine** to enter the search string.
4. Click the Find Next button to find the first occurrence of the word *magazine*.

   If you do not use the Find command to locate your word, you can click before, after, or within the word to indicate the word you want to look up. You can also double-click the word.

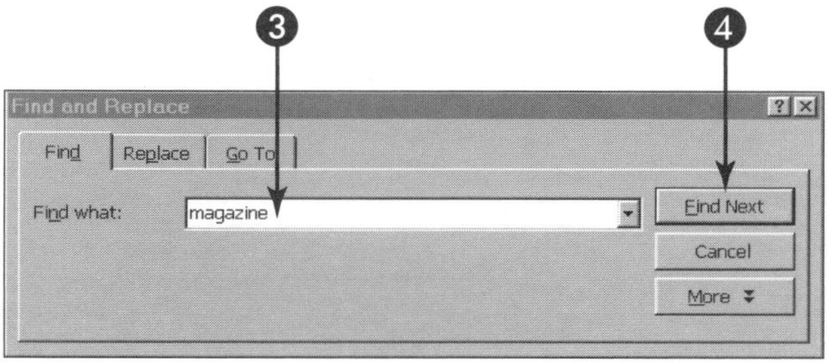

5. Select the Tools menu and highlight Language.
6. Click Thesaurus in the Language submenu (or press Shift+F7).

   The Thesaurus dialog box opens. The Looked Up text box displays the selected word. Below this box, you see a list of meanings with their parts of speech enclosed in parentheses. To the right of the Looked Up box, you see a list of synonyms.

Finding synonyms with the thesaurus

7. Look halfway down the list of synonyms to see the word *publication*, and then click it.
8. Click Replace to change the word in the document.
9. Save your changes and close the document.

If you want to see additional synonyms, open the thesaurus, select a synonym in the Replace with Synonym list, and click the Look Up button. Word will display a list of different synonyms.

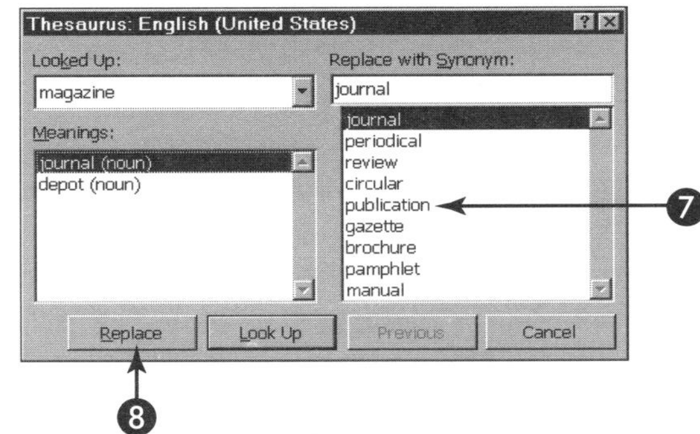

VISUAL BONUS: WORD'S PROOFING TOOLS

The Spelling shortcut menu offers many options for correcting your misspelled words.

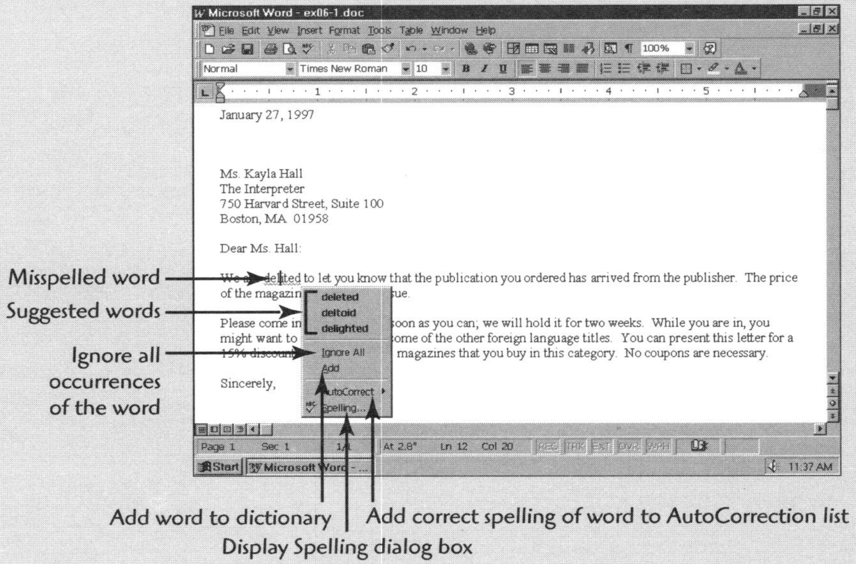

Misspelled word

Suggested words

Ignore all occurrences of the word

Add word to dictionary

Display Spelling dialog box

Add correct spelling of word to AutoCorrection list

Spelling shortcut menu

Finding synonyms with the thesaurus

The Grammar shortcut menu offers several ways to correct grammar, style, usage, and punctuation.

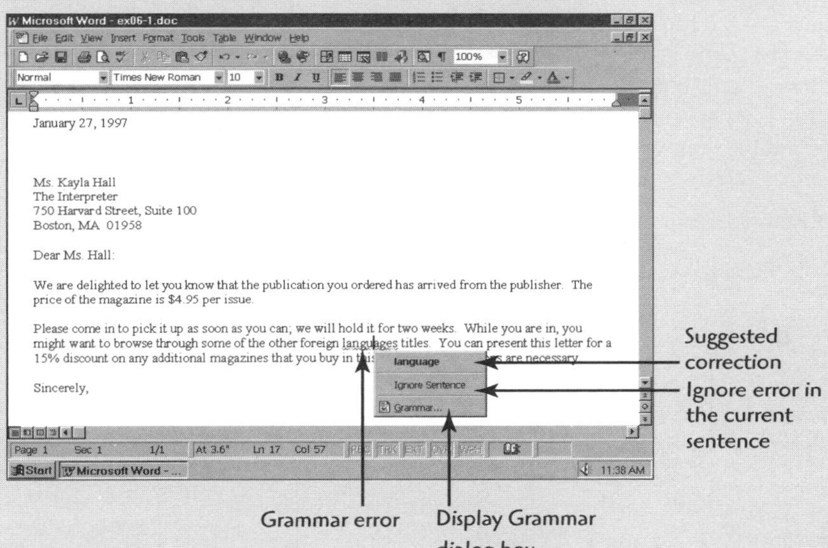

Grammar shortcut menu

The Thesaurus dialog box lets you find synonyms, antonyms, words related to the word you're looking up, and the parts of speech for the meanings of a word.

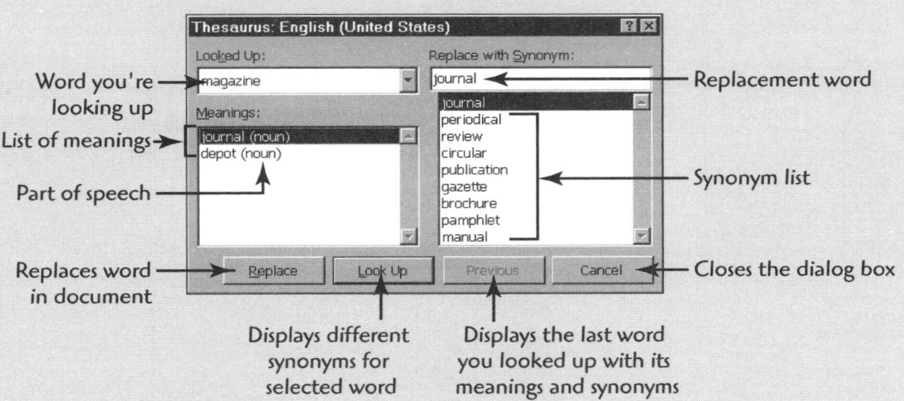

Thesaurus dialog box

Skills challenge

SKILLS CHALLENGE: PROOFING IT ALL

This exercise gives you a chance to practice the skills you've learned in this lesson. You correct the spelling and grammar errors, as well as find synonyms in the thesaurus, using a draft version of the memo you created earlier in Lesson 5. Answer the bonus questions to review the skills and help you determine your understanding of the topics covered. The answers to the bonus questions are located in Appendix C.

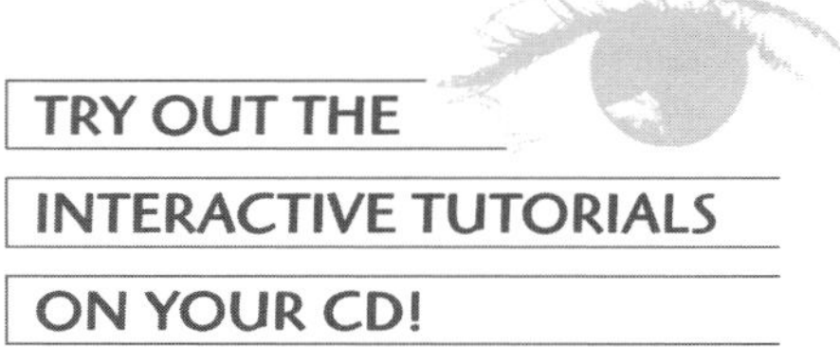

1. Open the file EX06-2.DOC.
2. Correct all the spelling errors flagged in the document.

If spelling checker flags a proper noun, what are your two choices for removing the wavy red underline?

3. Correct all the grammar errors flagged in the document.

2 *What is the easiest method for correcting grammar errors?*

4. Locate the word *agenda* with the Find command.

Name the three methods for selecting a word you want to look up in the thesaurus.

5. Replace the word *agenda* with a synonym.

   Your document should now look like the accompanying illustration.

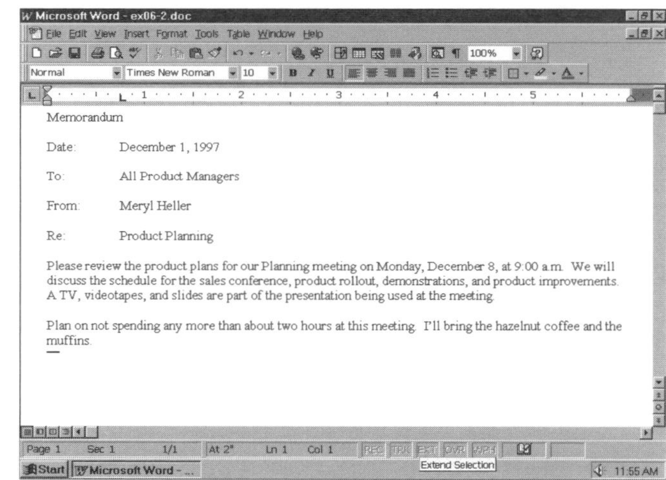

6. Save the file.
7. Close the file.

TROUBLESHOOTING

Now you've explored the proofing tools that Word has to offer. The following table offers solutions to several issues you might have encountered in working on these skills.

Problem	Solution
I chose the wrong option from the Spelling shortcut menu.	Click the Undo button on the Standard toolbar immediately after you choose the wrong option. Then start over.
The Standard Writing grammar rules are not strict enough.	You can change the grammar rules for the Standard Writing style by selecting Tools ➢ Options. Click the Grammar tab, choose Settings, and then select the options you want.
I write more casually and find that the Standard Writing style doesn't suit my needs.	Choose a different writing style by selecting Tools ➢ Options, clicking the Grammar tab, and choosing Casual from the Writing Style drop-down list.
I chose a word in the synonym list and looked it up, but didn't find a word I want. Now I want to get back to the original word I looked up.	Click the Previous button in the Thesaurus dialog box.

Wrap up

WRAP UP

Before moving on to the next lesson let's review the skills you learned:

- Using AutoCorrect to check spelling
- Using the grammar checker
- Finding synonyms with the thesaurus

For more practice with the proofing tools, create a flyer to announce that you have some furniture for sale.

The next lesson shows you how to embellish the text in your documents by applying character formatting.

Formatting Fonts and Paragraphs

GOALS

In this lesson, you learn the following skills:

- Adding bold, italics, and underlines
- Changing fonts
- Changing font sizes
- Setting margins
- Setting tabs
- Indenting text
- Aligning text
- Adjusting line spacing

Get ready

GET READY

For this lesson, you will need the file EX07-1.DOC from the One Step folder.

When you finish the last exercise in this lesson, you will have produced a document that looks like the accompanying illustration.

GREAT AMERICAN PUBLISHERS
100 Seaside Avenue
Greenwich, CT 06345
203-555-7800

January 27, 1997

Ms. Kayla Hall
The Interpreter
750 Harvard Street, Suite 100
Boston, MA 02110

Dear Ms. Hall:

We are delighted to let you know that the magazine you ordered has arrived from the publisher. The price of the magazine is $4.95 per issue.

Please come in to pick it up as soon as you can; we will hold it for two weeks. While you are in, you might want to browse through some of the other foreign language titles. You can present this letter for a 15% discount on any additional magazines that you buy in this category. **No coupons are necessary**.

This month we are featuring the most popular foreign language magazine on the market. Here is a small sample of one of the great articles in it:

Before you travel to a foreign country, study the language of the country you are visiting. Buy foreign language cassette tapes, books, and videotapes or borrow them from your local library. Also check out language schools and college courses offered in a foreign language. Before you know it, you will be speaking the language with ease.

Sincerely,

Erisa Evans
Magazine Reference Manager

CHANGING CHARACTER FORMATTING

After you edit your text, you have to make sure all of that hard work gets noticed. When used appropriately, fonts not only make your document more readable, they also help set a style and tone for text. Applying bold, italics, or underline formatting to these fonts adds emphasis to your words, highlighting important points and making your document more attractive.

A font is a typeface and size set for letters, numbers, and special characters. One font might be used for headings in a document, and another for the body text. However, a good rule to follow is to use no more than two fonts on a single page. Otherwise, your document becomes busy and difficult to read. In the Normal template, which is the one applied when you create a new document, the default font is Times New Roman and the font size for text is 10 points.

A point is a standard measurement of type size; it equals 1/72 of an inch. For example, characters in a 10-point font size are 10/72 of an inch tall. Typically, business letters use either a 10- or 12-point setting for text.

You can use the Formatting toolbar to choose a font and adjust its size. You can also use it to apply bold, italic, and underline formatting. All the buttons on the Formatting toolbar are shortcuts to items that appear in the Format menu. The Format menu offers more formatting options than the toolbar. For one thing, you can use the Font dialog box, which is accessed through the Format menu, to fine-tune your fonts.

There are a number of advantages to using the Font dialog box. You can make all your font formatting changes in one fell swoop instead of using each individual tool on the toolbar. You can also

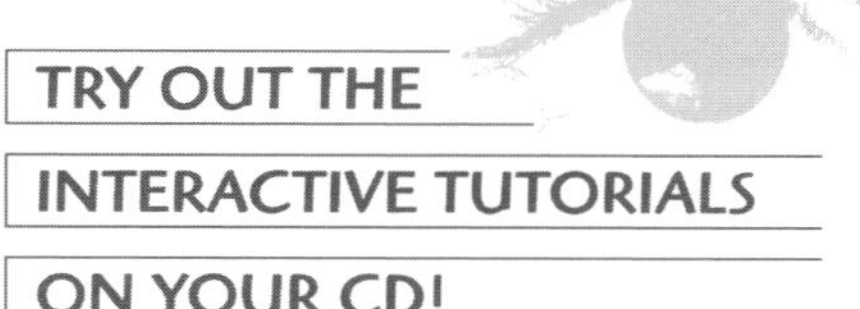

preview the font changes before applying them, and you can apply effects that aren't available on the Formatting toolbar (for example, Superscript, Shadow, and Small Caps).

You can use the fonts provided by Word and fonts designed especially for your printer. You can also buy font software packages that give you a myriad of fonts from which to choose. If Word doesn't have a screen version of the printer font you select, it substitutes a font. In such cases, the printout looks different from what you see onscreen.

You can apply a new font to a single word or any amount of text you want to change. You can change the font color by either using the Font Color tool at the right end of the Formatting toolbar or the Font Color options in the Font dialog box. Many font colors are available in various shades, hues, and patterns that you can use to spiff up your documents. You can display text colors on a color monitor even if you print the document on a black-and-white printer. However, if you have a color printer, you'll benefit more from changing font colors.

Adding bold, italics, and underline

By adding font styles such as bold, italics, and underline to your text, you can enhance and emphasize individual characters, words, or as much text as you want

For the following exercises, you'll use the EX07-1.DOC file from the One Step folder. This file contains the business letter you've worked with in earlier lessons. We'll emphasize some of the text by applying bold, italics, and underline. This can be done either with buttons on the Formatting toolbar (shown in the accompanying illustration), or the Format Font command. In this exercise, we use the toolbar buttons and the menu commands.

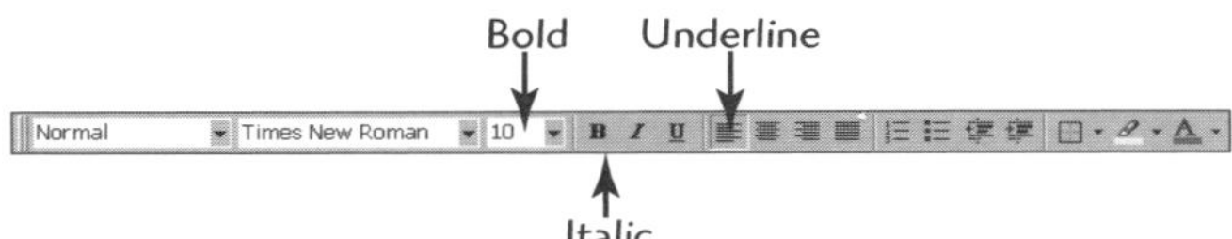

1. Open the file EX07-1.DOC.
2. In the second paragraph, select *No coupons are necessary*.

3. Click the Bold button on the Formatting toolbar (or press Ctrl+B).
4. Select the last paragraph.
5. Click the Italic button on the Formatting toolbar (or press Ctrl+I).
6. In the second paragraph, select *15% discount.*
7. Click the Underline button on the Formatting toolbar (or press Ctrl+U).
8. Click anywhere in the document to deselect the text.

   Your document should now resemble the one in the accompanying illustration.

The font style buttons on the Formatting toolbar are toggles. To undo formatting, select the text and click the button again.

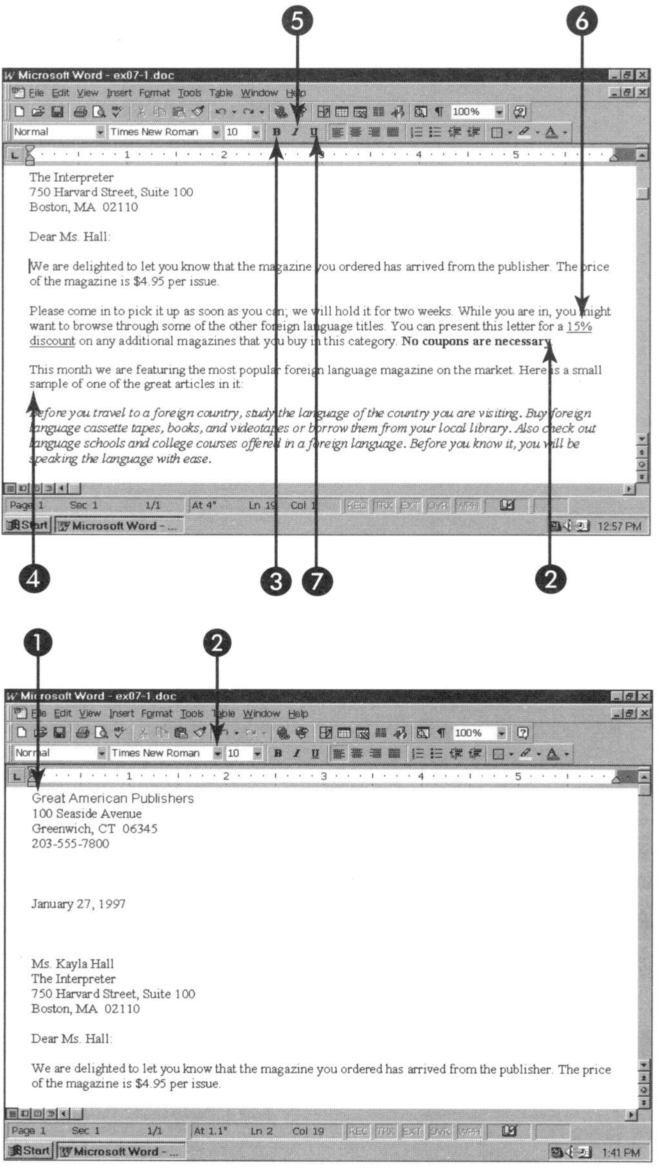

Changing the font

A font specifies the overall look of the character set. The default font is Times New Roman, but you can change it to Arial, Courier, Impact, or choose from a multitude of other fonts. Varying fonts helps draw attention to important words and phrases in a document. For example, you can change the font for a title and subtitle to make them stand out at the top of the document. Often the letterhead of a document looks better when it is emphasized by formatting. In this exercise, you change the font used in the letterhead.

1. Select the company name in the letterhead.
2. Click the Font drop-down arrow on the Formatting toolbar (the Font box contains the name of the current font, Times New Roman).

   The fonts in the list may vary, depending on your printer and any additional fonts you have installed.

3. Drag the scroll bar to the top of the list.
4. Choose Arial. This font is used often for letterheads. It offers a clean, easy-to-read look.
5. Click anywhere in the document to deselect the text.

When you select fonts for a document, the most recently used fonts will be listed at the top of the Font drop-down list, with a line between them and the alphabetical listing of all fonts. Because it's best to limit yourself to a few fonts and use them consistently in a document, it's a good idea to have this list handy. The list also saves you from having to scroll through the longer list each time you want to apply a particular font.

Let's also change the font for the letterhead address. This time, you'll use the Font dialog box to make the change. This will let you preview the appearance of the font before you apply it.

6. Select the letterhead address.
7. Select the Format menu.
8. Click Font. The Font dialog box appears.
9. In the Font list, drag the scroll bar to the top.
10. Choose Arial.

    The Preview box at the bottom of the dialog box shows you how the text will look if you apply the font.

11. Click OK.

    As you can see, the text for the letterhead address appears in the Arial font.

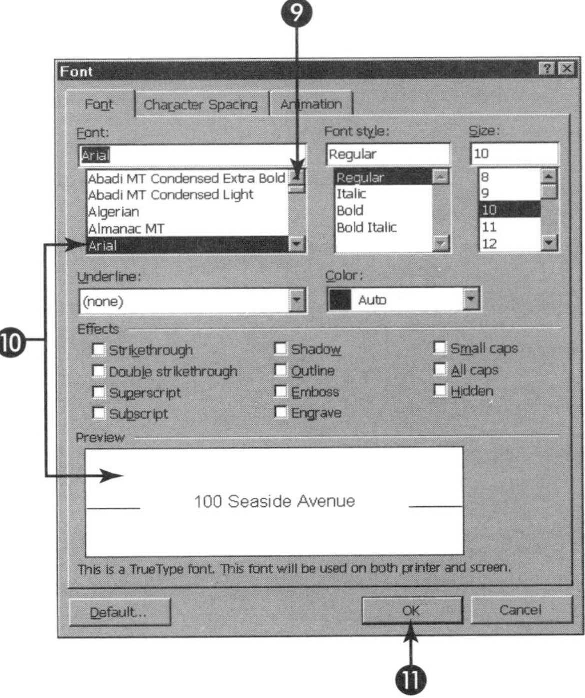

Changing the font size

Changing the font size

The font size controls the height of the font characters. The default font size for the Times New Roman font is 10 points. A point is equal to 1/72 of an inch. Changing the font size is handy when you want to bring attention to a title by increasing its font size. Next, let's change the font size of the company name in the letterhead.

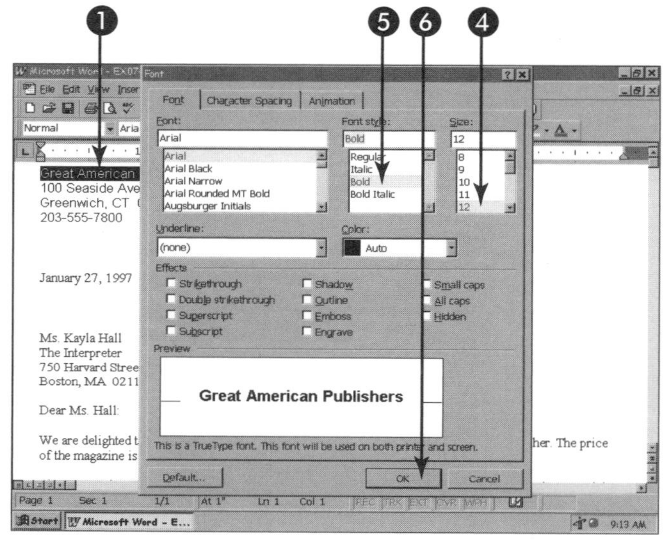

1. Select the company name in the letterhead.
2. Select the Format menu.
3. Click Font.
4. In the Size list, choose 12.

   The font sizes in the list may vary, depending on your printer and the selected font.
5. In the Font Style list, choose Bold.
6. Click OK to accept both changes you made to the text.

   The dialog box closes. The 12-point font looks good, but let's make it a little larger using the Formatting toolbar. Notice the text is still selected.
7. Click the Font Size drop-down arrow on the Formatting toolbar, and select 14.
8. Click anywhere in the document to deselect the text.

   The document now looks like the accompanying illustration.

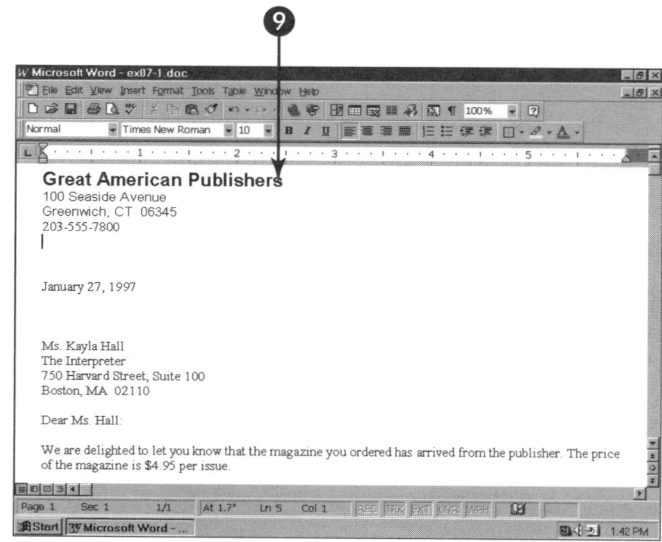

Some formatting styles, especially bold and shadows, increase the width of the characters and may change the way the text wraps.

Let's apply small capitals to the company name in the letterhead.

9. Select the letterhead company name.

⑩ Press Ctrl+Shift+K.

⑪ Click anywhere in the document to deselect the text.

The company name in the letterhead appears in small capitals.

You can use keyboard shortcuts for some other effects besides small capitals: Ctrl+Shift+plus sign for Superscript; Ctrl+equal sign for Subscript; Ctrl+D for Shadow, and Ctrl+Shift+A for All Capitals.

VISUAL BONUS: FONT DIALOG BOX

The Font dialog box enables you to change the font, font size, and font style. You can also apply effects and make other changes to selected text.

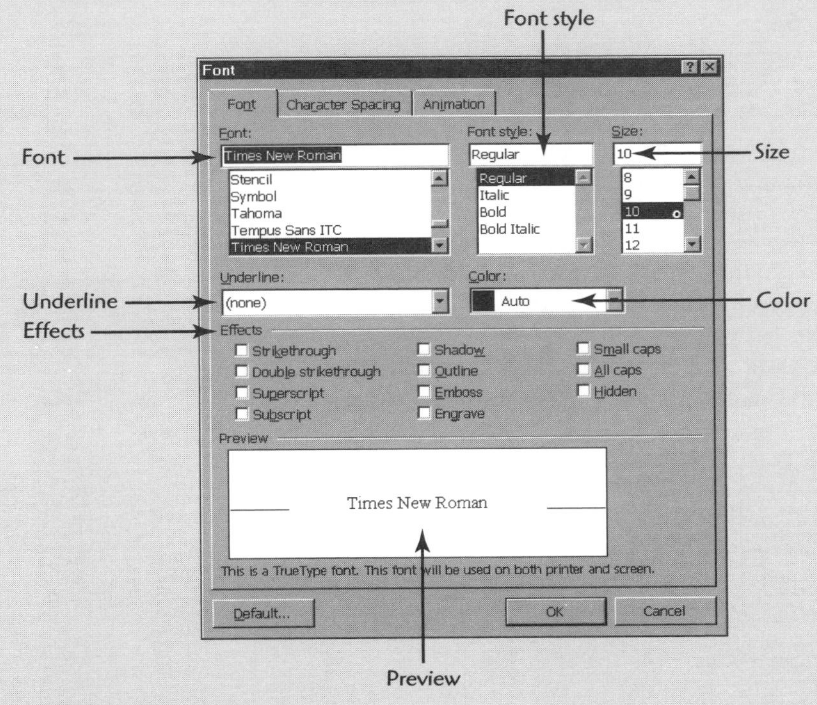

Font style
Font
Size
Underline
Color
Effects
Preview

Font dialog box

Setting tabs

SETTING TABS AND MARGINS

Setting tabs is useful for indenting paragraphs and lining up columns of numbers and text.

You can set different types of tab stops: left (default), center, right, or decimal tabs. Each time you press the Tab key on the keyboard, Word moves your text to the next tab stop. Word has preset tab stops every one half inch. For example, there is a left tab at 1/2″, 1″, 1-1/2″, 2″, and so on, all the way across the ruler. If you don't want to use the preset tabs, you can set new tab stops.

You can set tab stops in the Format➢Tabs dialog box. But, an easier way to set tab stops for the entire document is to use the ruler at the top of the document window. If you want to set tab stops for just one paragraph, you select the paragraph and then make the tab stop changes on the ruler.

Margins are the empty spaces around the four edges of a page. Setting margins in Word is very easy compared to setting them on a typewriter. With a typewriter, once you set the margins and type the document, nothing can be changed without some retyping. In Word, however, you can change the margins before, during, or after you enter text.

Word presets the top and bottom margins at 1″ and the left and right margins at 1.25″. You can adjust the margins for a single paragraph or an entire document.

The business letter that you've been working on in earlier exercises contains block text. This means that all lines begin at the left margin. Let's indent the paragraphs to make the letter easier to read.

Setting tabs

Word has default tabs at half-inch intervals from the left margin. However, you can set left, center, right, decimal, and dot leader tabs. Let's use the Tab key to indent the first paragraph in the business letter.

1. In the first paragraph, click before the *W* in *We*.

2. Press the Tab key to insert a tab.

   Word inserts the tab and moves the insertion point to the beginning of the tab stop. Notice that the first sentence in the

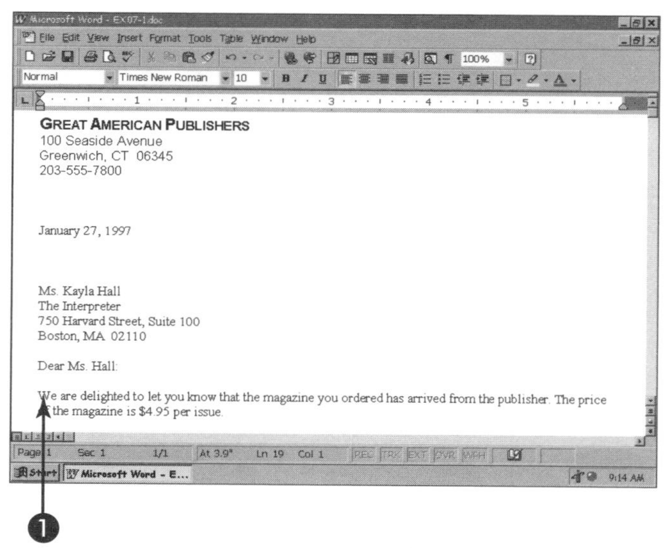

paragraph now starts 1/2" from the left margin. The paragraph is indented too far from the left margin, so let's undo the tab insertion.

3. Press Ctrl+Z.

   Word removes the tab and moves the insertion point back to the left margin. As you can see, the first sentence in the paragraph now starts at the left margin. Let's practice setting and removing tab stops.

4. Click the 1/4" mark—the second tick from the left end of the ruler—to set a tab at 1/4" .

   A tab marker, represented by the letter L for a left tab stop appears under the 1/4" tick mark.

5. Press the Tab key to insert a tab and indent the paragraph 1/4" from the left margin.

6. In the second paragraph, click before the *P* in *Please*.

7. Click the 1/4" mark—the second tick from the left end of the ruler—to set a tab at 1/4" .

8. Click the 3/4" mark—the sixth tick from the left end of the ruler—to set a tab at 3/4".

9. Press the Tab key twice to insert two tabs and indent the paragraph 3/4" from the left margin.

   Now, let's remove a tab stop from the ruler.

10. Point to the Left Tab marker (L) at the 3/4" mark on the ruler, hold down the left mouse button, and drag the marker down and off the ruler.

    Word moves the insertion point to the next tab stop. Now your paragraph is indented at 1/2".

11. Press Backspace.

    Word moves the insertion point to the next tab stop. Now your paragraph is indented at 1/4".

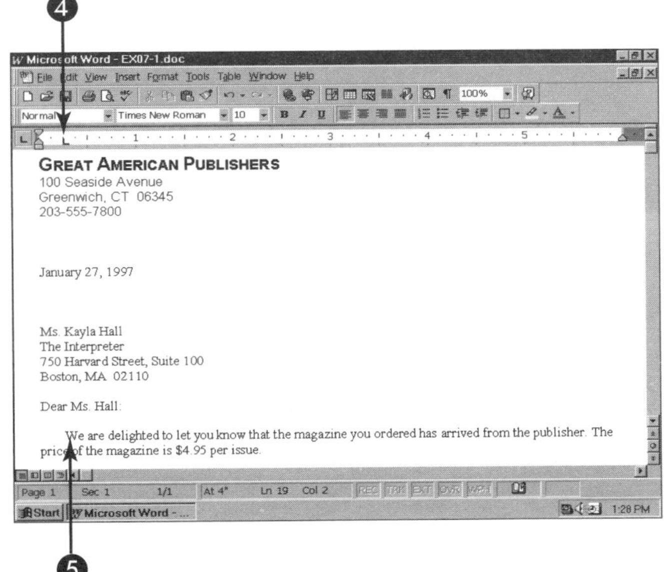

Setting tabs

⑫ Set a tab at 1/4" for the third paragraph and indent the paragraph at 1/4".

Your document now looks like the accompanying illustration.

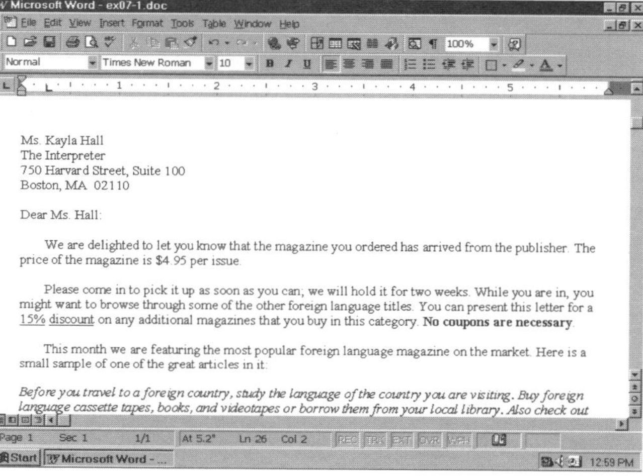

Ms. Kayla Hall
The Interpreter
750 Harvard Street, Suite 100
Boston, MA 02110

Dear Ms. Hall:

We are delighted to let you know that the magazine you ordered has arrived from the publisher. The price of the magazine is $4.95 per issue.

Please come in to pick it up as soon as you can; we will hold it for two weeks. While you are in, you might want to browse through some of the other foreign language titles. You can present this letter for a 15% discount on any additional magazines that you buy in this category. **No coupons are necessary.**

This month we are featuring the most popular foreign language magazine on the market. Here is a small sample of one of the great articles in it:

Before you travel to a foreign country, study the language of the country you are visiting. Buy foreign language cassette tapes, books, and videotapes or borrow them from your local library. Also check out

NOTE

To clear all the tabs in one fell swoop, select Format ➢ Tabs and click the Clear All button.

SETTING TAB STOPS WITH LEADERS

You can also set tab stops with leader characters. A leader character is a solid, dotted, or dashed line that *leads up* to tabbed text. When you press Tab, Word fills the space with leader characters. Leader characters are frequently used in a table of contents or index and are excellent for creating the lines for fill-in forms. For example, a dotted line leads your eyes across the space between a chapter name and the page number on which the chapter begins. To set a tab leader, select the paragraphs to which you want to add leader characters before the tab stops. Select Format ➢ Tabs to display the Tabs dialog box. In the Tab Stop Position box, type the position for a new tab, or choose an existing tab stop. In the Alignment section, choose an alignment type for the text that appears at the tab stop. For a table of contents, choose Right alignment. In the Leader section, choose a leader option, and click Set.

Setting margins

The default for the top and bottom margin is one inch. The default for the left and right margin is 1.25 inches. Word lets you adjust the top, bottom, left, and right margins at any time. First let's check the top margin setting indicator in the document.

1. Click before the *G* in *Great* in the letterhead.

   Look at the fourth indicator from the left end of the Status bar (at the bottom of your screen). At 1" tells you the vertical position of the insertion point and where the first line of the document will start printing on paper. Now let's set the top margin at 1 1/2".

2. Select the File menu.
3. Choose Page Setup.

   The Page Setup dialog box opens, and you see the Margins tab displayed. Notice the text boxes for each of the four margins—Top, Bottom, Left, and Right. Top is selected.

4. Type **1.5** to specify a 1.5" top margin.
5. Click OK.

   Now the indicator on the Status bar has changed to At 1.5". Your document will begin one and one-half inches down from the top of the paper when printed.

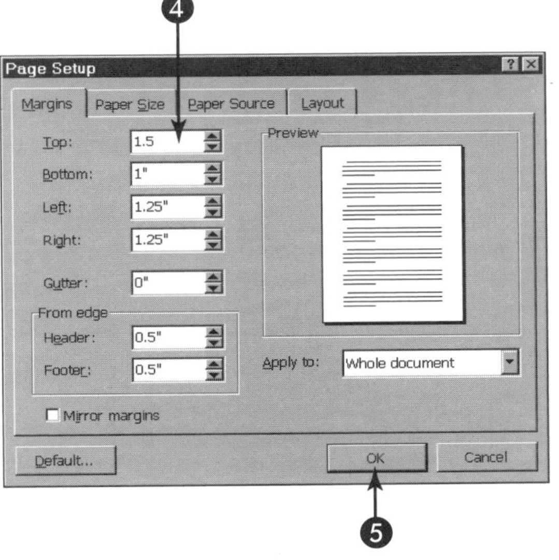

Setting margins

ADDING HYPHENATION

When you're finished writing and editing your document, you may want to use Word's Hyphenation feature to add hyphenation. To hyphenate a word means to split a long word at the end of a line. That way, you can eliminate gaps in a ragged right margin and get the text to fit better on the page. There are two ways to hyphenate text: manually and automatically.

To hyphenate your text manually, select Tools ➢ Language, and select Hyphenation to display the Hyphenation dialog box. Then click the Manual button. Word begins the search and identifies a word or phrase to hyphenate. At this point, you can click Yes to insert the hyphen in the location Word suggests, or you can use the arrow keys to move the insertion point to the location you want and then click Yes.

If you do not want to hyphenate the entire document, simply select the specific text you want to hyphenate. Word will search only that selection.

To hyphenate your text automatically, follow these steps:

1. Select Tools ➢ Language, and select Hyphenation to display the Hyphenation dialog box.
2. Choose the Automatically Hyphenate Document option.
3. In the Hyphenation Zone box, specify the amount of space to leave between the end of the last word in a line and the right margin.

   If you enter a high zone number such as 1" to make the hyphenation zone wider, you reduce the number of hyphens. If you enter a low zone number such as .25" (the default hyphenation zone) to make the hyphenation zone narrower, you reduce the gaps in a ragged right margin.
4. In the Limit Consecutive Hyphens To box, specify the number of consecutive lines that Word can hyphenate (the default is No Limit).
5. Click OK to begin automatic hyphenation.

VISUAL BONUS: THE RULER

The ruler enables you to set and change tabs. The Tab Alignment button at the left end of the ruler enables you to change the tab alignment. The tab markers indicate where tab stops are set.

The ruler

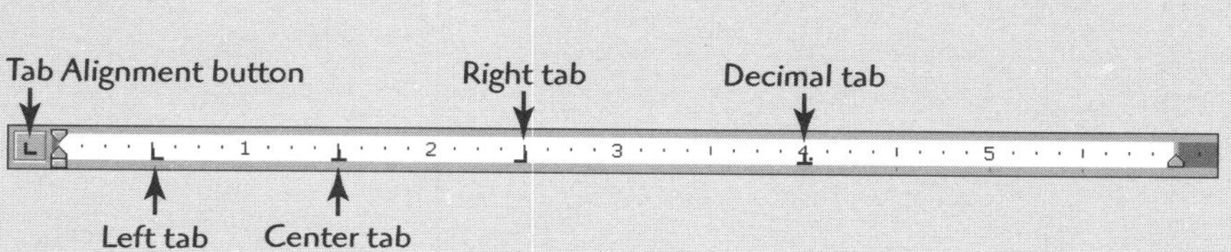

INDENTING, ALIGNING, AND SPACING TEXT

There are times when you want to adjust how text is placed so it stands out on the page.

One of the most effective ways to emphasize information is to change the way it is placed on the page. For example, indenting text on both sides creates white space around the text so it's easy to notice. For this type of indenting, you do not use the Tab key. (If you indent by inserting a tab next to each line of text, you have to readjust the tabs and text each time you make an addition or deletion of text.)

To indent a block of text, use indent settings so that the whole block shifts to start from a distance relative to the margin. If you add or delete text, Word adjusts the paragraph so the text lines up correctly. If you decide to move the indented text, the block of text will still be indented. If you reset the margin, the indented text stays indented relative to the new margin setting.

When you indent paragraphs, don't forget to pay attention to the Alignment choices on the Formatting toolbar. The Alignment options are also available in the Format ➢ Paragraph dialog box. You can align text on the left, center, or right, or you can justify it on both margins.

Left alignment is the default. Left alignment means that text is aligned flush with the left margin and appears *ragged right* on the page or column. Left alignment is used for conventional and office correspondence. Center alignment centers text between the left and right margins. Right-aligned text appears flush with the right margin.

Justified alignment spreads text between the left and right margins by expanding or contracting the space between words so text runs flush against both margins. This can cause rather odd spacing between characters in words, and some people don't like the Justify alignment for this reason. However, because all lines begin and end at exactly the same spot on either side of the page, the text forms a uniform block without the ragged edge of the left or right alignment. Justified text, which has an orderly look, is generally used in multiple-column newsletters, newspapers, and magazines.

When you adjust the layout of text in your documents, you may also want to change the line spacing. In most cases, documents are single-spaced. However, you can choose from Single, 1.5 lines,

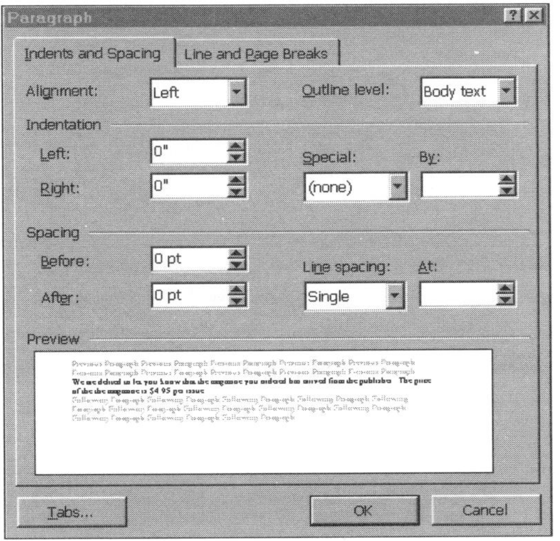

Double, At Least (the current point size), Exactly, and Multiple. Double-spacing is excellent for a draft, a manuscript, or a script so you can mark your changes more easily on the printed pages. The At Least option specifies the minimum amount of space between lines. Word adds additional space as needed. The Exactly option specifies a fixed amount of space between lines. In Exact mode, Word doesn't add additional space, even if it's needed. The Multiple option increases or decreases the amount of space between lines (in points or lines).

Indenting text

You can align paragraphs relative to the margin with the indenting feature. Let's see how indents work. You should still be in the file EX07-1.DOC.

Notice that a little hourglass-like symbol appears on the ruler, right at the left margin's edge. This symbol is actually made up of three parts:

- The top triangle is the First Line Indent marker. If, for instance, you select a paragraph and move the First Line Indent symbol one half an inch on the ruler, the first line of the paragraph moves in that far but the rest of the lines stay where they are.
- The bottom triangle is the Hanging Indent marker. A hanging indent is the opposite of a first line indent. If you select a paragraph and move the Hanging Indent marker half an inch to the right, the first line begins at the same spot, but all the following lines move in a half inch from it. Hanging indents are useful for bulleted or numbered lists and bibliographic entries.
- The small box beneath the hanging indent is the Left Indent symbol. If you select a paragraph and move the left indent half an inch to the right, the whole paragraph moves in one half inch. Any hanging or first line indent settings are maintained, relative to the new left indent position.

The keyboard shortcut for creating a hanging indent is to press Ctrl+T. To undo the hanging indent, press Ctrl+Shift+T.

Let's indent the quotation to make it stand out better.

1. Click before the *B* in *Before* at the beginning of the last paragraph to position the insertion point where you want a left indent.
2. Click and drag the Left Indent marker to the $^{1}/_{2}$" mark on the ruler.

Notice the whole hourglass configuration consisting of the First Line Indent, Hanging Indent, and Left Indent markers is at the $^{1}/_{2}$" mark on the ruler. By moving this entire symbol, you move all lines in a block of text to line up along a single indent setting, as shown in the accompanying illustration.

For faster indenting, based on the default $^{1}/_{2}$" default tab stop, you can use the Indent tools on the Formatting toolbar. Just click the Increase Indent button on the Formatting toolbar to indent a paragraph to the next tab stop on the ruler. Click the Decrease Indent button on the Formatting toolbar to move the indented paragraph to the previous tab stop. You can also press Ctrl+M to indent the current paragraph $^{1}/_{2}$ inch. Press Ctrl+Shift+M to undo the $^{1}/_{2}$-inch indent.

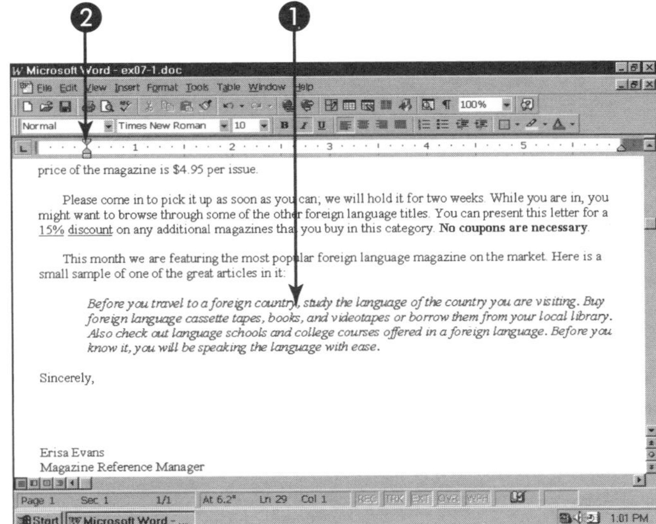

Aligning text

The default alignment setting for text you type in a Word document is at the left margin. When you're positioning text on a page you sometimes want to realign it. That is, you may want the text to be aligned in the center of your page, or flush with the right margin. This can be done either with buttons on the toolbar shown in the accompanying illustration, or the Alignment options in the Paragraph dialog box. In this exercise, we use the toolbar buttons.

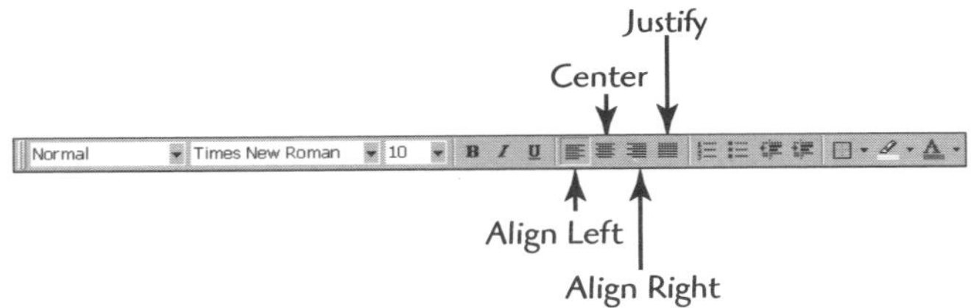

Adjusting line spacing

Let's work with the letterhead and date. We'll try the center, right, and left alignment options, and see what works best.

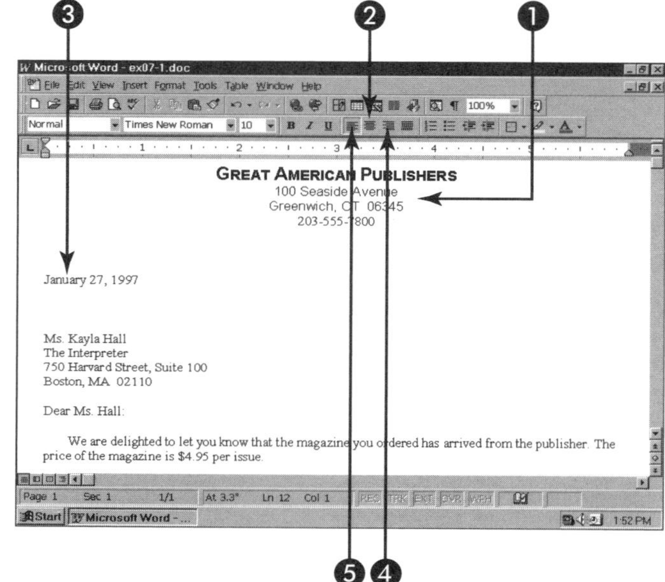

1. Select the letterhead.
2. Click the Center button on the Formatting toolbar (or press Ctrl+E).

   As you can see, the text is centered between the left and right margins.
3. Select the date.
4. Click the Align Right button on the Formatting toolbar (or press Ctrl+R).

   The date looked better where it was.
5. Click the Left Align button on the Formatting toolbar (or press Ctrl+L) to return the date to the left margin.
6. Click anywhere in the document to deselect the text.

   These alignment changes should make your document look like the accompanying illustration.

To change aligned text back to "normal" text, select the text and click the Align Left button on the Formatting toolbar, which is the preset alignment scheme.

Adjusting line spacing

Another way to change the appearance of paragraphs on a page is to adjust the line spacing between lines of text. Let's make the quotation easier to read by adding more space between the lines.

1. Select the last paragraph.
2. Select the Format menu.
3. Click Paragraph.

Adjusting line spacing

The Paragraph dialog box appears. The settings in this dialog box are applied to selected text, or, if no text is selected, they change the line spacing for all text you enter from this point on.

Notice that the Paragraph dialog box also offers an alternative to the method described in the previous section for setting indentations. You can indent selected text by setting the Indentation measurements, and you can choose special effects, such as a hanging or first line indent.

4. In the Spacing section, click the Line spacing drop-down arrow to display the line spacing list.
5. Select 1.5 lines to apply 1.5 lines of spacing to this paragraph.

   The Preview box shows how the first line of selected text will be spaced from the second line using this setting.
6. Click OK.
7. Click anywhere in the document to deselect the text.

   The new spacing is shown in the accompanying illustration.
8. Save the changes and close the document.

   If you want an entire document to be spaced differently from the default single spacing, change the line spacing setting before you begin typing any text. If you want to change spacing after you have entered text, you need to select the text and then use the Format Paragraph command to make changes to it. A shortcut for selecting all the text in your document is to hold down the Ctrl key and click in the left margin or press Ctrl+A.

A quick way to specify single spacing is to press Ctrl+1; for 1.5 lines, press Ctrl+5.

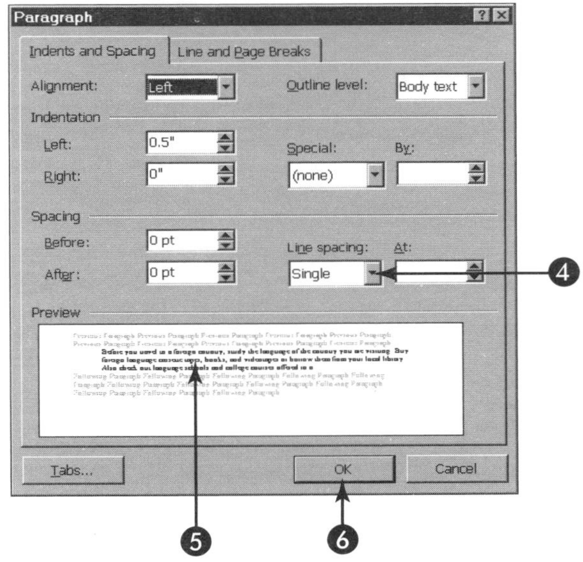

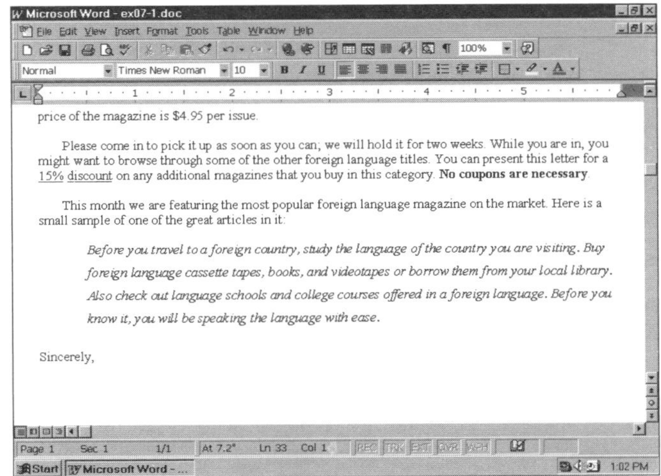

Skills challenge

SKILLS CHALLENGE: FORMATTING A MEMO

In this review exercise, you practice all the skills you've learned in this lesson to create a simple memo from scratch. Answer the bonus questions to review the skills and help you determine your understanding of the topics covered. The answers to the bonus questions are located in Appendix C.

TRY OUT THE INTERACTIVE TUTORIALS ON YOUR CD!

1. Create a new document.
2. Set a left tab stop at 3/4″.

By what increment are left (default) tab stops set on the ruler?

3. Change the top margin to 2″.
4. Type the following text:

Memorandum. Press Enter twice.

To: [Tab] **All Marketing and Product Managers**. Press Enter.

Date: [Tab] **December 1, 1997**. Press Enter.

From: [Tab] **Meryl Heller**. Press Enter.

Re: [Tab] **Food and Beverage Planning**. Press Enter twice.

Please review the food and beverage plans for our planning meeting on Monday, December 8, at 9:00 a.m. We will discuss the agenda for the sales conference, product rollout, demonstrations, and product improvements. Press Enter twice.

I'll bring the hazelnut coffee and the muffins. Plan on spending no more than two hours at this meeting. See you there!

5. Tab in the first paragraph at 3/4″.
6. Tab in the second paragraph at 3/4″.
7. Name the file **MYMEMO**.

8. Save the file.
9. Select *Memorandum*.
10. Apply boldface to the selected text.
11. Select the Format menu.
12. Choose the Font command.
13. Change the text to Courier New.
14. Change the font size to 16 point.
15. Click OK to apply the font changes.
16. Select *Food and Beverage Planning* in the *Re* line.
17. Apply boldface to the selected text.
18. Apply italic to the selected text.

    Your document should now look like the accompanying illustration:

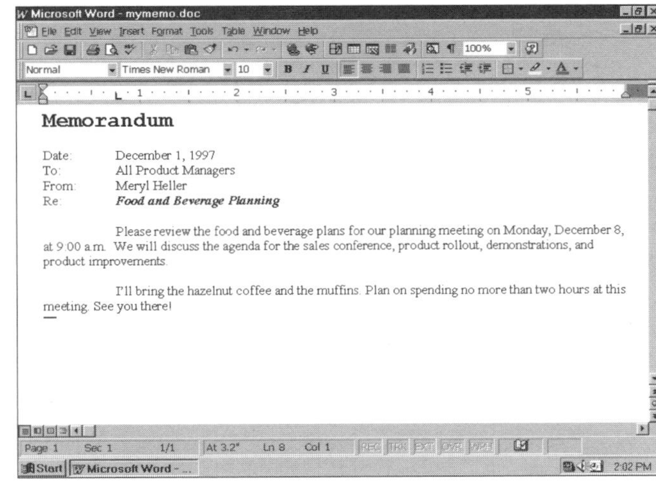

Identify the two fonts used in this document. How was each applied?

19. Select both paragraphs.
20. Remove the tab marker at 3/4" on the ruler.
21. Delete the tab at the beginning of each paragraph.
22. Use the Left Indent marker to indent both paragraphs at the 1/2" tab stop on the ruler.

What is the quickest way to indent paragraphs based on the default 1/2" tab stops?

23. Select *Memorandum*.
24. Center the selected text.

Besides using the Center button on the Formatting toolbar, what is the alternate way to change text alignment?

Troubleshooting

25. Select the memo headings that include the *Date, To, From,* and *Re* lines.

26. Change the line spacing to Double.

Which menu command do you use to change line spacing?

Your document should now look like the accompanying illustration.

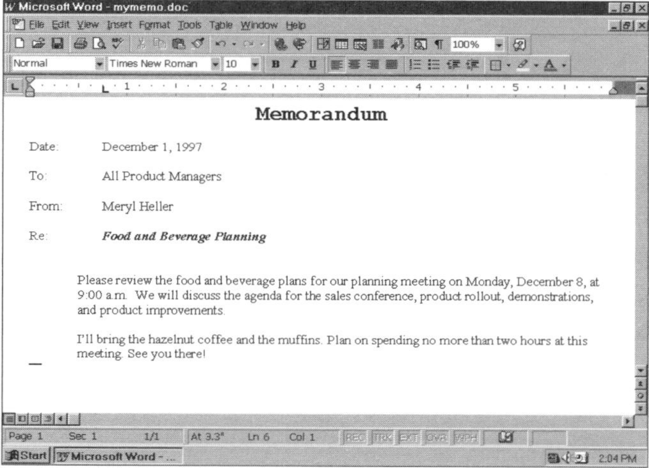

27. Save the changes.

28. Close the file.

TROUBLESHOOTING

Now you've got some simple formatting skills to help you produce handsome documents. The following table offers solutions to several issues you might have encountered in working on these skills.

Problem	Solution
How can I change the default font when I start a document?	Before you type any text, choose a new font in the Font box on the Formatting toolbar.
I set several tabs and now want to get rid of them all.	Drag each tab marker down off the ruler or select Format ➢ Tabs and click the Clear All button.
I applied a font to text and got a lot of little pictures.	Some fonts, such as Wingdings, are made up of symbols, not of letters and numbers. Select another font.
I changed the font size of the text, and now the lines run together.	Select Format ➢ Paragraph and increase the amount of line spacing.

WRAP UP

In this lesson, you've gotten hands-on experience with several skills, including the following:

- Changing the font style, font, and font size
- Setting tabs and margins
- Indenting text
- Aligning text
- Adjusting line spacing

If you want to become more proficient with these skills, create a product announcement to release a new and improved product.

In the following lesson, you are introduced to more Word formatting features that can make any kind of document look professional.

Creating Lists, Headers, and Footers

GOALS

In this lesson, you learn the following skills:

- Creating a bulleted list
- Creating a numbered list
- Numbering pages
- Adding headers and footers
- Formatting headers and footers

Creating a bulleted list

GET READY

To work through this lesson, you will need the files EX08-1.DOC and EX08-2.DOC from the One Step folder.

When you've finished the exercises in this lesson, you will have created a document that looks like the accompanying illustration.

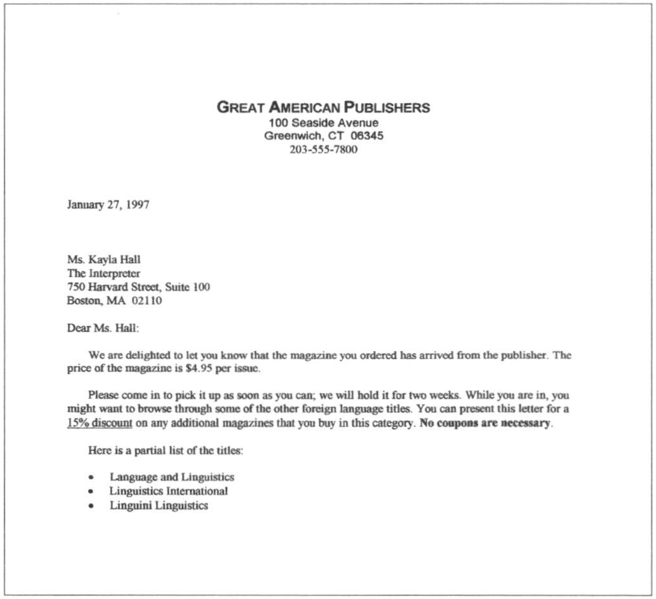

GREAT AMERICAN PUBLISHERS
100 Seaside Avenue
Greenwich, CT 06345
203-555-7800

January 27, 1997

Ms. Kayla Hall
The Interpreter
750 Harvard Street, Suite 100
Boston, MA 02110

Dear Ms. Hall:

We are delighted to let you know that the magazine you ordered has arrived from the publisher. The price of the magazine is $4.95 per issue.

Please come in to pick it up as soon as you can; we will hold it for two weeks. While you are in, you might want to browse through some of the other foreign language titles. You can present this letter for a 15% discount on any additional magazines that you buy in this category. **No coupons are necessary.**

Here is a partial list of the titles:

- Language and Linguistics
- Linguistics International
- Linguini Linguistics

Erisa Evans

This month we are featuring the most popular foreign language magazine on the market. Here is a small sample of one of great articles in it:

Before you travel to a foreign country, study the language of the country you are visiting. Buy foreign language cassette tapes, books, and videotapes or borrow them from your local library. Also check out language schools and college courses offered in a foreign language. Before you know it, you will be speaking the language with ease.

Here are directions to Great American Publishers.

1. Superhighway north
2. Exit 3, The Boulevard
3. Left at first traffic light onto Seaside Avenue

Sincerely,

Erisa Evans
Magazine Reference Manager

CREATING BULLETED AND NUMBERED LISTS

Word offers several tools to assist you in presenting lists of information. Lists help readers follow the progression of an idea, a series of steps, itemized text, and so on. Word enables you to create bulleted lists and numbered lists.

One good way to bring attention to special information on a page is to break it down into phrases or short sentences and put bullets next to each important point. However, if you're presenting a series of step-by-step instructions, a numbered list is usually more effective.

With Word's Bullets and Numbering command, you can choose the type of bullet or numbering scheme that you want to insert in a list. The numbering feature automatically renumbers your list to accommodate additional entries.

You can create a list from scratch or select existing text and turn it into a list with the Bullets button or Numbering button on the Formatting toolbar. Each new paragraph gets a new bullet or number.

With Word's automatic formatting feature, you can create bulleted and numbered lists as you type. If you type an asterisk, one or two hyphens, a greater-than symbol (>), or an arrow created with a greater-than sign and a hyphen or equal sign (-> or =>), Word turns the text into a bulleted list. If you type a number followed by a period, hyphen, closing parenthesis, or greater-than sign (>), and then a space or tab and text, Word turns the text into a numbered list.

Creating a bulleted list

For the following exercises, you'll use the file EX08-1.DOC from the One Step folder. This file has a version of the business letter you've worked with in previous lessons. The boss has informed us that we

Creating a bulleted list

need to include a bulleted list of magazines in the letter. There are three methods for creating a bulleted list:

- You can create the list automatically as you type. This is the easiest method.
- You can type the list, select all the text in the list, and then select Format ➢ Bullets and Numbering. Choose the bullet type and click OK.
- You can type the list, select all the text in the list, and then click the Bullets button on the Formatting toolbar.

Let's type asterisks for the bullets in this exercise to see how automatic bullets work.

1. Open the file EX08-1.DOC.
2. Click at the beginning of the blank line below the second paragraph, and press Enter to insert another blank line.
3. Set a tab at $^1/_4$" on the ruler.
4. Press Tab to start a new paragraph and type **Here is a partial list of the titles:**
5. Press Enter twice.
6. Press the asterisk key (*) and then press Tab. Type the following items to create a bulleted list:

   Language and Linguistics. Press Enter.

   Linguistics International. Press Enter.

   Linguini Linguistics. Press Enter twice.

   Word automatically recognizes the combination of an asterisk, tab, and text as you type and converts your asterisk to a bullet. Then it bullets each subsequent item you type. Pressing Enter twice after the last item in the list tells Word that you want to turn off the automatic bullets feature.

   Now let's indent the bulleted items so that they line up with the rest of the text in the memo.

7. Select all the bulleted items.

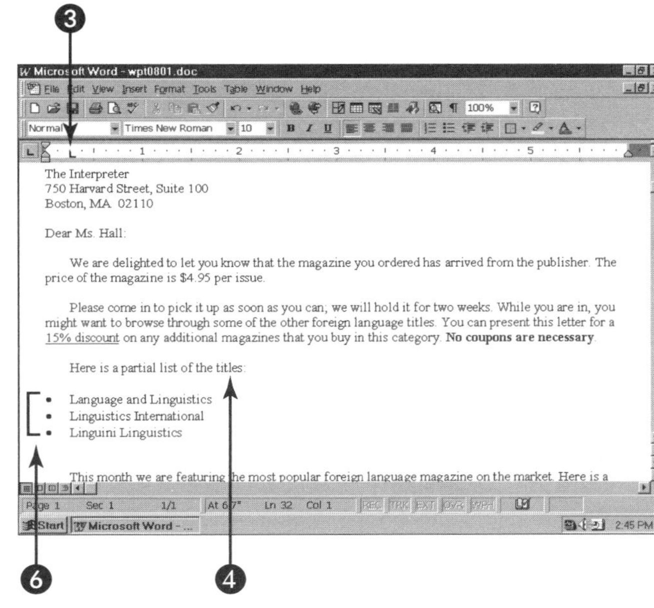

8. Click the Increase Indent button (the button with several horizontal lines and a right arrow) on the Formatting toolbar.

9. Delete one of the two paragraph marks between the bulleted list and the next paragraph to remove the extra blank line.

Your bulleted list should now look like the one in the accompanying illustration.

If you insert new items in the list, Word will bullet the list entries automatically. If you want to remove only the bullets from the list and leave the text, click at the beginning of the text for each item, and then press Backspace.

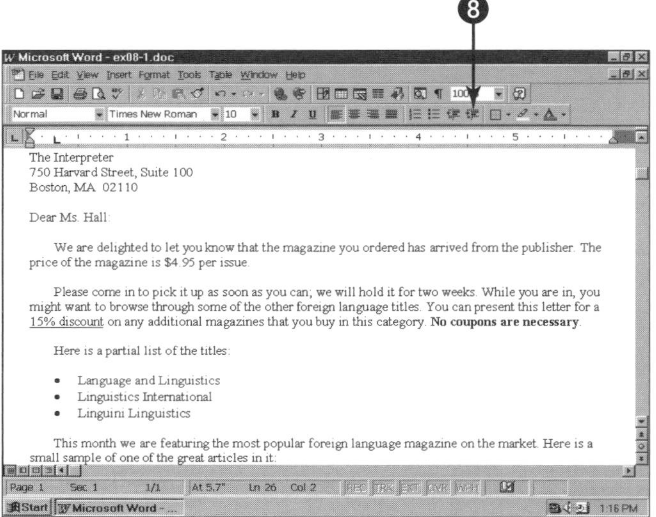

Creating a numbered list

A numbered list is similar to a bulleted list, but instead of bullets, numbers in sequential order precede the items. For example, if you type a list containing six items, you can have Word add numbers to the items in the list, numbered 1 through 6. The steps for creating a numbered list are similar to those for creating a bulleted list. There are three methods for creating a numbered list:

- You can create the list automatically as you type. This is the easiest method.
- You can type the list, select all the text in the list, and then select Format ➢ Bullets and Numbering. Click the Numbered tab, choose the numbering scheme you want, and then click OK.
- You can type the list, select all the text in the list, and then click the Numbering button on the Formatting toolbar.

The boss has asked us to create a numbered list that contains directions to the publisher. Let's create a numbered list as we type.

1. Click at the beginning of the blank line below the last paragraph.

2. Press Enter.

Creating a numbered list

3 Set a tab at 1/4″ on the ruler.

4 Press Tab and type **Here are directions to Great American Publishers.** Press Enter twice.

5 Type the following items to create a numbered list:

1. Press Tab.

Superhighway north. Press Enter.

Exit 3, The Boulevard. Press Enter.

Left at first traffic light onto Seaside Avenue. Press Enter twice.

When you type a number, followed by a period and a tab, Word automatically starts a numbered list and then numbers each subsequent item in the list as you type. Pressing Enter twice after the last item in the list tells Word that you want to turn off the automatic numbering feature.

Now let's indent the numbered list to align it with the preceding paragraph.

6 Select all the numbered items.

7 Click the Increase Indent button (the button with several horizontal lines and a right arrow) on the Formatting toolbar.

8 Delete one of the two paragraph marks below the numbered list to remove the extra blank line.

Your numbered list should now match the one in the accompanying illustration.

If you insert or delete items in the list, Word renumbers the list entries automatically. If you would like to remove only the numbers from the list and leave the text, click at the beginning of the text for each item, and then press Backspace.

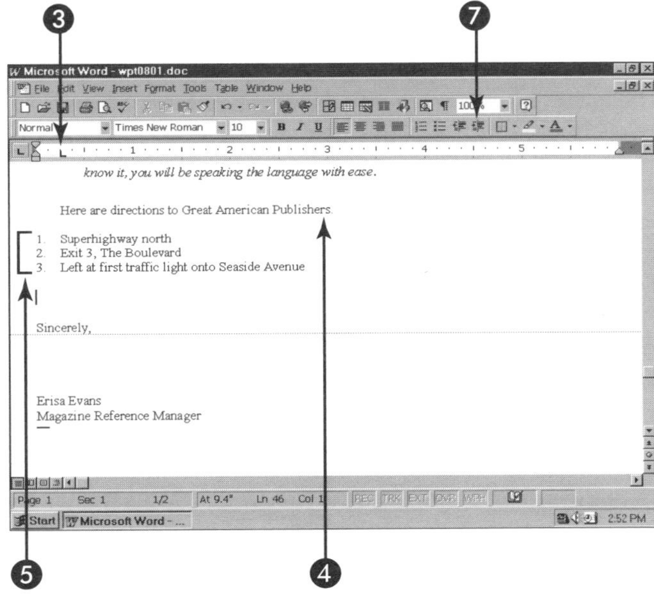

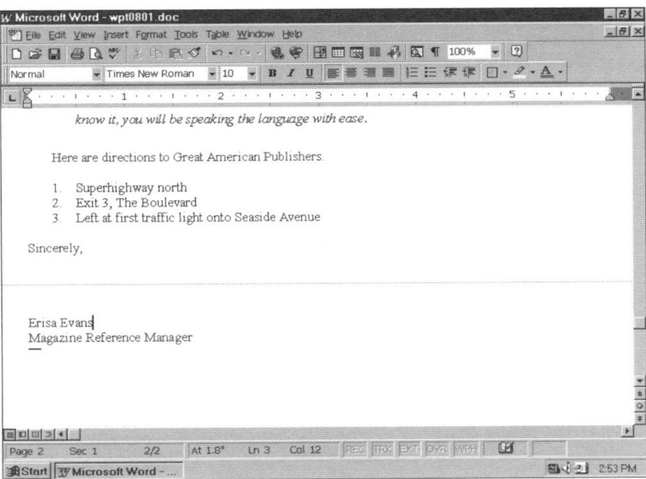

Numbering your pages

NUMBERING PAGES

Manuscripts, reports, booklets, newsletters, and other multiple-page documents require page numbering. Word's page numbering feature automatically inserts page numbers and prints the page numbers in the position you specify. That way, you don't have to enter and manage the page numbers manually.

When you add page numbers with the Insert ➢ Page Numbers command, you can specify whether to add the page numbers to the top of each page (to a header) or to the bottom of each page (to a footer). You can also specify the alignment of the number. Page numbers do not appear in Normal view, but they do appear in Page Layout view, Print Preview, and the document printout.

Numbering your pages

Let's divide the letter into two pages, and then number them.

1. Click the paragraph mark following the bulleted list.
2. Press Ctrl+Enter to insert a page break.
3. Select the Insert menu.
4. Click Page Numbers.

   Word opens the Page Numbers dialog box. The default position for page numbers is Bottom of Page (Footer), and the default alignment is Right.

5. Click the Alignment drop-down arrow to display a list of alignment choices.
6. Choose Center.
7. Click in the Show Number on First Page checkbox.

   To prevent a page number from printing on the first page, you need to remove the check mark in this checkbox. Usually, the first page in a document doesn't have a page number, especially if the page contains a cover letter or title page.

8. Click OK.

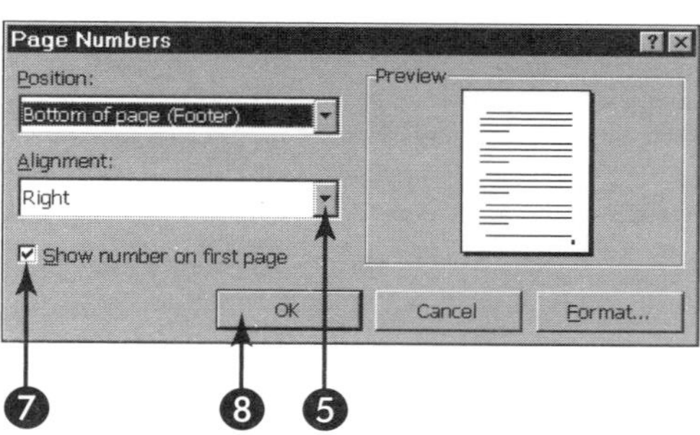

Word switches to Page Layout view so that you can see the page numbers. The page number appears in light gray.

9. Scroll to the bottom of page 1 to see that there is no page number.
10. Scroll to the bottom of page 2 to view the page number.
11. To see more of your page, click the Zoom drop-down arrow on the Standard toolbar and choose 50%. When you switch to Normal view the zoom percentage will automatically return to 100%. The bottom of the second page in your document should now look like the one in the accompanying illustration.

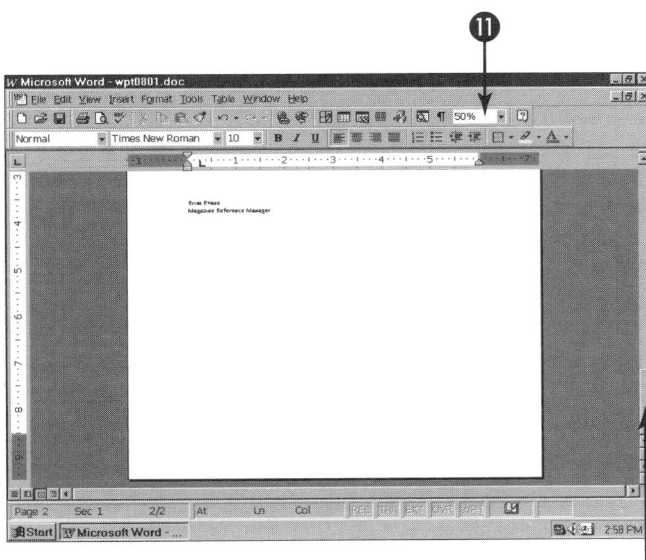

You can change the formatting for the page numbers by clicking the Format button in the Page Numbers dialog box. Word displays the Page Number Format dialog box. From the Number Format list, you can select Arabic numerals (1,2,3 . . .), which is the default, lowercase or uppercase letters, or lowercase or uppercase Roman numerals.

CREATING HEADERS AND FOOTERS

Word enables you to add headers and footers so that you can print information at the top and bottom of every page of the printout. You can create your own header and footer information, include text, and add special commands to control the appearance of the header or footer. Word will adjust the page to make room for the headers and footers.

If you have a document that is divided into multiple sections, you can define individual headers and footers for each section. Word also enables you to create different headers or footers for odd and even pages or for the first page in a document or section.

Creating headers and footers

Headers and footers print information, such as chapter headings, dates, or page numbers below the top margin or above the bottom margin of every page of a document. Header and footer information

Creating headers and footers

appears onscreen in Page Layout view and Print Preview. Let's add a header to this document so that the reader always knows who created the work.

1. Switch to 100% zoom and select the View menu.
2. Click Header and Footer.

   The Header area and Header and Footer toolbar are displayed.
3. Type **Erisa Evans** in the Header area.

   Now we'll move to the Footer area and insert the filename using Word's AutoText feature. AutoText entries are listed in the Insert AutoText menu on the Header and Footer toolbar (for more information on the toolbar, see the "Visual Bonus" section.
4. Click the Switch Between Header and Footer button (the button with a page and a yellow bar above and below it) on the Header and Footer toolbar.
5. Click the Insert AutoText drop-down arrow to open the AutoText menu.
6. Choose File name to insert the filename in the Footer area automatically.
7. Click the Close button on the Header and Footer toolbar.
8. Scroll up and down page 2 to see the header and footer information. Headers and footers only appear in Page Layout view.

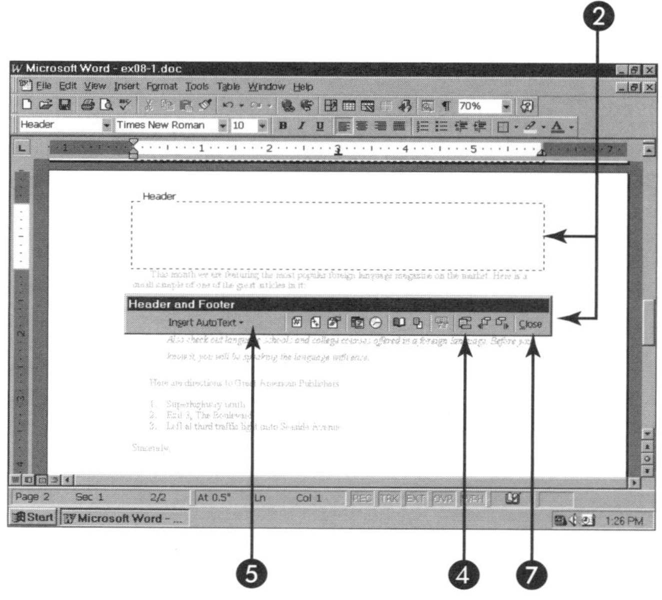

You can create different (alternate) headers or footers for odd and even pages, or for the first page in a document or section. To do so, select File ➢ Page Setup and click the Layout tab. Choose the Different Odd and Even option and click OK. Display the Even Page Header area or Even Page Footer area and type your information. Click the Show Next button on the Header and Footer toolbar to move to the Odd Page Header and Even Page Header. Then enter the information you want.

VISUAL BONUS: HEADER AND FOOTER TOOLBAR

After you select View ➢ Header and Footer, you'll see the Header and Footer toolbar. It contains tools for creating, navigating between, and formatting headers and footers.

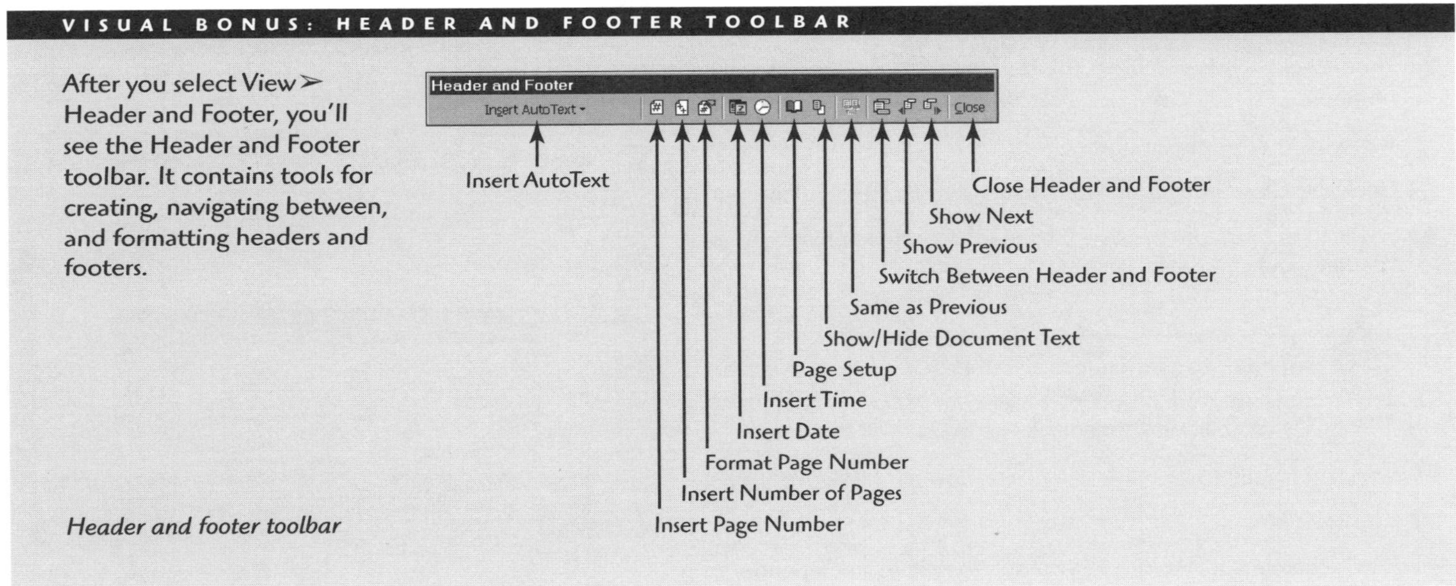

Header and footer toolbar

Formatting headers and footers

Once you create your headers and footers, you can make changes to them. Use Word's editing and formatting commands as you normally would use them on text in a document. In this exercise, we'll add bold to the page number.

1. Select the View menu.
2. Choose Header and Footer.
3. Click the Switch Between Header and Footer button on the Header and Footer toolbar.
4. In the Footer area, click the page number to display its border.
5. Double-click the number *2* in the page number border.

Formatting headers and footers

6. Click the Bold button on the Formatting toolbar.
7. Then, click anywhere else in the document to deselect the page number.

   Word makes the page number bold.
8. Click the Close button on the Header and Footer toolbar.
9. Scroll to the bottom of page 2 to see the boldface page number (darker gray).

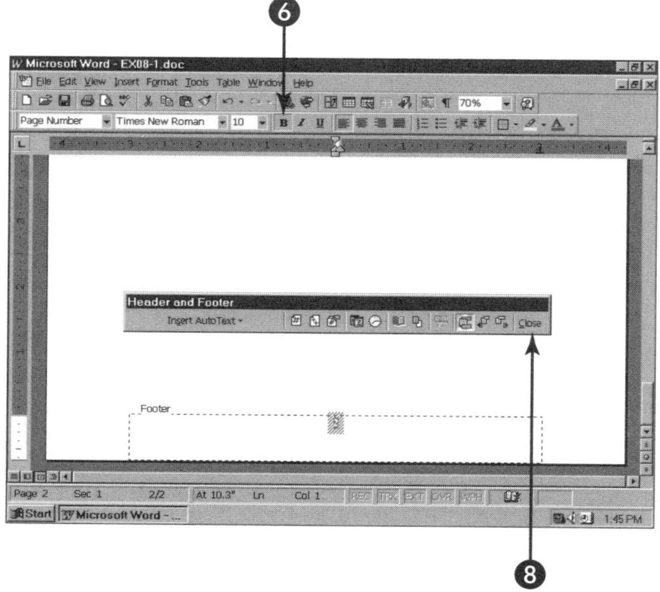

If it is too difficult to see in Page Layout or Normal view, click the Print Preview button on the Standard toolbar, and then click the bottom of the page.

10. Save the changes you made.
11. Close the file.

If you change your mind and you don't want to use a header or footer, select the text in the Header or Footer area and press Delete.

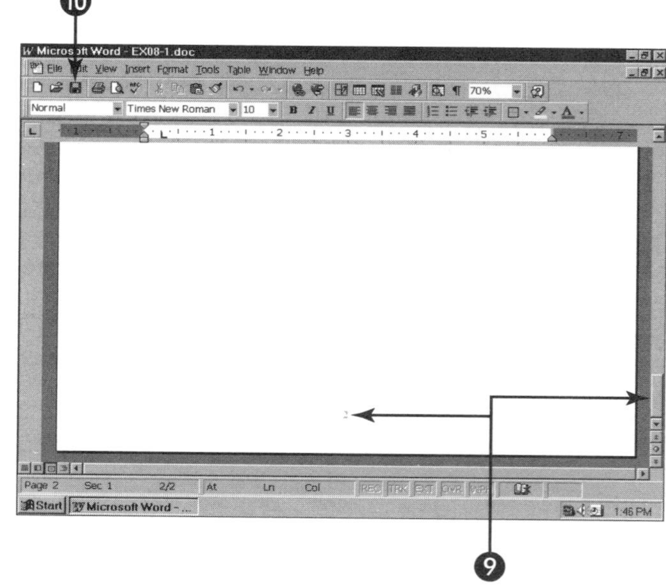

If you print a document that contains header and footer information, and something unexpected prints at the top or bottom of your document, check the Header or Footer area. Most likely there is a typo or some mistake made in the header or footer information. For example, if you have too much white space between the header text and where your page text begins, you may need to edit your header to remove any extra spaces (indicated by paragraph marks).

SKILLS CHALLENGE: CREATING A LAUNDRY LIST

This final exercise will give you practice with all the skills you've learned in this lesson. You'll work with a version of the memo you used in previous lessons. Answer the bonus questions to review the skills and help you determine your understanding of the topics covered. The answers to the bonus questions are located in Appendix C.

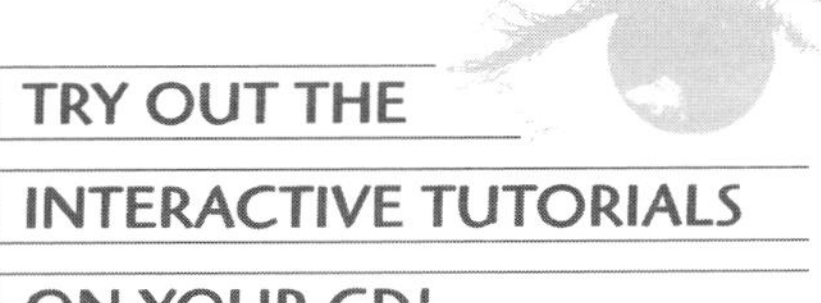

TRY OUT THE INTERACTIVE TUTORIALS ON YOUR CD!

1. Open the file EX08-2.DOC.
2. Scroll down to the bottom of the document.
3. Create a new page.
4. Type **Here's a list of the topics that we will discuss and videotape:**.
5. Press Enter twice.
6. Press asterisk (*) and then Tab.
7. Type the following bulleted list:

   sales conference. Press Enter.

   product rollout. Press Enter.

   demonstrations. Press Enter.

   product improvements. Press Enter twice.

   Name the three ways to create a bulleted list.

8. Create a third page.
9. Type **Here are instructions for running the VCR:**.
10. Press Enter twice.
11. Type **1.** and then press Tab.

Skills challenge

12. Type the following numbered list.

    Turn on TV. Press Enter.

    Turn on VCR. Press Enter.

    Insert videotape. Press Enter.

    Press Play. Press Enter twice.

13. Add page numbers to your document using the default settings. Do not number the first page.

When you add page numbers to a document, what alignment types does Word offer?

14. In the header, type **Food & Beverage Planning Meeting**.

After you insert page numbers, what view is the document in?

15. In the footer, insert the current date.
16. Press the spacebar, and insert the current time.

How do you move back and forth between the header and footer areas?

17. Close the Header and Footer toolbar.

    The accompanying illustration shows the bottom of page 2 and top of page 3 in the document.

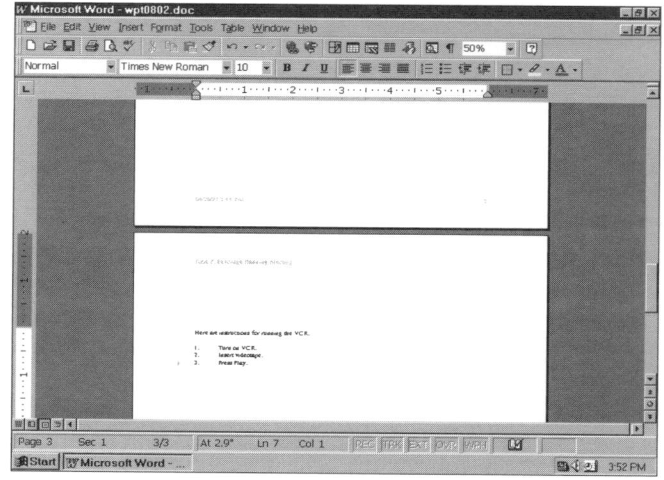

18. Save the changes and close the file.

TROUBLESHOOTING

Completing this lesson indicates that you've learned how to format your documents with Word's formatting tools and procedures. The following table offers explanations for several problems you might have encountered in learning these skills.

Problem	Solution
I typed an asterisk and the text for the first bullet item and pressed Enter. Word didn't convert the asterisk to a bullet.	You left out one important step—you have to press Tab or the spacebar after the asterisk in order for Word to create the bulleted list automatically.
I inserted page numbers in my document, but I don't want the page number on the title page.	Select Insert ➢ Page Numbers and click in the Show Number on First Page checkbox to remove the check mark in the box.
I added page numbers, and the date and time to a header and footer, but {PAGE}, {DATE}, and {TIME} appear in the header and footer.	Word inserts fields for the page number, date, and time items. The fields update the page numbers when you change the document, and update the date and time when you print the document. Press Alt+F9 to manually update the fields.
The page text prints right up against the header text.	Insert a paragraph mark or two to create some blank lines between the header text and the page text.

Wrap up

WRAP UP

In this lesson, you've had hands-on experience with several skills, including the following:

- Creating bulleted and numbered lists
- Numbering pages
- Creating and editing headers and footers

If you would like more practice with these skills, create a packing list for your next business trip.

The next lesson shows you some nifty formatting shortcuts that will make your life easier when you format Word documents.

LESSON 9

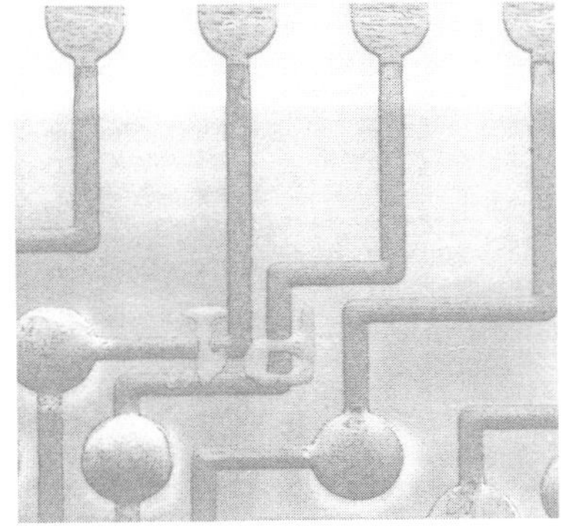

Taking Shortcuts

GOALS

In this lesson, you learn the following skills:

- Applying a style
- Viewing the contents of a style
- Creating a style
- Using the Repeat command
- Copying formats
- Using a template
- Creating AutoText
- Applying AutoText

Get ready

GET READY

For this lesson, you will need the files EX09-1.DOC and EX09-2.DOC from the One Step folder.

When you complete the exercises in this lesson, you will have applied styles to your business letter, which is shown in the accompanying illustration.

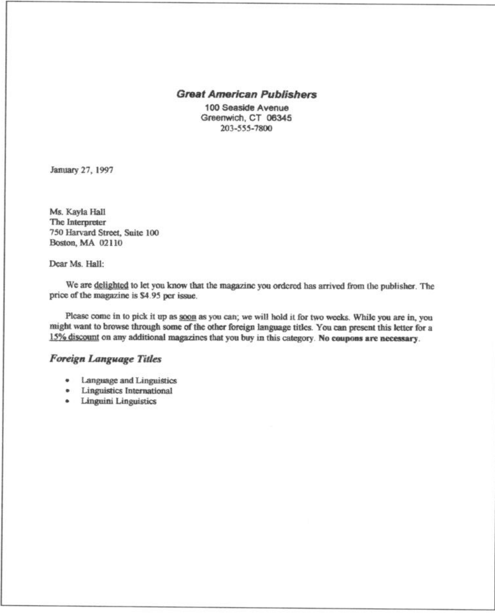

Great American Publishers
100 Seaside Avenue
Greenwich, CT 06345
203-555-7800

January 27, 1997

Ms. Kayla Hall
The Interpreter
750 Harvard Street, Suite 100
Boston, MA 02110

Dear Ms. Hall:

We are delighted to let you know that the magazine you ordered has arrived from the publisher. The price of the magazine is $4.95 per issue.

Please come in to pick it up as soon as you can; we will hold it for two weeks. While you are in, you might want to browse through some of the other foreign language titles. You can present this letter for a 15% discount on any additional magazines that you buy in this category. **No coupons are necessary.**

Foreign Language Titles

- Language and Linguistics
- Linguistics International
- Linguini Linguistics

Erisa Evans

Quotation

This month we are featuring the most popular foreign language magazine on the market. Here is a small sample of one of the great articles in it:

Before you travel to a foreign country, study the language of the country you are visiting. Buy foreign language cassette tapes, books, and videotapes or borrow them from your local library. Also check out language schools and college courses offered in a foreign language. Before you know it, you will be speaking the language with ease.

Directions to Great American Publishers

1. Superhighway north
2. Exit 3, The Boulevard
3. Left at first traffic light onto Seaside Avenue

Sincerely,

Erisa Evans
Magazine Reference Manager

Result9.doc 2

WHAT IS A STYLE?

Until now you've made only one character and paragraph formatting change at a time. The Formatting toolbar and the keyboard shortcuts make formatting so easy that you might not bother looking for other shortcuts. But if you always stop at the Formatting toolbar, you're missing out on some of Word's most impressive formatting tools.

One way to dramatically increase the results of your efforts is to use styles. A style is simply a combination of character and paragraph formatting settings that you can name, save, and apply to your text. Instead of individually formatting every part of every paragraph or chunk of text, you can use a style to format certain elements all at once. The more complex or changeable your document, the more you need styles. You can use a style as many times as you need. Styles ensure that your document's formatting remains consistent, and they simplify making changes to paragraphs you have already formatted.

Styles are even more important in Word 97 than in previous versions of Word because they are now the foundation for many of Word's most exciting new automatic features. For instance, Word can automatically add heading numbers to every section in your document, providing that you've added styles to identify your headings. Word can also add chapter numbers to all your document's page numbers, but only if you format your chapter headings with a unique style.

You may not be aware of it, but the documents you've created already use styles. Styles are built into templates on which you base your document. A template is a sort of boilerplate containing a number of styles. When you apply a particular template to a document, headings, text, margins, and other elements will appear in preset styles. For example, when you create a new document using the default Normal template, Word automatically applies the accompanying styles. The

Normal style includes the following character and paragraph formatting settings : 10-point Times New Roman, English (U.S.) language, character scale at 100 percent, flush left alignment, single line spacing, pagination widow/orphan control, and Body Text for the outline level.

The other three styles in the Normal template are Heading 1, Heading 2, and Heading 3. There are more than 90 additional character and paragraph styles available in the Normal template, even though they aren't usually obvious on the screen.

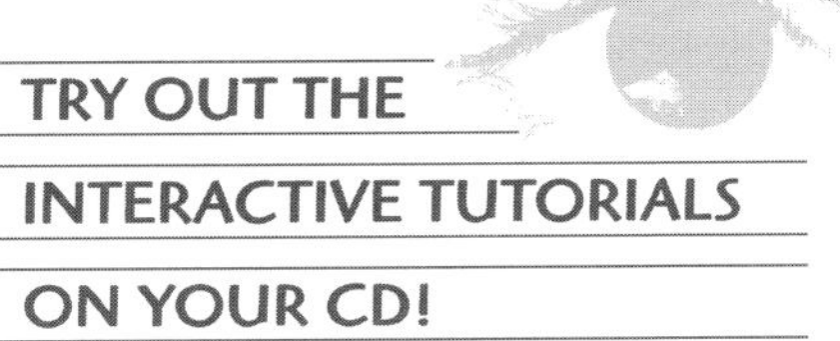

Applying a style

Word comes with many styles that you can apply to your text. For example, you might want to apply a style to a major heading, a bulleted list, or a paragraph. You can also define a group of character and paragraph formats and save them as a style. In the following exercises, you'll use the file EX09-1.DOC from the One Step folder. This file has a version of the business letter you've worked with in previous lessons. Let's select the heading on page 1 and apply a style to it.

1. Open the file EX09-1.DOC.
2. Select the company name in the letterhead.
3. Click the Style drop-down arrow on the Formatting toolbar (it currently says Normal for normal body text).

   A list of Word's default styles appears.

4. Choose Heading 2.

   Word applies the following style settings to the text: Arial font, 12-point font size, a bold italic font style, and left alignment.

5. Click the Center button on the Formatting toolbar to recenter the company name.

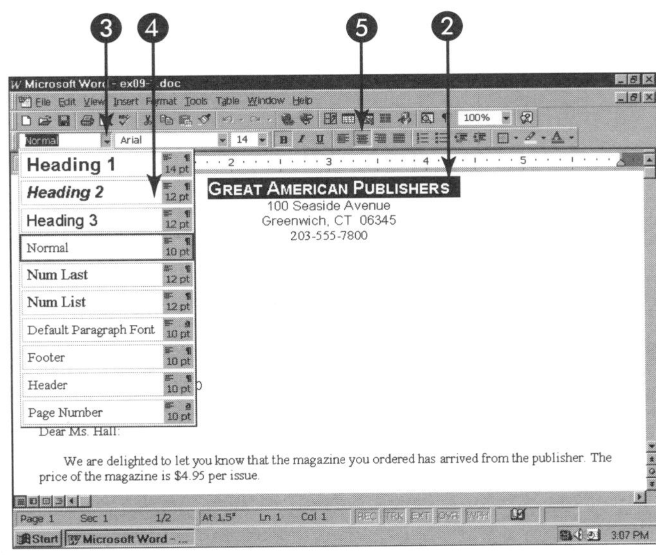

Viewing the contents of a style

If you select the wrong style, select the text (if it's not still selected), and choose the style you want from the Style drop-down list on the Formatting toolbar.

If you want to apply a style only to a single paragraph, you don't have to select text. Position the insertion point anywhere in the paragraph and select the style. The entire paragraph (that is, from the beginning of the paragraph to the paragraph mark at the end of the paragraph) changes to the new style.

Viewing the contents of a style

Any formatting that you add to text individually and manually, or any of the items from the Format menu's dialog boxes can be included in a style. To help you decide which style you want to apply to any of your text, we'll view the contents of a style.

1. Leave the heading selected.
2. Select the Format menu.
3. Choose Style to open the Style dialog box.

   Word opens the Style dialog box.
4. Notice the Paragraph Preview box and Character Preview box on the right side of the dialog box. These boxes show you what the paragraph and character formatting will look like when the style is applied to your text.
5. Take a look at the current style's description at the bottom of the dialog box. Most of Word's default styles are simple. They contain a font, font size, and font style. More elaborate styles contain additional character and paragraph formatting, bulleted and numbered lists, borders and shading, tabs, and columns.
6. Click Cancel to close the dialog box.
7. Click anywhere to deselect the text.

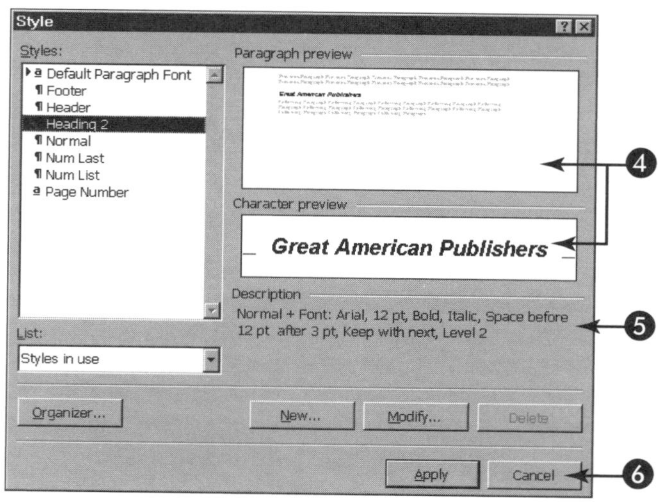

VISUAL BONUS: STYLE PREVIEW

Word gives you more ways than one to quickly see how a style looks. You've already seen the Paragraph and Character preview boxes in the Style dialog box. You can also get a sneak preview of styles by clicking the Style drop-down arrow in the Formatting toolbar. Word displays the Style Preview list. Each style name appears in the font, font size, font style, and alignment that will be used when you apply that style (some formatting features, such as line spacing, will not be displayed).

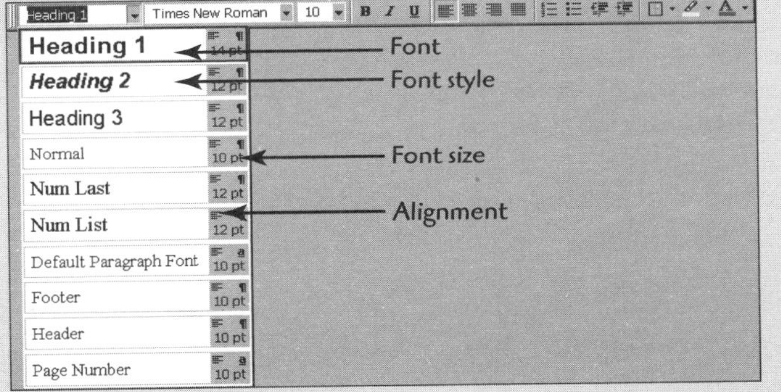

Style preview

Creating a style

You can create a new style yourself and use it in future documents. There are two ways to create a style:

- Base a new style on text that is already formatted. This method is the easier way to create a style because you already know how the basic style looks when it's applied to text. To base a new style on an existing format, select the formatted text. Then, click in the Style box on the Formatting toolbar, type the new style name, and press Enter.
- Use the Style dialog box to create a style from scratch.

Creating a style

Let's use the Style dialog box so that you can see all the formatting elements that go into creating a style from scratch, as well as get hands-on control over every part of your style.

1. Click anywhere in the first line of the inside address.
2. Select the Format menu.
3. Choose Style to open the Style dialog box.
4. Click the New button.

   The New Style dialog box appears.

If there is an existing style that has some of the elements you'd like in the new style, you can save time by selecting it from the Based On drop-down list in the New Style dialog box. Then you can change the formatting features you want to change, and leave the formatting that suits your needs. If there isn't a style that has some of the components you want, leave the Based On setting at Normal. This style has only font, font size, and alignment settings so you can customize it easily.

Word's Widow/Orphan Control prevents widows and orphans by moving them to another page. A widow is an isolated line at the top of a page, such as the last line of a paragraph, that can be moved to the bottom of the preceding page. An orphan is an isolated line at the bottom of a page, such as a heading or the first line of a paragraph, that can be moved to the top of the next page.

5. Make sure that Normal is selected in the Based On drop-down list.
6. To name the new style, type **MyStyle** in the Name text box, replacing the words *Style 1*.

   Look at the Description area at the bottom of this dialog box. It says Normal + Widow/Orphan Control. You can now add whatever formatting settings you want to the Normal style.
7. Click the Format button. The Format menu opens.

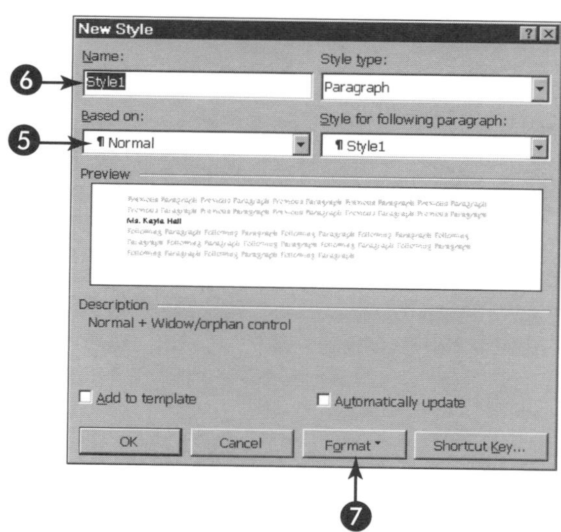

8. Choose Font. The Font dialog box appears.
9. Select the Bold Italic font style and change the font to 12 pt.
11. Click OK to return to the New Style dialog box.

    Notice the description in the Style dialog box now says Normal + Font: 12 pt, Bold, Italic, Widow/Orphan Control. You can use the Format button to repeat this procedure and make changes to other types of formats.

11. Click OK to save the new style.
12. Click the Close (X) button to close the Style dialog box.
13. Select the heading *Foreign Language Titles* on page 1.
14. Open the Style drop-down list on the Formatting toolbar. Notice that your new style is now on the list.
15. Choose MyStyle. The MyStyle style name appears in the Style box on the Formatting toolbar. The selected text becomes bold, italic, and 12 pt.

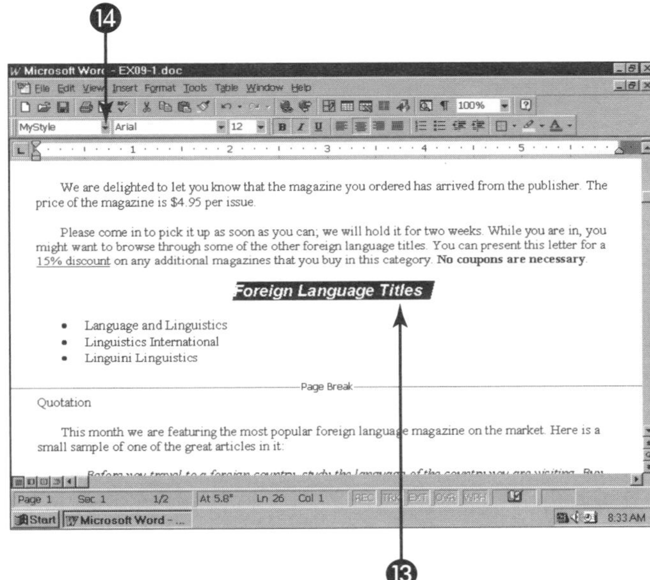

If you no longer need a particular style, you can delete it. Open the Style dialog box, select the style you want to eliminate, click the Delete button, and choose Yes.

FAST FORMATTING

When you finally get a page the way you want it, why reinvent the wheel to create other pages? Word figures you'll eventually get around to creating exactly what you want and offers some tools to help you achieve the same excellence time after time without redoing all that work. The power of the Repeat command and the Format Painter tool are only a keystroke and a click away.

Using the Repeat command

Using the Repeat command

The Repeat key repeats your most recent action. It is excellent for repeating a format command such as bold, italic, applying a style, and so on. We'll see how it works.

1. Select **Directions to Great American Publishers** on page 2.
2. Press F4 (Repeat key). This repeats the previously applied style.
3. Select *delighted* in the first sentence on page 1.
4. Click the Underline button on the Formatting toolbar.
5. Select *soon* in the first sentence in the second paragraph.
6. Press F4.
7. Click anywhere to deselect the text.

   Now your document should look like the accompanying illustration.

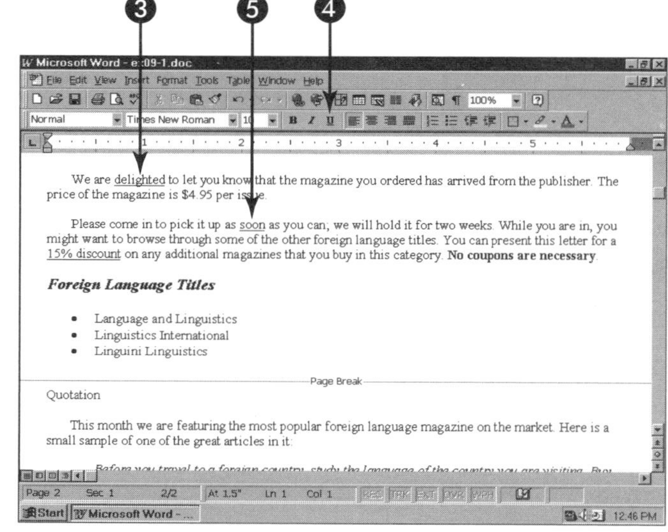

Copying formats

The Format Painter is a mini formatting copier that is good for very simple formatting. You will find it's easy to copy the format of one piece of text to another using the Format Painter tool.

1. Select the heading *Foreign Language Titles.*
2. Click the Format Painter button (the button that looks like a paintbrush) on the Formatting toolbar.

   The mouse pointer changes to a small paintbrush symbol (with an I-beam next to it) that you use to copy the format of the selected text to any text you drag your mouse pointer over.
3. Drag the mouse pointer across *Quotation* at the top of page 2.
4. Click anywhere to deselect the text.

   Your document should now look like the accompanying illustration.

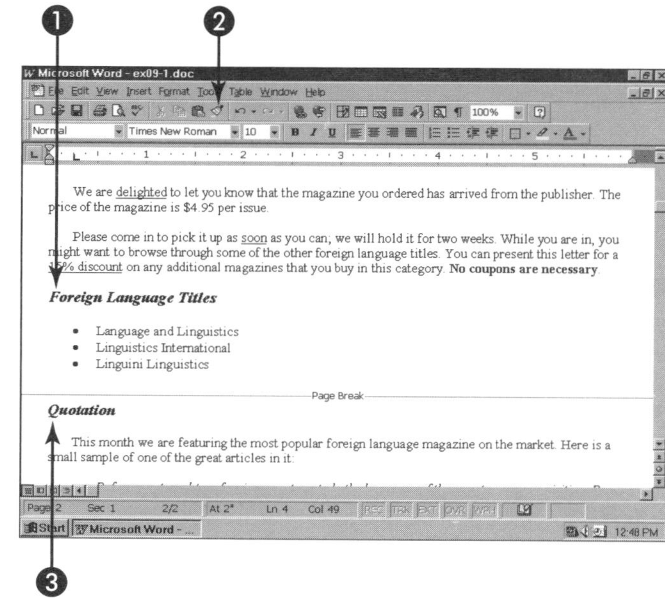

5 Save your changes and close the file.

TEMPLATES AND AUTOTEXT

A template provides a pattern for shaping a document. When you create a new document, you can use a template that contains boilerplate text, styles, AutoText items, graphics, WordArt, macros, a menu, key, and toolbar assignments. You can use a template to standardize types of documents that you frequently use.

By default, Word uses the NORMAL.DOT template, which contains the standard settings when you create a new document. However, you can choose to create documents with other templates. Word provides several families of templates that are organized in categories on the tabs in the New dialog box: General, Publications, Other Documents, Letters & Faxes, Memos, and Reports. If you don't see any or all of these tabs, you will need to install the templates using Add/Remove Programs in the Windows Control Panel.

AutoText is a great feature for speeding up text entry. This feature enables you to store text or graphics as an AutoText entry, assign a name to it, and then use it as many times as you want. For example, you might want to use AutoText for a frequently used address, distribution list for memos, or a company logo.

Using a template

Word supplies you with a wide variety of templates. Each template is based on a pattern for shaping a document. Templates can help you keep a set of special documents consistent. For example, you might want to use a template to create all your fax cover sheets. Let's use a template to create a fax cover sheet.

1 Select the File menu.

2 Click New.

The New dialog box opens. From here you can select a template category.

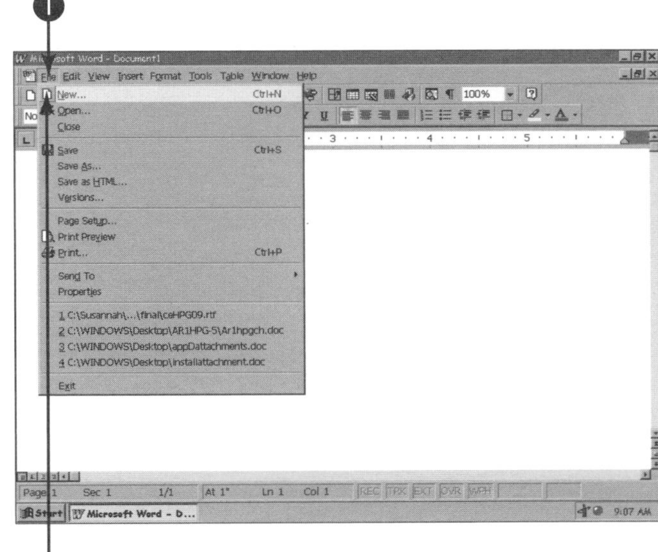

3. Click the Letters & Faxes tab.

   The Letters & Faxes tab contains several templates.

4. Click Elegant Fax.dot

   A small picture of the elegant fax appears in the Preview box on the right side of the dialog box.

5. Click OK.

   The fax cover sheet appears with prompts asking you to click and type.

6. Click in a box and type to fill in the following information:

   Company Name: **Great American Publishers**

   To: **Kayla Hall**

   From: **Erisa Evans**

   Company: **The Interpreter**

   Fax Number: **617-555-1122**

   Total No of Pages Including Cover: **3**

7. Right-click Erisa and choose Ignore All on the Spelling shortcut menu.

   Your document should now look like the accompanying illustration, which is shown in Page Layout view.

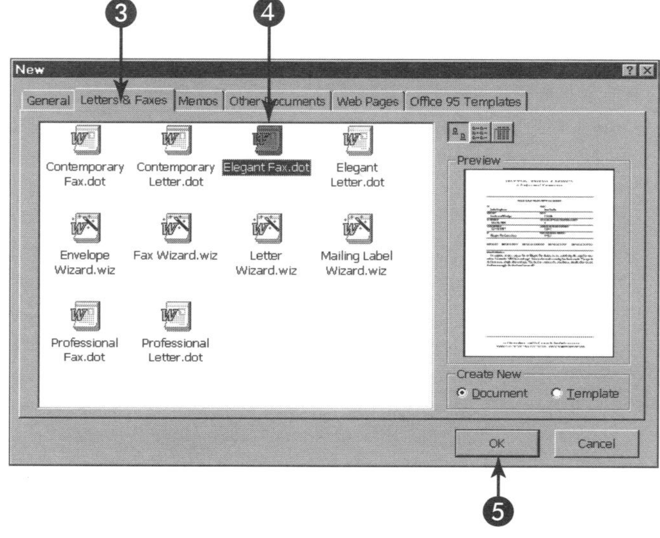

Creating AutoText

AutoText enables you to store and retrieve frequently used text in your documents. Let's use AutoText to store the company name and address in the letterhead.

1. Select all the text in the Notes/Comments section at the bottom of the fax cover sheet.

2. Press Delete.

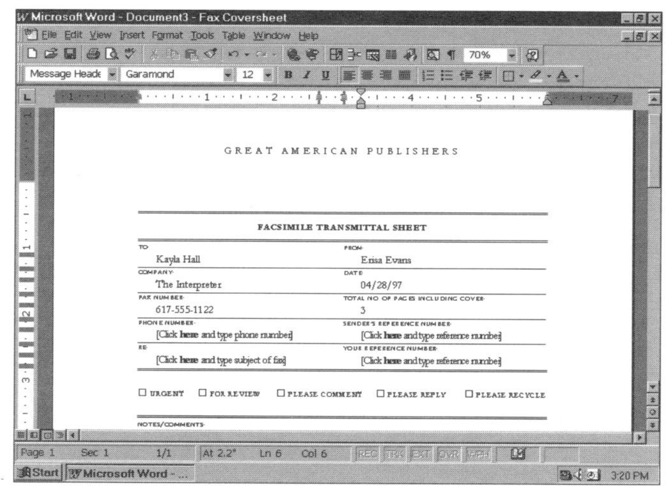

3 Type **Please send your check to the following address:** and press Enter.

4 Select the Window menu.

5 Choose EX09-1.DOC at the bottom of the Window menu.

This switches to the document that contains the address.

6 Select the company name and address in the letterhead.

7 Select the Insert menu.

8 Choose AutoText.

9 Choose New (or press Alt+F3).

The Create AutoText dialog box appears. Notice that Word displays the first 14 characters of the selected text as the suggested AutoText entry name.

10 To name the entry, type **company address** in the text box, replacing the words *Great American*.

11 Click OK to save the AutoText entry.

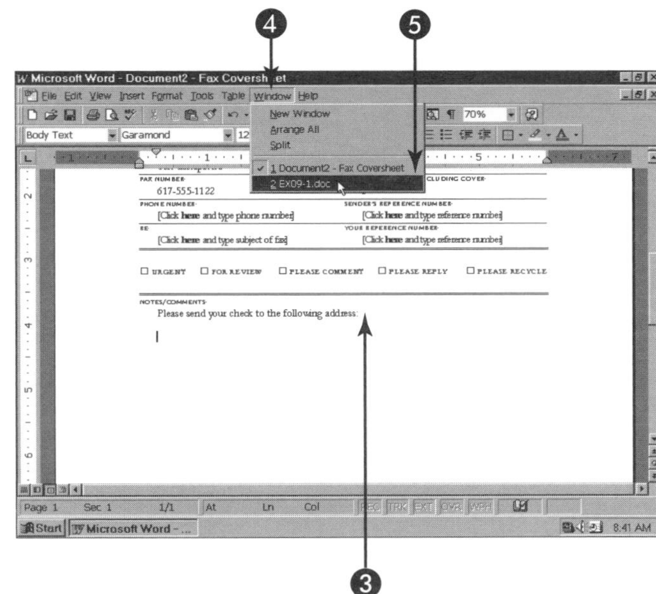

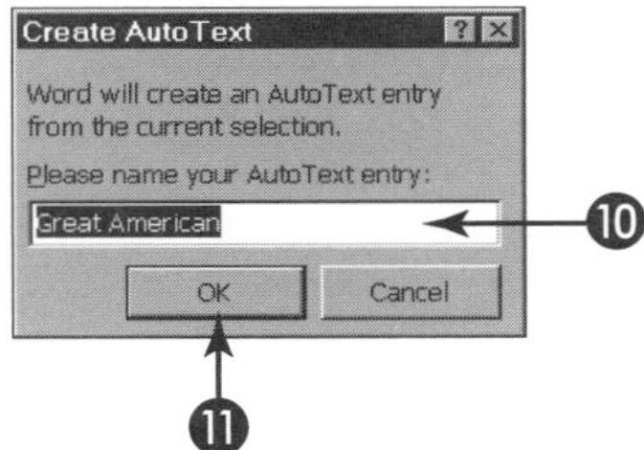

Applying AutoText

Once you create the AutoText entry, you can use it as many times as you want in any document. Now we'll use the AutoText entry to insert the company name and address in the fax cover sheet.

1 Select Window, and choose the fax cover sheet document.

2 Scroll to the bottom of the fax cover sheet document.

3 Select the Insert menu.

4 Choose AutoText.

5 Choose AutoText again.

The AutoCorrect dialog box appears. The AutoText tab is selected and there is a list of AutoText entries. You can insert, add, and delete AutoText entries.

Skills challenge

6. Double-click *company address*.

   Word inserts the AutoText entry, as shown in the accompanying (bottom) figure.

7. Select the File menu.
8. Choose Save As.
9. Name the document **Fax Cover**.
10. Close the document.
11. Save the changes to your business letter.
12. Close the document.

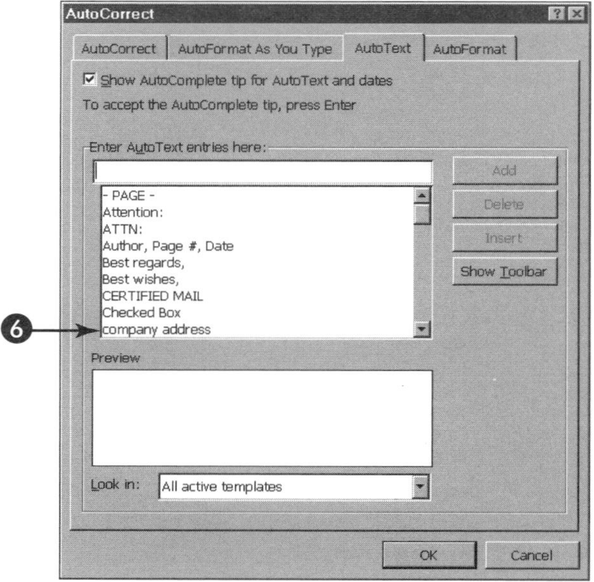

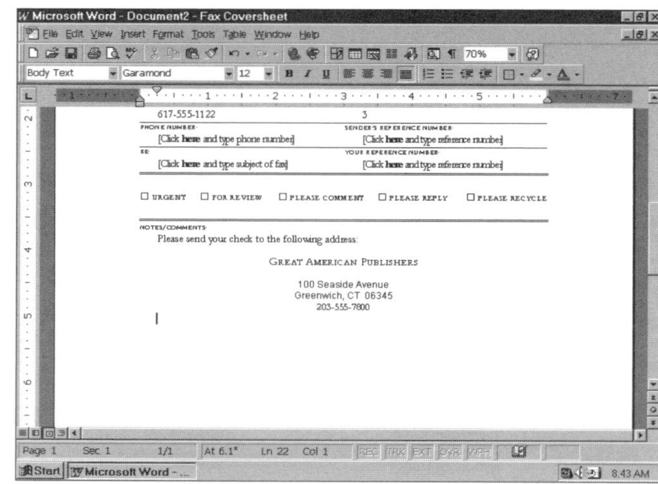

SKILLS CHALLENGE: TAKING FORMATTING SHORTCUTS

This review exercise gives you plenty of practice with formatting shortcuts that you've picked up in this lesson. You use the memo you've worked with in earlier exercises. Answer the bonus questions to review the skills and help you determine your understanding of the topics covered. The answers to the bonus questions are located in Appendix C.

1. Open EX09-2.DOC.
2. Select *Memorandum*.
3. Open the Style list on the Formatting toolbar and view the styles listed.

What is the name of the default template attached to every new document you create?

4. Apply the Heading 1 style.
5. Select the Format menu.
6. Choose the Style command. Take a look at the current style's (Normal) description in the Style dialog box.

Skills challenge

In addition to the style description, what formatting can you preview in the Style dialog box?

7. Click the New button.
8. Create a new style based on the Normal style.
9. Name the new style **MEMOHEAD**.

What button do you click in the New Style dialog box to add more formatting elements to a style?

10. Change the font style to Bold Italic and 11 pt.
11. Click OK to save the style.
12. Close the Font dialog box.
13. Then, close the Style dialog box.
14. Select the word *Date* in the memo.
15. Apply the MEMOHEAD style.
16. Click the Format Painter tool on the Formatting toolbar.

What is the mouse pointer shape that you see when you perform the Format Painter operation?

17. Drag over *To* in the memo heading to apply the formatting.
18. Select *From* in the memo heading.
19. Press F4 (Repeat key).
20. Select *Re* in the memo heading.
21. Press F4 (Repeat key).

    Your memo should now look like the one in the accompanying illustration.

22. Save your changes.
23. Close the file.

    Now you'll create a cover sheet to send with the memo.

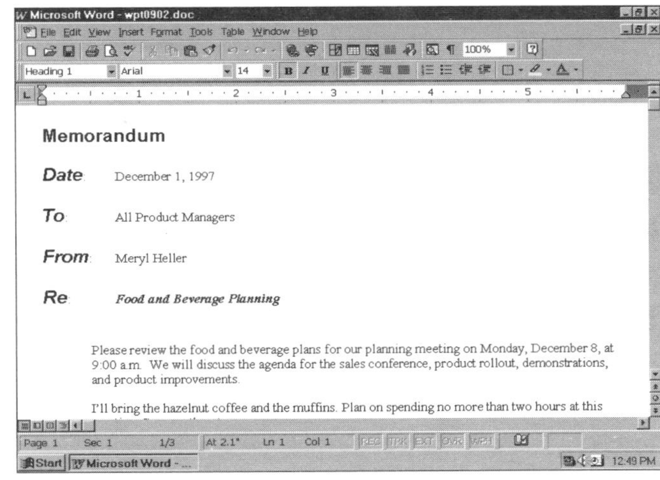

Troubleshooting

24. Use the Professional Fax template to create a fax cover sheet.
25. Apply the *company address* AutoText entry to fill in the company name at the top of the fax cover sheet.
26. Click and type to fill in the fax cover sheet.
27. Open the File menu.
28. Choose the Save As command.
29. Name the document Fax Cover 2.
30. Save the document.

Which command do you use to create an AutoText entry?

Your memo should resemble the one in the accompanying illustration.

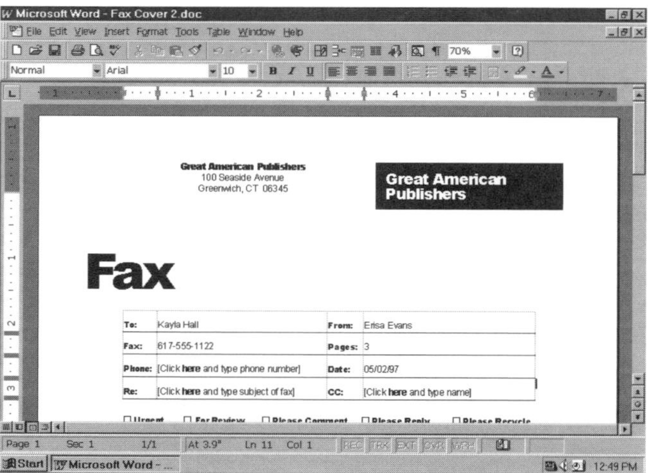

31. Close both files.

TROUBLESHOOTING

Finishing this lesson shows you've learned shortcuts that will come in handy when formatting your documents. The following table offers explanations for several issues you might have come across when stepping through these skills.

Problem	Solution
I saved a style and now I can't find it.	Styles that aren't part of a document's template have to be loaded into the document. Select Format ➢ Style Gallery and choose your style from the list there.
I created a new style, but I no longer need it.	Select Format ➢ Style, choose the style you want to delete, click the Delete button, and choose Yes to confirm the deletion.

Problem	Solution
I copied some formatting with the Format Painter tool and I don't like the results in the new location.	Click the Undo button on the Standard toolbar immediately after you finish painting the format.
I used the F4 (Repeat key) to repeat a style, typed some text, selected the text, and pressed F4 again. But the style was not repeated.	The F4 (Repeat key) repeats the last command you executed. Repeating a format with the F4 key works best when formatting is consecutive without any other actions in between.
I only have the Blank Document template in the New dialog box.	Use Add/Remove Programs in the Windows Control Panel to install the rest of the templates.
When I press Alt+F3 to create a new AutoText entry, nothing happens.	You must select the text you want to store in an AutoText entry before you can create the entry.

WRAP UP

Before you take a break, let's review what you've learned in this lesson:

- Applying, viewing, and creating styles
- Using the Repeat command
- Copying formats
- Using a template
- Creating an AutoText entry
- Applying an AutoText entry

If you want more practice with these skills, experiment with creating your own résumé.

In Lesson 10, you work with graphics to make your documents a bit slicker.

PART III

Enhancing What You've Got

This part shows you how to add pictures and organize information in your documents. You'll learn how to draw, create columns, and format a table and an outline.

This part contains the following lessons:

- Lesson 10: Shaping Up with Graphics
- Lesson 11: Creating Columns
- Lesson 12: Organizing Information with Tables, Outlines, and Organization Charts

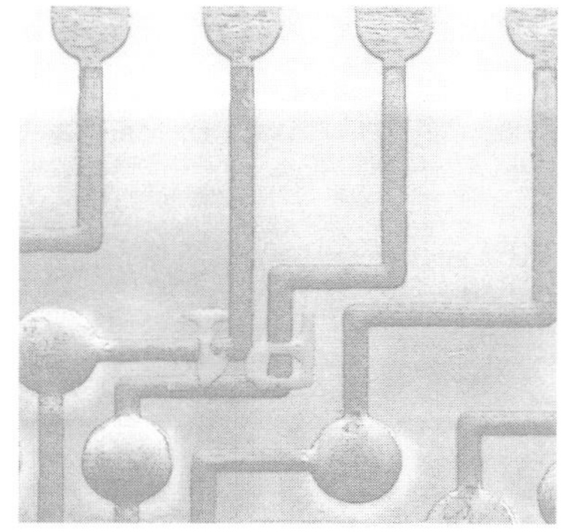

Shaping Up with Graphics

GOALS

In this lesson, you learn the following skills:

- Inserting clip art
- Adding WordArt
- Drawing shapes and lines
- Creating and modifying 3-D shapes
- Selecting objects
- Moving objects
- Resizing objects
- Changing line styles
- Changing color and patterns

Get ready

GET READY

For this lesson, you will need the files EX10-1.DOC and EX10-2.DOC from the One Step folder.

When you're done with the exercises in this lesson, you will have added graphics to your business letter as shown in the accompanying illustration.

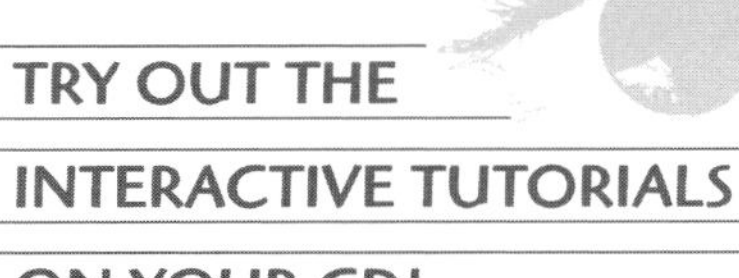

TRY OUT THE
INTERACTIVE TUTORIALS
ON YOUR CD!

ADDING OBJECTS

As they say, a picture is worth a thousand words. And how! In Word, you can blend graphics with text to add excitement and visual interest to your page layout. Word provides several ways to get graphics into your documents. You can insert an evocative piece of clip art, add WordArt, or create your own drawing with Word's drawing tools. Take your pick. Any way you do it, you add emphasis and visual impact to your documents. Graphics can liven up any document. For example, you could insert a food graphic in the Whole Foods report.

Word's clip art library contains more than a thousand professionally prepared pictures. You can insert these pictures instantly into your document. Also, many import file types and various graphics formats are supported by Word. You can even insert a graphic that you created in another program. A Word graphic image file has the file extension WMF, which stands for Windows Metafile.

WordArt enables you to choose from many preset special text effects to add designs and shapes to plain text. WordArt manipulates fonts in any way, shape, or form — it squeezes them, bends them into shapes, stretches them, adds shadows, borders, and a host of other text effects. WordArt is wonderful for creating desktop publishing effects, especially for creating logos.

The drawing tools are invaluable for creating an image from scratch. You can use the tools to create lines and shapes, color them in, and apply patterns to them. The drawing tools can help you create a piece of art that you can be proud of.

Whole Foods

Proposal and Marketing Plan

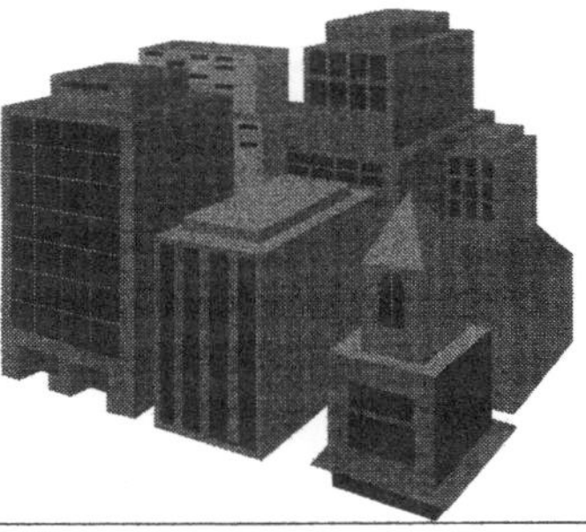

Whole Foods' Best Opportunity for West Region Expansion

Inserting clip art

You can insert clip art pictures in your document with the Insert Picture command. For example, you could insert a graphic in a report to spice it up. In the following exercises, you'll be working with the EX10-1.DOC file from the One Step folder. This file contains the Whole Foods report you've worked with before. Your first task is to insert a piece of clip art.

1. Open the file EX10-1.DOC.
2. On the title page, click before the *W* in *Whole.*
3. Open the Insert menu.
4. Choose the Picture command.
5. Select Clip Art.

   Word opens the Microsoft Clip Gallery dialog box. The clip art gallery shows you all the clip art for all the graphics categories, by default. However, you can display just the clip art images you want by choosing a specific graphics category. Let's try that now.

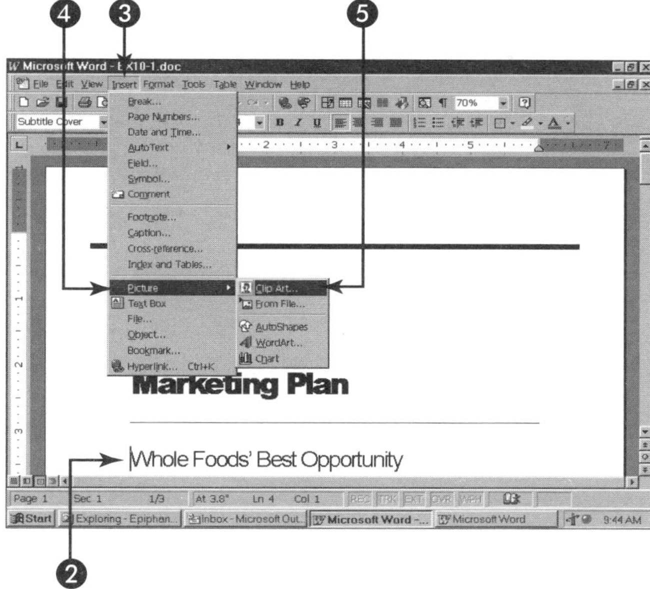

If there are no images in the Microsoft Clip Gallery, it is probably because they were not installed or have been deleted. If so, you will need to install the clip art through Add/Remove Programs in the Control Panel.

If you want more clip art to choose from, you can buy packages of clip art (in black and white or color) from software stores and mail-order catalogs. These clip art "libraries" are packaged by topics such as animals, business, holidays, music, people, and so on. If you want more professional artwork, look for photo collections, which are usually sold on CDs.

6. Click the Clip Art tab to bring it to the front, then, in the categories list (on the left), choose *Buildings*.
7. Click the Skyscraper Large Tall picture.

   The Clip Art Keyword information appears at the bottom left in the dialog box. This information helps you find the image, if you need to use it again.
8. Click the Insert button to insert the picture.

   Word places the graphic in your document in the default position and size. You can tell the graphic is still selected because it has small squares called selection handles surrounding it.
9. Click outside the graphic to deselect it.

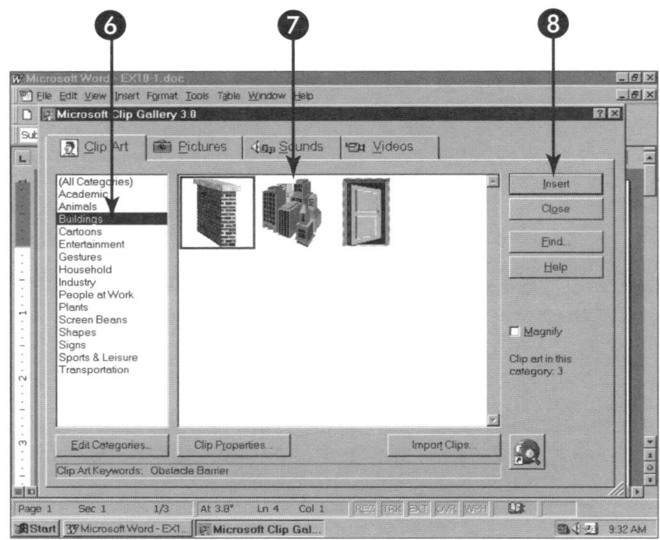

If you no longer want the graphic in your document, simply select the graphic by clicking it and pressing the Delete key.

Adding WordArt

WordArt enables you to create desktop publishing effects for your text. You can create company logos by adding designs and shapes to plain text. In this exercise, you will add a Whole Foods logo to the report.

1. Click in the left margin above *Proposal and*.
2. Select the Insert menu.
3. Choose Picture.
4. Select WordArt.

   You see a gallery of WordArt text in all shapes, sizes, and colors.
5. Click the WordArt text sample in the first row, third column.
6. Click OK.

   The Edit WordArt Text dialog box appears, as shown in the accompanying illustration.

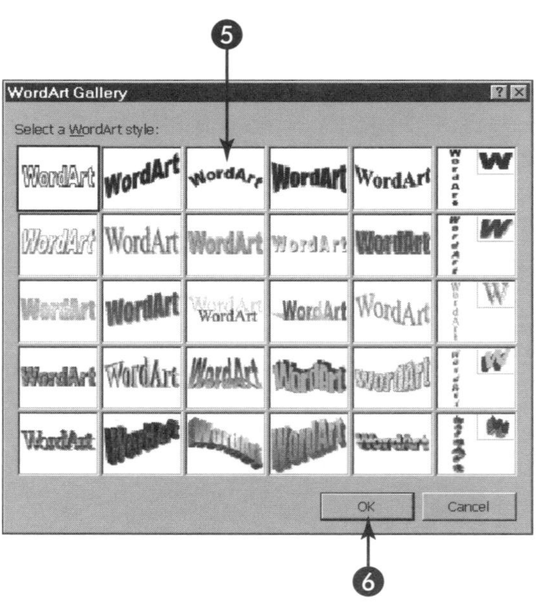

❼ Type **Whole Foods** in the Text box, replacing the words *Your Text Here*.

❽ Click OK.

The WordArt insert lands on top of the text *Proposal and Marketing Plan*. We'll move the text to a more attractive position later in this lesson.

Now you've created your own logo for Whole Foods, Inc. Even though it appears in color onscreen, the printout will be black-and-white unless you have a color printer. Notice the WordArt toolbar near the logo. The WordArt toolbar appears near whatever you've just inserted. It contains tools for editing and formatting your WordArt objects.

❾ Click outside the WordArt object to deselect it and hide the toolbar.

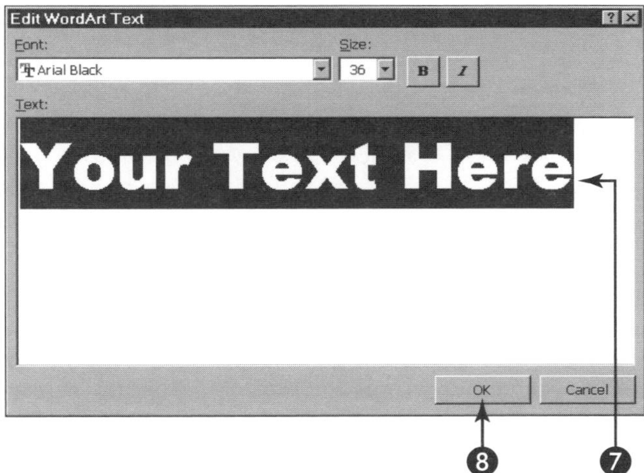

Drawing shapes and lines

Despite the huge variety of great clip art that is available, you still might not be able to find that perfect image. Or perhaps you'd just prefer to create your own art. In either case, you don't have to be a talented artist to create vibrant, eye-catching graphics. With Word's drawing tools, you can start with a simple drawing and then build on it. Let's see how creative we can be.

❶ Press Ctrl+End to move to the bottom of the document.

❷ Press Ctrl+Enter to create a page break.

Now you have a clean slate to draw on—page 4.

Drawing shapes and lines

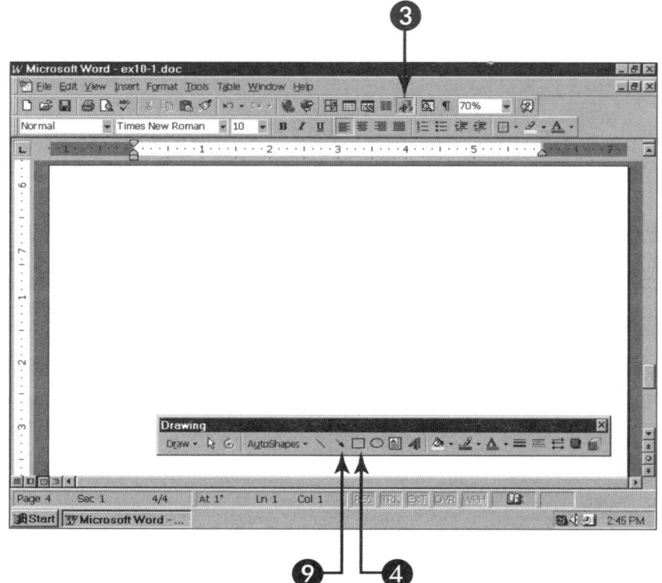

3. Click the Drawing button (the button with a blue A, and two shapes, one yellow and one aqua) on the Standard toolbar.

   The Drawing toolbar appears across the bottom of the screen, and Word automatically switches to Page Layout view (if you're not already in that view), as shown in the accompanying illustration. The drawing tools enable you to create an almost endless variety of shapes. For a greater variety of shapes, use the AutoShapes tool on the Drawing toolbar.

4. Click the Rectangle tool near the middle of the Drawing toolbar.

   Your mouse pointer now looks like a crosshair.

5. Eyeballing the vertical and horizontal rulers, click approximately where 1″ on the horizontal ruler and 1″ on the vertical ruler meet. This is where you want the shape to begin.

6. Drag the crosshair across to approximately 4″ on the horizontal ruler and down to 3″ on the vertical ruler.

7. Release the mouse button.

   Voila! You've drawn your first rectangle. You can see that this object is selected because there are selection handles at the sides and corners of it. At this point, you can shrink or stretch the shape, add color to it, add patterns, and change the line style. If you want to delete the rectangle, press Delete or Backspace.

8. Click anywhere on the page to deselect the rectangle.

To draw a perfect square, click the Rectangle tool, and then hold down the Shift key while dragging the crosshair to where you want to end the square.

9. Click the Arrow tool (next to the Rectangle tool) on the Drawing toolbar.

⑩ Click inside the lower right corner of the rectangle object, and then drag up a couple of inches.

Now you have an arrow pointing up toward the top of the rectangle.

⑪ Click the Text Box tool (a page with an A and lines on it) on the Drawing toolbar.

⑫ Hold down the Shift key and drag the crosshair inside the rectangle to draw a 1″ × 1″ box.

⑬ Release the mouse button.

⑭ Type **Highest Sales!** in the box.

⑮ Click outside the objects to deselect them.

Your artwork should resemble the accompanying illustration.

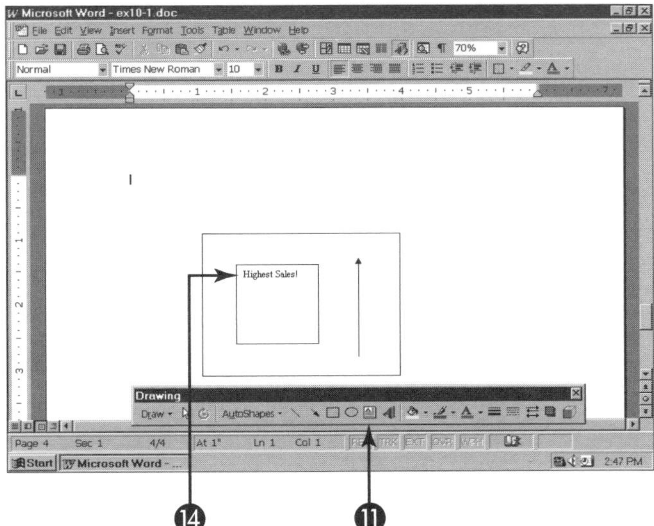

Drawing shapes and lines

VISUAL BONUS: DRAWING TOOLBAR AND 3-D SETTINGS TOOLBAR

The Drawing toolbar contains tools and Draw menu commands you'll need for creating artwork. And even if you never create a drawing, you still might find some of these tools invaluable for drawing lines and shapes.

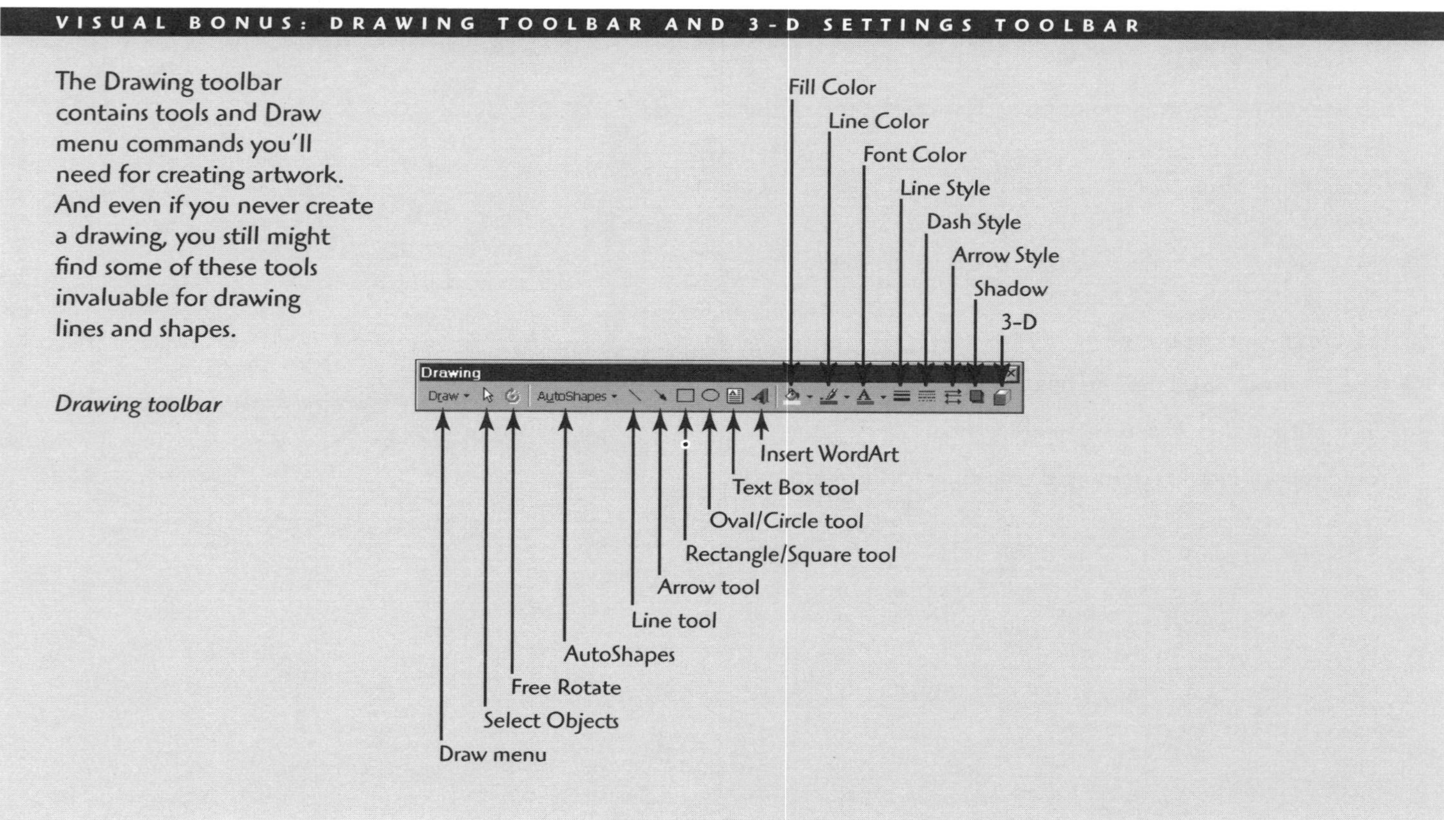

Drawing toolbar

Creating and modifying a 3-D shape

This toolbar enables you to adjust a 3-D shape's orientation in 3-D space by tilting it, and change its surface qualities, color, thickness, and lighting setting.

3-D Settings

3-D Color
Surface
Lighting
Direction
Depth
Tilt Right
Tilt Left
Tilt Up
Tilt Down
3-D On/Off

3-D Settings toolbar

Creating and modifying a 3-D shape

Word provides 20 predefined 3-D shapes. We'll change the rectangle to a 3-D shape in our drawing.

1. Click the rectangle to select it.
2. Click the 3-D button at the far right of the Drawing toolbar.

   A palette of ready-made 3-D shapes appears.
3. Choose 3-D Style 1 in the first row, first column.

   The 3-D shape appears in the drawing. Now let's modify the 3-D shape.
4. Click the 3-D button at the far right of the Drawing toolbar.
5. From the 3-D menu, choose 3-D settings.

   The 3-D Settings toolbar appears.

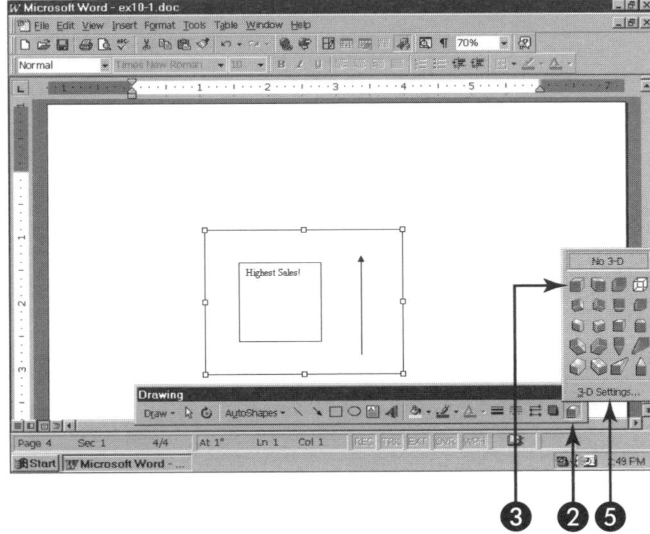

6. Click the Depth button on the 3-D Settings toolbar.
7. Choose 144 points.
8. Click outside the object to deselect it.

   The 3-D shape should look like the accompanying illustration.

9. Click the Close (X) button on the 3-D Settings toolbar to hide the toolbar.
10. If you no longer want the object to be 3-D, select the 3-D shape, click the 3-D button on the Drawing toolbar, and choose No 3-D.

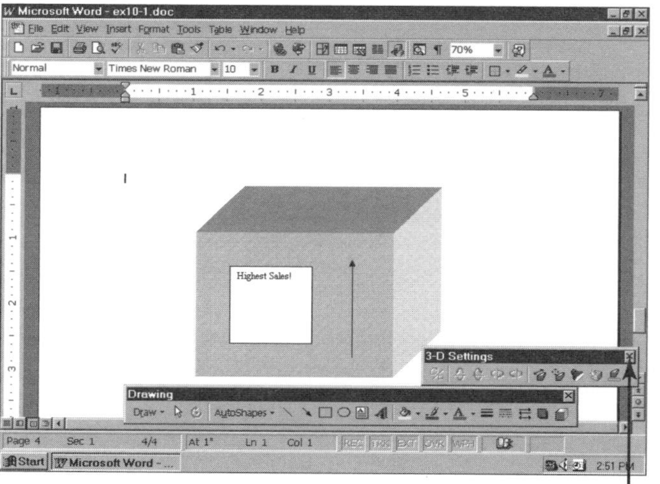

WORKING WITH OBJECTS

After you add an object to your document, you might want to make some alterations to it. Before you can work with an object, you must select it. After you select an object, you can make adjustments such as moving the object exactly where you want it to go. You can also stretch or shrink an object to any shape or size you want. The next few exercises give you a chance to practice these types of alterations.

Selecting objects

You can either select a single object or multiple objects. Let's see how easy it is to select objects.

1. Move the mouse pointer to any side of the rectangle's border until you see the mouse pointer arrow and a four-headed arrow.
2. Click the rectangle's border.

   You've selected one object. You can tell an object is selected because selection handles appear along the sides and corners of the picture.

3. Click outside the object to deselect it.
4. Click the text box.

You've selected a different object. But suppose you want to work on more than one object at a time? No problem. You can select multiple objects. Now let's select a second object.

5. Move the mouse pointer to any side of the rectangle's border until you see the mouse pointer arrow and a four-headed arrow.
6. Hold down the Shift key and click the rectangle's border.

   Each selected object displays selection handles, as shown in the accompanying illustration. At this point, you can make any changes you want to both objects at once.

7. Click outside the objects to deselect them.

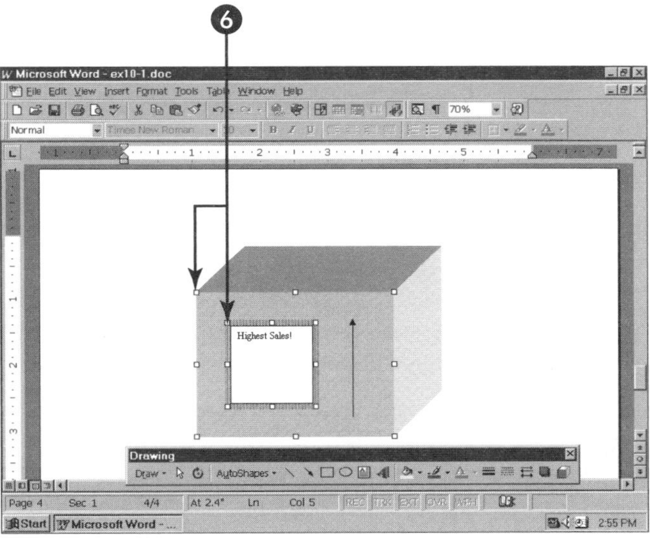

Moving objects

You can move an object wherever you want in the document. First you need to select the object, and then you can use the mouse to move the object to a new location. In this exercise, the images have been placed in the document, but they need to be moved to a better position.

1. Press Ctrl+Home to move to the top of the document.
2. Click the Whole Foods logo.
3. Move the mouse pointer over the logo until you see the mouse pointer arrow and the four-headed arrow.
4. Click and hold down the mouse button and drag the object so that its dashed line border is directly above the thick horizontal line at the top of the document.
5. Release the mouse button.
6. Scroll down a few lines.
7. Click the skyscraper graphic.
8. Click and hold down the mouse button, and drag the object to the right about 1/2 inch.
9. Release the mouse button.
10. Click outside the object to deselect it.

    Your report should now resemble the accompanying illustration.

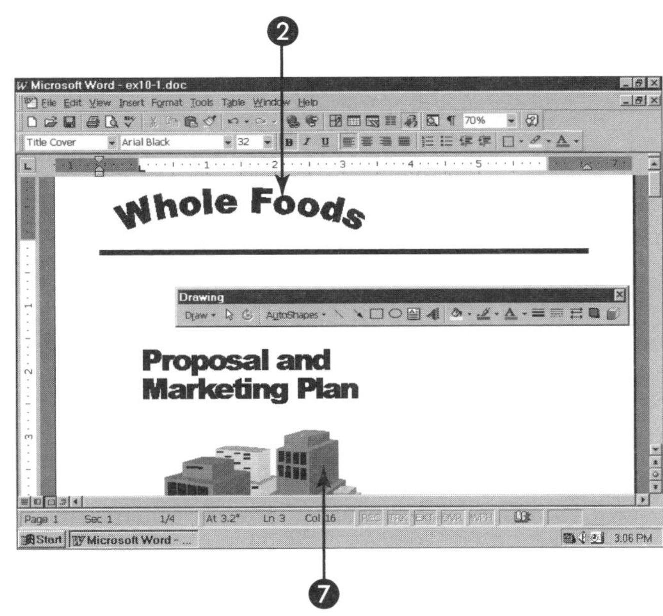

If you moved the object to the wrong location, there's no need to worry. You can move the picture to a new location by following the steps above. You can also use the Undo drop-down menu to back up to the original location.

Resizing objects

Word lets you enlarge or reduce the size of an object. After you select an object, you can use its sizing handles (squares) and the mouse to resize the object. Now that the pictures in your document are in place, you can do one more improvement to make them picture-perfect—you can resize them. Let's make the skyscrapers shorter and wider.

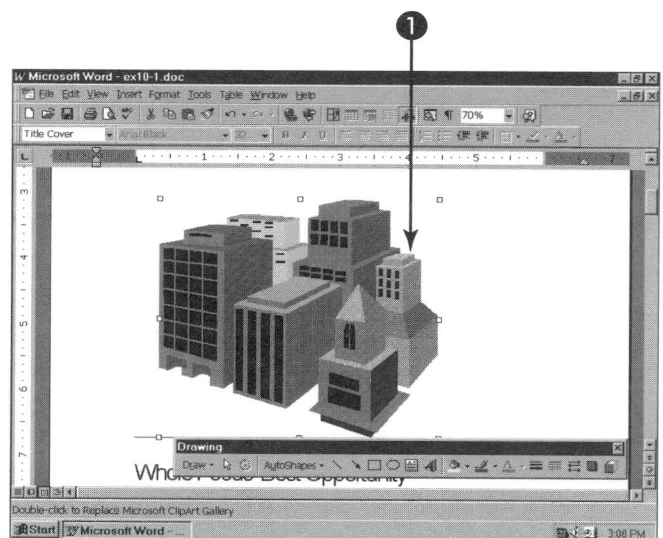

1. Click the skyscraper graphic to select it.
2. Move the mouse pointer to the top middle selection handle until you see a double-headed arrow.
3. Drag the object down about $^1/_2$ inch to make the object shorter.
4. Move the mouse pointer to the right middle selection handle until you see a double-headed arrow.
5. Drag the object to the right about one inch to make the object wider.

For faster resizing, you can click and drag a corner selection handle to simultaneously stretch or shrink two sides of an object.

6. Click outside the object to deselect it.

Your document should now resemble the accompanying illustration.

The text box in the drawing is too large. Let's resize it.

7. Press Ctrl+End or scroll down to page 4.
8. Click the text box to select it.
9. Point to the lower right corner selection handle until you see a double-headed arrow.
10. Drag the corner of the object up and to the left to make the box almost the same size as the text.

    If you resize the object and it looks distorted, you can follow the steps above or use Undo to change the picture back to its original size.

FORMATTING OBJECTS

When you draw on a piece of paper or canvas, you can easily change your picture by using the eraser on your pencil or coloring with paint, oils, crayons, colored pencils, or whatever you have available. You can make similar changes with Word's object formatting commands. You can change line styles by choosing from a variety of thicknesses, dotted lines, and broken lines. You can even change the direction of arrows at the ends of a line.

If you want to brighten up your objects, or give them a different look and feel, you can use Word to fill a shape with a solid color or pattern. Changing colors and patterns can be a lot of fun whether you have some artistic ability or if you just enjoy experimenting.

Changing line styles

There are several line styles that you can apply to a line. They include single, double, and triple lines, and dotted and dashed lines.There is also an assortment of thicknesses ranging from 1/4 pt to 6 pt. The arrow inside the rectangle looks a little scrawny. Let's make it stand out more by thickening the line.

Changing colors and patterns

1. Click the arrow object to select it.
2. Click the Line Style tool (the button with several horizontal lines) on the Drawing toolbar.

   You see an array of line style choices, as shown in the accompanying illustration. The current thickness (3/4 pt) is highlighted.
3. Choose 6 pt thickness.
4. Click outside the object to deselect it.

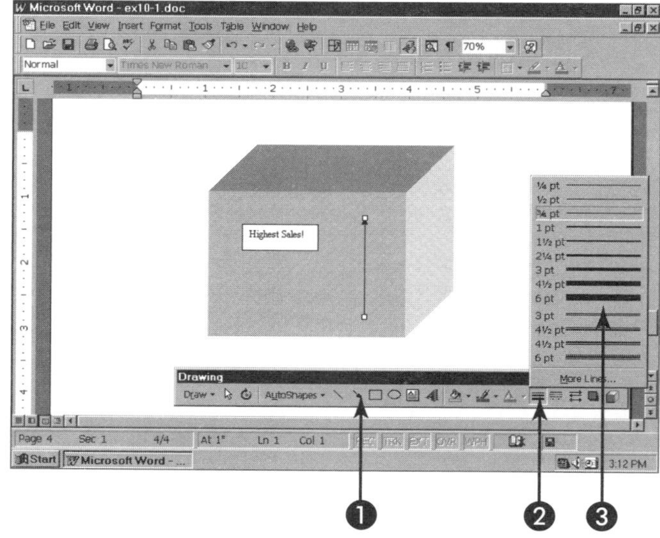

Changing colors and patterns

You can choose from numerous colors and patterns to add pizzazz to your objects. Now you'll discover how easy it is to fill a shape with a color and pattern.

1. Click the rectangle object to select it.
2. Click the drop-down arrow on the Fill Color tool on the Drawing toolbar. A palette of colors appears.
3. Click the pink color, fourth row down, first column on the left.

   The rectangle is filled with pink.
4. Click the Fill Color tool drop-down arrow on the Drawing toolbar again.
5. Select Fill Effects.
6. Click the Pattern tab.

   A palette of patterns appears.

   Click the 40% Polka Dot pattern in the last row, first column.
8. Click OK.
9. Click outside the object to deselect it.

   The front of the 3-D rectangle now contains the pattern you chose, as shown in the accompanying illustration.
10. Save your changes.
11. Close the file.

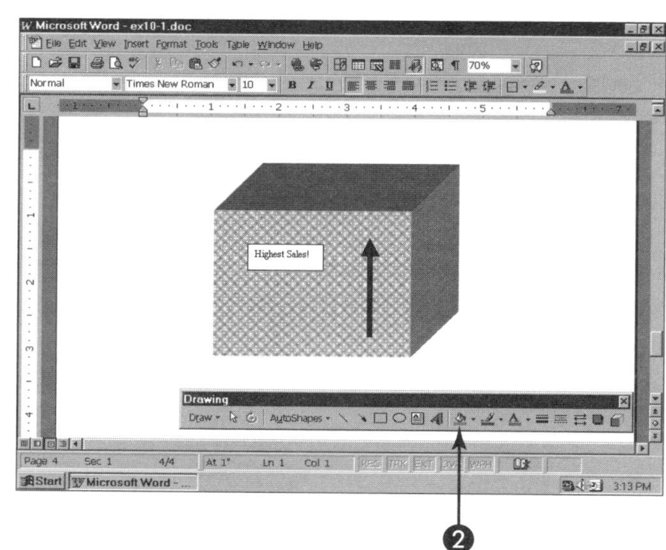

SKILLS CHALLENGE: CREATING A SIMPLE DRAWING

In this exercise, you get to practice the graphics skills that you learned in this lesson. You use the memo you've worked with in earlier exercises. Answer the bonus questions to review the skills and help you determine your understanding of the topics covered. The answers to the bonus questions are located in Appendix C.

1. Open the file EX10-2.DOC.
2. Press Ctrl+End or scroll to the bottom of the memo.
3. Open the Insert menu.
4. Select the Picture command.
5. Select Clip Art.
6. Choose the Academic category.
7. Choose the Leadership graphic (the conference table with people seated around it; Clip Art Keywords: Lecture).
8. Insert the graphic.

How can you tell that an object is selected?

9. Press Ctrl+Home.
10. Open the Insert menu.
11. Select the Picture command.
12. Select WordArt.
13. Choose the WordArt text sample in the fourth row, first column.
14. Click OK.
15. Type **Memo**.
16. Click OK.

What is the purpose of the WordArt toolbar?

Skills challenge

⑰ Move the WordArt object to the top of the document, above the memo heading, as shown in the accompanying illustration.

How do you move an object?

⑱ Press Ctrl+End, and then create a new page.

⑲ On page 2, use the Oval tool to create a circle approximately 1 inch in diameter (remember to press Shift while dragging to draw an exact circle shape).

⑳ Use the Arrow tool to create an arrow to the right of the circle, pointing left (remember to drag from right to left).

㉑ Resize the circle to make it larger by $^1/_2$ inch (remember to press Shift while dragging).

What's a quick way to resize an object?

㉒ Use the Line Style tool to change the arrow's line thickness to 3 points.

㉓ Use the Fill Color tool to fill the circle with the Aqua color and the Large Checker Board pattern.

㉔ Click outside the object to deselect it.

㉕ Close the Drawing toolbar.

What are the two steps that display the patterns palette?

Your simple drawing should look like the one in the accompanying figure.

㉖ Save your changes.

㉗ Close the file.

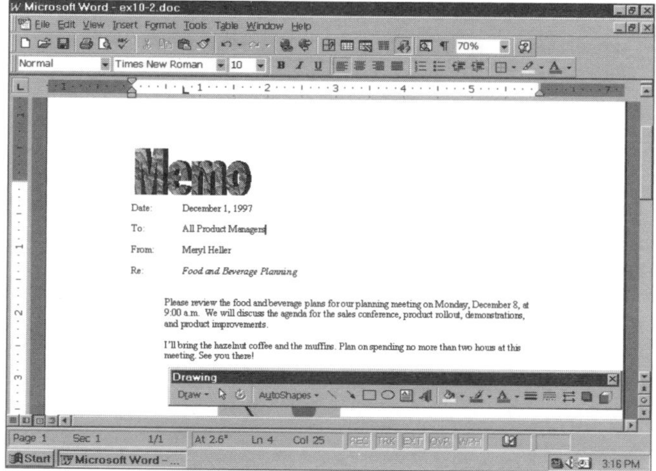

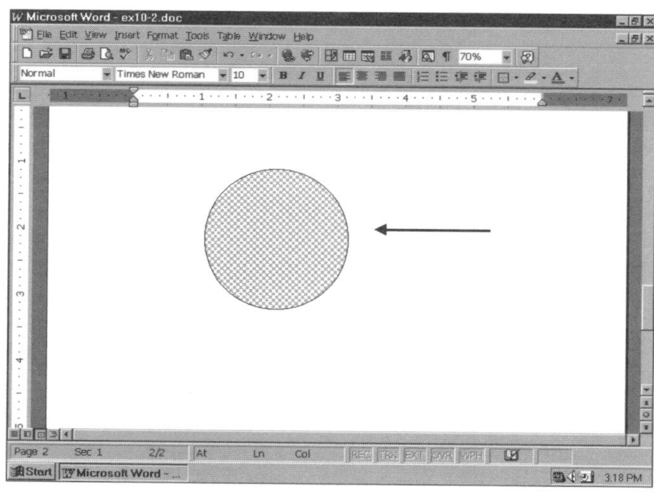

TROUBLESHOOTING

Now that you've completed this lesson, you can use graphics to produce documents with a professional flair. The following table offers solutions to several problems you might have encountered when going through these skills.

ON YOUR CD!

Problem	Solution
I inserted a piece of clip art and it's not the one I need.	Select the graphic and press Delete. Then start over to insert the clip art you want.
The WordArt text is overlapping and hiding some text.	Click the WordArt object and drag it to a better position.
I drew an oval shape and the lines look jagged.	To create an exact oval or circle, hold down the Shift key while dragging the crosshair.
I applied a line color of white to my object and the object disappeared.	By default, Word draws objects with black lines and a white background. The white line color blends into the white background causing the object to disappear. With the object selected, use the Line Color tool on the Drawing toolbar to choose a different line color.

Wrap up

WRAP UP

In this lesson, you've learned the following skills:

- Inserting clip art
- Adding WordArt
- Drawing shapes and lines
- Creating and modifying 3-D shapes
- Selecting, moving, and resizing objects
- Changing line styles
- Changing color and patterns

If you want more practice with these skills, experiment with creating your own simple drawing on a wedding invitation.

In the next lesson, you learn how to create columns in your documents.

Creating Columns

GOALS

In this lesson, you learn the following skills:

- Creating columns
- Editing columns
- Adding section breaks
- Adding a border to a paragraph
- Shading a paragraph

Get ready

GET READY

For this lesson, you will need the files EX11-1.DOC and EX11-2.DOC from the One Step folder.

When you've completed the exercises in this lesson, you will have created the bulletin shown in the accompanying illustration.

TRY OUT THE INTERACTIVE TUTORIALS ON YOUR CD!

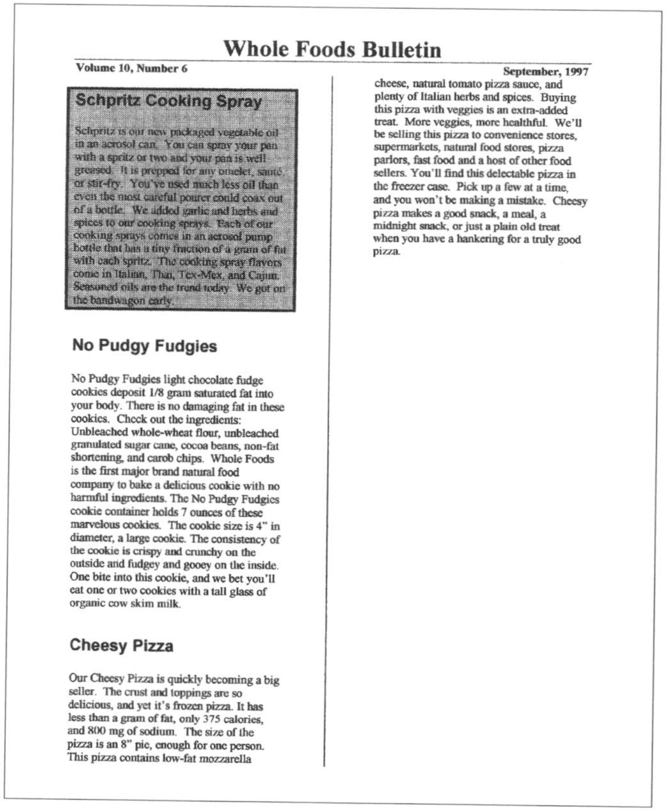

Whole Foods Bulletin

Volume 10, Number 6 | September, 1997

Schpritz Cooking Spray

Schpritz is our new packaged vegetable oil in an aerosol can. You can spray your pan with a spritz or two and your pan is well greased. It is prepped for any omelet, sauté, or stir-fry. You've used much less oil than even the most careful pourer could coax out of a bottle. We added garlic and herbs and spices to our cooking sprays. Each of our cooking sprays comes in an aerosol pump bottle that has a tiny fraction of a gram of fat with each spritz. The cooking spray flavors come in Italian, Thai, Tex-Mex, and Cajun. Seasoned oils are the trend today. We got on the bandwagon early.

No Pudgy Fudgies

No Pudgy Fudgies light chocolate fudge cookies deposit 1/8 gram saturated fat into your body. There is no damaging fat in these cookies. Check out the ingredients: Unbleached whole-wheat flour, unbleached granulated sugar cane, cocoa beans, non-fat shortening, and carob chips. Whole Foods is the first major brand natural food company to bake a delicious cookie with no harmful ingredients. The No Pudgy Fudgies cookie container holds 7 ounces of these marvelous cookies. The cookie size is 4" in diameter, a large cookie. The consistency of the cookie is crispy and crunchy on the outside and fudgey and gooey on the inside. One bite into this cookie, and we bet you'll eat one or two cookies with a tall glass of organic cow skim milk.

Cheesy Pizza

Our Cheesy Pizza is quickly becoming a big seller. The crust and toppings are so delicious, and yet it's frozen pizza. It has less than a gram of fat, only 375 calories, and 800 mg of sodium. The size of the pizza is an 8" pie, enough for one person. This pizza contains low-fat mozzarella cheese, natural tomato pizza sauce, and plenty of Italian herbs and spices. Buying this pizza with veggies is an extra-added treat. More veggies, more healthful. We'll be selling this pizza to convenience stores, supermarkets, natural food stores, pizza parlors, fast food and a host of other food sellers. You'll find this delectable pizza in the freezer case. Pick up a few at a time, and you won't be making a mistake. Cheesy pizza makes a good snack, a meal, a midnight snack, or just a plain old treat when you have a hankering for a truly good pizza.

CREATING COLUMNS

Creating columns in Word is easy. You type the text, select the Format Columns command, and Word automatically converts that text into newspaper-style columns. Newspaper-style columns are sometimes referred to as *snaking columns*. Snaking columns contain text that goes from the bottom of one column to the top of the next column. Two-column documents are handy for newspapers, newsletters, bulletins, magazine articles, lists, and indexes.

Once you tell Word how many columns you want in your document, you can enter the text into the columns. As you type the text, Word fills the column until you reach the bottom of the page, and then it continues (wraps) the text to the top of the next column.

Word's Format Columns command lets you define your columns. For example, you can change the number of columns, the space between columns, the width of the columns, and other options in the Columns dialog box. You can also put a vertical line between columns to separate them visually.

You edit the text in columns the way you normally would for any other text—insert, overtype, delete, copy, and move. You can format the text in columns. And, you can move around columns with the navigation keys.

When you want to change different elements in one part of a document, such as columns, margins, page setup, page number formatting and positioning, or headers and footers, you can divide a document into sections. Sections can be a single paragraph long or can stretch for many pages. A headline for a newsletter could be its own section, and a set of columns of text under the headline could be another section. In long documents, an index could be a section by itself, with a different header, footer, and page numbering scheme.

Creating columns

You insert section breaks to denote sections. A section break indicates where you want one section to end and another section to begin.

Creating columns

Word enables you to create newspaper columns where text begins at the top of the column, continues to the bottom of that column, and then continues from the top of the next column. In the following exercises, you'll work with the file EX11-1.DOC from the One Step folder. This file contains text for the Whole Foods, Inc. bulletin. Your mission is to present the text in two columns. It's not mission impossible.

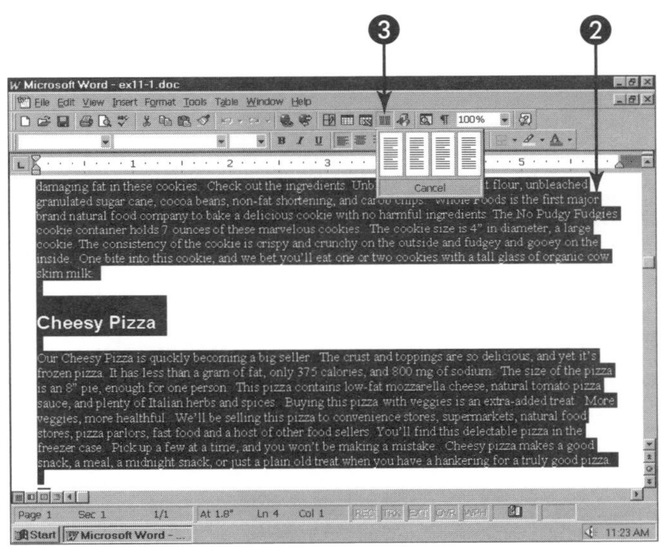

1. Open the file EX11-1.DOC.
2. Select all the text in the document, except the title line, volume number, and date.
3. Click the Columns button (the button with two columns) on the Standard toolbar.

   Word displays a four-column toolbar below the Columns button.
4. Hold down the left mouse button and drag over the columns to highlight two columns.

   The words 2 Columns appear at the bottom of the Columns toolbar.
5. Release the mouse button.

If you decide you no longer want columns, select the text in the columns, click the Columns button on the Standard toolbar, and highlight one column.

6. Click anywhere to deselect the text.

You're now in Page Layout view, as shown in the accompanying illustration. Notice that the zoom is usually set at 70 percent. Word automatically changes the zoom to a pre-set number; usually 70 percent, when you work with columns in Page Layout view.

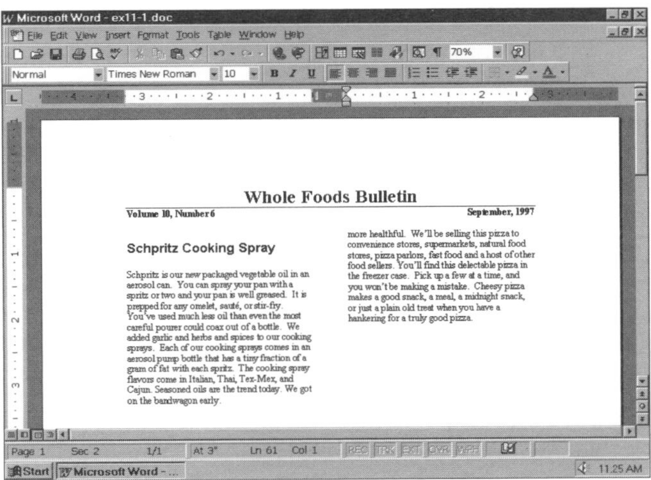

Editing columns

Editing columns

Once you set up your columns, you can makes changes to the characteristics of the columns. For example, you can change the number of columns, add a line between columns, and make the columns equal in width. Perhaps this bulletin would look better if the columns were a little skinnier and had a line between them. Let's edit the columns to have those characteristics.

1. Position the insertion point anywhere in a column.
2. Select the Format menu.
3. Click Columns to open the Columns dialog box.
4. Click the Equal Column Width checkbox.
5. For column 1, click the Width down arrow until 2.5 appears.

   The width for column 2 decreases to 2.5 inches automatically because the Equal Column Width feature is checked.
6. Click the Line Between checkbox.

   Look at the Preview box to see how the columns look now. The two columns are wider and have a vertical line between them.
7. Click OK.

   You can see the narrower columns of text and the vertical line separating them in the accompanying illustration.

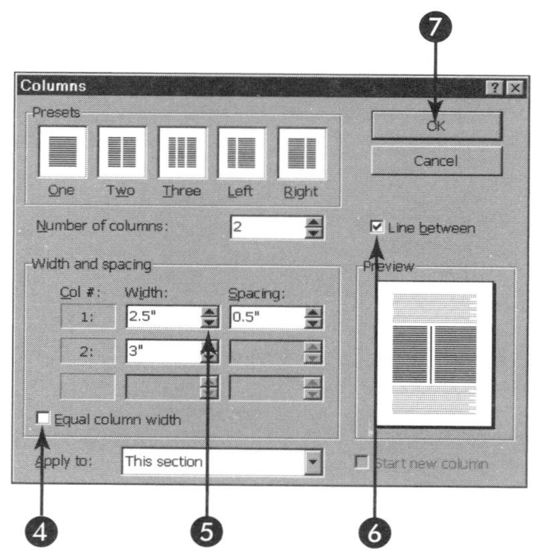

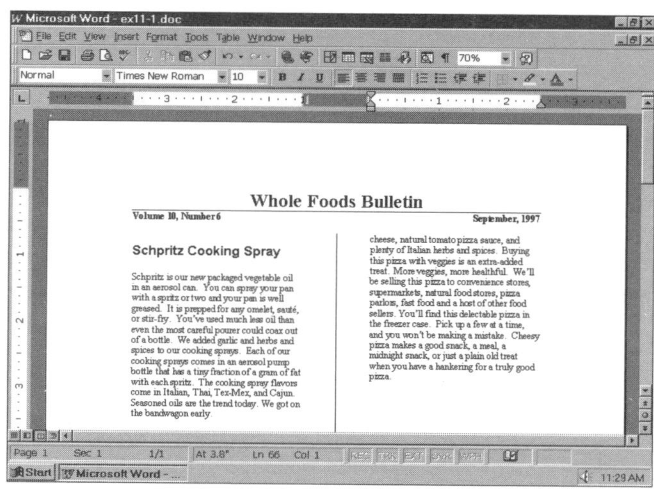

Adding section breaks

Section breaks indicate where you want one section to end and another section to begin in documents. Let's divide the document into two sections.

1. Click the Normal View button on the Status bar to switch to Normal view.
2. Scroll to the bottom of the document (or press Ctrl+End).
3. Select the Insert menu.

Adding section breaks

4 Click Break.

The Break dialog box appears. There are the following four types of section breaks:

- Next Page: Begins the new section at the top of the next page
- Continuous: Begins the new section on the same page as the preceding section without inserting a page break
- Even Page: Begins the new section at the top of the next even-numbered page
- Odd Page: Begins the new section at the top of the next odd-numbered page

5 In the Section breaks area, choose the Next Page option.

6 Click OK.

Word divides the document into sections (see the accompanying illustration) with a section break mark; that is, a double dotted line with the words *Section Break (Next Page)*. The section break type is enclosed in parentheses. At the left end of the Status bar, Word displays the section that currently contains the insertion point. For example, Sec 2 represents Section 2 in the document.

Now let's change the number of columns to one in Section 2.

7 Place the insertion point back in Section 2, and select the Format menu.

8 Click Columns.

9 In the Presets section, choose One.

10 Click OK.

11 Type **The newsletter will be distributed every Monday at 7 a.m.**

The text appears in one column in Section 2.

To delete a section break, in Normal view, position the insertion point below the section break mark (double dotted line) and press Backspace.

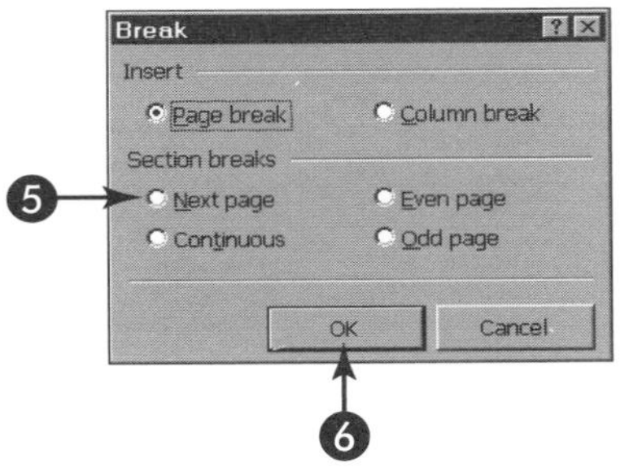

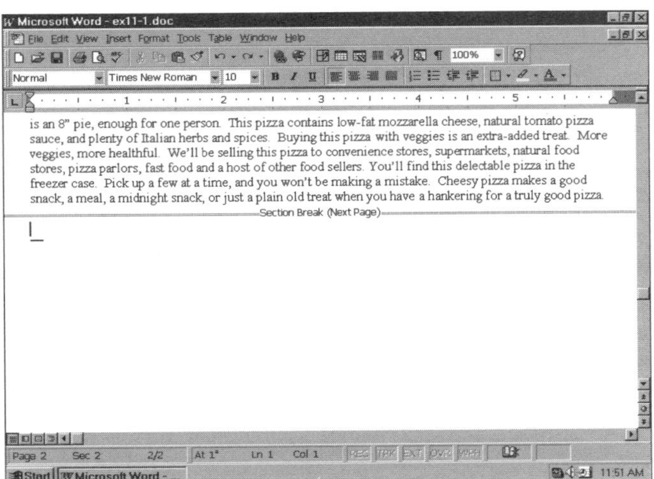

Adding section breaks

FORMATTING A SECTION

Word's section layout features help you set up the beginning of sections, vertical alignment (how the top of a section aligns with the top margin), line numbering, and suppression of endnotes. To format a section, position the insertion point in the section you want to format. Select File ➢ Page Setup and click the Layout tab. You can also double-click the section break mark (double dotted line) at the top of the section to display the Page Setup dialog box and the Layout tab. Choose any options in the Layout tab to format a section, and then click OK.

VISUAL BONUS: COLUMNS DIALOG BOX

The Columns dialog box is where you make choices about the formatting of your columns.

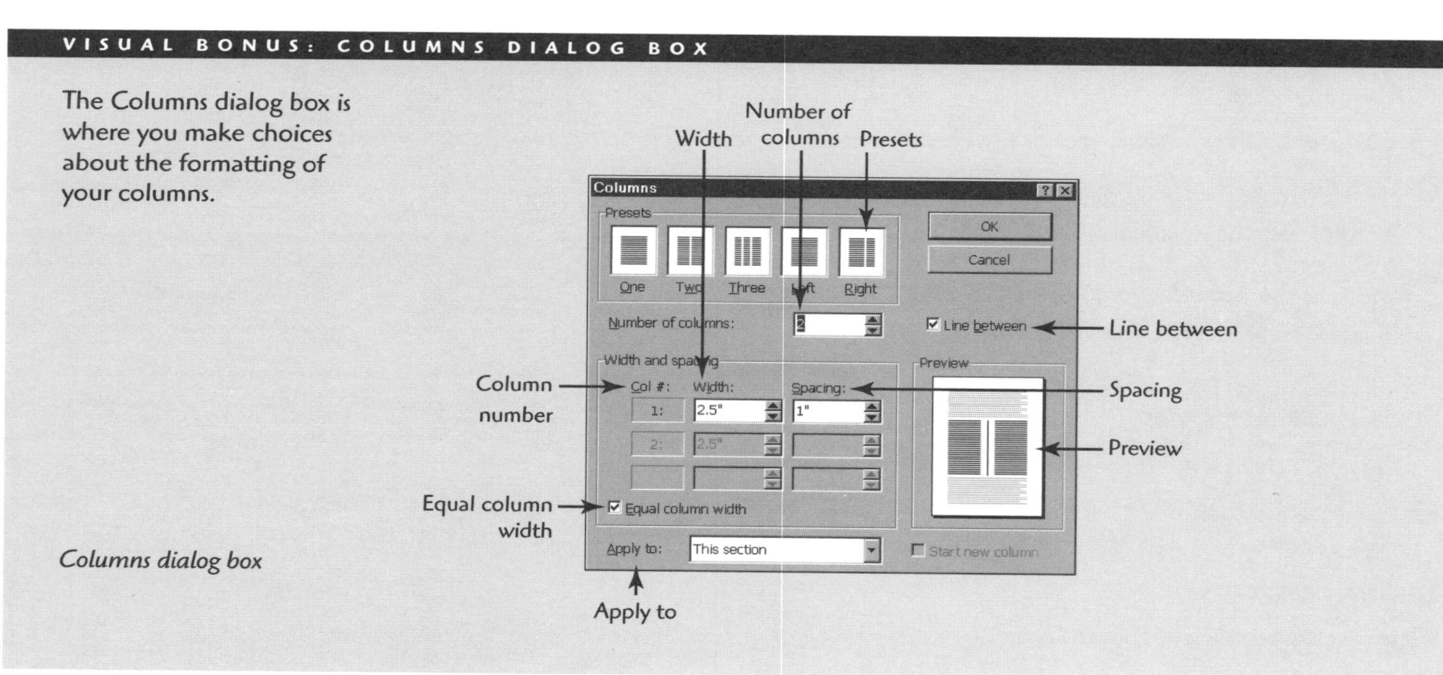

Columns dialog box

Adding a border to a paragraph

ADDING BORDERS AND SHADING

If you want to emphasize document headings or sections of a document, you can add borders and shading to your paragraphs. The Borders and Shading feature enables you to add borders, emphasis lines, and shading to paragraphs. Word can only add borders and shading to text that ends with a paragraph mark. For example, you might want to add a single thick border around a paragraph. Or you might want to add a double underline below headings to bring attention to them. You can also add lines to separate parts of a document.

With Word's automatic formatting feature, you can place a border above a paragraph by typing three or more dashes, underscores, or equal signs above the paragraph. Dashes create a thin line, underscores create a thick line, and equal signs create a double line.

Adding a border to a paragraph

Borders are lines and boxes you can use to enclose paragraphs, graphics, or table cells. One of the many things you can do with the Borders and Shading command is put boxes with either a single or double line around paragraphs. We'll put a box around the first article in the bulletin to make it stand out.

1. Select the first heading and paragraph, *Schpritz Cooking Spray*.
2. Click the Border tool's (the Outside Border button, by default) drop-down arrow on the Formatting toolbar.

   Word displays the border choices in a toolbar.
3. Click the Outside Border button in the first row and first column on the Border toolbar.

   Word outlines the edges of the paragraph with a single line. That line looks too thin for our purposes, so let's thicken it up.

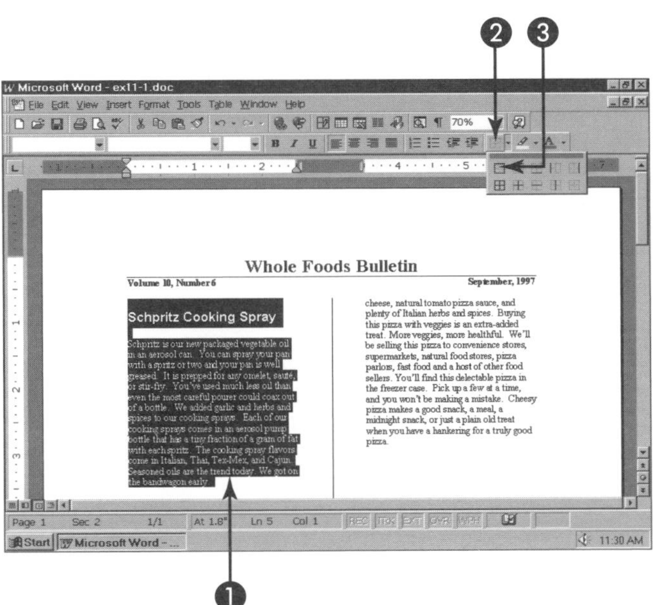

Adding a border to a paragraph

You can also add lines at the top, center, bottom, left, or right side of paragraphs with either a single, double, dashed, or dotted line. Click the Outside Border, Top Border, Bottom Border, Left Border, Right Border, All Borders, Inside Border, Inside Horizontal Border, or Inside Vertical Border button on the Borders palette to tell Word where to place the line.

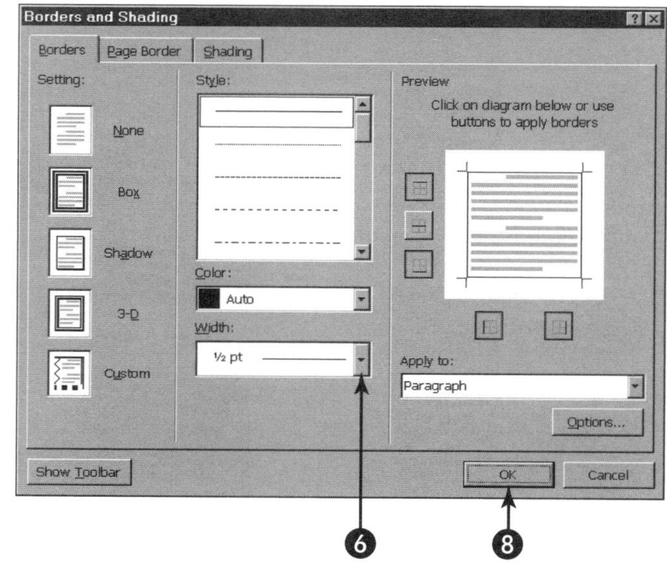

4. Select the Format menu.
5. Click Borders and Shading.

   The Borders and Shading dialog box opens.
6. Click the drop-down arrow in the Width box.

   A list of line widths appears. The list is similar to the Line Style list on the Drawing toolbar that you used in Lesson 10.
7. Choose 2 1/4 point.
8. Click OK.
9. Click outside the selected paragraph to deselect it.

   The border is now bolder and easier to see, as shown in the accompanying illustration.

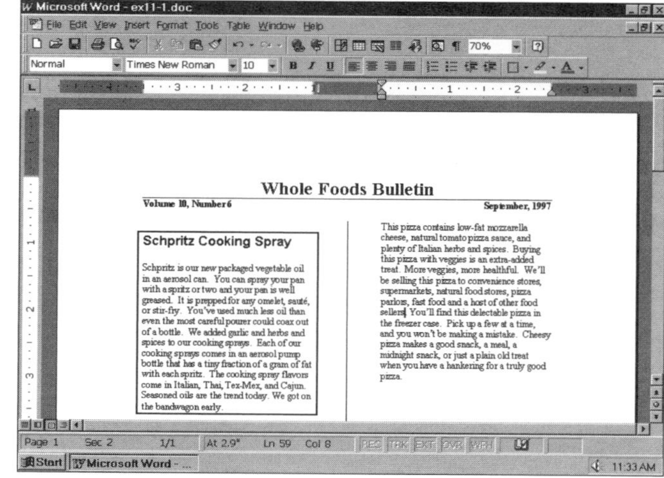

If you want to remove the border, click the Borders drop-down arrow on the Formatting toolbar. Then click the No Border button.

VISUAL BONUS: BORDER CHOICES

When you click the Borders drop-down arrow on the Formatting toolbar, you see several border choices. By default, the Outside Border is selected.

Borders toolbar

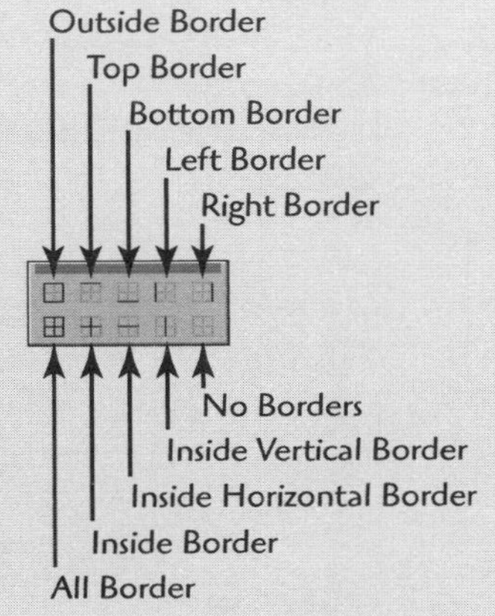

Shading a paragraph

Shading a paragraph can draw attention to certain text in your document. Perhaps you want to shade a title, a quotation, or a note surrounded with a border. Shading comes in all kinds of colors ranging from grays to typical palette colors. Let's shade the paragraph that is surrounded with a border.

1. Select the heading and paragraph enclosed in the border.
2. Select the Format menu.
3. Click Borders and Shading.
4. Click the Shading tab.
5. In the Fill section, click the fill color in the second row, first column to fill the box with 15 percent Gray.

   The name of the shading you chose appears to the right of the color palette and the color appears in the sample text in the Preview box on the right side of the dialog box.
6. Click OK.

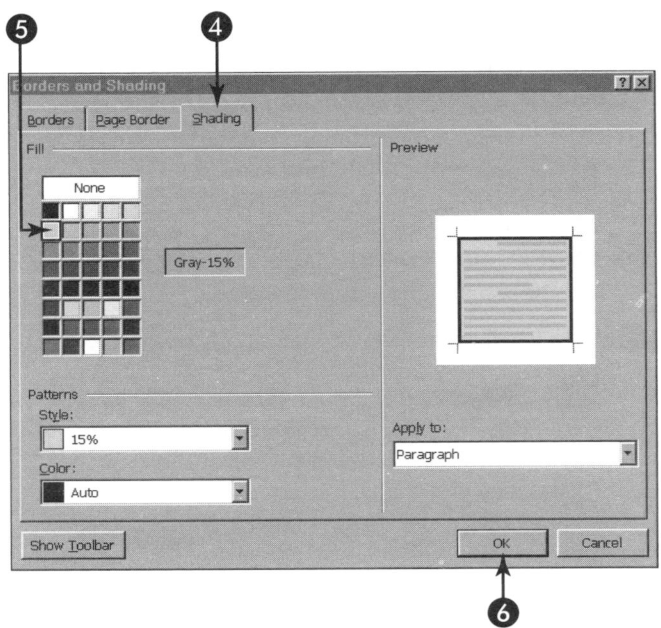

Skills challenge

7. Click outside the selected paragraph to deselect it.

   Compare your screen to the accompanying illustration. Depending on your printer, the shading might print differently than it appears onscreen, or it might not print at all. If you don't have a color printer, be careful not to choose too dark a color that might obscure your text.

8. Save your changes and close the file.

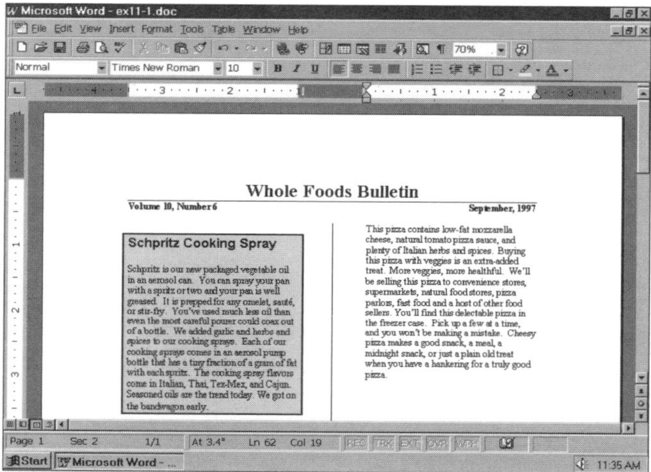

If the shading doesn't tickle your fancy, you can either pick a new shade or clear the shading altogether. Select the text box, select Format ➢ Borders and Shading, and click the Shading tab. In the Fill section, choose a new shade or None.

SKILLS CHALLENGE: CREATING A SIMPLE NEWSLETTER

This final exercise provides a recap of the columns and borders skills you learned in this lesson. You use a document that contains text for the Whole Foods newsletter. Answer the bonus questions to review the skills and help you determine your understanding of the topics covered. The answers to the bonus questions are found in Appendix C.

1. Open the file EX11-2.DOC.
2. Select all the text in the document, except the newsletter title, volume number, and date at the top.
3. Click the Columns button on the Standard toolbar.

What is the maximum number of columns you can create using the Columns button on the Standard toolbar?

4. Choose two columns.
5. Select the Format menu.
6. Click the Columns command.
7. Choose the Equal Column Width option.

> **2** *What feature in the Columns dialog box lets you change the size of columns?*

8. Make both columns 2.5 inches wide.

   Insert a vertical line between the columns.

10. Select the last heading and paragraph (last article in the right column).
11. Click the Borders button on the Formatting toolbar.
12. Choose an outside border.

> **3** *If you want to get rid of a border, what do you choose in the Border toolbar?*

13. Select the Format menu.
14. Choose the Borders and Shading command.
15. Click the Shading tab.
16. Pick Gray 12.5 percent in the first row, last column.

    Your newsletter should resemble the one in the accompanying illustration.

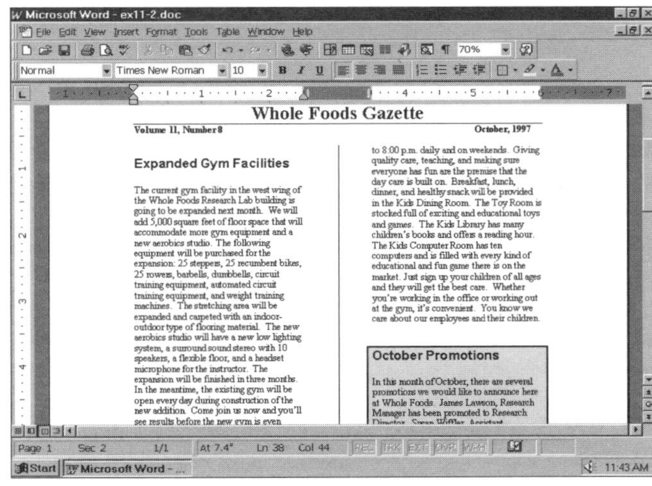

17. Switch to Normal view.
18. Scroll to the end of the document
19. Insert a Next Page section break.
20. Save your changes.
21. Close the file.

Troubleshooting

TROUBLESHOOTING

Now you've learned how to create columns and add borders and shading to paragraphs in your documents. The following table offers solutions to several problems you might have encountered when acquiring these skills.

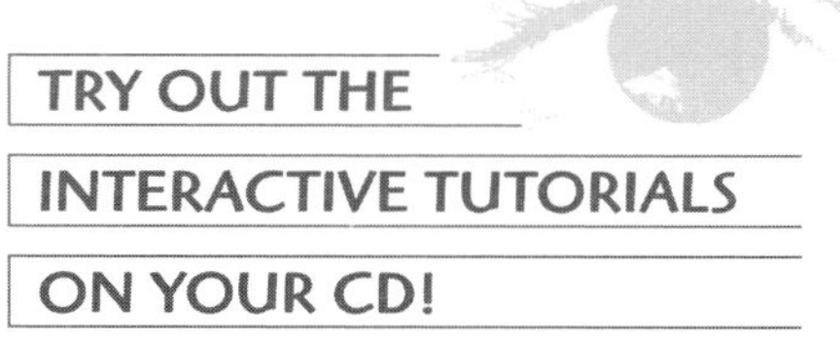

Problem	Solution
I created two columns and now I need a third column.	Select all the text in the two columns, click the Columns button on the Standard toolbar, and choose three columns.
I would like to make the left column narrower than the right column.	Select Format ➢ Columns and choose the Left option in the Presets section.
I added a top border to a short line of text and the line extends all the way across the page. I really wanted the border above the text only.	Border lines extend to the paragraph mark at the end of a line. To insert a line above the text only, click the Drawing tool on the Standard toolbar, click the Line tool, and drag the crosshair above the text to draw a line the length you want.
I shaded a paragraph with black and now I can't see my text.	The default color for text is black; therefore, the text blended with the black shading. To fix this, select Format ➢ Borders and Shading and select a lighter color shading.

WRAP UP

In this lesson, you've learned the following skills:

- Creating columns
- Editing columns
- Adding section breaks
- Adding a border to a paragraph
- Shading a paragraph

If you want more practice with these skills, experiment with creating your own simple neighborhood newsletter.

In the lesson coming up, you learn how to set up tables, outlines, and organization charts in Word.

Organizing Information with Tables, Outlines, and Organization Charts

GOALS

In this lesson, you learn the following skills:

- Inserting a table
- Entering, selecting, and aligning text in a cell
- Changing fonts for text in a table
- Rotating text in a table
- Inserting and deleting rows and columns
- Adjusting column width
- Using Table AutoFormat
- Creating and modifying an outline
- Viewing outline headings
- Numbering an outline
- Creating and changing an organization chart

Inserting a table

GET READY

For this lesson, you need the files EX12-1.DOC and EX12-2.DOC from the One Step folder.

When you're done with the exercises in this lesson, you will have created a table like the one shown in the accompanying illustration.

Whole Foods
Cereal Comparison Study

Cereal	*Sugar*	*Fiber*
Wheat Os	0.5 g	3 g
Wheat Pops	0.6 g	1 g
Wheat Bran	0.2 g	10 g

CREATING A TABLE

Creating a table is a great way to list items and show relationships so readers can grasp information quickly. You can also use tables to summarize facts and figures—for example, a two-column table with your competition's product features in one column and your product features in the other. Tables are often used in annual reports, sales reports, and order forms.

The Table feature enables you to create a table and then enter text and numbers (similar to a spreadsheet) without defining tab settings. Tables are easier to work with than tabs if you have to set up a grid of information with columns and rows.

If you need to edit your table, you simply click in the table area and then make your changes. You can make any adjustments to your table, from the simplest change (correcting a typo) to the more involved (inserting and deleting rows and columns, changing the format, column width, row height, and so on). Use the Tab key or arrow keys to move from one cell to another within the table. To correct typos and make simple changes to the data, use the standard editing conventions, such as overtype, insert, delete, copy, and move.

Some formatting changes you can make to text in a table include changing alignment and font size, and rotating text.

TRY OUT THE
INTERACTIVE TUTORIALS
ON YOUR CD!

Inserting a table

There are three ways to create a table:

- **Insert Table**—You can create a simple table by using the Insert Table tool on the Standard toolbar. This tool enables you to specify the number of rows and columns you want. You start with a blank table and fill in the cells.

■ **Draw Table**—You can create a more complex table using Word's Draw Table feature. This feature enables you to draw a table using the mouse. In Draw Table mode, the mouse pointer looks like a pen. You can create cells with different heights and widths.

■ **Convert Text to Table**—Use this feature if you have text that you want to convert into a table. Before you convert the text, separate the columns with tab spaces and indicate the ends of rows with paragraph marks (press Enter). Then select the text and choose Table ➢ Convert Text to Table. Finally, select the options you want in the Convert Text to Table dialog box.

In the following exercises, you'll use the file EX12-1.DOC from the One Step folder. This file contains a title and subtitle for a Whole Foods comparison study. Your job is to create a simple table that compares three cereals.

1. Open the file EX12-1.DOC.

   Notice the document is in Page Layout view.

2. Press Ctrl+End.

3. Click the Insert Table button on the Standard toolbar.

   Word displays a grid below the Insert Table button.

4. Hold down the left mouse button and drag over the grid to highlight three columns and three rows.

   You see a 3×3 Table at the bottom of the grid. This tells Word to create a three-column table with three rows.

5. Release the mouse button.

   Word inserts a table with three columns and three rows.

What if you no longer want the table you just created? To delete the table, you can click the Undo button on the Standard toolbar. Or, you can click and drag over the entire table to select it, and then press Delete.

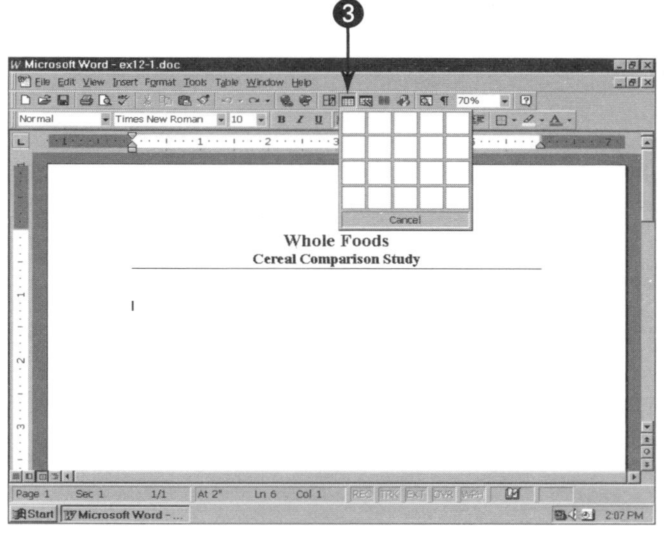

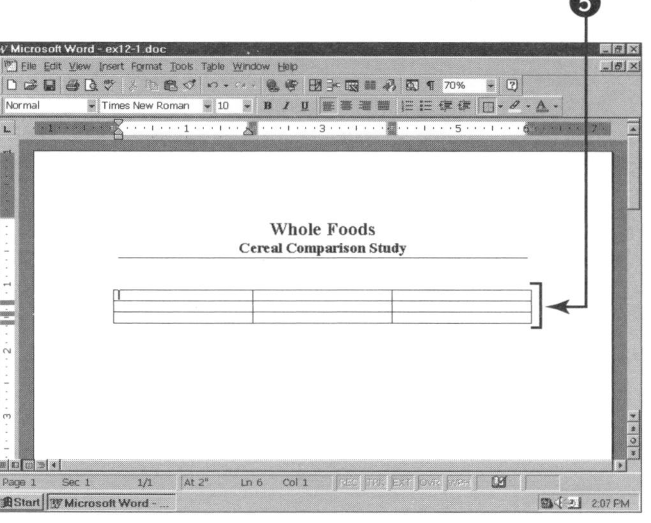

Entering text in a cell

Entering text in a cell

A Word table contains columns and rows and looks like a spreadsheet. The intersection of a row and a column in the table is called a cell. You can enter text and numbers in cells by typing the information and then pressing Tab to move to the next cell. The insertion point is in the first cell in the first row. This is where we'll begin entering text in the table.

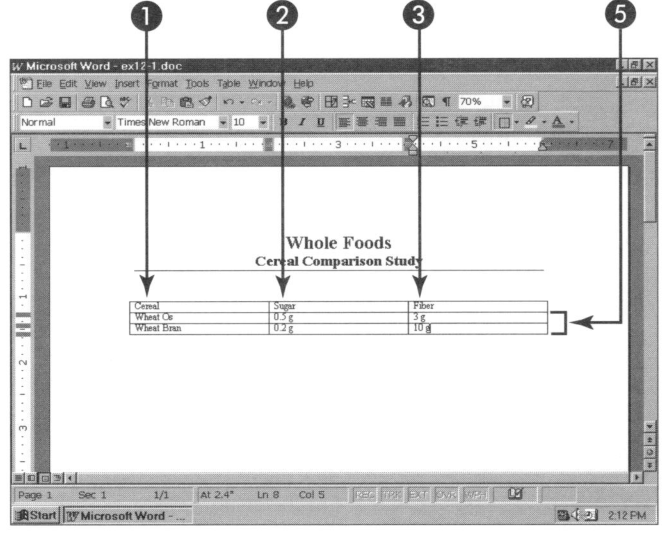

Cereal	Sugar	Fiber
Wheat Os	0.5 g	3 g
Wheat Bran	0.2 g	10 g

1. Type **Cereal** and press Tab.

TIP

Pressing Shift+Tab will move you back to the preceding cell.

2. Type **Sugar** and press Tab.
3. Type **Fiber**.

   This completes the headings for the table.
4. Press Tab.

   This moves the insertion point to the first cell in the next row.
5. Type the following table entries:

   Wheat Os. Press Tab.

   0.5 g. Press Tab.

   3 g. Press Tab.

   Wheat Bran. Press Tab.

   0.2 g. Press Tab.

   10 g

As you can see, all the cells have entries.

Selecting and aligning text

You can make corrections to text and numbers in the table as you would in a normal document. Keep in mind that pressing Enter within a cell inserts a line break, and doesn't move you to the next cell.

You can convert a table to text by selecting the table, and then selecting Table ➢ Convert Table To Text. Then choose the character you want to use to separate the columns.

Selecting and aligning text

Generally, numbers should be aligned right in a column. The numbers in the last two columns of this table are aligned left. Your assignment is to select those numbers and right-align them using the Align Right button on the Formatting toolbar. You already know how to use this tool because you right-aligned text in an earlier lesson.

1. Move the mouse pointer to the top border of the first cell in the second column until you see a thick down arrow.
2. Click to select the second column, and then drag to the right to select the last column, too.
3. Click the Align Right button on the Formatting toolbar.

   Word aligns the text and numbers on the right side of each cell.
4. Click anywhere in the table to deselect it.

Your table should look like the one in the accompanying illustration.

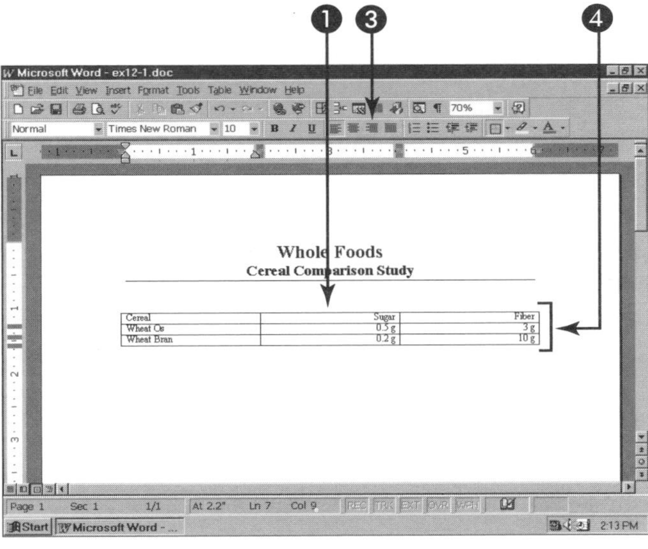

Cereal	Sugar	Fiber
Wheat Os	0.5 g	3 g
Wheat Bran	0.2 g	10 g

Changing fonts for text in a table

Changing fonts for text in a table

You can change the font and font size for text in a table just as you would for any other text in a document. The font size in the table is too small. Let's change it.

1. Move the mouse pointer to the left margin next to the first row.
2. Click and drag down to select all the cells in the table.
3. Click the Font Size drop-down arrow on the Formatting toolbar.
4. Choose 14 pt.
5. Click anywhere in the table to deselect it.

Your table should look like the one in the accompanying illustration.

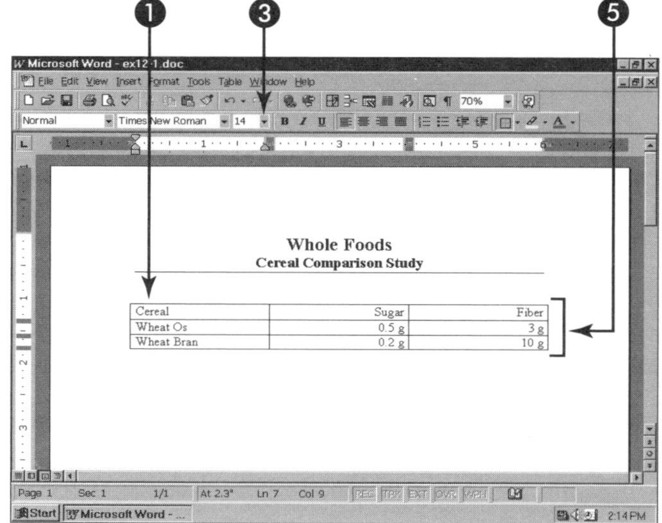

Rotating text in a table

Word enables you to rotate text so that the words are facing the right or the left. Let's rotate the text for a column heading.

1. Double-click the column heading *Cereal.*
2. Select the Format menu.
3. Click Text Direction.

   The Text Direction - Table Cell dialog box opens.
4. Choose the vertical box on the left.

   Word displays a sample of the rotated text in the Preview box on the right.
5. Click OK.

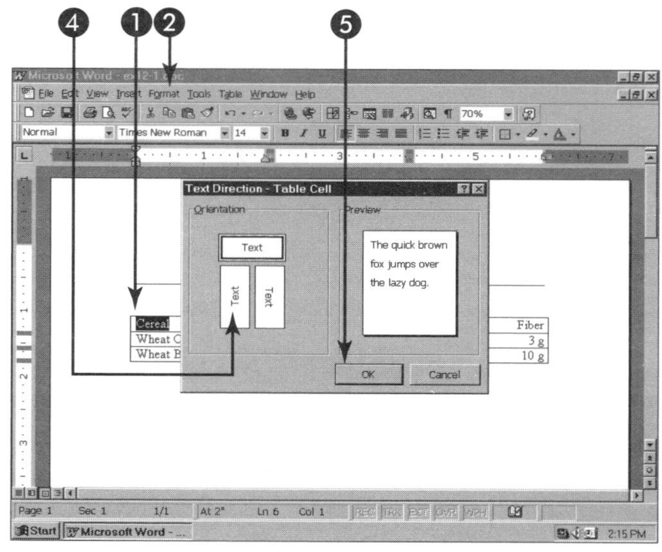

6 Click anywhere in the table to deselect it.

Your table should look like the one in the accompanying illustration.

The column heading doesn't look very good. In general, rotated text is best for long column headings that label narrow columns (for example, columns with single characters such as Y for Yes and N for No, and single numbers). But there is no problem. We'll undo the rotated text.

7 Press Ctrl+Z to undo the rotated text.

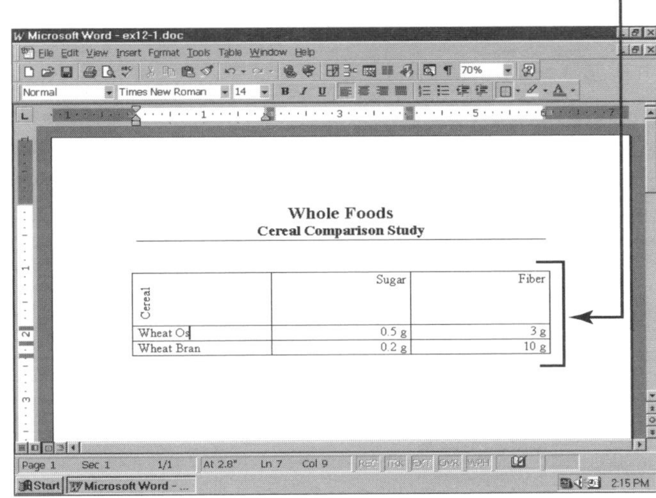

Inserting and deleting rows and columns

The Table ➢ Insert Rows command lets you insert rows and columns. The Table ➢ Delete Rows command allows you to delete rows and columns.

Suppose that, after creating your table, you decide to add a new row or column of text or spacing. Adding white space between rows or columns makes the table easier to read. Or, perhaps you want to delete rows of text or empty space. Let's practice these tasks here.

1 Click in any cell in the last row.

To access the Table commands, you have to put the insertion point within the table. Also, the insertion point must be in the row below where you want the new row to appear.

2 Select the Table menu.

3 Click the Insert Rows command.

You've inserted a new row in the table. The last row shifts down to adjust accordingly.

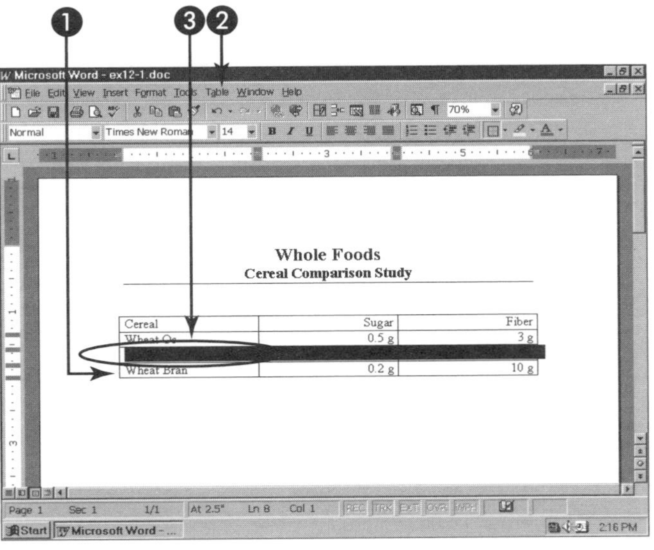

Click the Insert Rows button on the Standard toolbar to insert rows in a table. To create a new last row in the table, put the insertion point in the cell of the last row and column of the table, and press Tab.

Inserting and deleting rows and column

4 Click in the first cell of the new row.

5 Type the following cell entries:

Wheat Pops. Press Tab.

0.6 g. Press Tab.

1 g

The steps for inserting a column are similar to the steps for inserting a row. Let's insert a new column between the first and second columns.

6 Move the mouse pointer to the top of the second column until you see a thick down arrow.

7 Click at the top of the second column to select the entire column.

8 Select the Table menu.

9 Click Insert Columns.

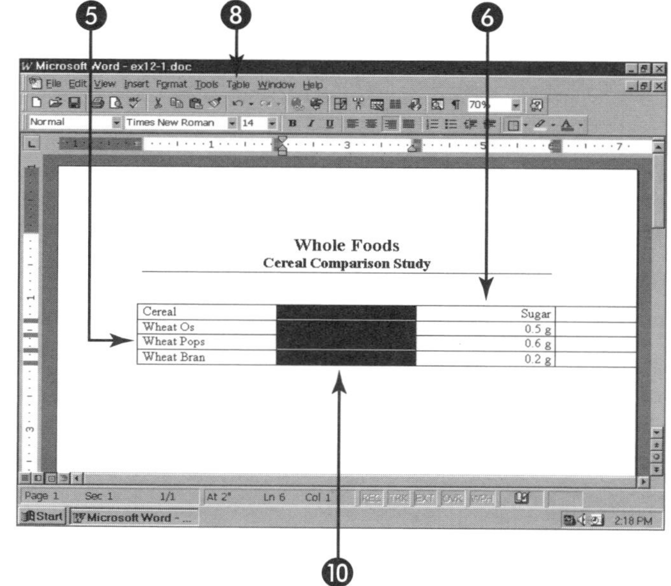

You can also click the Insert Columns button on the Standard toolbar to insert columns quickly.

10 Click in any cell to deselect the column.

There's your new column. Notice that the last two columns shifted to the right to accommodate the new column. Now let's delete the new column.

11 Move the mouse pointer to the top of the blank column until you see a thick down arrow.

12 Click at the top of the blank column.

The entire column is selected and highlighted.

13 Select the Table menu.

14 Click Delete Columns.

The entire column disappears. The table contains four rows and three columns now.

To quickly delete a row, click in the left margin of the row you want to delete. Then select Table ➢ Delete Rows.

INSERTING OR DELETING MORE THAN ONE COLUMN OR ROW AT A TIME

What if you want to insert or delete more than one column or row at a time? Here's how you do it:

- To insert more than one row at a time, click in the left margin of the row where you want to begin inserting a few rows. Then drag down over the number of rows you want to insert. Select Table ➢ Insert Rows.
- To insert more than one column at a time, click at the top of the column where you want to begin inserting a few columns. Then drag across the number of columns you want to insert. Select Table ➢ Insert Columns.
- To delete more than one row at once, click in the left margin of the first row you want to delete. Then drag down to highlight the number of rows you want to delete. Select Table ➢ Delete Rows.
- To delete more than one column at once, click the top of the first column you want to delete. Then drag across to highlight the number of columns you want to delete. Select Table ➢ Delete Columns.

Adjusting column width

Adjusting column width

After the text has been entered, the columns may need to be widened to accommodate long entries or made skinnier to close up white space. You can select Table ➢ Column Width to adjust column width, or you can use the mouse. In this exercise we'll use the mouse because it's more visual and it's also quicker.

1. Move the mouse pointer to the border line between the first and second columns until you see double vertical bars with a left and right arrow.
2. Click and drag the column border to the right to the 2 1/2" mark on the horizontal ruler.
3. Move the mouse pointer to the outside border line of the last column until you see double vertical bars with a left and right arrow.
4. Click and drag the column border to the left to the 5 1/4" mark on the horizontal ruler.

Compare your table to the one in the accompanying illustration.

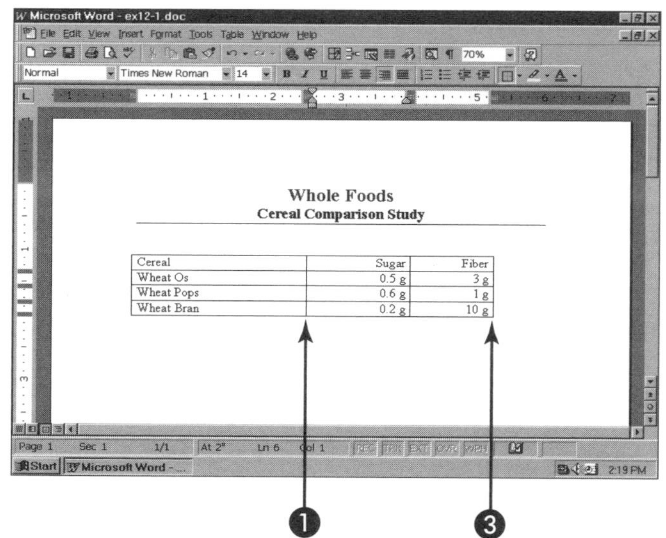

You can use the same technique to make a row shorter or taller. If a row is too tall or short, move the mouse to the row border until the pointer changes to a double horizontal bar with an up and down arrow. Then drag the row border to change the height.

FORMATTING A TABLE

By default, Word displays a 1/2-pt single line border to outline the rows and columns in a table as you work onscreen. This border prints. If you don't want to print the border and still want to display lines for guidance, you can remove the border and display gridlines onscreen. Gridlines do not print.

The Table ➢ Show/Hide Gridlines command is a toggle to turn the gridlines on or off. When you print the table, the lines do not appear on your printout. However, you can add different types of borders or lines around individual cells, groups of cells, or an entire table that will print. Adding borders increases the readability of a table.

You can easily format your table using the formatting commands and tools you already know—Borders and Shading, Alignment, Font, Font Size, Font Style, and Font Color. But deciding what options you want and executing each of these formatting commands individually could take a lot of time. Luckily, there's Word's Table AutoFormat command. In one fell swoop, you can use Table AutoFormat to make your tables look beautiful.

Displaying gridlines

The gray gridlines that outline table cells are a visual aid onscreen, but they do not print. In this exercise, we'll remove all the border lines to display gridlines.

1. Select all the cells in the table.
2. Select the Format menu.
3. Click the Borders and Shading command and click the Borders tab to bring it to the front.
4. In the Setting section, choose None.
5. Click OK.
6. Click anywhere in the table to deselect it.

   As you can see, Word outlines the rows and columns with gray gridlines.

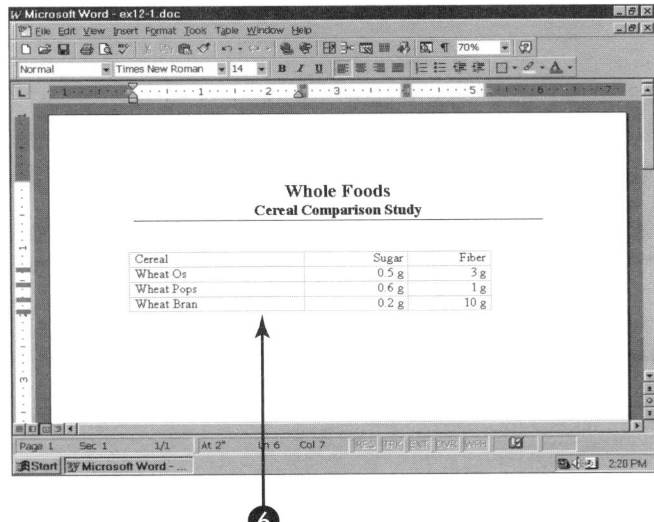

Using Table AutoFormat

The Table AutoFormat command lets you apply all different types of formatting to your table. The formatting includes font, font size, column width, color, line style, and much more. Let's see how easy it is to use Table AutoFormat.

1. Select all the cells in the table.
2. Select the Table menu.

Using Table AutoFormat

3 Click Table AutoFormat.

You see the Table AutoFormat dialog box, as shown in the accompanying illustration. The available formats appear in a list on the left side of the dialog box. The Preview box is on the right. You can select the formatting by clicking in the checkbox next to each format you want to apply or omit from the AutoFormat settings.

4 Choose Colorful 2.

5 In the Formats to apply section, clear the check mark in the AutoFit checkbox.

Turning off the AutoFit option retains the current column widths and row heights.

6 Click OK.

7 Click anywhere in the table to deselect it.

The new formatting is shown in the accompanying illustration. If the formatting doesn't suit your taste, you can always repeat the steps to change it.

8 Save your changes.

9 Close the file.

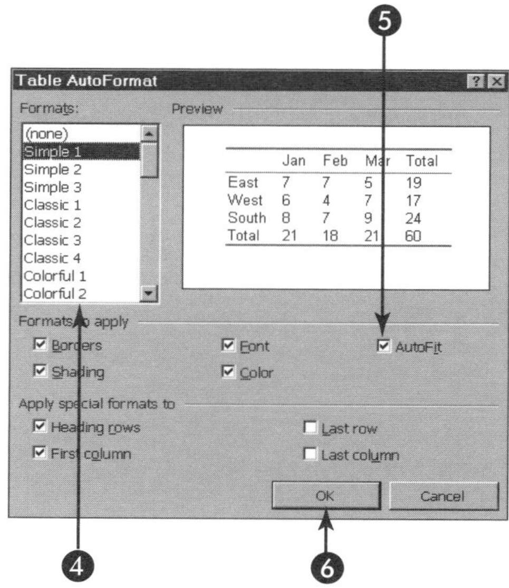

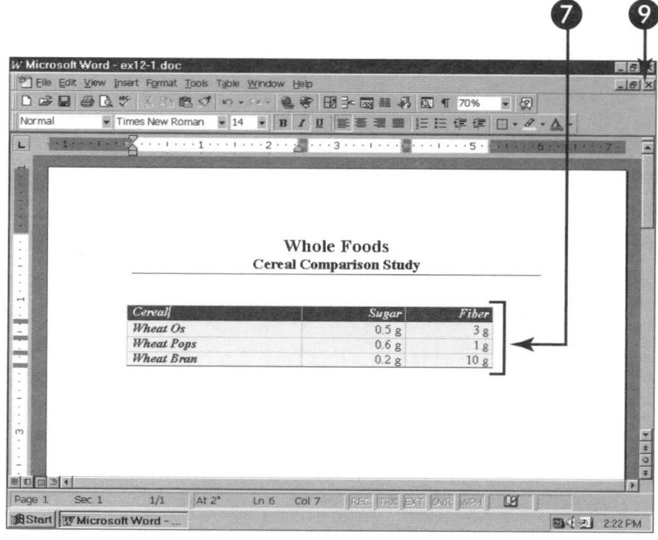

CREATING AND MODIFYING AN OUTLINE

In Lesson 4 you learned how to switch to Outline view and view your document in outline format. Now you'll learn how to build an outline from scratch. Outlines can help you organize your ideas as you compose a new document by letting you view only the headings. Later, an outline can help you reorganize and edit your document.

Using Table AutoFormat

An outline consists of three elements: headings, subheadings, and body text. Word treats headings independently. Associated subheadings are not promoted and demoted along with the headings. Body text always remains associated with its heading. There are nine possible outline heading levels: Heading 1, Heading 2, Heading 3, and so on, through Heading 9. Each heading level can have one level of body text. The headings have different formatting styles that make it easier for you and others to quickly determine the organization of your document.

When you create or edit a Word outline, you can promote and demote headings and subheadings, and demote headings and subheadings to body text. When you promote a heading (and its body text), Word moves the heading (and its body text) to a higher level number. When you promote body text, Word moves the body text to the heading level of the preceding heading. Demoting a heading moves the heading to a lower level number. Demoting a heading to body text moves the heading to a lower level number and changes the heading to body text.

You can collapse parts of your document so only the headings show, and you can restrict the view of your outline to specific levels of headings. Click any of the ten buttons on the right side of the Outline toolbar—the buttons numbered from 1 to 10 and the All button. To change the order of the headings, you can move one or more headings up or down in the outline, and you can easily move an entire section—headings, subheadings, and any body text.

If you work with numbered outlines for bids, proposals, or legal documents, you can have Word add numbers to the outline for you. Word numbers the elements in an outline with any one of the various outline number styles such as numbers and letters, Roman numerals, and the word *chapter* with numbers. If you move elements of an outline to another position in the document, and add or delete elements, Word renumbers the elements for you.

Creating an outline

Creating an outline

You can create an outline in Word using Outline view and the Outline toolbar. In this exercise, we create a simple outline for a Whole Foods employee handbook.

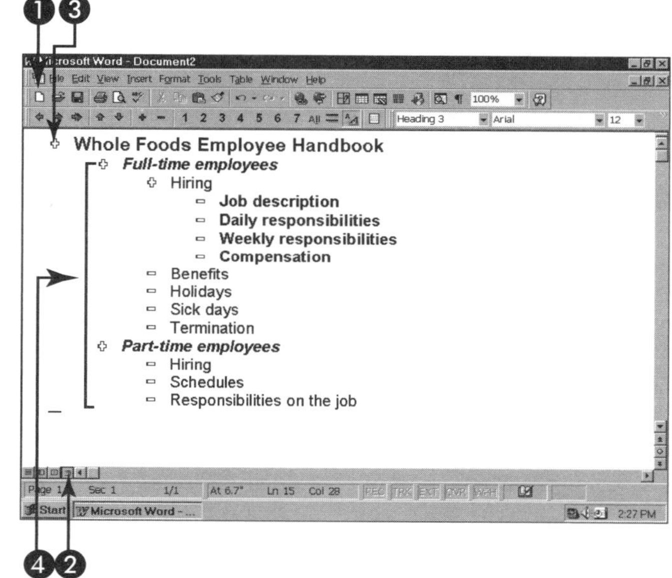

1. Create a new document.
2. Click the Outline View button on the Status bar. A minus sign appears at the top of the document near the insertion point.

   This is where you begin typing the first heading in the outline. The Outline toolbar appears at the top of the document window. (See the Visual Bonus in the next section for details on the Outline toolbar.)
3. Type **Whole Foods Employee Handbook**, and press Enter.
4. Type the following outline items:

   Press Tab, type **Full-time employees**, and then press Enter.

   Press Tab, type **Hiring**, and then press Enter.

   Press Tab, type **Job description**, and then press Enter.

   Type **Daily responsibilities**, and then press Enter.

   Type **Weekly responsibilities**, and then press Enter.

   Type **Compensation**, and then press Enter.

   Press Shift+Tab, type **Benefits**, and then press Enter.

   Type **Holidays**, and then press Enter.

   Type **Sick days**, and then press Enter.

   Type **Termination**, and then press Enter.

Press Shift+Tab, type **Part-time employees**, and then press Enter.

Press Tab, type **Hiring**, and then press Enter.

Type **Schedules**, and then press Enter.

Type **Responsibilities on the job**.

You have entered four levels of headings in the outline. A plus sign next to a heading indicates that subheadings are associated with the heading. A minus sign means there are no subheadings below the heading.

VISUAL BONUS: OUTLINE TOOLBAR

In Outline view, the Outline toolbar appears below the Formatting toolbar. This toolbar contains tools for modifying and viewing an outline in various ways.

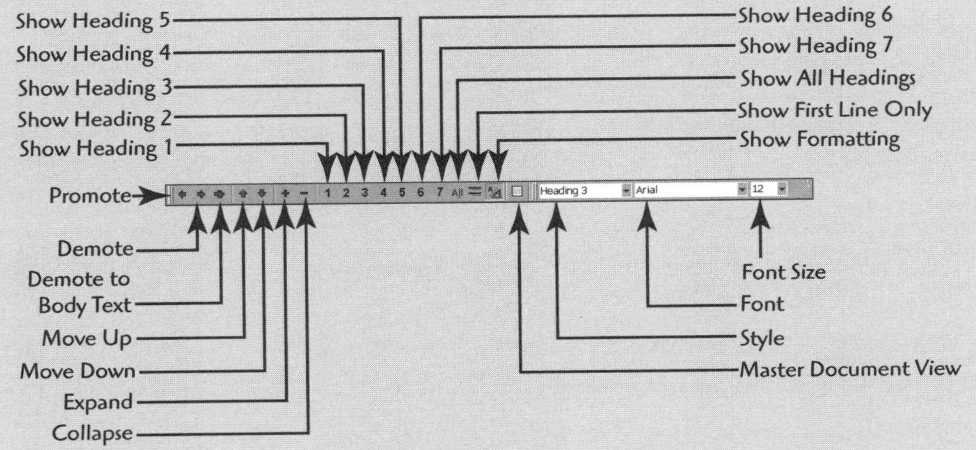

Show Heading 5
Show Heading 4
Show Heading 3
Show Heading 2
Show Heading 1
Promote
Demote
Demote to Body Text
Move Up
Move Down
Expand
Collapse
Show Heading 6
Show Heading 7
Show All Headings
Show First Line Only
Show Formatting
Font Size
Font
Style
Master Document View

Outline toolbar

Modifying an outline

Modifying an outline

Often, you will need to make changes to your outline to better organize your ideas and incorporate any changes. You can promote or demote headings and body text, move headings up or down, or even move entire sections of headings wherever you want in the outline. Let's modify the outline and use some of the buttons on the Outline toolbar.

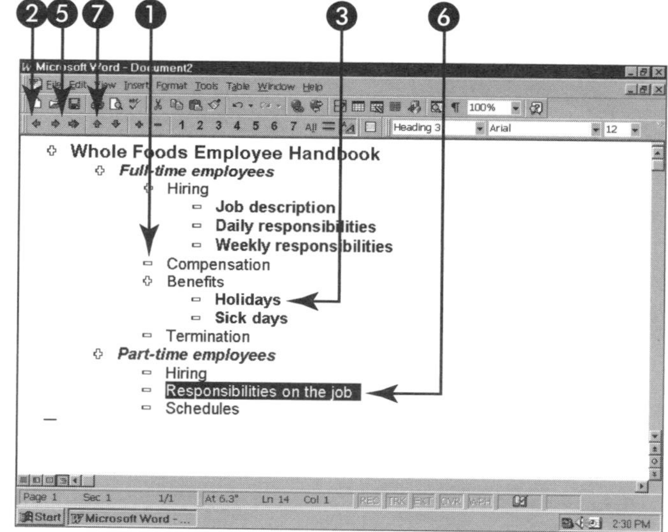

1. Click anywhere in the heading *Compensation*.
2. Click the Promote button on the Outline toolbar.

   Word promotes the heading from level 4 to level 3.
3. Move the mouse pointer to the left margin next to *Holidays*.
4. Click and drag down to select *Holidays* and *Sick days*.
5. Click the Demote button on the Outline toolbar.

   Word demotes the headings from level 3 to level 4.

To quickly promote a heading, click anywhere in the heading, and press Shift+Tab. To quickly demote the heading, press Tab.

6. Click anywhere in the heading *Responsibilities on the job*.
7. Click the Move Up button on the Outline toolbar.

   Word moves the heading up one line. Notice that *Schedules* moves down one line.

A fast way to move a heading up or down is to move the mouse pointer to the plus or minus sign next to the heading until you see a four-headed arrow, and then drag the heading up or down. As you drag the heading, you'll see a horizontal line and a right arrow that you can use as a guide to place the heading exactly where you want it to appear in the outline.

Viewing outline headings

You can view the headings in your outline in different ways by using the tools on the Outline toolbar. For example, you can collapse and expand headings, show all the headings or only the headings you want to display in the outline. Follow these steps to see how it works.

1. Click anywhere in *Hiring* in the *Full-time employees* section.
2. Click the Collapse button on the Outline toolbar.

   Word collapses the subheadings. You see a wavy line next to the heading. This wavy line means that the heading has collapsed subheadings.
3. Click the Expand button on the Outline toolbar.

   Word shows the subheadings.
4. Click the Show Heading 3 button on the Outline toolbar.

   Words shows the first three levels of headings in the outline.
5. Click the Show All Headings button on the Outline toolbar.

   Words shows all the headings again.

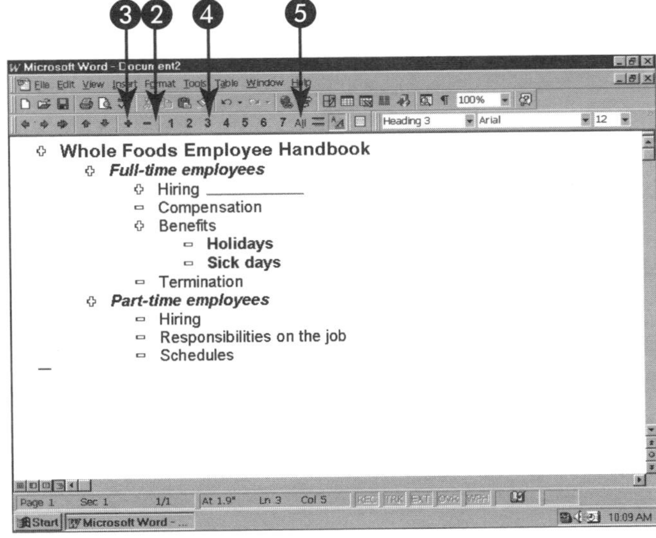

Numbering an outline

Numbering an outline

You can number an outline with the Format Bullets and Numbering command. If you change the heading in the outline, Word automatically renumbers the outline accordingly. Let's number the outline.

1. Select all of the text in the outline.
2. Select the Format menu.
3. Click Bullets and Numbering.

   The Bullets and Numbering dialog box appears.
4. Click the Outline Numbered tab.

   The Outline Numbered tab appears in front.

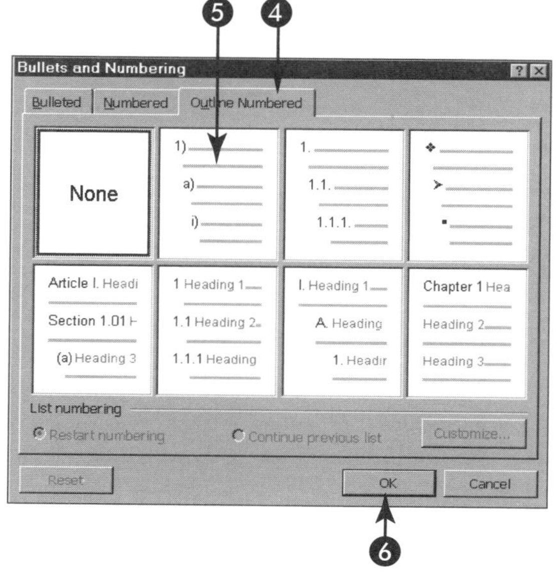

A quick way to apply outline numbering is to right-click any heading in the outline and choose Bullets and Numbering on the shortcut menu.

5. Choose the numbering scheme in the first row, second column.
6. Click OK.
7. Click anywhere in the outline to deselect it.

   Word inserts numbers and letters next to the headings and subheadings in the outline.

   Now let's move a heading to see how Word renumbers the outline.
8. Click anywhere in *Compensation.*
9. Click the Move Up button on the Outlook toolbar three times.

   Word renumbers the outline.
10. Save the document, name it **MY OUTLINE**, and then close the file.

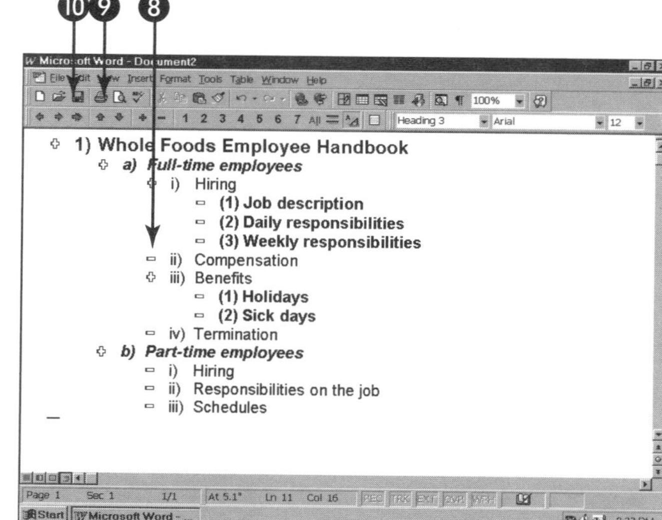

CREATING AN ORGANIZATION CHART

You can build an organization chart in a Word document using the MSOrganization Chart 2.0. program, which you can access with the Insert Object command. When you create an organization chart, Word treats it as an object in a document. The organization chart program enables you to illustrate the structure of authority and responsibility (the chain of command) in an organization. You don't have to draw boxes and lines with the program because it automatically inserts the boxes and lines for you. After you build the organization chart, you can change the font, font size, and font color for the text in the boxes, the box style, the line style, and the background color for the chart.

Creating an organization chart

The Microsoft Organization Chart program in Word enables you to create an organization chart from scratch. You can show the levels of hierarchy and various members or departments within your company in a chart with boxes and lines. Let's create an organization chart for Whole Foods Inc. and see how it works.

1. Create a new document.
2. Select the Insert menu.
3. Click the Object command.

   The Insert Object dialog box appears. By default, the Create New tab is selected, which is what we want. The Object Type list contains all the programs that you can use in Word to create a new object in a document.

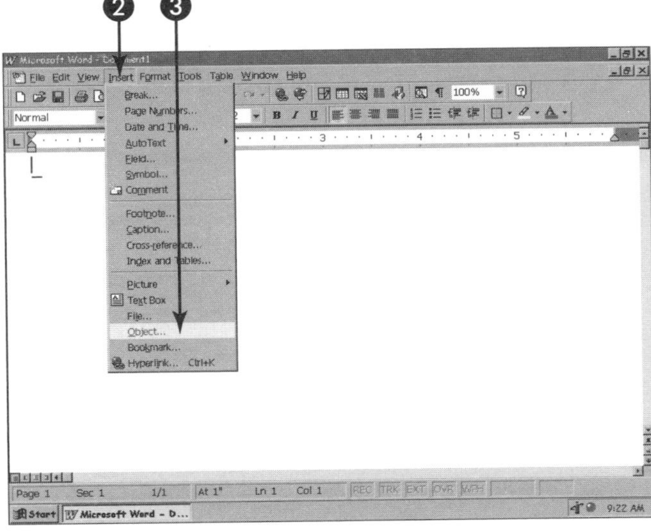

Creating an organization chart

❹ Scroll down the Object Type list until you see MS Organization Chart 2.0, and select it.

If you don't see MS Organization Chart 2.0 in the Object Type list, it means that the program is not installed. You can run the Microsoft Word setup program again to install the organization chart program.

❺ Click OK.

The Microsoft Organization Chart window appears.

❻ Click the Maximize button in the upper right corner of the Microsoft Organization Chart window.

The full-size window shows placeholder text in boxes, and lines connecting the boxes. The *Type name here* placeholder text in the top box is now highlighted so that you can type a name right over it.

❼ Type a name, and press Enter.

❽ Then, type a title for an individual who should be included in this box.

❾ For the rest of the boxes, select the placeholder text and type names and titles for the individuals whom you want to include in these boxes.

❿ Select the *Chart Title* placeholder text, and type **Whole Foods Inc.**

⓫ Select the File menu.

⓬ Click Close and Return to Document.

A prompts asks if you want to update the object.

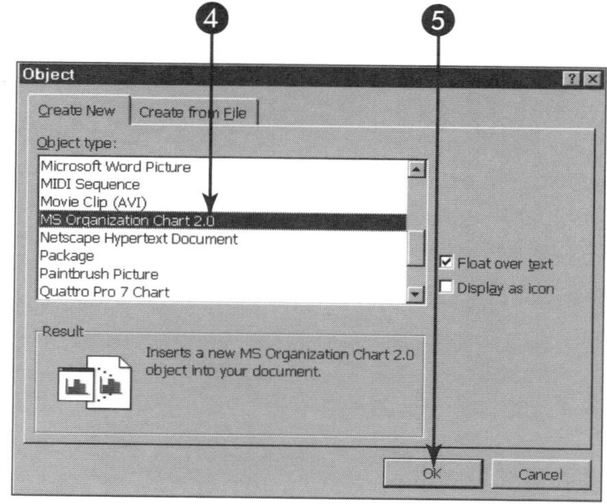

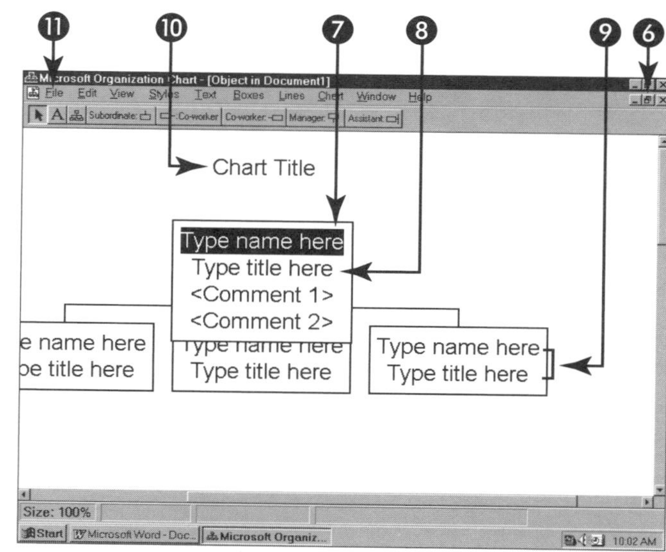

⓭ Choose Yes.

The organization chart is saved and appears in the document. This object is selected.

You can add more boxes to your organization chart, if you wish. There are several types of boxes you could add: a subordinate box, a coworker box, a manager's box, and an assistant box. To add boxes, click the button on the Organization Chart toolbar that matches the relationship to an existing box that you want to create. For example, to add a subordinate to a box that is already on the chart, click the Subordinate button and then click the box to which you want to attach it. A box with placeholder text appears in the chart. Then you can fill in the name and title in the box.

To delete a box, select it and press the Delete button.

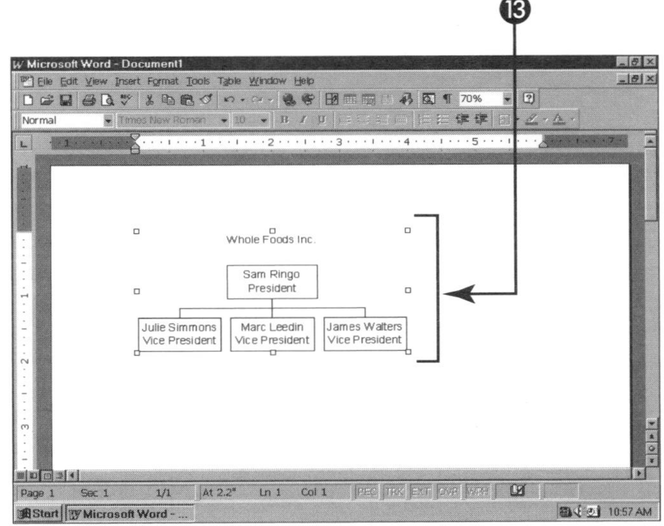

Changing an organization chart

After you add and remove boxes in your organization chart, you can format it with the Styles, Text, Boxes, Lines, and Chart commands in the Microsoft Organization Chart menu bar. Let's format the chart by adding a shadow to the boxes and changing the line style of the connecting lines.

1. Double-click any text in the chart.
2. Click the Maximize button in the upper right corner of the Microsoft Organization window to maximize it.
3. Press Ctrl+A to select all the boxes in the chart.
4. Select the Boxes command.
5. Click Shadow.
6. Select a shadow style from the shadow palette.
7. Open the Edit menu.
8. Choose the Select command.

Skills challenge

9. Choose Connecting Lines.
10. Select the Lines command.
11. Choose Thickness.
12. Choose a line style from the palette.
13. Open the File menu.
14. Choose the Exit and Return to Document command.

    A prompts asks if you want to update the object.
15. Choose Yes.
16. Select the File menu.
17. Choose Save.
18. Name the document **MY ORG CHART**.

    Your organization chart should now look like the one in the accompanying illustration.

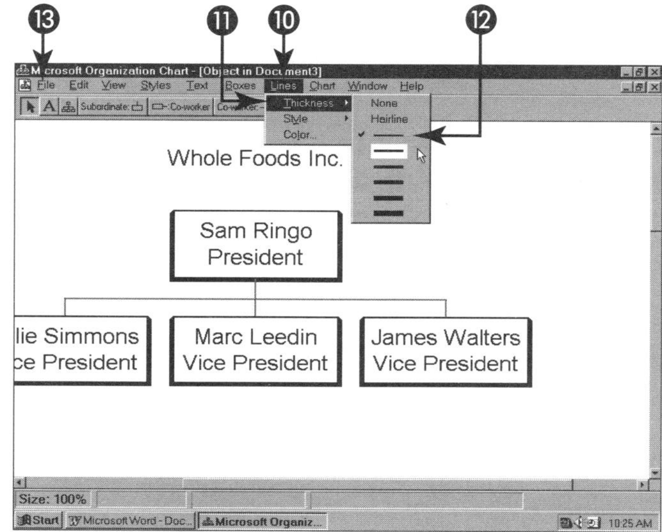

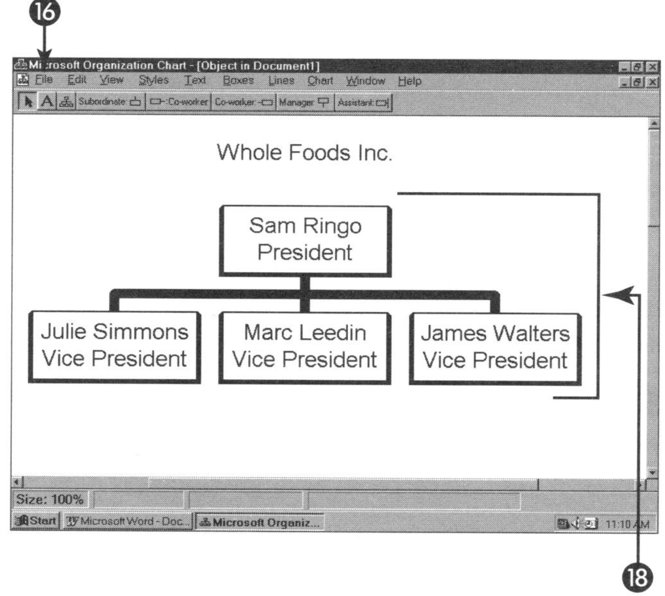

NOTE

Because an organization chart is handled as an object in a Word document, you can move and resize the organization chart, just as you would any object in Word. To move the organization chart, select it, and drag it to the new location. To resize the organization chart, move the mouse pointer to a side border or corner until you see a double-headed arrow. Then drag the border to stretch or shrink the chart.

SKILLS CHALLENGE: BUILDING AN ORDER FORM

This final exercise reviews the skills that you've learned in this lesson. You will build a Whole Foods order form, and then enter a hypothetical order. Answer the bonus questions to review the skills and help you determine your understanding of the topics covered. The answers to the bonus questions are located in Appendix C.

Skills challenge

TRY OUT THE
INTERACTIVE TUTORIALS
ON YOUR CD!

1. Open the file EX12-2.DOC.
2. Press Ctrl+End.
3. Click the Insert Table button on the Standard toolbar.
4. Create a table with four columns and four rows.

What does the mouse pointer symbol look like when you're in Draw mode?

5. Type the following column headings in the first row.

Product Name. Press Tab.

Code. Press Tab.

Qty. Press Tab.

Cost. Press Tab.

What key combination can you use to move backward from one cell to another?

6. Type the following orders into the form.

Strawberry Surprise. Press Tab.

SS015. Press Tab.

2500. Press Tab.

1250. Press Tab.

Lemon Lulu. Press Tab.

LL018. Press Tab.

1000. Press Tab.

500. Press Tab.

Berry Breeze. Press Tab.

BB020. Press Tab.

1500. Press Tab.

750

Skills challenge

So far, your order form should resemble the one in the accompanying illustration.

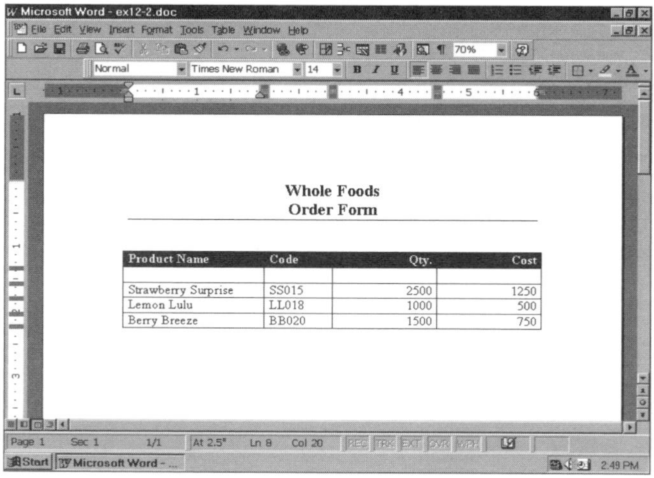

7. In the last two columns, right-align the headings and all the numbers.
8. Insert a new row between the first and second row to add space.

Where do you put the insertion point when you want to insert new rows?

9. Insert a new column between the second and third columns.

Describe the mouse pointer that appears when you move to the top of a column to select an entire column.

10. Delete the new blank column.
11. Select the entire table.
12. Change the font size to 14 pt for all the text.
13. Remove the border lines.
14. Open the Table menu.
15. Choose the Table AutoFormat command.
16. Scroll down the Formats list and choose Grid 8.
17. Turn off the AutoFit option.
18. Use the mouse to widen the first column to display the long entries (2″ on the horizontal ruler).

Describe the mouse pointer that appears when you move to a column border to adjust column width.

19. Click anywhere in the table to deselect it.

Now your order form should look like the one in the accompanying illustration.

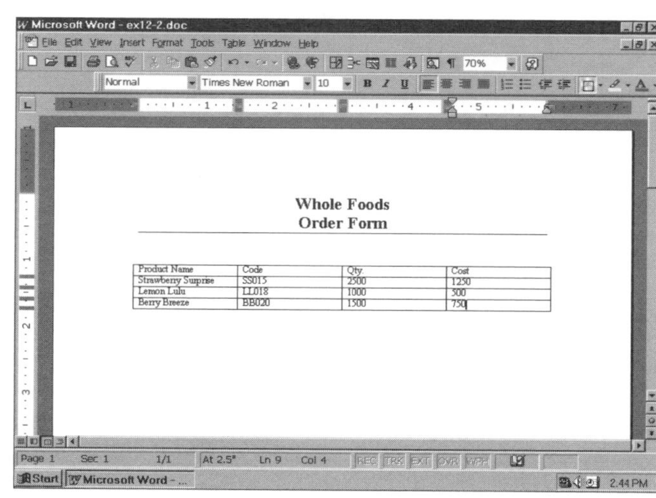

20. Save your changes.
21. Close the file.

TROUBLESHOOTING

Now that you've completed this lesson, you know how to create tables. The following table offers solutions to several problems you might have encountered when learning these skills.

Problem	Solution
There is an extra line in my table that I don't want.	Click the Eraser button on the Tables and Borders toolbar. The mouse pointer changes to an eraser symbol. Drag the eraser over the line you don't want. The line disappears.
I wanted to use a command on the Table menu or the Tables and Borders toolbar, but the commands and tools were dimmed.	The insertion point has to be in the table before you can use any commands on the Table menu or tools on the Tables and Borders toolbar.
I selected a cell and wanted to delete an entire row. A dialog box appeared asking me if I want to shift cells or delete an entire row.	Select the Delete An Entire Row option. Because you selected only one cell and not the entire row, Word thinks you want to delete only one cell. If you want to delete an entire row, be sure to select all the cells in that row.
One of the table autoformats is great for my table, except for a couple of formats.	In the Table AutoFormat dialog box, choose the autoformat you want, click the checkboxes for the formatting you want to omit from the autoformat, and click OK.

Wrap up

WRAP UP

In this lesson, you've practiced the following skills:

- Inserting a table
- Entering text in a cell
- Selecting and aligning text
- Changing fonts for text in a table
- Rotating text in a table
- Inserting and deleting rows and columns
- Adjusting column width
- Using Table AutoFormat
- Creating and modifying an outline
- Viewing outline headings
- Numbering an outline
- Creating and changing an organization chart

If you want more practice with these skills, create your own order form for items you want to buy from a mail order catalog.

In the following lesson, you learn how to print your documents.

PART IV

Outputting Your Results

In this part, you'll learn how to print your documents, use mail merge, and make use of Word and the World Wide Web. You'll also learn how to use other Office applications with Word.

This part contains the following lessons:

- Lesson 13: Printing Your Word Document
- Lesson 14: Working with Mail Merge
- Lesson 15: Using Word to Create a Web Page
- Lesson 16: Integrating Other Microsoft Office Applications

Printing Your Word Document

GOALS

In this lesson, you learn the following skills:

- Selecting paper size and orientation
- Centering a page vertically
- Previewing a document
- Printing from the Print dialog box
- Printing envelopes and labels

Get ready

GET READY

For this lesson, you will need the files EX13-1.DOC and EX13-2.DOC from the One Step folder.

When you've completed the exercises in this lesson, you will have printed the business letter shown in the accompanying illustration.

GREAT AMERICAN PUBLISHERS
100 Seaside Avenue
Greenwich, CT 06345
203-555-7800

January 27, 1997

Ms. Kayla Hall
The Interpreter
750 Harvard Street, Suite 100
Boston, MA 02110

Dear Ms. Hall:

We are delighted to let you know that the magazine you ordered has arrived from the publisher. The price of the magazine is $4.95 per issue.

Please come in to pick it up as soon as you can; we will hold it for two weeks. While you are in, you might want to browse through some of the other foreign language titles.

Foreign Language Titles

- Language and Linguistics
- Linguistics International
- Linguini Linguistics

You can present this letter for a 15% discount on any additional magazines that you buy in this category. **No coupons are necessary.**

Directions to Great American Publishers

1. Superhighway north.
2. Exit 3, The Boulevard.
3. Left at first traffic light onto Harvard Street.

Sincerely,

Erisa Evans
Magazine Reference Manager

PREPARING TO PRINT

In Word, you can print your documents just as you typed them, or you can enhance the printout using several page layout options. When you select Word's Page Setup command, the Page Setup dialog box offers four tabs: Margins, Paper Size, Paper Source, and Layout. You learned how to set the margins in Lesson 7. As for the Paper Size options, the default paper size is Letter 8 1/2×11, but you can choose Legal, A4 (European size paper), envelopes, or a customized paper size. Another Paper Size option is Orientation: Portrait (vertical), which is the default, or Landscape (horizontal).

The Paper Source options enable you to specify how the first page and other pages will be fed through your printer. You can select Default Tray, Auto Sheet Feed, Envelope Feed, or Manual Feed, depending on the printer model you have.

Most of the Layout options were discussed in previous lessons. You learned about the Section Start options in Lesson 11 and the Headers and Footers options in Lesson 8. One other Layout option is to align the text between the top and bottom margins with the Vertical Alignment command. By default, Word aligns text with the top margin. However, letters often look better on the page when they are centered top to bottom. Centering text on a page also works well for special documents, such as invitations, and for document, chapter, or report titles on a title page. If you want, you can justify the text on a page to distribute the text equally between the top and bottom margins. The Justified option is excellent for a title page.

Print Preview is like looking through the lens of a camera to see what you're going to photograph. In Print Preview, you see document pages onscreen as they will appear printed on paper, including page numbers, headers, footers, fonts, font sizes and styles, orientation, vertical alignment, and margins. Previewing your document is an excellent way to catch formatting errors, such as incorrect margins and overlapped text. You cannot edit your document in Print Preview. However, you can change the indents, column markers, and margins on the horizontal ruler. You will save paper and time by previewing your document before you print.

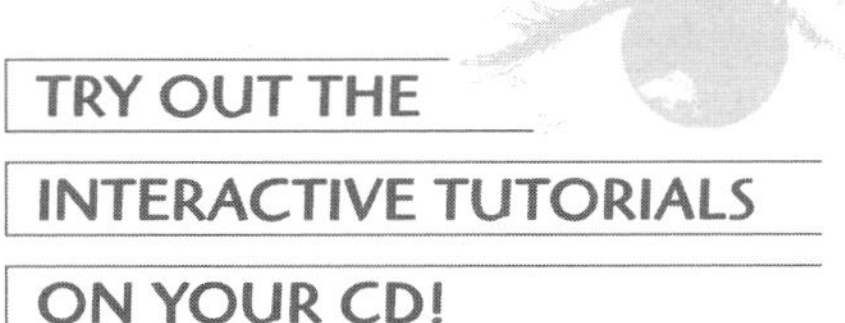

TRY OUT THE INTERACTIVE TUTORIALS ON YOUR CD!

Centering a page vertically

There are three types of vertical alignment. By default, the Top vertical alignment option aligns the first line in the document with the top margin. However, you can choose the Center vertical alignment option to center text between the top and bottom margins. The Justified vertical alignment option expands the space between paragraphs to align the first line with the top margin and the last line with the bottom margin. In the following exercises, you'll use the file EX13-1.DOC from the One Step folder. This file contains a version of the two-page business letter you've used in earlier lessons. First we'll combine the two pages into one. Then we'll center the letter vertically to improve its appearance.

1. Open the file EX13-1.DOC.
2. Scroll down and place your cursor on the page break.
3. Press Delete to remove the page break.
4. Select the File menu.
5. Click Page Setup.
6. Click the Layout tab.

   You see all the Layout options in the Page Setup dialog box, as shown in the accompanying illustration.

7. Click the Vertical Alignment drop-down arrow.
8. Choose Center.
9. Click OK.

   You cannot see the vertical alignment change onscreen. However, you will be able to see the change in Print Preview, which we discuss in the next exercise.

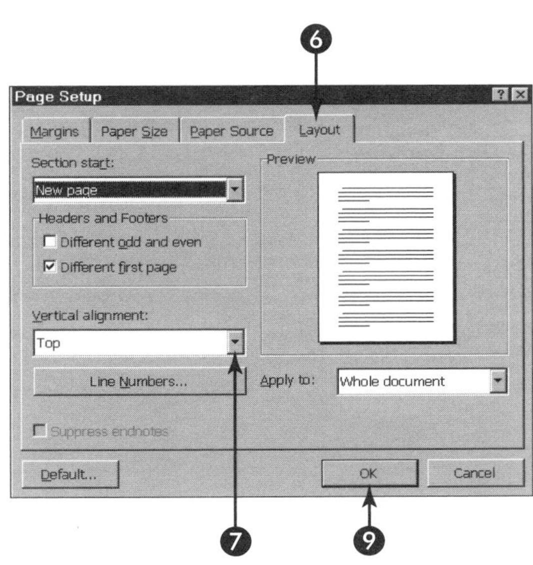

13 Printing Your Word Document

Previewing a document

Previewing a document

The Print Preview feature displays onscreen what the document will look like when printed— graphics and all. Let's examine the business letter in Print Preview before we print it.

1. Click the Print Preview button (contains a piece of paper with a magnifying glass) on the Standard toolbar.

   You see a preview of how your document will look when you print it, as shown in the accompanying illustration. Notice that the text is centered vertically on the page. The mouse pointer is a magnifying glass with a plus sign (+). This mouse pointer lets you magnify any portion of the page. As you can see, the zoom magnification in the Zoom box on the Print Preview toolbar is 31 percent.

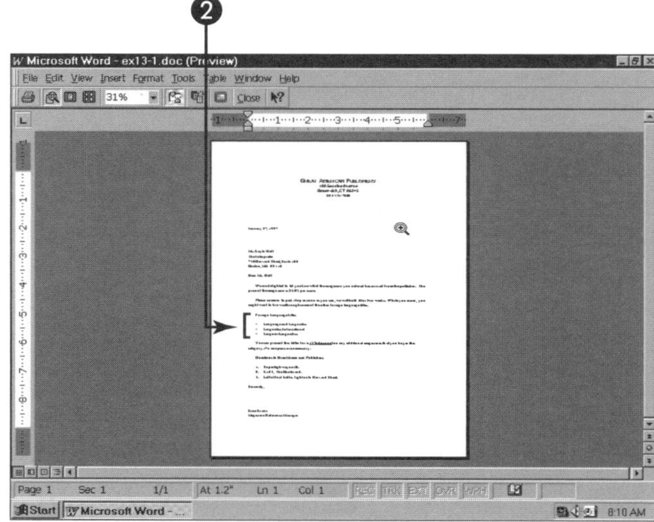

The zoom percentage is for viewing the page only; it doesn't have anything to do with the size of the document on the printed page.

2. Move the mouse pointer to the bulleted list in the center of the page.
3. Click the bulleted list.

   Word zooms in on the middle portion of your page and magnifies the text to 100%, as shown in the Zoom box in the accompanying illustration. The 100% magnification is the size that your document prints on your printer. Notice that the mouse pointer becomes a magnifying glass with a minus sign. This mouse pointer enables you to zoom out and shrink the text on the page.

4. Click the text again.

   The text returns to its normal display magnification.

5. Click the Close button to exit Print Preview.

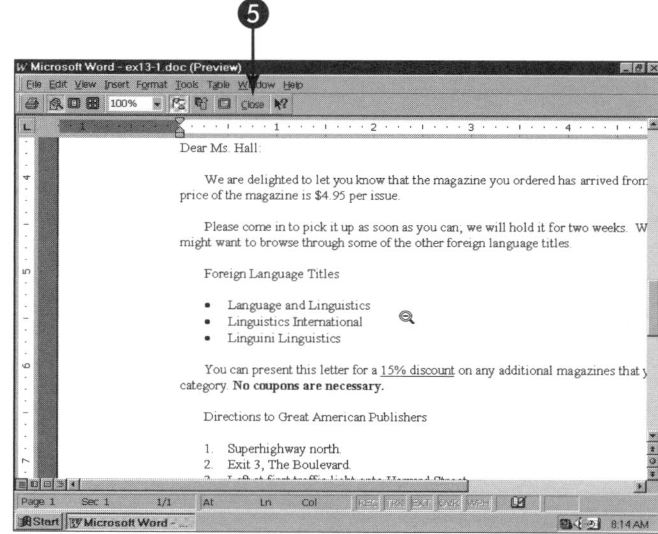

Previewing a document

The Zoom box on the Print Preview toolbar enables you to specify how large or small a document appears on the screen. This Zoom feature is similar to the Zoom you used in Lesson 4 to zoom in and out of your document.

VISUAL BONUS: PRINT PREVIEW

By clicking the Print Preview button on the Standard toolbar you get to see how your document will look when it's printed. The Print Preview toolbar at the top of the screen gives you tools to view and print your document. Although you cannot edit your document in Print Preview, you can adjust indents, margins, and columns.

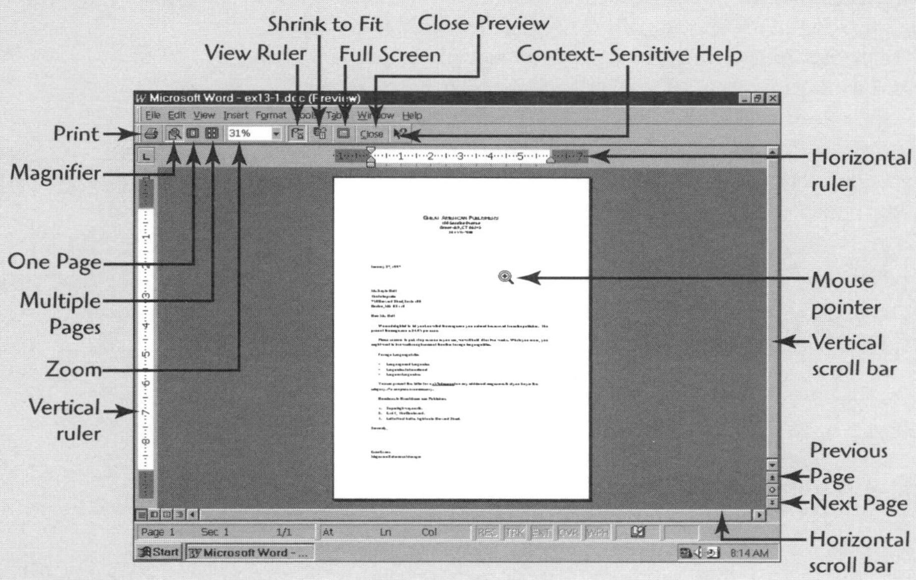

Shrink to Fit
Close Preview
View Ruler
Full Screen
Context- Sensitive Help
Print
Magnifier
One Page
Multiple Pages
Zoom
Vertical ruler
Horizontal ruler
Mouse pointer
Vertical scroll bar
Previous Page
Next Page
Horizontal scroll bar

Print Preview

Printing from the Print dialog box

PRINTING YOUR DOCUMENT

There are several ways to print your document:

- Select the File ➢ Print command.
- Press Ctrl+P.
- Click the Print button on the Standard toolbar.

When you select the File Print command or press Ctrl+P, Word displays the Print dialog box. This dialog box enables you to print some or all the pages within a document, the current page, a range of pages, specific separate pages, or selected text. You can also specify the number of copies of the printout, and you can collate pages when you print multiple copies of a multipage document. You can even print a document to another file.

If your print options are already set up for printing the document, you can simply click the Print button on the Standard toolbar. Word doesn't display the Print dialog box and prints the document immediately. This printing method is useful for quick printing, but you can't change any options.

Printing from the Print dialog box

In this exercise, you learn how to print your document from the Print dialog box. If you have already set up your print options and you're in the document, you can just click the Print button on the Standard toolbar to print your document.

Printing from the Print dialog box

Before you use your printer with Word, check the Print Setup options. Often, you will need to provide more details about your printer so that Word can use the options and capabilities that are available with your particular printer. To check the Print Setup options, select File ➢ Print, and click the Properties button at the top of the Print dialog box. The Properties dialog box displays three tabs: Paper, Graphics, and Device Options. (You may have additional tabs, depending on your printer.) Change any printer options you want, and click OK.

❶ Open the File menu.

❷ Choose the Print command.

You can also press Ctrl+P to print.

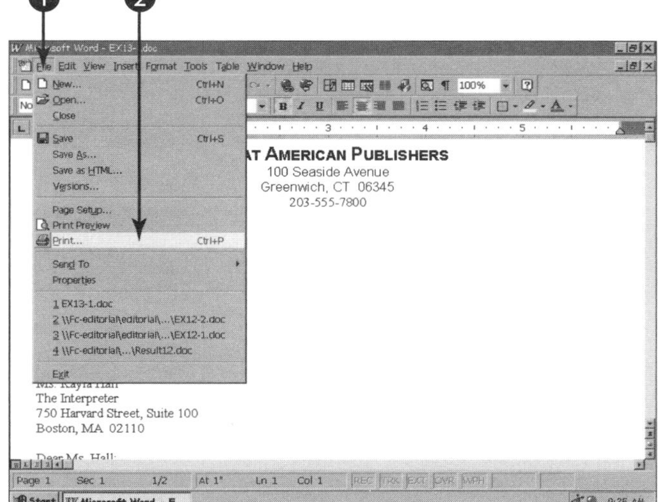

Word opens the Print dialog box. This dialog box contains options with which you can control your print jobs. The current printer appears at the top of the dialog box.

Your computer may be set up to run on different printers, depending on your output needs. For example, you may want to use a laser printer when you need a high-quality printout; at other times, the output from your ink-jet printer may be sufficient.

Printing from the Print dialog box

❸ Make sure the correct printer is selected. To select a different printer, click the Name drop-down arrow and choose a printer from the printer list.

If you want to fax your document to someone else, select the fax option in the printer list, such as Microsoft Fax or WinFax. Word will lead you through a series of wizard dialog boxes to send the fax.

Now it's time to choose which pages you want to print. In the Page range area, you have the following four options:

- All is selected by default. If you select this option, Word will print all the pages in your document.
- The Current Page option prints only the page where the insertion point is.
- The Selection option is only available if you have selected a block of text in your document. If you choose this option, Word prints only the block of text.
- The Pages option enables you to select specific pages. For example, if you type 1-3, Word prints pages 1 through 3. To print disconnected pages, enter a comma between the page numbers and page ranges. For instance, you could type 1,5,8, 9-12,20.

❹ For this exercise, select Current Page.

Next, you must decide how many copies to print. The default is 1 copy. To print multiple copies, enter a number in the Number of Copies text box, or click the Number of Copies up arrow until you see the number you want.

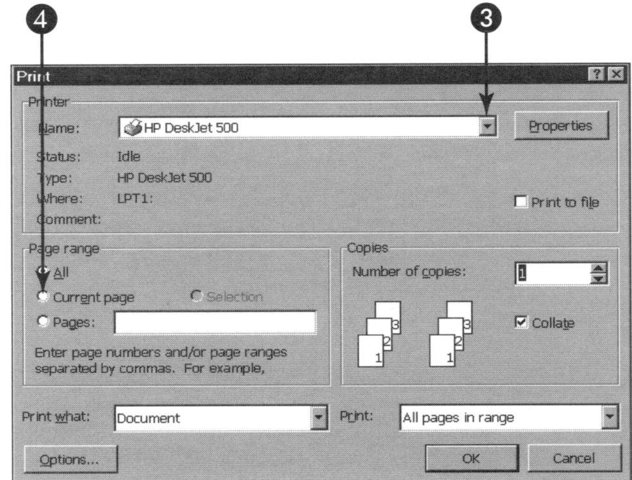

Printing from the Print dialog box

5 Type **2** in the Number of Copies text box.

The Collate option is selected. By default, Word prints a complete copy of the document before the next copy of the document begins to print. Because Word creates the number of copies you specify and then sends all the copies of the document to the printer, the printing takes longer. To speed printing, clear the check mark in the Collate checkbox.

The Print to File option enables you to print the document to another file or route it to someone else on your company's network. This option is also useful when you want to create a file you can take to a computer that has a printer but no copy of Microsoft Word. Let's leave this checkbox empty.

6 Click OK.

Word begins to print your document. While a document is printing, Word displays a Printer icon at the right end of the Windows Taskbar.

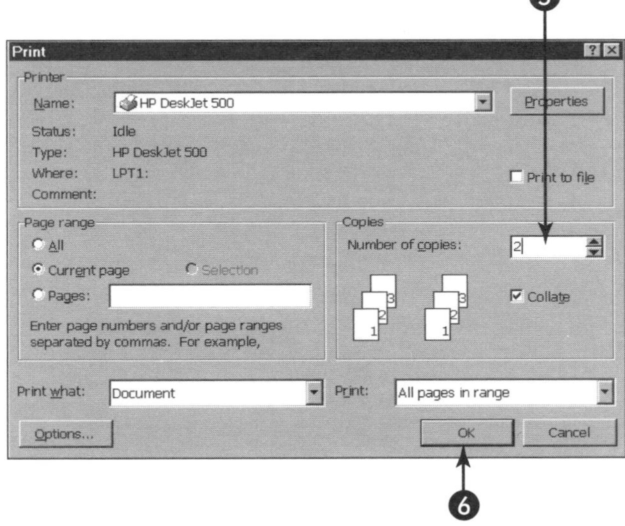

It's a good habit to save your documents before printing—just in case a printer error or other problem occurs. That way, you won't lose the work.

7 Save your changes.

CANCELING PRINTING

You can cancel a print job either before it prints or while it prints. Canceling a print job often does not work for documents such as the one in this exercise, unless you are on a network or have other documents lined up to print. Word prints a short document faster than you can cancel it.

While a document is printing, Word displays a Printer icon at the right end of the Windows Taskbar. To stop a document from printing, double-click the Printer icon to display the Print Queue dialog box. Then click the document name, and select Document ➢ Cancel Printing from the menu bar in the dialog box to cancel the print job. Click the Close (X) button to close the dialog box.

Printing an envelope

PRINTING ENVELOPES AND LABELS

Word gives you a quick way to print addresses on envelopes. You can print addresses on different sizes of envelopes immediately, or include the envelope in a document and print it later. You can even specify a return address. Word also enables you to specify or customize the envelope size.

The Labels feature creates mailing labels for you. You can print an address on a single label or print a sheet of labels with the same address. You can even specify Avery or other brand mailing labels and the label type so that the addresses print neatly on the labels you feed into your printer.

Printing an envelope

The Tools Envelopes and Labels command lets you set up and print addresses on envelopes. This exercise shows you how to print an envelope for the business letter.

1. Select the inside address in the letter (Kayla Hall's name and address).
2. Select the Tools menu.
3. Click the Envelopes and Labels command.

   You see the Envelopes and Labels dialog box. The Envelopes tab is selected and the inside address appears in the Delivery Address box.
4. Click in the Return Address box.
5. Type the following address, replacing Kayla Hall's information:

   Erisa Evans. Press Enter.

   Great American Publishers. Press Enter.

   100 Seaside Avenue. Press Enter.

   Greenwich, CT 06345.
6. Click Print.

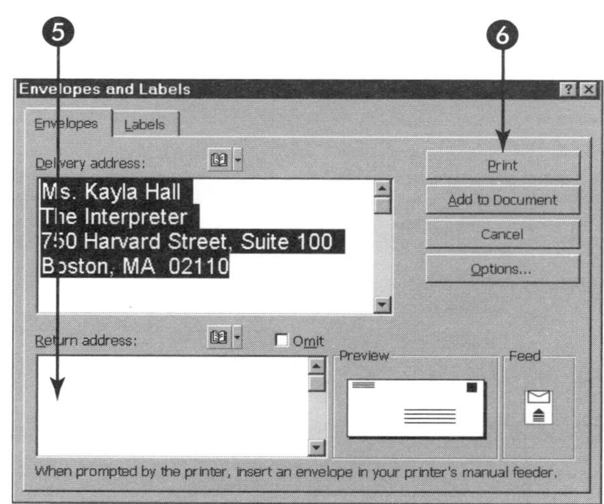

TIP

The default envelope size is a Size 10 (4 1/8" × 9 1/8") business envelope. If you want to specify a different envelope size, click the Options button in the Envelopes and Labels dialog box. Word displays a list of different envelope sizes. Choose the envelope size you want, or choose Custom to customize one of your own. Then click OK.

7. If you have a manual feed printer, feed the envelope into the printer.
8. Then, press the On Line button on the printer.

Printing a label

With the Tools Envelopes and Labels command you can set up and print addresses on labels. In this exercise, you learn how to print a single label for the inside address in the business letter.

1. Select the inside address in the letter (Kayla Hall's name and address).
2. Select the Tools menu.
3. Click the Envelopes and Labels command.
4. Click the Labels tab.The inside address appears in the Address box.
5. In the Print section, choose the Single Label option.

TIP

The default label is Avery standard, 2160 Mini Address, but if you want to specify a different label brand and type, click the Options button in the Envelopes and Labels dialog box. Word displays a list of different label brands and types. Choose the label you want or choose Custom to customize a label. Then click OK.

6. Click Print.
7. If you have a manual feed printer, feed the label into the printer, and then press the On Line button on the printer.

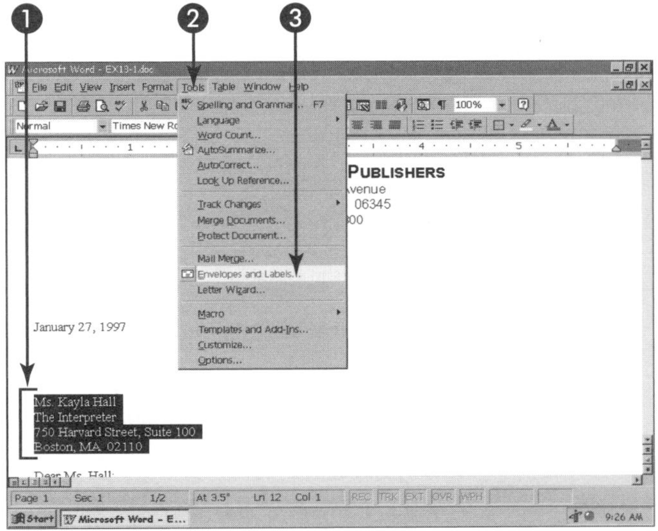

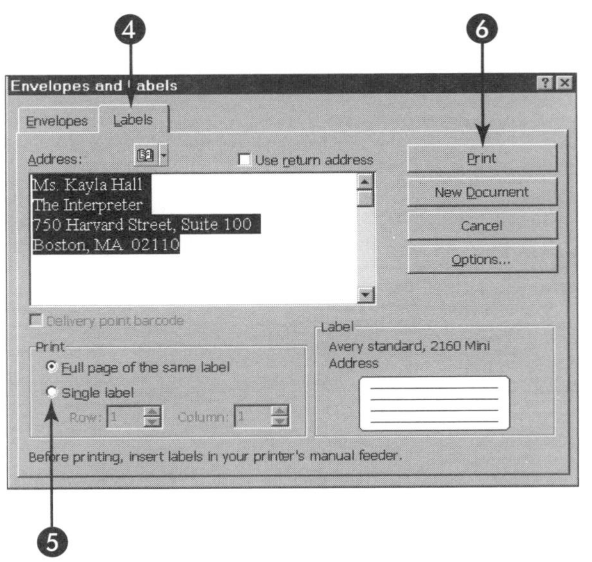

8. Save your changes.
9. Close the file.

SKILLS CHALLENGE: PRINTING A REPORT

In this review exercise, you practice the printing skills that you've picked up in this lesson. Your mission is to preview and print the Whole Foods report. Answer the bonus questions to review the skills and help you determine your understanding of the topics covered. The answers to the bonus questions are located in Appendix C.

1. Open the file EX13-2.DOC.

What command lets you change the layout options?

2. Click the Print Preview button on the Standard toolbar.
3. Click the Next Page button to view each page in the document.
4. On page 3, click the table to zoom in.
5. Click in the text to zoom out.
6. Click the Close Preview button to exit Print Preview.
7. Open the File menu.
8. Choose the Print command.
9. Specify printing pages 1 and 2.

If you want to print only pages 1 and 3, how would you enter the page numbers in the Page text box?

10. Specify printing 2 copies.
11. Click OK to start printing.
12. Print an envelope that includes Great American Publishers' delivery address and your own return address.

13 Print a single label that includes your own address.

Which command prints envelopes and labels?

14 Save your changes.

15 Close the file.

TROUBLESHOOTING

Now that you've completed this lesson, you know how to preview and print documents, envelopes, and labels. This table offers solutions to several problems you might have encountered when learning these skills.

Problem	Solution
My document doesn't print on my printer.	If you have difficulty printing, be sure to check that the correct printer is selected in the Print dialog box.
I changed some layout options and now every page in my document has been affected.	Page setup settings affect the whole document, unless you specify otherwise. There is an Apply To option (with Whole Document selected, by default) in the Page Setup dialog box. You can choose From This Point Forward to indicate where you want the page setup option to start taking effect.
I usually print my documents in a portrait (vertical) orientation, but now I need to print a document in a landscape (horizontal) orientation.	In the Page Setup dialog box, choose the Paper Size tab, and in the Orientation section, choose Landscape.

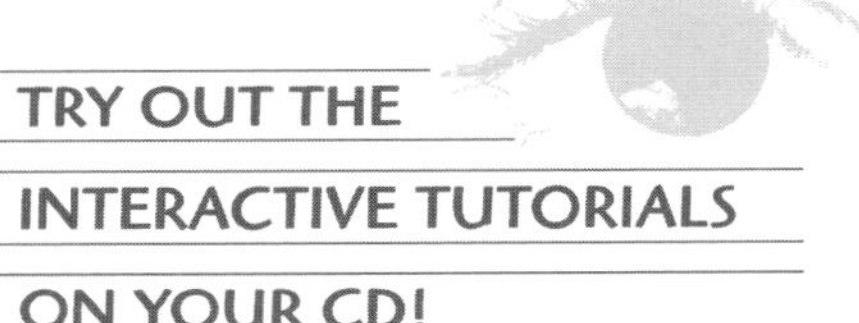

Wrap up

Problem	Solution
My printed pages always have an inch border around the sides when I print my documents on a laser printer. I would like to start printing my text closer to the edge of the paper.	Go into File ➢ Page Setup and change your margins. Be aware though that a laser printer cannot print closer than 1/4 inch to the page edge. You won't be able to print anything in that region.

WRAP UP

In this lesson, you practiced the following skills:

- Centering a page vertically
- Previewing a document
- Printing from the Print dialog box
- Printing envelopes and labels

If you want more practice with these skills, print all the documents you've created in the One Step at a Time lessons.

The next lesson gets you acquainted with Word's Mail Merge feature.

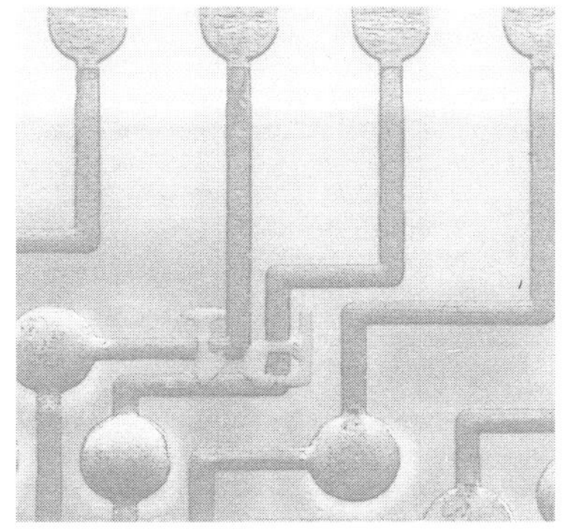

Working with Mail Merge

GOALS

In this lesson, you learn the following skills:

- Creating a main document
- Creating a data source
- Entering names and addresses
- Placing merge fields in your main document
- Viewing and checking a mail merge
- Merging to a printer or document

Get ready

GET READY

For this lesson, you will need the files EX14-1.DOC and EX14-2.DOC from the One Step folder.

When you're finished with the exercises in this lesson, you will have printed the product announcement shown in the accompanying illustration.

To: Sarah Jacobs

City: New York

Soap That Is Really Clean

Whole Foods is proud to announce a new bar soap called Safe Soap. It's made simply with shea and mango butters and herbal extracts. Butter soaps smell good enough to eat and will make your skin feel soft and touchable. Available in 3.5-ounce bars, look for flavors of Ginger Snap Mango, Vanilla Bean Truffle, and our favorite, Pink Grapefruit & Champagne. The flavor of the month is Banana Boat.

WHAT IS MAIL MERGE?

Mail Merge is a feature that enables you to personalize form letters for mass mailings, product announcements, customer letters, reports, invitations, and contribution solicitations. With Mail Merge, you can also merge a list of names and addresses to create invoices and mailing labels, and to fill in standard forms. For example, you can print phone lists and customer lists; you can even print addresses on envelopes.

Instead of typing many individual letters and changing the variable information in each letter, you can tell Word to merge the letter and the variable information, which saves you typing and time.

Creating a form letter with Mail Merge involves a number of steps. It is, however, easier than it looks. The exercises in this lesson build on each other. Therefore, it is important that you follow all the exercises in this lesson to complete the merge process.

SETTING UP MAIL MERGE

Two files make up a basic merge procedure: the main document and the data source file. The main document contains the unchanging text and the codes that control the merge. The data source contains the variable information, such as names and addresses, that you want to insert into the main document.

There are several tasks you need to follow to create a merge letter. First, you create the main document. Next, you create the data source. Word provides several predefined fields to use in the data source, or you can create your own. Once you save the data source, you're ready to enter records. There are a couple of terms you'll need to know regarding a data source: record and field. A *record* is one set of information, such as all the information about one person. Each individual element in the record, such as the first name, the last name, or the phone number, is stored in a *field*.

After you enter records, the next step is to type the text of the main document (if you have text from an existing document, you can skip this step). The main document contains the letter's text—the information you want each letter to contain. The main document also includes the codes that control the merge. You need to know the names of the fields you created in the data source so that you can insert the right code into the main document.

After you create the main document, you save the file.

Here are the main steps for a mail merge operation:

1. Create the main document.
2. Create the data source.
3. Enter records in the data source fields.
4. Type the text of the main document.
5. Place merge fields in the main document.
6. View and check a mail merge.
7. Merge to a printer or document.

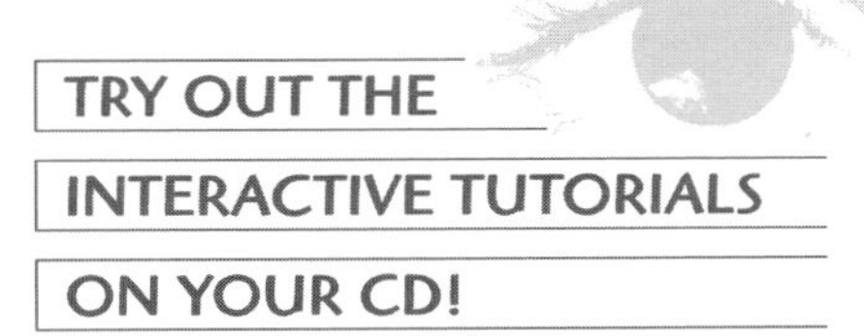

Creating the main document

The first step involved in setting up a mail merge is to create the main document. The main document contains field names and the information that remains constant. In the following exercises, you'll work with the EX14-1.DOC file stored in the One Step folder. This file contains a Whole Foods product announcement. We'll use it as our main document.

1. Open the file EX14-1.DOC.
2. Select the Tools menu.
3. Click the Mail Merge command.

You see the Mail Merge Helper dialog box. This dialog box enables you to create a main document and data source, and

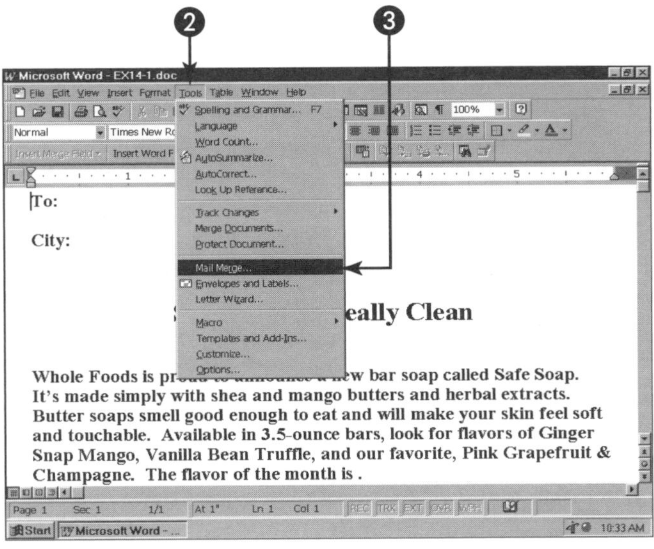

merge the two files. Beneath the Create button in this dialog box, you see the Merge Type is Form Letters, and the main document is EX14-1.DOC. Since we provided you with a main document, Word knows it's a form letter and displays the document name. When you want to create a new document, you could follow Steps 4-6 below. Otherwise, we'll now skip to Exercise 2.

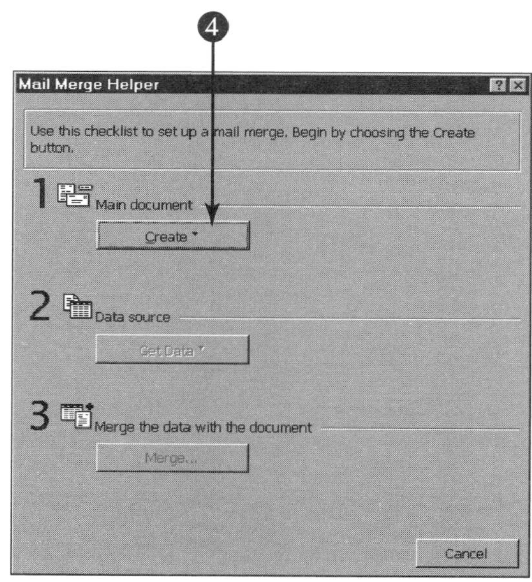

4. Click the Create button.

   Word displays a drop-down list of options. You can choose the type of main document you want to create from this list.

5. Choose Form Letters.

   Word asks whether you want to open a new document or create the document within the active window. Because we're going to use the product announcement document, let's go with the active window choice.

6. Choose Active Window.

   You're back to the Mail Merge Helper dialog box. Next you create the data source, as explained in Exercise 2.

Creating a data source

The second step in creating a mail merge is to create a data source document. The data source document contains the variable information, such as names and addresses, that you merge into the main document. Let's create a data source that will contain names and addresses for the product announcement.

1. Click the Get Data button in the Mail Merge Helper dialog box.
2. Choose Create Data Source from the drop-down list of data source options.

If you have created a Contacts list in Microsoft Outlook (a component of the Microsoft Office 97 suite), a personal address book in the Microsoft

Exchange (a component of Windows 95), or a Contacts list in Schedule+ (a component of the Microsoft Office 95 suite), you can use these records as a data source. To use addresses from an address book, choose Use Address Book from the Get Data menu. Then choose the appropriate address book and follow the instructions as prompted.

The Create Data Source dialog box opens. This dialog box includes a Field Name list with common field names. Instead of trying to figure out all the fields you'll need, you can eliminate the default fields you don't want. Also, you can add new field names. Let's do that now.

3. Type **Flavor** in the Field Name text box.
4. Click the Add Field Name button.

   Word adds this field to the bottom of the list for your data source. Now we'll start deleting unnecessary fields.
5. Scroll to the top of the Field Names in the Header Row list.
6. Click Title.
7. Click the Remove Field Name button to remove the field.
8. Select and remove these predefined fields: JobTitle, Company, Address1, Address2, State, PostalCode, Country, HomePhone, and WorkPhone.

   Now we have only the fields we need: FirstName, LastName, City, and Flavor.

The last field name you delete appears in the Field Name text box, even though you have removed it from the header row list.

9. Click OK to complete the Field Name list.
10. Name the file **SOAPDATA**.

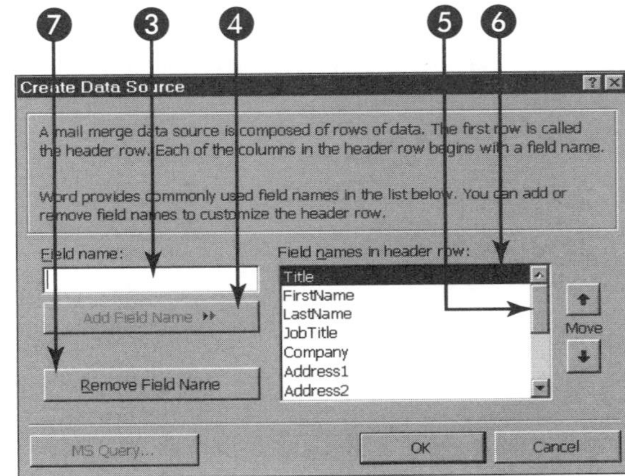

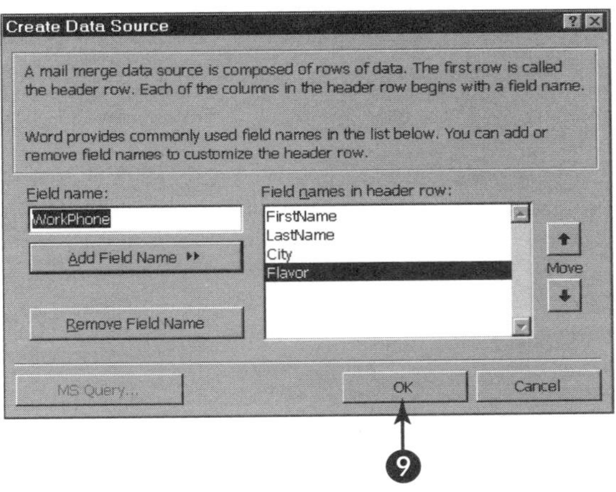

Entering a data source

⓫ Save the file.

Word reminds you that no records have been created. In other words, no entries have been made in the name, city, and flavor fields. In the next exercise, you add records to your data source file.

⓬ Click the Edit Data Source button.

The Data Form dialog box appears (see the accompanying figure).

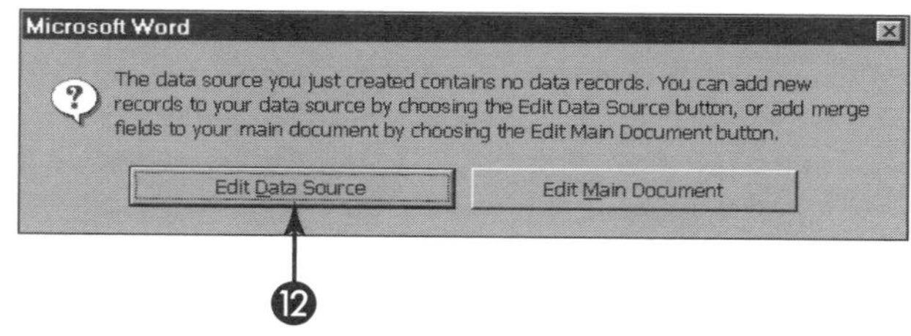

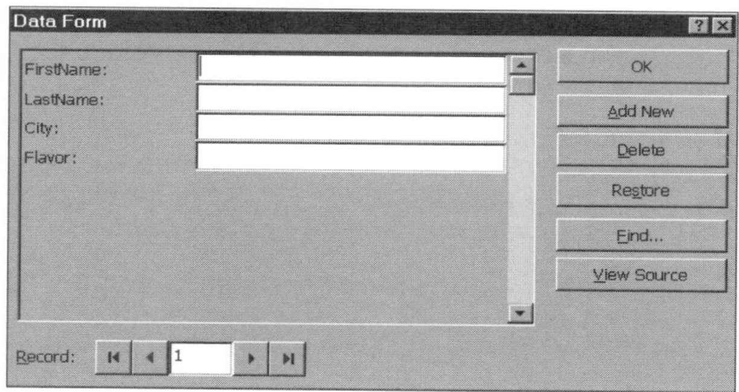

Entering names and addresses

After you create a data source document, the next step in the mail merge process is to enter the variable information, such as names and addresses. Each complete set of variable information is known as a record. Let's enter three names and addresses to add records to the data source file.

If you have already created a data source file, then in the Mail Merge Helper dialog box, click the Edit button in the Data Source section.

❶ Type the following fields into the appropriate text boxes.

Sarah. Press Tab.

❷ **Jacobs**. Press Tab.

❸ **New York**. Press Tab.

❹ **Banana Boat**

❺ Click the Add New button.

The current record is added to the data source document. The text boxes clear, and the record count is incremented by one. Now you can enter the next record.

❻ Type the following fields into the appropriate text boxes for the second record.

Casey. Press Tab.

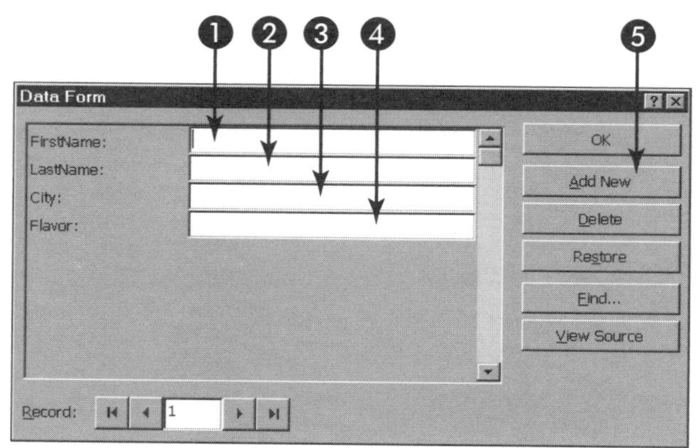

TIP

To move backward, press Shift+Tab. If you make a mistake while typing, correct it as you would in any other document.

7 **Brenner**. Press Tab.

8 **Chicago**. Press Tab.

9 **Papaya Smoothie**

10 Click the Add New button.

TIP

It's a good idea to save the file periodically when you're adding records. Just select File ➢ Save or press Ctrl+S.

11 Type the following information for the last record.

Matt. Press Tab.

12 **Trifaro**. Press Tab.

13 **Boston**. Press Tab.

14 **Blueberry Breeze**

15 Click OK.

When you click OK, Word adds the last record to the data source and closes the Data Form dialog box. You're returned to the main document. The Mail Merge toolbar is displayed between the ruler and the Formatting toolbar.

16 Mail Merge Helper displays a warning message that there are no merge fields in our main document. Click the Edit Main Document button in the dialog box to remove the message.

In the next exercise, we'll insert merge fields in the main document.

TIP

To delete a record, use the Record scroll arrows at the bottom of the Data Form to display the record you want. Then click the Delete button.

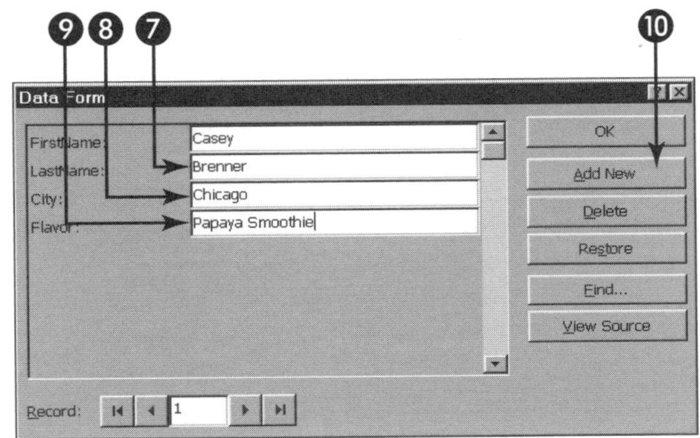

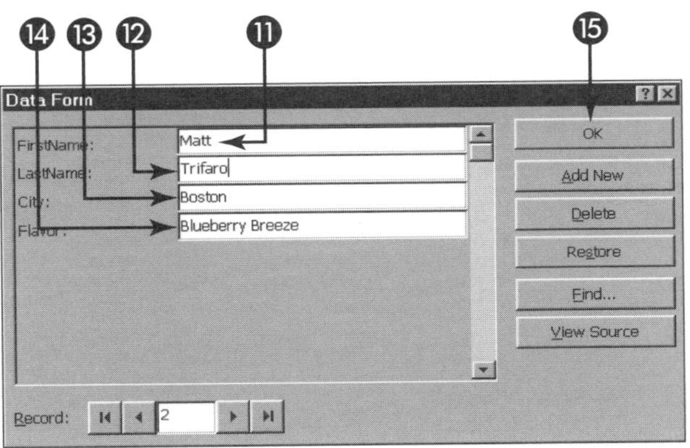

Placing merge fields in your document

The main document contains field names. Each field name corresponds to a field name in the data source document. After you create the main document, you can either use existing text or type a document from scratch. In this exercise, the text for the product announcement is already in place so you don't have to do a lot of typing. The only thing left to do is insert the merge fields in the main document. Let's try that.

1. Click after the colon in *To:*.
2. Press Tab.
3. Click the Insert Merge Field button on the Mail Merge toolbar. You see a drop-down list of field names. They should look familiar. Word copied these field names from the data source you created.
4. Choose FirstName. This inserts the field name enclosed in double-arrow brackets, referred to as a field code. This code tells Word to insert the first name in each record into the first field of the main document.
5. Press the spacebar.
6. Click the Insert Merge Field button on the Mail Merge toolbar.
7. Choose LastName.
8. Click after the colon in *City:*.
9. Press Tab.
10. Insert the third field name, City.
11. Click before the period in the last sentence.
12. Insert the last field name, Flavor.

    Your main document should now look like the one in the accompanying illustration.
13. Save the file.

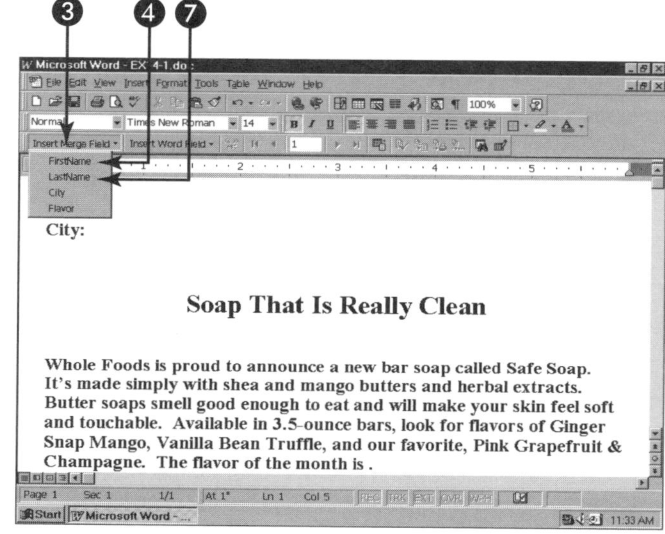

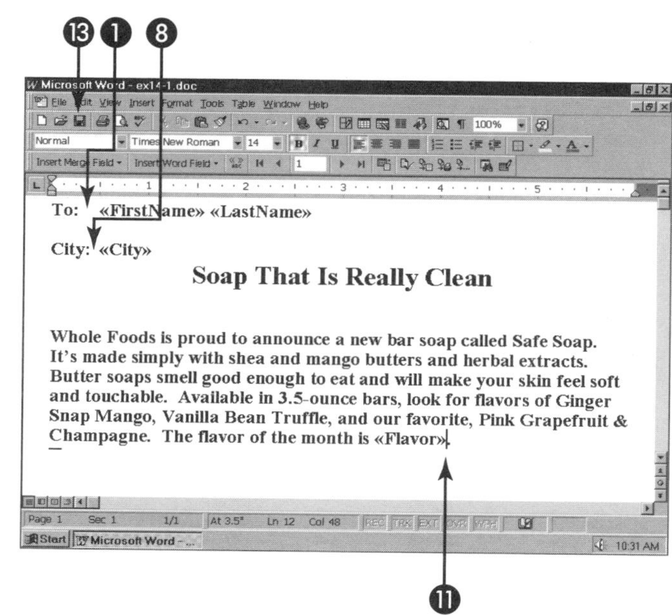

Placing merge fields in your document

VISUAL BONUS: MAIN DOCUMENT AND DATA SOURCE

The main document contains the constant text and the merge codes that tell Word where to insert the variable information. The Mail Merge toolbar located at the top of the main document provides a set of tools for merging and printing your merge documents.

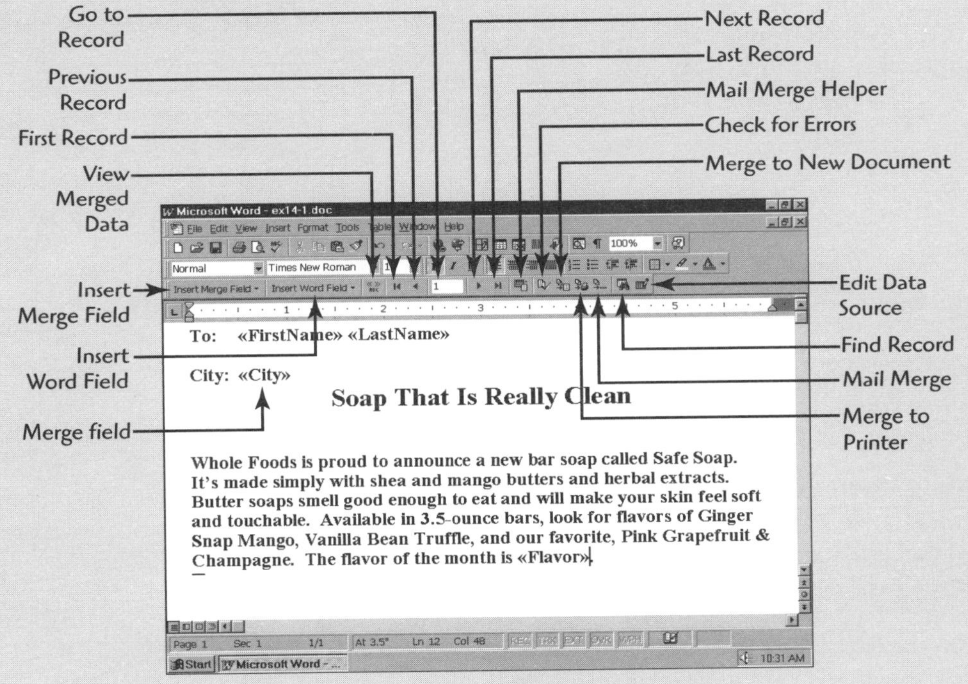

Main document

continued

VISUAL BONUS: MAIN DOCUMENT AND DATA SOURCE (continued)

The data source file stores the variable information that you want to insert into the main document. A complete set of information is called a record. Each piece of information is stored in a field. You enter records in the data form.

Data source

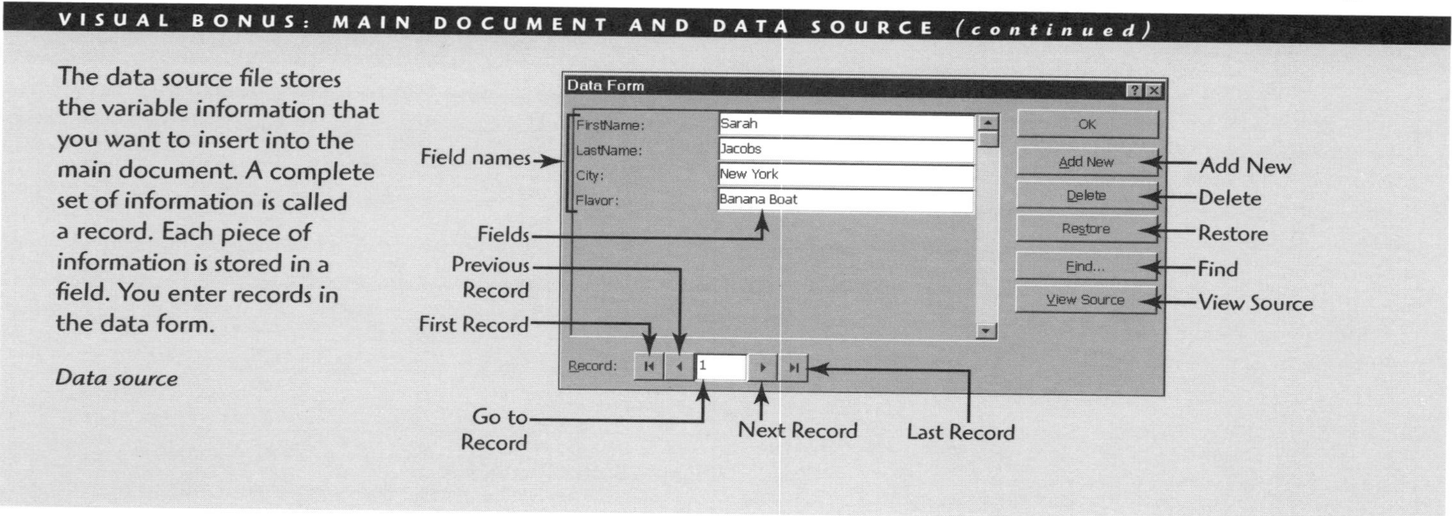

MERGING THE DOCUMENT AND DATA

The final step is to merge the data source file with the main document file. The merge fields in the main document instruct Word to move into the data source, copy the appropriate fields, and insert them into the letter. A new file will be created that contains a letter for each record in the data source. You can either save or print the new file.

Viewing and checking a mail merge

One advantage of Word's Mail Merge feature is you can view your merge documents and check them for errors before you merge the data. Let's see how this feature works.

1. From the main document, click the Check for Errors button on the Mail Merge toolbar.

   The Checking and Reporting Errors dialog box opens.

2. You have the following three choices in this dialog box:

   - Simulate the merge and report errors in a new document. Word checks for errors without producing the resulting merged documents.
   - Complete the merge, pausing to report each error as it occurs. If Word finds any error during error checking, it pauses and displays a message to inform you about the error. That way, you can correct each error in the documents during the error checking process. This option produces the resulting merged documents.
   - Complete the merge without pausing. Report errors in a new document. If Word finds errors, it will display a message at the end of the error checking process. That way, you need to go back into each document and correct the errors. This option produces the resulting merged documents.

   Choose the second option.

3. Click OK. Word merges the documents and displays the product announcements in a new document called Form Letters1 (see the accompanying figure). It is error-free!
4. Save the file.
5. Close your file.

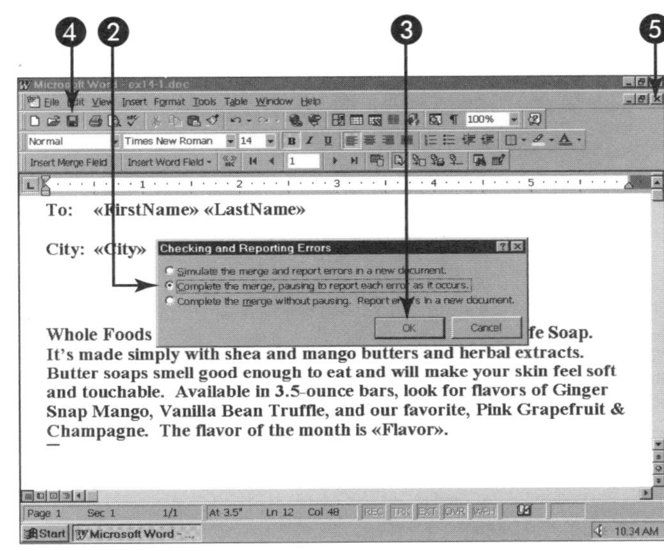

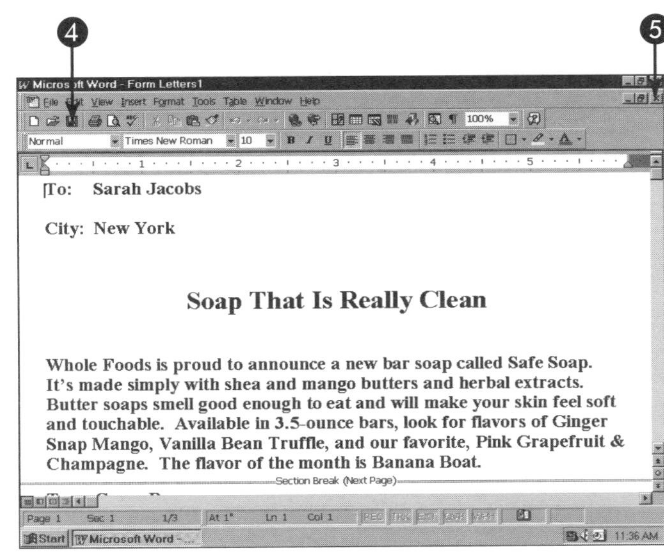

Printing to a printer or document

The last step in the merge process is merging the main document file and the data source file. Word creates a new file that contains a letter for each record in the data source. You can save the new file or just print it. The Mail Merge feature offers many options for controlling how a merge is performed. For example, you can merge to the printer or merge all letters into a document with each letter on a separate page. Let's merge the documents to the printer and print some exquisite product announcements.

1. In the main document, click the Merge to Printer button on the Mail Merge toolbar. The Print dialog box appears.

Skills challenge

❷ Click OK to start printing the product announcements.

❸ Close the files.

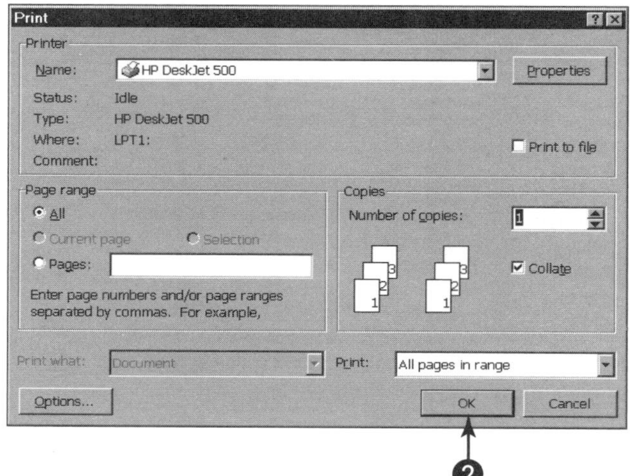

Word's Mail Merge feature offers numerous options that you may want to experiment with on your own. Some of these options include sorting the data records and using a Microsoft Access database or Microsoft Outlook's Contact list for the data source. This lesson provides only the simplest of examples. If you want more information, see the Microsoft Word 97 documentation.

SKILLS CHALLENGE: PRODUCING FORM LETTERS

This final exercise reviews the mail merge skills that you've learned in this lesson. Your task is to produce a personalized memo to inform employees about the Whole Foods exhibit at a trade show. EX14-2.DOC contains a memo to which you will add merge fields. Answer the bonus questions to review the skills and help you determine your understanding of the topics covered. The answers to the bonus questions are in Appendix C.

❶ Open the file EX14-2.DOC.

What are the three main functions of the Mail Merge Helper?

❷ Select the Tools menu.

❸ Click the Mail Merge command.

❹ Click the Create button.

❺ Choose Form Letters.

How do you add more records to your mail merge?

❻ Click the Active Window button.

7. In the Mail Merge Helper dialog box, click the Get Data button.
8. Choose Create Data Source.
9. Type **Code** in the Field Name text box.

How do you look at the first record in your data source?

10. Click the Add Field Name button.
11. Keep the following field names: FirstName and LastName. Remove the rest of the field names by clicking each one and clicking the Remove Field Name button.

    The Field Names in the Header Row list should look like the one in the illustration.

How do you delete a record from your data source?

12. Click OK.
13. Name the file **MEMODATA** and save it.
14. Click the Edit Data Source button in the warning dialog box.
15. Type the following records into the data form.

    Drew. Press Tab.

    Zeller. Press Tab.

    3684
16. Click the Add New button.
17. Type the second record in the data form:

    Tawanda. Press Tab.

    Mobley. Press Tab.

    9241
18. Click the Add New button.

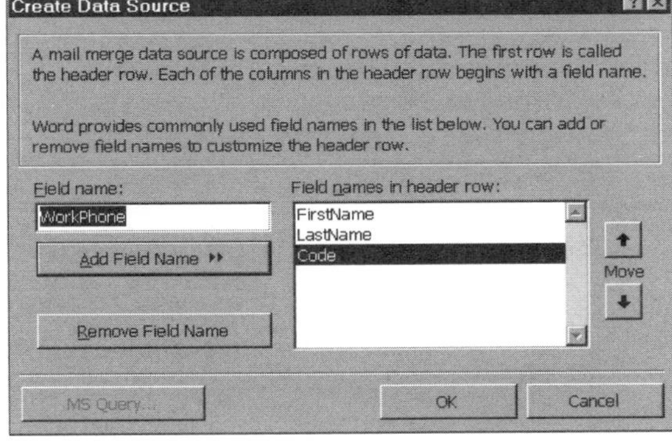

19. Type the third record into the data form.

    Lucy. Press Tab.

    Hanes. Press Tab.

    6388

20. Click OK.
21. In the main document, click where you want to insert a merge field, click the Insert Merge Field button on the Mail Merge toolbar.
22. Choose a field name.

    Your letter with merge fields in the main document should look like the letter in the illustration.

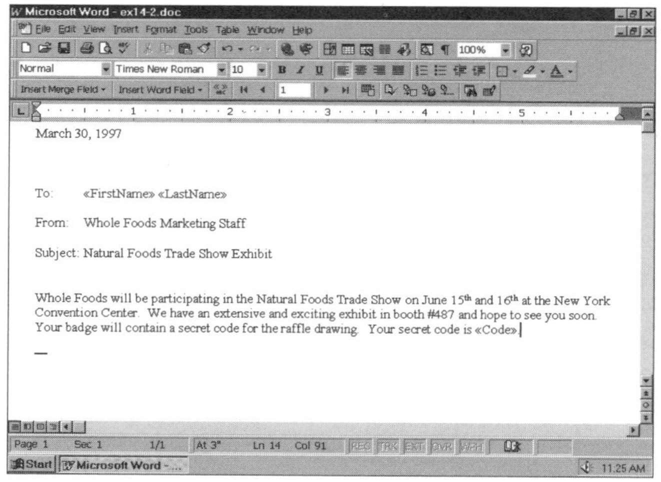

23. Save the main document.
24. Click the Check for Errors button on the Mail Merge toolbar.
25. Choose the second option.
26. Correct any errors, if necessary.
27. Close the new document that contains the memos without saving it.
28. Click the Merge to Printer button on the Mail Merge toolbar.
29. Click OK to print the merge memos.
30. Save your changes.
31. Close the files.

TROUBLESHOOTING

Now that you've completed this lesson, you know about Word's powerful Mail Merge feature. The following table offers solutions to several problems you might have encountered when learning these skills.

TRY OUT THE
INTERACTIVE TUTORIALS
ON YOUR CD!

Troubleshooting

Problem	Solution
I mistakenly entered a merge field in the wrong place in the main document.	Select the text (including the brackets) for the merge field, use Ctrl+X or the Edit menu to cut the misplaced field, and then paste it in the correct location in the document.
When I merged my main document and data source, I didn't get the correct results.	Observe where the errors occur in the merged document. Then check the merge fields in the data source and the merge fields in the main document. Typically, the errors occur in the data source. If you find errors, correct them and run the merge again. If you find no errors, have someone else check the merge fields. Sometimes another pair of eyes can catch the mistakes that you just can't see because you're so familiar with the documents. Make any necessary corrections, and run the merge again.
I want to add a record, but I already closed the Data Form dialog box.	Click the Edit Data Source button on the Mail Merge toolbar. Then enter your record.
I need to make some changes to a record that I've already added to my data source.	In the Data Form dialog box, use the scroll arrows or type the record number into the Go to Record box to find the record you want to edit. Make the necessary changes to the record and click OK.

Wrap up

WRAP UP

In this lesson, you practiced the following skills:

- Creating a main document
- Creating a data source
- Entering names and addresses
- Placing merge fields in your document
- Viewing and checking a mail merge
- Merging to a printer or document

If you want more practice with these skills, create a form letter announcing your promotion at work.

In the last lesson coming up, you are introduced to the exciting new features in Word that let you create Web pages in Word and browse the Web directly from Word.

Using Word to Create a Web Page

GOALS

In this lesson, you learn the following skills:

- Converting a Word document into a Web page
- Adding audio to your Web document
- Adding video to your Web document
- Viewing a Web page with online layout view
- Sending a Web page to an FTP site
- Browsing the Web
- Creating a hyperlink
- Browsing through files that contain hyperlinks

Get ready

GET READY

For this lesson, you will need the files EX15-1.DOC and EX15-2.DOC from the One Step folder. You will also need to obtain the address of an FTP site from your Webmaster or a site's system administrator.

When you've completed the exercises in this lesson, you will have produced the Web page shown in the accompanying illustration.

Whole Foods Gazette

Volume 11, Number 8 **October, 1997**

Expanded Gym Facilities

The current gym facility in the west wing of the Whole Foods Research Lab building is going to be expanded next month. We will add 5,000 square feet of floor space that will accommodate more gym equipment and a new aerobics studio. The following equipment will be purchased for the expansion: 25 steppers, 25 recumbent bikes, 25 rowers, barbells, dumbbells, circuit training equipment, automated circuit training equipment, and weight training machines. The stretching area will be expanded and carpeted with an indoor-outdoor type of flooring material. The new aerobics studio will have a new low lighting system, a surround sound stereo with 10 speakers, a flexible floor, and a headset microphone for the instructor. The expansion will be finished in three months. In the meantime, the existing gym will be open every day during construction of the new addition. Come join us now and you'll see results before the new gym is even finished. Stay fit and you stay healthy.

New Day Care Center

We are finally getting the day care center that we have been requesting for the past two years. In the east wing of the Whole Foods Administration building, we have dedicated an entire wing to the day care center. There are 10 day care center providers who are trained and licensed. They are on staff from 7:00 a.m. to 8:00 p.m. daily and on weekends. Giving quality care, teaching, and making sure everyone has fun are the premise that the day care is built on. Breakfast, lunch, dinner, and healthy snacks will be provided in the Kids Dining Room. The Toy Room is stocked full of exciting and educational toys and games. The Kids Library has many children's books and offers a reading hour. The Kids Computer Room has ten computers and is filled with every kind of educational and fun game there is on the market. Just sign up your children of all ages and they will get the best care. Whether you're working in the office or working out at the gym, it's convenient. You know we care about our employees and their children.

October Promotions

In this month of October, there are several promotions we would like to announce here at Whole Foods. James Lawson, Research Manager has been promoted to Research Director. Susan Wiffler, Assistant Marketing Manager has been promoted to Marketing Manager. Brent Silver, Marketing Communications Director has been promoted to Vice President of Marketing Communications. Laura Marco, Operations Assistant has been promoted to Operations Supervisor. Deborah Carter, Human Resources Recruiter has been promoted to Human Resources Manager. We thank all of you for your continued hard work and contributions to Whole Foods. You make the company what we are today.

WORD AND THE WEB

You can publish a Word document as a Web page so that other people on the World Wide Web can see your work. In order to place Web pages on the Web, you need to have an ISP (Internet service provider) that provides you with space for Web pages, or you need access to a Web service established at your company. You can ask the Webmaster (or whoever manages the Web servers) at your company where to place your Web pages.

You can use an existing Word document for a Web page by saving it as a Web page. Word closes the document, and then reopens it in HTML (HyperText Markup Language) format. The alternative is to create your own Web page in Word from scratch, and then format it the way you want. No matter which method you use, you can publish many types of documents on the Internet—for example, a company newsletter or a product brochure.

Every Web page is basically a plain text file with formatting instructions for the text, graphics, and links added to it. This file is called the HTML source because the instructions are written in HTML format. The Web recognizes the Web page similarly to how you would see it in Word's Online Layout view.

The Online Layout view in Word enables you to see your document as it will look in a Web browser. (A browser is a program with which you can read information on the Internet.) As you saw in Lesson 4, this view makes the text easy to read because it's large and wraps to fit the window. You can edit and format text in Online Layout view.

You can even add audio and video to your Web page in Word. That way, the reader of your Web page can play a sound file or view a video while visiting the Web site.

After you convert a Word document to a Web page, you can publish your Web page on the Internet by sending the page to an FTP (file transfer protocol) site on the Internet. FTP is a protocol that the Internet uses to send files between your computer and other computers on the Internet. Computers that offer files for download are called FTP sites. Using FTP is a fast and reliable way to download files from other Internet computers and to upload files for yourself.

After you publish the document, you see the document as it would appear in a Web browser. Then you can get on the Internet while you're in Word and view your own Web page. Other users will also be able to view your Web page.

Converting a Word document in a Web page

You can take a Word document and easily convert it into a Web page by using the File Save As HTML command. In the following exercises, you'll use the EX15-1.DOC file in the One Step folder. This file contains the Whole Foods newsletter you worked with earlier. We'll convert it into a Web page.

1. Open the file EX15-1.DOC.
2. Select the File menu.
3. Choose the Save As HTML command.

   You see the Save As HTML dialog box. Notice the HTML document choice in the Save As Type list. The My Documents folder appears in the Look In box. Let's store the HTML document in the My Work folder.

4. Use the Up One Level button on the Save toolbar to display the My Work folder.
5. Highlight the current file name in the File Name text box.
6. Type **mywebdoc** in the File Name text box.
7. Click the Save button.

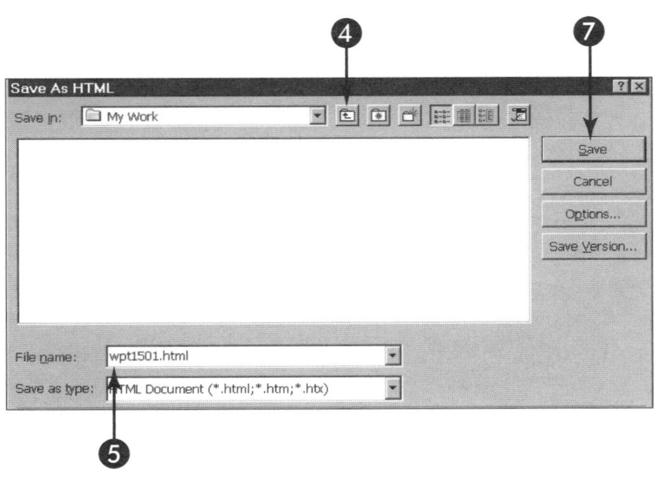

Word converts the document to HTML format so it can be published on the Web (see the accompanying illustration). The document appears with the name Whole Foods Bulletin in the title bar. This is the computer's name for the document. Yours may differ from the one listed here because Word creates a name based on information from your computer.

HTML automatically adds blank lines under paragraphs and headings. You can avoid ending up with too many blank lines in your Web page by deleting the blank line after each paragraph in the original document, not the HTML document. Then, select Format ➢ Paragraph, and increase the number of points in the After box in the Spacing area. A suggested size is 6 points.

When you save a document as an HTML document, Word saves any graphics and other objects in separate files.

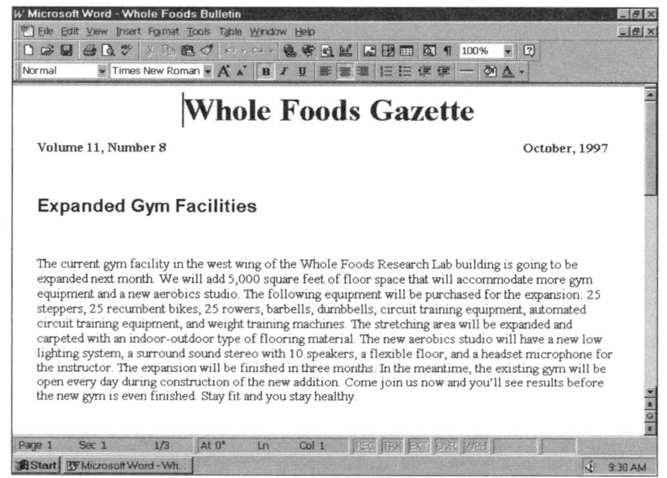

Adding audio to your Web document

You can add an audio clip to your Web document so that any reader who visits your Web page on the Internet can play a sound file. Perhaps you want the sound to be a backdrop for the Web site. When the Web page is opened or returned to, the background sound will be played automatically. It's a good idea to add the sound to a Web page that is less frequently visited than the home page. The repetition of a sound each time the reader jumps to the home page can become irritating. In this exercise, we'll add an audio clip to our Web document.

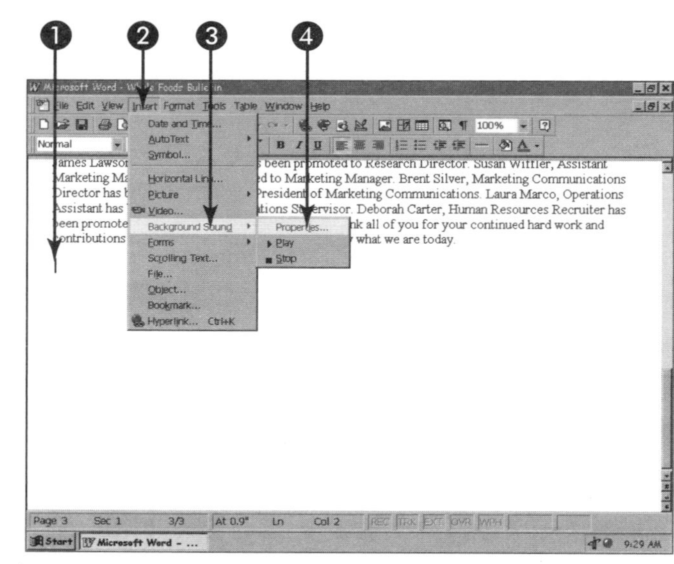

1. Press Ctrl+End to move the insertion point to the end of the Web document.

   This positions the insertion point where you want to insert the audio clip.

2. Select the Insert menu.
3. Choose the Background Sound command.
4. Click Properties.

   The Background Sound dialog box opens.

5 Click the Browse button.

The File Open dialog box appears. You see a list of sound files that are stored on your hard disk drive. Word will accept most of the popular Internet sound formats, such as WAV, MID, AU, AIF, RMI, SND, and MP2 (MPEG audio). But keep in mind that not all Web browsers support all these formats. For instance, WAV files are Windows-specific and are used infrequently on the Internet.

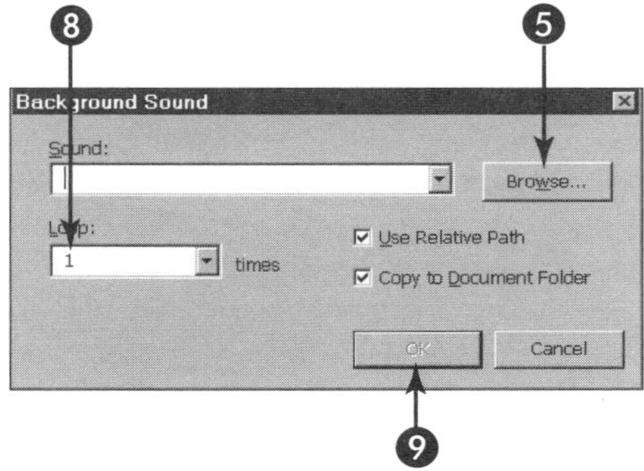

If you want to use sound files that are stored on a CD-ROM, choose the CD-ROM drive in the File Open dialog box, usually D:, and then choose the sound file you want to insert in your Web document.

6 Choose crash.au.

7 Click Open.

The sound filename appears in the Sound text box. The next option you can change is the Loop option. This specifies the number of times you want to repeat the sound. You can choose either to repeat the sound up to five times or to repeat it infinitely. If you choose the Infinite option, the sound will always be in the background when people visit your Web site.

8 In the Loop drop-down list, specify the number of times you want to repeat the sound.

9 Click OK.

The sound immediately plays.

To test the sound while you're developing your Web page, select Insert ➢ Background Sound, and choose Play. When you want to stop playing the sound, select Insert ➢ Background Sound, and choose Stop.

Adding video to your Web document

Word enables you to add a video clip to your Web document so that people who visit your Web site can watch a video clip. When the user opens the Web page, the video is downloaded. You can specify that the video is played either when the visitor opens the Web page or uses the mouse to point to the video, or both. Not all Web browsers can play a video, so you can opt to show only certain images or just text in the video. This exercise shows you how to add a video clip to your Web document.

1. Select the File menu.
2. Click Save or press Ctrl+S to save your document.

   (It's a good idea to save your document before you insert a video clip in it.)

For this exercise, leave the insertion point at the end of the Web document. Otherwise, you can insert a video clip anywhere you want in the Web document.

3. Select the Insert menu.
4. Choose the Video command.

   The Video Clip dialog box opens.

5. Click the Browse button.

   The File Open dialog box appears. You see a list of the video files that are stored on your hard disk drive. The video files have the file extension AVI, MOV, or any of many others.

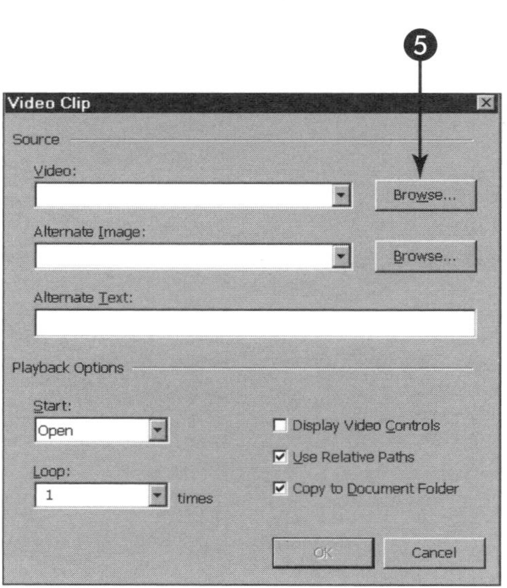

If you want to use video files that are stored on a CD-ROM, choose the CD-ROM drive in the File Open dialog box, usually D:, and then choose the video file you want to insert in your Web document.

6. Choose gulls.avi.

7 Click OK.

The video filename appears in the Video text box.

Video files are large and slow when they are loaded in and played on the Internet. Instead of choosing an entire video file for your users to see, you may want to select an alternate still image. In the Alternate Image text box, choose an image you want or click the Browse button and choose a still image. If you want to enter text that appears if your users don't want to display graphics, enter the text in the Alternate Text box. Be sure that your audience can play AVI files. Certain browsers can play AVI files but others cannot. You can find some sample AVI files on the Microsoft Office 97 Installation CD-ROM or you can purchase video files on CD-ROM from other manufacturers.

In the Playback Options section, the Start option lets you specify when the video will start. You can choose from three Start options: Open, Mouse-over, and Both. The Open option plays the video when the Web page opens. The Mouse-over option plays the video when the mouse pointer moves over the video. The Both option plays the video when the Web page opens and when the user points to the video.

8 In the Start drop-down list, choose a Start option.

The Loop option specifies the number of times you want to repeat the video. You can choose either to repeat the video up to five times or infinitely. If you choose the Infinite option, the video plays continuously when people visit your Web site. Be careful about choosing the Infinite option because when the video plays over and over again it can become annoying.

9 In the Loop drop-down list, specify the number of times you want to repeat the video.

10 Click the Display Video Controls checkbox to display the video controls Start and Stop while you're developing your Web pages.

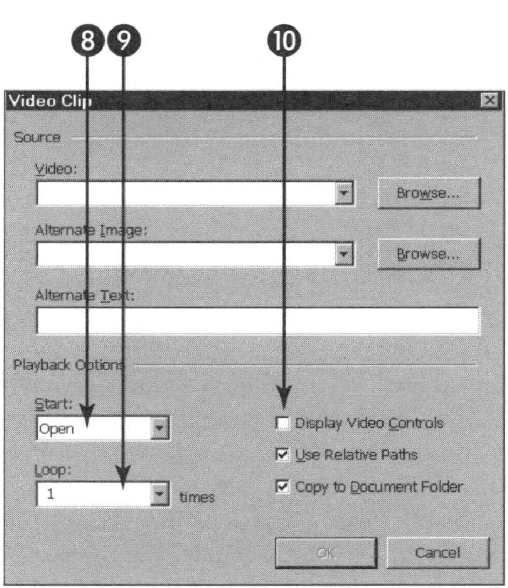

Viewing a page in Online Layout view

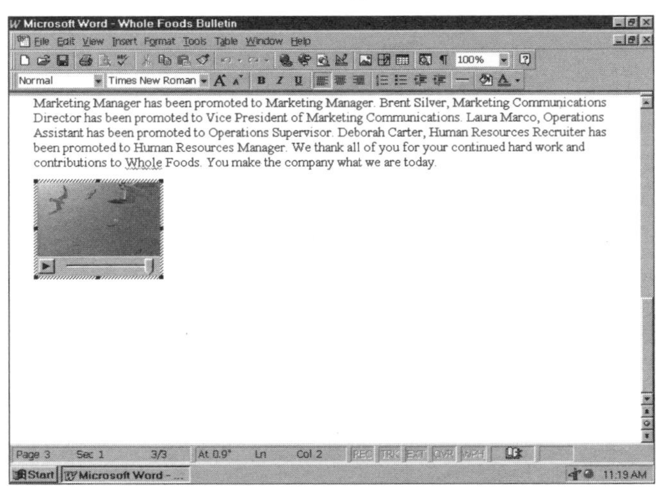

11. Click OK. Your screen should look similar to the accompanying figure.

    If you didn't choose an alternate image or alternate text, Word displays a warning message. Click Continue to proceed. The video file appears as an icon in your Web document, and the video will play back. If you chose the Mouse-over Start option, the video will play back when you move your mouse over the video in your Web page. When you want to stop playing the video, choose the Stop video control in your Web page.

Viewing a Web page with Online Layout view

Word's Online Layout view shows a version of the Web page that is similar to what it will look like in a Web browser. Your Web page might look different in a browser such as Netscape, Internet Explorer, or America Online than it does in Word, depending on how your browser interprets HTML codes. Let's look at our document in Online Layout view.

1. If your document isn't already in Online Layout view, click the Online Layout View button on the View toolbar.

   As you can see, the document contains large text and wraps to the View window so that you can see the end of every line of text (not the way it wraps for printing where you might not see some text on the far right side of the screen). Compare your screen to the accompanying illustration.

To make sure the text in the HTML document that appears in Online Layout view is always legible, you can change the minimum size for the font. In Online Layout view, select Tools ➢ Options and click the View tab. Enter the minimum font size you want in the Enlarge Fonts Less than box. Keep in mind that fonts less than 12 points are difficult to read. To increase the font size for text manually, select the text you want to enlarge, and click the Enlarge Font Size button (the button with the letter A and an up arrow) on the Formatting toolbar. To decrease the font size for text, select the text, and click the Decrease

Font Size button (the button with the letter A and a down arrow) on the Formatting toolbar.

2. Use the scroll bars to see the rest of the document.

TIP

In Online Layout view, you see the Document Map on the left side of the window. This pane contains an outline for the document. You can use it to move around your document and track where you are in the document. (The Document Map feature is not always automatically associated with Online Layout view. With some documents, you have to turn on Document Map by selecting the View ➢ Document Map command.)

3. Click New Day Care Center in the Document Map pane.

   The New Day Care Center article appears in the right pane.

4. Select the View menu.
5. Click the Normal command to return to Normal view.
6. Close the document.

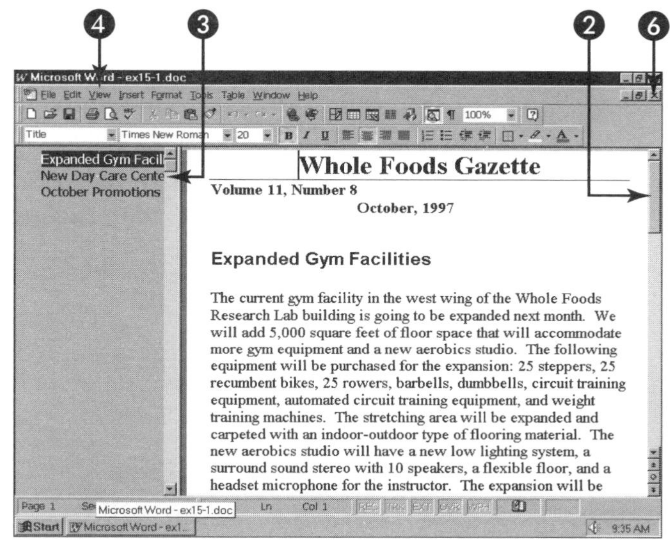

Sending a Web page to an FTP site

Now we need to tell Word about the FTP sites you want to access. For this lesson, you will need to obtain the address of an FTP site from your Webmaster or a site's system administrator.

1. Select the File menu.
2. Click Save As.
3. In the Save As dialog box, click the Save In drop-down arrow.
4. Choose Add/Modify FTP Locations.

   The Add/Modify FTP Locations dialog box appears.

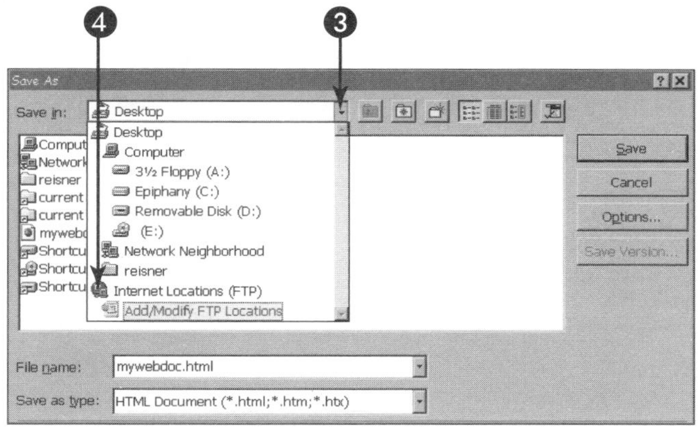

Sending a Web page to an FTP site

5 In the Name Of FTP Site text box, type the FTP site address.

FTP addresses begin with `FTP://`*. For example,* `FTP://FTP.AOL.COM` *is the FTP site for America Online. If you don't know the correct FTP site name, ask the site's system administrator.*

If you have a personal account at the FTP site, click the User option button in the Log On As area. Then enter your user name and password. Otherwise, leave the default option, Anonymous, selected. Anonymous users are given access only to certain public areas of a site. In most cases, you connect as an anonymous user if you want to download files; an anonymous user may not be able to upload files.

6 Click the Add button to add the FTP site.

As you can see, the new FTP site appears in the FTP sites box at the bottom of the Add/Modify FTP Locations dialog box.

7 Click OK.

Notice the name of the new FTP site appears in the Save In box. Now let's send the Web page from Word to the FTP site.

8 Connect to the Internet using any ISP you have.

9 In Word's Save As dialog box, choose the FTP location.

10 Make sure the filename MYWEBDOC.HTML is in the File Name text box.

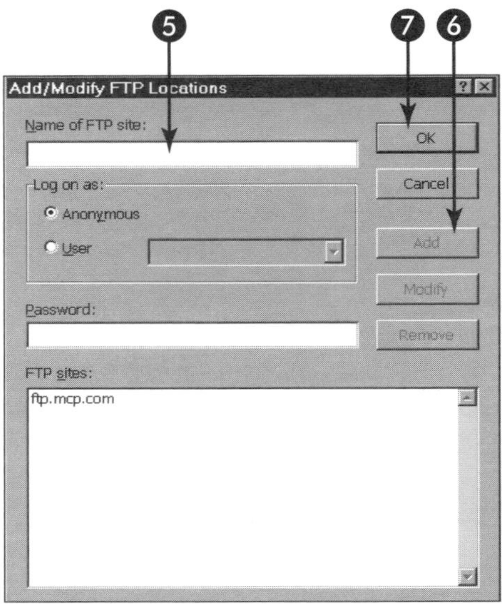

You can also type the URL for the file in the File Name text box, as in `ftp://ftp.aol.com/mywebdoc.html`.

Sending a Web page to an FTP site

11 Click the Open button to upload the file to the FTP site.

You are connected to the top level of the FTP site.

12 Move through the folders to find the one you want to use, and then select the folder.

13 Click the Save button.

Your HTML document is saved in the selected folder. However, any associated GIF, sound, or video files are not saved with the HTML document in the FTP site. You need to transfer them separately with an FTP program. Or better yet, you can use the Publish to the Web wizard that comes with Microsoft Office 97 Service Release 1 to transfer all file types to a server.

VISUAL BONUS: THE WEB TOOLBAR

The Web toolbar provides tools for browsing Web pages backward and forward, refreshing the current page, searching the Web, storing Web pages in the Favorite Places folder, and entering a URL (uniform resource locator). A URL is similar to a filename or address. The Web uses it to locate the Web page.

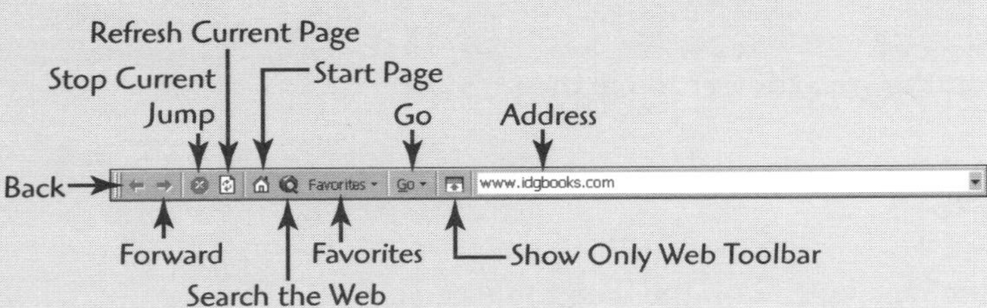

The Web toolbar

Browsing the Web

Browsing the Web

You can browse the Web to your heart's content directly from Word. You don't have to leave the program and start the Internet Explorer or any other browser you might normally use. Just use the Web toolbar in Word. You can enter a URL and search for a specific Web page or browse around the Web at any time. In this exercise, we'll browse for IDG Books Worldwide's Web site.

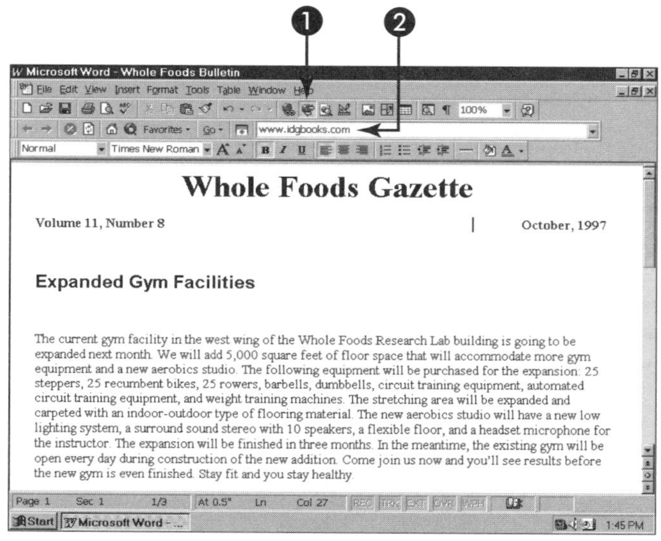

1. Click the Web Toolbar button on the Standard toolbar in Word.

   The Web toolbar appears onscreen.

If you have the Show/Hide ¶ feature turned on, be sure to turn it off by clicking the Show/Hide ¶ button on the Standard toolbar. Otherwise, your Web page will look quite messy.

2. Type **www.idgbooks.com** (the URL for IDG Books Worldwide) in the Address text box on the Web toolbar.
3. Press Enter. You might be prompted to connect to the Internet.

   The browser searches the Web and displays the Web page you requested.

4. Click a link in the IDG Books Worldwide Web page to open another Web page.
5. Click the Back button on the Web toolbar to see the previous Web page.
6. Click the Forward button on the Web toolbar to see the next Web page.
7. Click the Refresh Current Page button on the Web toolbar.

   This reloads the current Web page and updates it with the latest information.

CREATING HYPERLINKS

A hyperlink is a piece of text or graphic in a document that links to other documents or Web pages. You can have a Web wizard put hyperlinks in your Web page, or you can create your own hyperlinks to move to a Web page or a Word, Excel, PowerPoint, or Access file. You can even link to a specific location in a document. When you point to a hyperlink, Word displays the document path (for example, c:\winword\my documents\report.doc) or Internet address to which the link points. When you click a hyperlink, Word moves to the location to which the link points. A hyperlink appears as blue (default color) text in the document.

Hyperlinks are useful when you're distributing your document electronically and expect people to read it onscreen. Make sure that your readers will be able to access the documents to which you link. For example, if you link to a document on your local hard drive (C:) instead of a network drive, other people on your network won't be able to jump to the document, unless you make the entire contents of your machine available to other users on the network.

You can browse through files on your computer, on a network drive, or on the Internet that contain hyperlinks. The Web toolbar displays a list of the last 10 documents you jumped to by using the Web toolbar or a hyperlink. This feature makes it easy for you to return to these documents again.

Creating a hyperlink

In this exercise, we'll create a couple of hyperlinks to Web pages.

1. Create a new document and save it with the name **MY HYPERLINK**.

Creating a hyperlink

If you try to insert a hyperlink into a new document that hasn't been saved, Word displays a message informing you that the document must be saved before you can insert the hyperlink.

2. Type **The Internet address for IDG Books Worldwide is**, and press the spacebar.
3. Select the Insert menu.
4. Choose the Hyperlink command (or press Ctrl+K).

   The Insert Hyperlink dialog box opens.
5. In the Link to File or URL box, type **www.idgbooks.com**.
6. Click OK.

   The text you selected in the document is now a hyperlink and appears as blue text.
7. Point to the hyperlink.

   The mouse pointer becomes a hand, and a ScreenTip appears showing the URL.
8. Follow Steps 3–7 to create another hyperlink using the Internet address of one of your favorite Web sites.
9. Point to the hyperlink to display its URL.
10. Click the hyperlink you just created.

    Word displays the Web page in the Web browser.

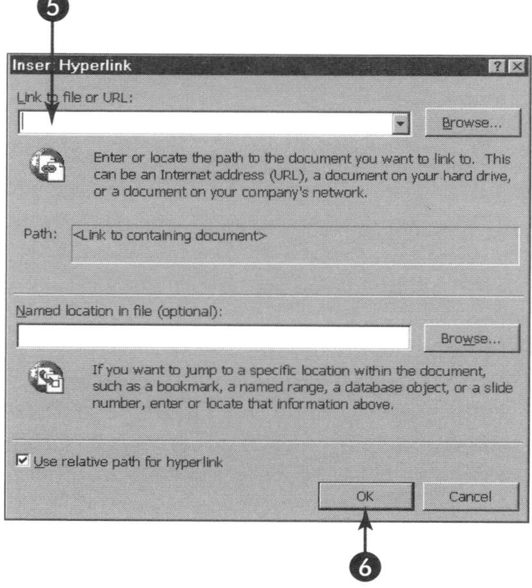

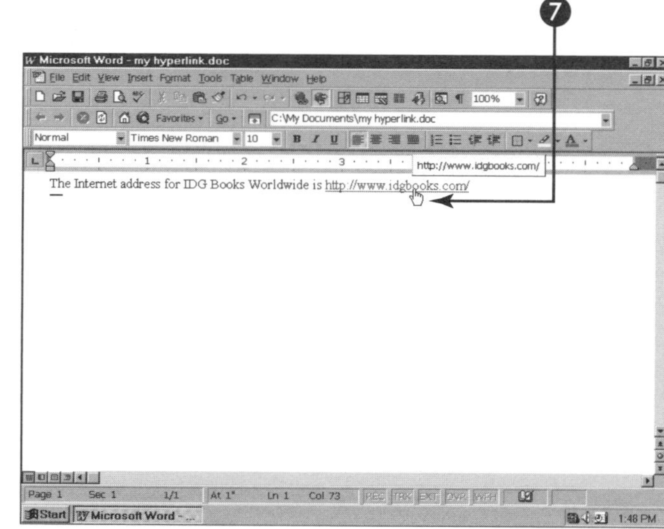

Browsing through files that contain a hyperlink

Let's browse through files that contain a hyperlink.

1. Click the Back button on the Web toolbar.

   You return to the Word document that contains the hyperlink.

2. Click the first hyperlink you created.

   Word displays the Web page in the Web browser.

3. Click the Back button on the Web toolbar.

   You return to the Word document that contains the hyperlink. The hyperlink text now appears in purple, indicating that you have visited the Web site associated with the hyperlink.

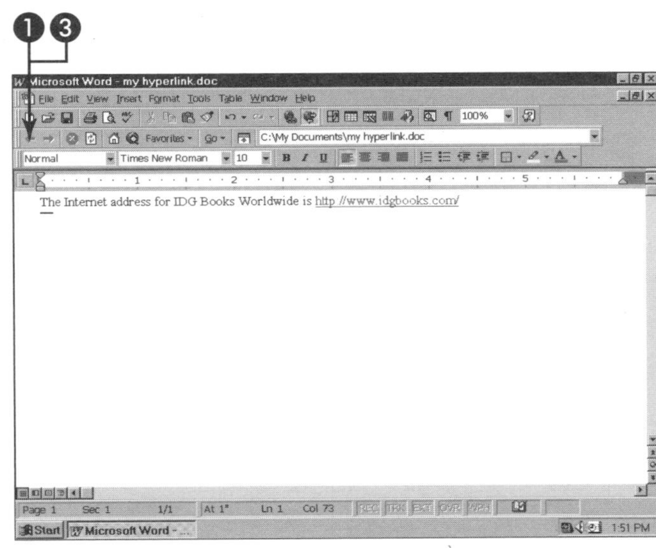

SKILLS CHALLENGE: PUBLISHING A WORD DOCUMENT AS A WEB PAGE

In this last exercise, you review the skills you've learned in this lesson. Your task is to publish a Web page on the Internet, and then browse the Web. EX15-2.DOC contains the Whole Foods bulletin that you've worked with before. Answer the bonus questions to review the skills and help you determine your understanding of the topics covered. The answers to the bonus questions are in Appendix C.

1. Open the file EX15-2.DOC.
2. Select the File menu.
3. Choose Save As HTML.
4. Type **wfbweb** to name the file and save it.
5. Add an audio clip to your Web document.
6. Add a video clip to your Web document.

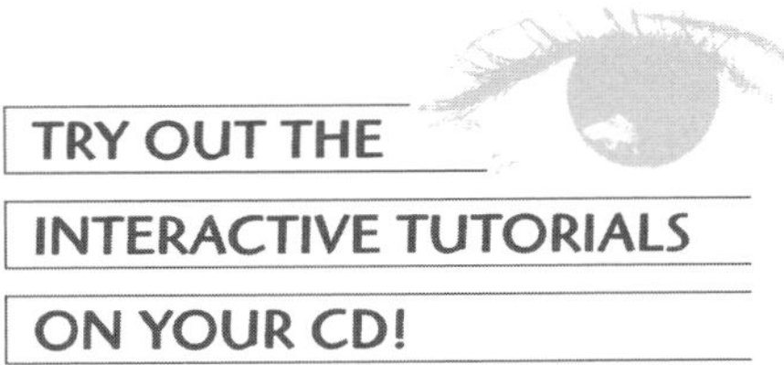

TRY OUT THE INTERACTIVE TUTORIALS ON YOUR CD!

Skills challenge

7. Click the Online Layout View button on the View toolbar.

Describe the two visual changes to text when it is displayed in Online Layout view.

8. Scroll around the document in Online Layout view.
9. Select the View menu.
10. Click Normal to return to Normal view.
11. Close the document.
12. Connect to the Internet using any ISP you have.
13. With the HTML document onscreen, select the File menu.
14. Choose Save As to open the Save As dialog box.
15. Choose an FTP location in the Save In list.
16. In the File Name text box, type **WFBWEB.HTML**.

How do you add an FTP location?

17. Click the Open button to upload the file to the FTP site.
18. Move to the folder where you want to store the Web document.
19. Select the folder.
20. Click the Save button to store the file in the folder.
21. Click the Web Toolbar button on the Standard toolbar in Word.
22. Type **www.idgbooks.com** (the URL for IDG Books Worldwide) in the Address text box on the Web toolbar.
23. Press Enter to view your Web page.
24. Open another Web page.
25. Click the Back button on the Web toolbar to see the previous Web page.

26. Click the Forward button on the Web toolbar to see the next Web page.

How do you reload and update the current Web page?

27. Create a new document.
28. Insert two hyperlinks to your Web pages on the Internet.
29. Browse through the files that contain hyperlinks.
30. Click the Web Toolbar button on the Standard toolbar to hide the toolbar.
31. Save the changes.
32. Close both files.

TROUBLESHOOTING

You've completed this lesson and learned about Word and the World Wide Web. This table offers solutions to several problems you might have encountered when learning these skills.

Problem	Solution
When I try to open my Web page files, I can't find them.	Web page files that were converted to HTML format have the file extension HTML. In the Open dialog box, choose All Files in the Files of Type box.
When I try to use my Web browser, I can't access the Internet.	You are probably experiencing either modem or network connection problems. Check your modem connection. Log on to your Internet service provider again. Consult your network administrator.

Wrap up

Problem	Solution
I tried adding an FTP site and Word displays an error message informing me that the FTP site doesn't exist.	All FTP addresses begin with FTP://. Be sure that you typed the FTP address correctly. Otherwise, ask the FTP site's system administrator for the correct FTP site name.
I logged on as an anonymous user to an FTP site. I can only access certain areas of the site, and I can't upload my Web pages.	Anonymous users are given access to only certain public areas of a site. You might find that you can download files from the FTP site, but you may not be able to upload files. Ask the FTP site's system administrator if you can have a user ID and password that gives you access to more FTP site areas and lets you upload files.

WRAP UP

In this lesson, you practiced the following skills:

- Converting a Word document into a Web page
- Adding audio to your Web document
- Adding video to your Web document
- Viewing a Web page with Online Layout view
- Sending a Web page to an FTP site
- Browsing the Web
- Creating a hyperlink
- Browsing through files that contain hyperlinks

If you want more practice with these skills, publish a favorite recipe as a Web page.

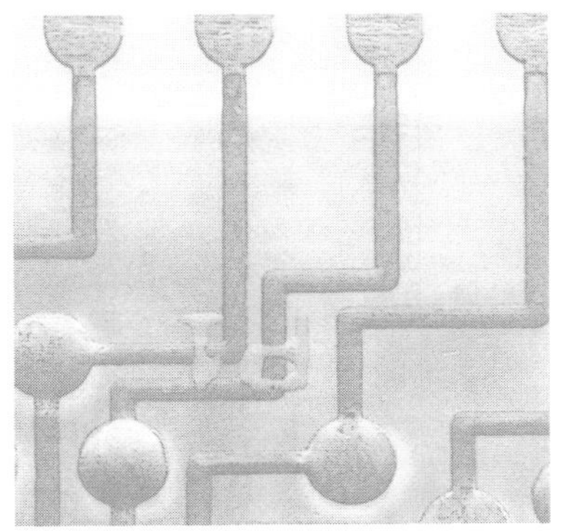

Integrating Other Microsoft Office Applications

GOALS

In this lesson, you learn the following skills:

- Creating a hyperlink to move between Office documents
- Copying and pasting between Office documents
- Linking Office documents
- Embedding Office documents
- Inserting an Excel worksheet into a Word document
- Inserting an Excel chart into a Word document
- Opening Word files in Outlook

Get ready

GET READY

For this lesson, you will need the files EX16-1.DOC, EX16-2.XLS, EX16-3.DOC, and EX16-4.XLS from the One Step folder. You will also need to have Microsoft Excel and Microsoft Outlook installed on your computer.

When you've completed the exercises in this lesson, you will have produced a Word document that contains an Excel worksheet and chart, as shown in the accompanying illustration.

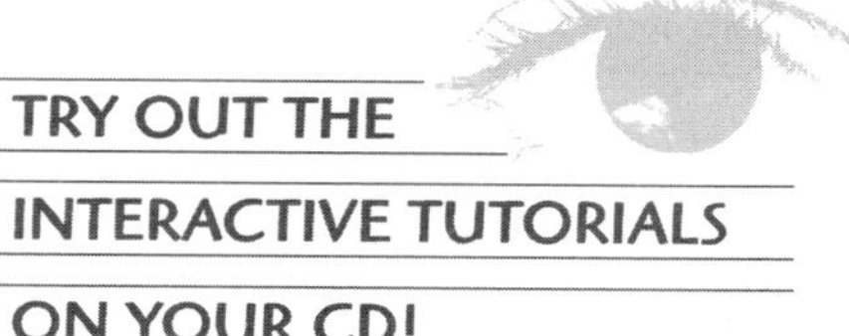

Whole Foods Inc.

Interoffice Memo

Date: 12/4/97
To: Sales Staff
Cc: Marketing Director
From: TRUDI REISNER
RE: Quarterly Sales

The quarterly sales report shows that sales have been healthy for the past year. There have been significant increases in each territory, indicating that the sales blitz and sales quota changes we experienced this year have improved sales. Here are the sales figures for all four quarters.

EX16-2.xls

Whole Foods Inc.
Quarterly Sales

	1st Quarter	2nd Quarter	3rd Quarter	4th Quarter	Total
Northeast	1,235	2,587	3,214	7,896	$ 14,932
South	5,624	3,698	1,236	6,541	$ 17,099
Midwest	3,214	1,478	5,478	6,512	$ 16,682
West	8,963	2,589	5,698	3,214	$ 20,464
Total	$ 19,036	$ 10,352	$ 15,626	$ 24,163	$ 69,177

8/4/97 1

SHARING MICROSOFT OFFICE APPLICATIONS

After you learn how to use Word, and if you already know how to use Excel and Outlook, you can use Microsoft Office to share information between applications. In Lesson 15 you learned how to create a hyperlink to jump to a Web page from a Word document. In this lesson, you will see how easy it is to create a hyperlink that moves you from one Microsoft Office application to another. You can also copy and paste text and graphics between Office documents.

Word enables you to *link* Office documents together to share information, as well as *embed* an Office document into another Office document. When you link and embed documents, you can update the information in the original document and the information in the second document is updated automatically to reflect the changes. Linking is the process of copying an object into an Office document; whenever the object is modified in the original application, the document that contains the object is automatically updated. For example, when you create a link between a Word document and an Excel worksheet, and you change the data in the Excel worksheet, Word automatically updates the worksheet data in the Word document, too.

With an embedded object, double-clicking the object causes the original program that created the object to start up, displaying the object ready for editing. For instance, you can embed an Excel worksheet into a Word memo, double-click the Excel worksheet that appears in the memo, and you'll see the Excel menus and toolbars, allowing you to make changes to the worksheet with Excel commands. When you're finished editing the worksheet, you can return to the Word menus and toolbars, and you will see the changes to the worksheet data in your Word memo.

You can also use the Word program with other programs in Microsoft Office. Suppose you create a memo in Word using a Word wizard and then you want to add an Excel worksheet to the memo to help illustrate and explain the text. Microsoft Office lets you insert the Excel chart into the Word document.

Another program you might want to share Word information with is Outlook, Microsoft's personal information manager. With Outlook you can do a multitude of things: manage your business and personal contacts, keep a schedule of your appointments and events, schedule meetings, track tasks involved in projects, send and receive e-mail messages, record any Outlook or Microsoft Office activity in a journal, and create sticky notes to remind yourself of things you need to do. Outlook's Journal feature lets you record and keep track of documents that you use in projects related to, for example, contact information, e-mail file attachments, or tasks. To share information between Word and Outlook, you can open Word files in Outlook.

Creating a hyperlink to move between Office documents

Creating a hyperlink to a Web page was discussed in Lesson 15, so you have experience creating a hyperlink already. In this exercise you use the Insert Hyperlink command again, but this time you create a hyperlink so that you can move among Office documents. In the following exercises, you'll use the EX16-1.DOC file in the One Step folder. This file contains the Whole Foods sales report. Let's create a hyperlink to move from the Word document to an Excel worksheet that contains Whole Foods' quarterly sales figures.

1. Open the file EX16-1.DOC.
2. Press Ctrl+End to move the insertion point to the end of the document.
3. Select the Insert menu.
4. Click the Hyperlink command (or press Ctrl+K).

   The Insert Hyperlink dialog box opens.

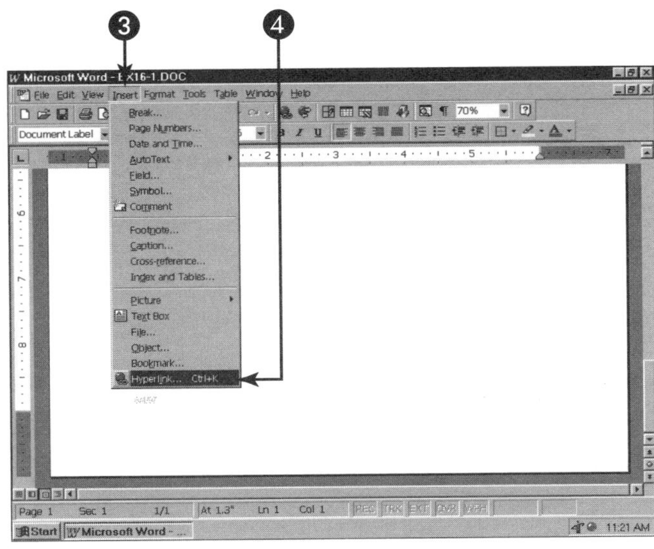

Copying and pasting

5. Enter the document pathname in the Link to File or URL box.
6. Click the Browse button.
7. Choose the One Step folder.
8. Choose the file named EX16-2.XLS.
9. Click OK.

If you know the file's pathname, you can enter it in the Link to File or URL box. For example, C:\My Documents\wfsales.xls.

10. Click OK in the Insert Hyperlink dialog box.

    The document name is now a hyperlink and appears as blue text.

11. Point to the hyperlink.

    The mouse pointer becomes a hand.

12. Click the hyperlink.

    Microsoft Excel opens and you see the Excel worksheet.

13. In Excel, select the File menu.
14. Click Exit.

    This closes the worksheet and Excel, and then returns you to the Word document.

15. Click the Microsoft Word button on the Windows taskbar.

    You see the Word document again. Notice the hyperlink text appears in purple, indicating that the hyperlink is selected.

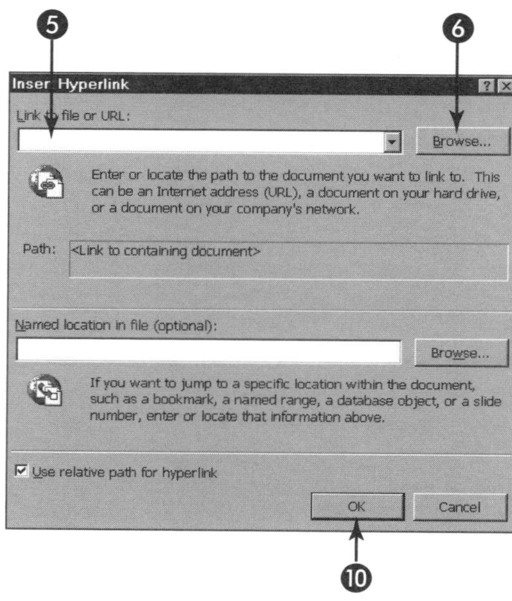

Copying and pasting between Office documents

You can copy data from one Office document and paste it into another. Perhaps you want to copy some sales figures from an Excel worksheet into a Word document that contains a report. In this exercise, you copy sales figures from an Excel worksheet into a sales report in Word. Let's use the hyperlink you created in Exercise 1 to

Linking Office documents

start Excel and open the sales worksheet. Then we'll copy and paste information between Office documents.

1. In the Word memo, click the hyperlink you created in Exercise 1 to switch to Excel.

   This starts Microsoft Excel and opens the sales worksheet.

2. Click in cell A1 and drag across and down to F9.

   You have selected a range of cells A1:F9. This is the data that we will copy into the Word document.

3. Open the Edit menu.
4. Click Copy (or press Ctrl+C).
5. Click the Microsoft Word button on the Windows taskbar to switch to Word.
6. Press Ctrl+End to move the insertion point to the bottom of the document. Press Enter twice.
7. Select the Edit menu.
8. Click Paste (or press Ctrl+V).

   The data appears in a table in the document, as shown in the accompanying illustration.

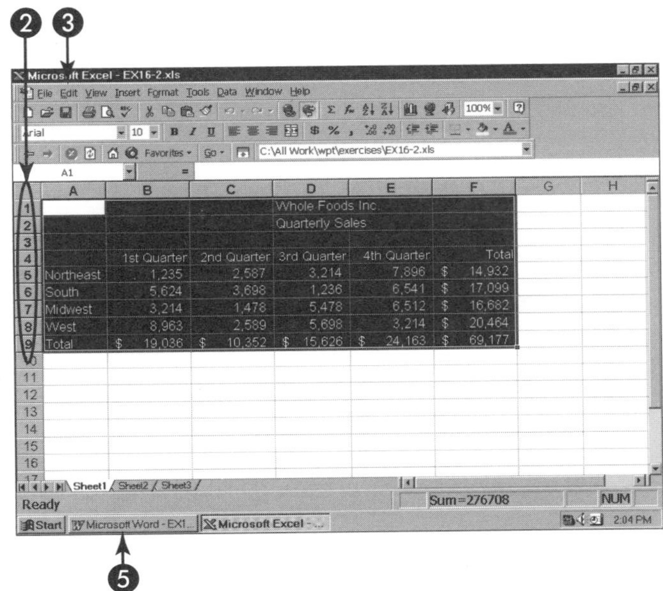

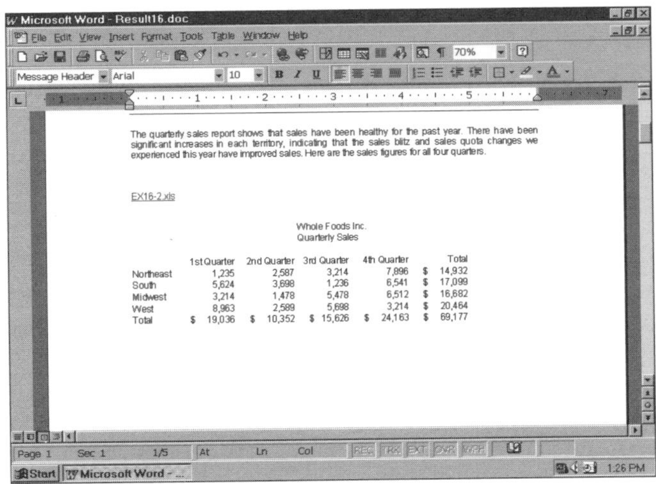

Linking Office documents

You can link Office documents. For example, you can take an existing Excel worksheet and copy and paste its contents or import it into a Word document. Then you can create a link between the Excel worksheet and the Word document so that each time the worksheet is updated in Excel, the worksheet data in Word is automatically updated to reflect any changes.

When you link Office documents, one document is called the *source* document and the other is called the *target* document. The source document contains the information you want to link; the target document receives the linked information. For example, if you want to link an Excel worksheet to a Word document, the worksheet file is the source document and the Word file is the target document.

Linking Office documents

When you link documents, the source document appears in the target document, but it is not physically there. For example, you can see an Excel worksheet in a Word document, but the worksheet still resides in Excel.

Let's link the Excel worksheet to our Word document.

❶ Press Ctrl+Enter to insert a page break.

The insertion point is at the top of page 2 in your memo.

❷ Click the Microsoft Excel button on the Windows taskbar to switch to Excel.

❸ Press Esc.

This removes the flashing marquis border around the selected range.

❹ Click in cell A4.

❺ Drag across and down to cell C9.

You have selected the range of cells A4:C9. This is the data that we will link to the Word document.

❻ Open the Edit menu.

❼ Click Copy (or press Ctrl+C).

❽ Click the Microsoft Word button on the Windows taskbar to switch to Word.

❾ Select the Edit menu.

❿ Click the Paste Special command.

The Paste Special dialog box appears. The selected range appears at the top of the dialog box.

⓫ In the As list, choose Microsoft Excel Worksheet Object.

⓬ Choose the Paste Link option.

⓭ Click OK.

⓮ If the Excel worksheet appears at the bottom of page 1, point to the worksheet; you will see a four-headed arrow. This arrow indicates that you can move the object.

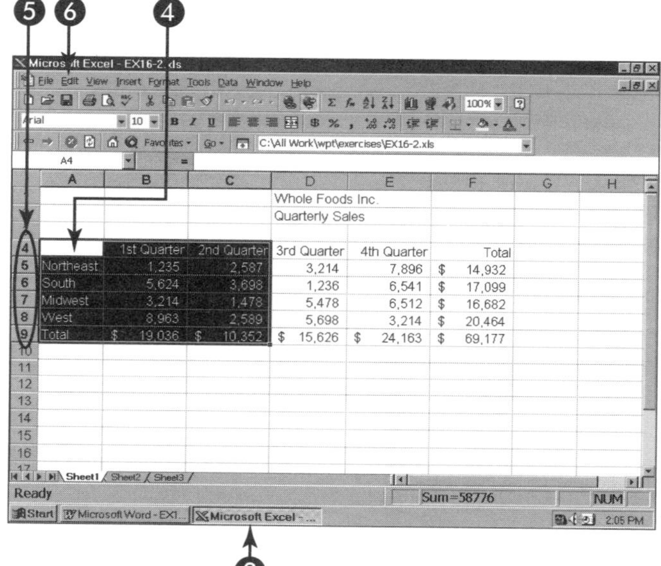

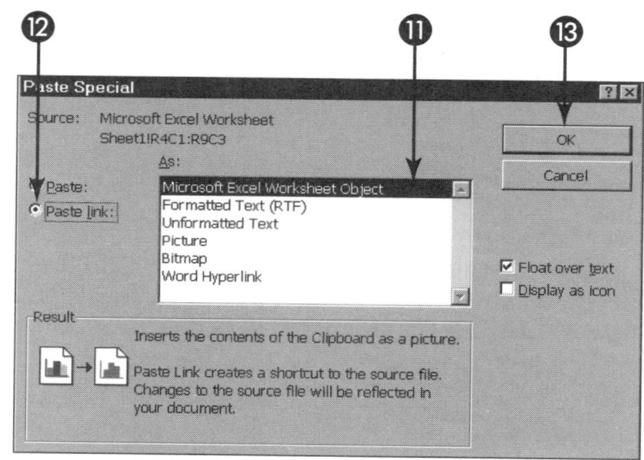

⑮ Now, drag the worksheet object to the top of page 2.

The Excel worksheet appears as an object in your Word document, as shown in the accompanying figure. Notice the white squares surrounding the worksheet's border. These squares are called selection handles, indicating that the object is selected.

If you want to change the information in the Excel worksheet object, just double-click the worksheet in the Word document. The link switches you to Excel, where you make your changes. Next, you can save and close the worksheet. Switch back to Word, and you will see that the linked worksheet reflects the changes you made in Excel.

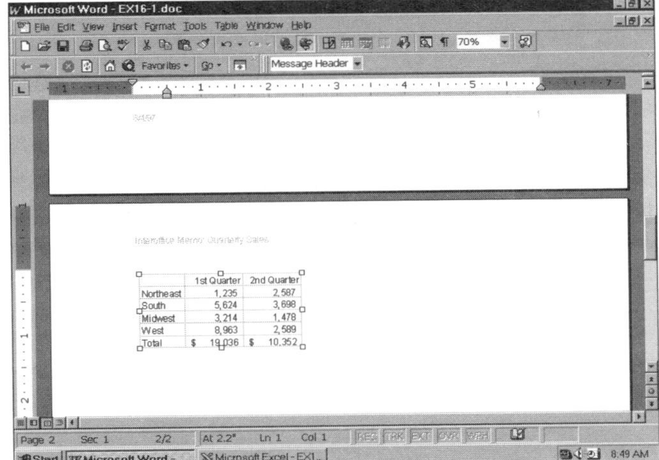

Embedding Office documents

When you take an existing Excel worksheet and copy and paste the information or import it into a Word document, you can embed the worksheet instead of linking it. By embedding the worksheet as an object, you can double-click the worksheet in Word, and the Word menus and toolbars are temporarily replaced by the Excel menus and toolbars. It's like working in a "super application," in which one window can perform many different types of applications' tasks— word processor to spreadsheet program and back. The advantage is that you can quickly and easily make changes to objects from different applications in the same window. This process is sometimes referred to as OLE (object linking and embedding). Any changes you make to the worksheet are automatically reflected in the worksheet in Word.

Embedding Office documents

Just like linking documents, you have a source document and a target document when you embed an object in a document. Embedding a document as an object physically places a document within another document. For example, if you embed an Excel worksheet in a Word document, the worksheet physically resides in Word as well as Excel. Let's embed the Excel worksheet in our Word document.

1. Click beneath the worksheet to move the insertion point.

   This moves the insertion point to the bottom of the memo.

2. Press Ctrl+Enter.

   You have inserted a page break. The insertion point is now at the top of page 3.

3. Click the Microsoft Excel button on the Windows taskbar to switch to Excel.

4. Press the Esc key to clear the flashing marquis border.

5. Then, click in cell A4 and drag down to cell F9.

   You have selected the range of cells A4:F9. This is the data that we will embed in the Word document as an object.

6. Select the Edit menu.

7. Click Copy (or press Ctrl+C).

8. Click the Microsoft Word button on the Windows taskbar to switch to Word.

9. Select the Edit menu.

10. Click Paste Special.

    The Paste Special dialog box appears. The selected range appears at the top of the dialog box.

11. In the As list, choose Microsoft Excel Worksheet Object.

12. Click OK.

    The Excel worksheet is now an embedded object in your Word document. Now let's change a couple of numbers in the Excel worksheet.

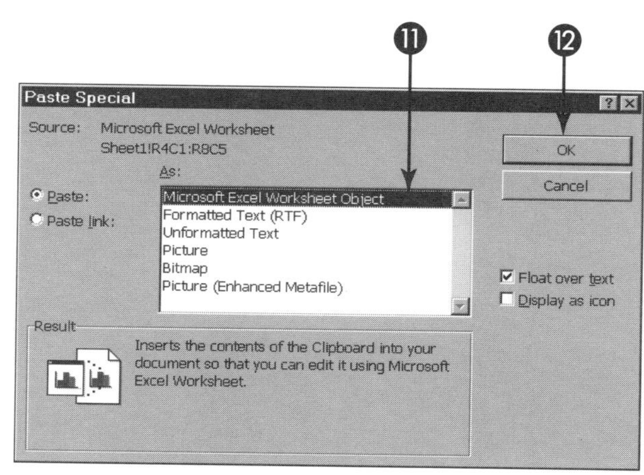

13 Double-click the worksheet object.

Notice the Word window takes on the appearance of an Excel window, displaying Excel's menus, toolbars, the Web toolbar, and the formula bar.

14 Click cell B5.

15 Type **2000**, and press Enter.

16 Next, click cell B7.

17 Type **3000**, and press Enter.

This changes two numbers in the Excel worksheet. Notice that the formulas in the Total column and Total row have been updated to reflect the new numbers.

18 Click outside the worksheet.

The Word toolbars appear. Notice the worksheet now contains the new numbers and the formulas have been recalculated automatically to reflect the changes you made. It's like magic!

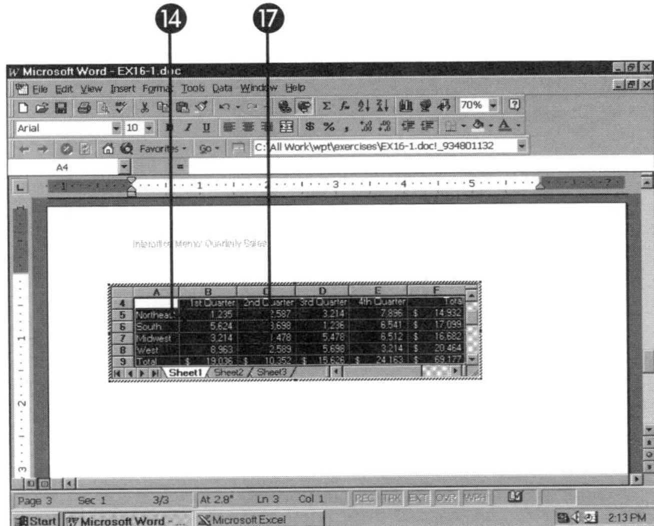

Keep in mind that when you embed a worksheet object, the entire workbook is really inserted. If you display the wrong worksheet in Word, simply double-click the worksheet in the Word document and click the worksheet tab you want. Then click outside of the worksheet area in Word.

Embedding Office documents

VISUAL BONUS: LINKING AND EMBEDDING OFFICE DOCUMENTS

Here's an example of an Excel worksheet that is linked to a Word document. The worksheet area appears in the Word document. You change the worksheet data in Excel. The worksheet data in Word is automatically updated to reflect your changes.

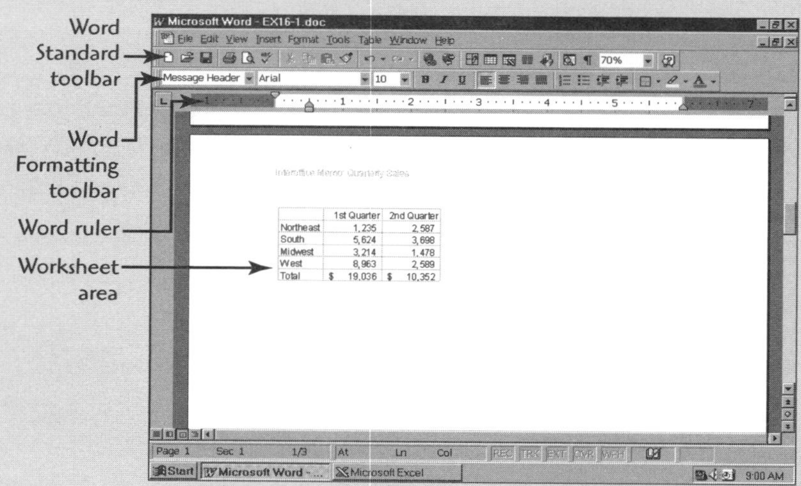

The linked document

This sample Excel worksheet is an embedded object that appears in a Word document. Notice the Word window takes on the appearance of an Excel window, displaying Excel's toolbars, the Web toolbar, and formula bar. The Excel worksheet physically exists in the Word document. You can change the worksheet data directly in Word. Then click outside the worksheet area to restore the Word toolbars.

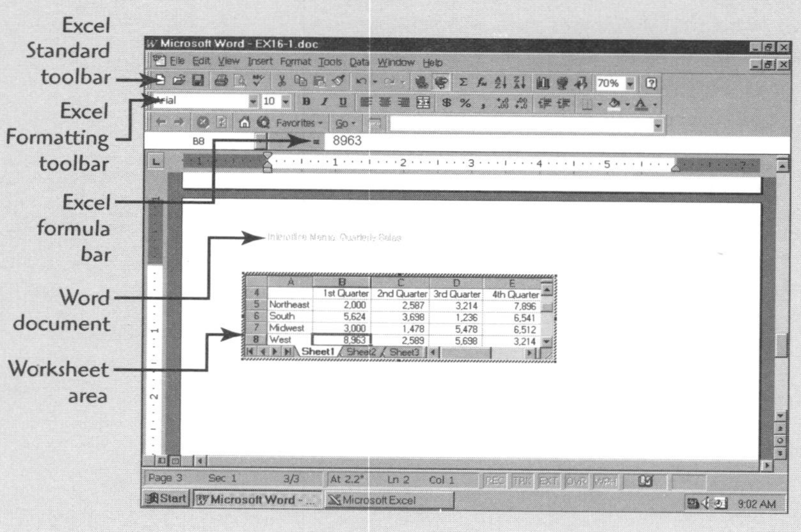

The embedded object in a document

Inserting an Excel worksheet into a Word document

Up until now you've copied and pasted an existing Excel worksheet into a Word document. But what if you want to create an Excel worksheet from scratch from within Word? You can do just that by using the Insert Microsoft Excel Worksheet command in Word. In this exercise, we will insert an Excel worksheet into a Word document.

1. Press Ctrl+End to move to the end of the document.
2. Press Ctrl+Enter to insert a page break and create page 4.
3. Click the Insert Microsoft Excel Worksheet button on the Standard toolbar.

   Below the Insert Excel Worksheet button, Word displays a grid with columns and rows.
4. Click in the first cell in the grid, and drag to the right to highlight four columns, and then drag down to highlight four rows.

   At the bottom of the grid, you see the words *4 x 4 Spreadsheet*, indicating that you have selected four columns and four rows.
5. Release the mouse button.

   Word displays an Excel worksheet called the worksheet area in your document. At the top of the document window is the Excel Standard toolbar, the Excel Formatting toolbar, the Web toolbar, and Excel's formula bar.
6. Enter data in your worksheet, as if you're working directly in Excel. (You can enter the data that appears in the accompanying illustration.)
7. When you're finished working in the worksheet area, click outside the worksheet area.

   The Word toolbars are restored. Your worksheet should have black selection handles around the outside border of the object.

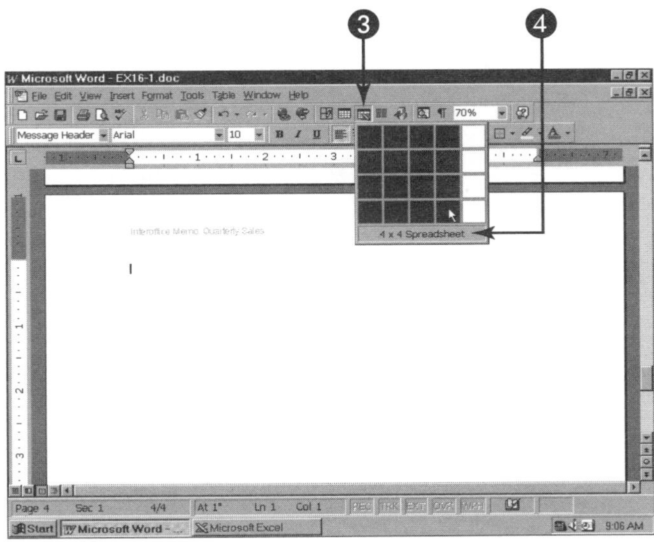

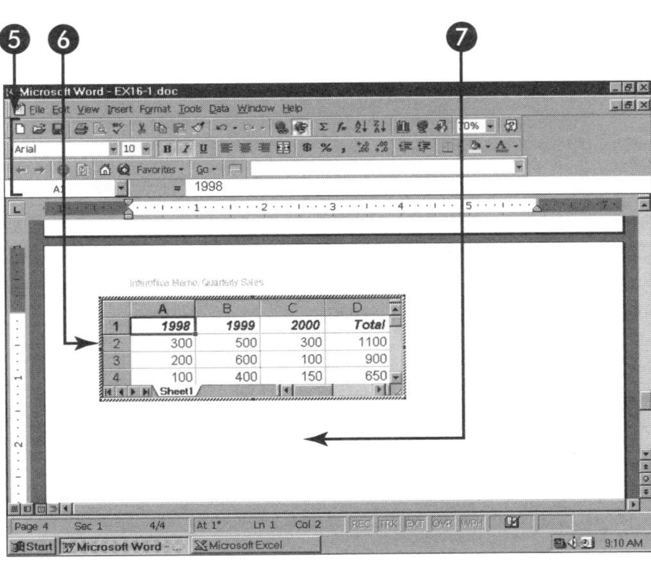

Inserting an Excel chart into Word

To edit the worksheet, you can double-click the worksheet area; the Excel toolbars will appear. Then you can make any changes to your worksheet. Click outside the worksheet area to restore the Word toolbars.

Inserting an Excel chart into a Word document

Not only can you insert a new Excel worksheet in Word, but you can also insert an Excel chart into a Word document in just a few easy steps. Let's insert an Excel column chart in your sales report in Word.

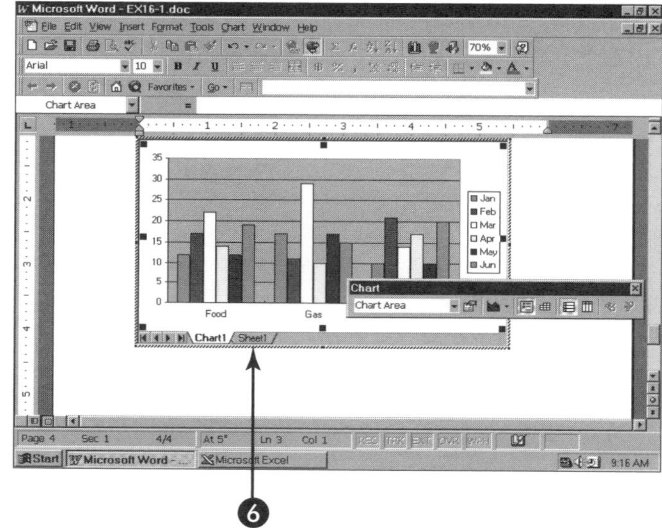

1. Press Ctrl+End to move to the end of the document, and press Enter twice.
2. Select the Insert menu.
3. Click Object.

   The Insert Object dialog box opens. Make sure the Create New tab is selected.
4. In the Object Type list, choose Microsoft Excel Chart.
5. Click OK.

   The Chart toolbar and a chart with placeholder text and numbers appear. The default chart type is a column chart. Notice the chart appears on the Chart 1 tab in the worksheet area. To change the placeholder data in the chart, you need to switch to the worksheet that contains the data that was charted.
6. Click the Sheet 1 tab in the worksheet area.

   A worksheet with columns and rows of data appears. The data is placeholder text with numbers that you can add to, change, or delete altogether. Let's delete the data and then use the worksheet data at the top of page 4 in your memo document.
7. Select all the data in the worksheet, and press Delete. Then enter the data you used previously that appears in Step 6 of Exercise 5.

   As you change the worksheet, the chart changes automatically to reflect the revised data.
8. Click the Chart 1 tab.

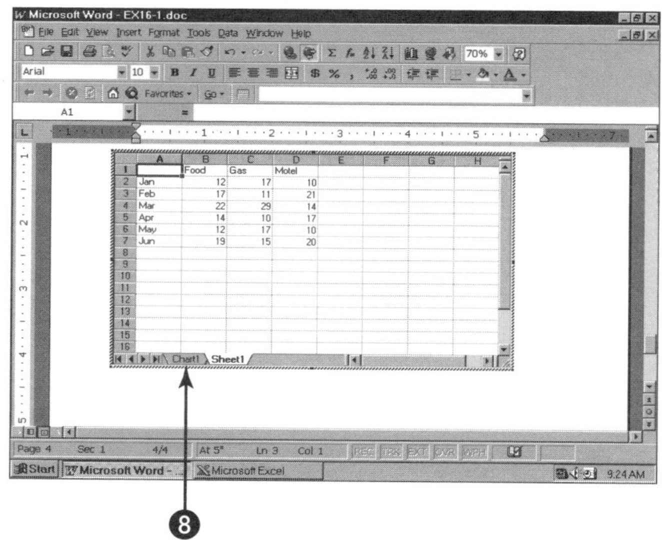

The chart contains the data you entered in the worksheet on the Sheet 1 tab, as you can see in the accompanying figure.

9. Save the file, and then close it.
10. Close Word, and then close Excel.

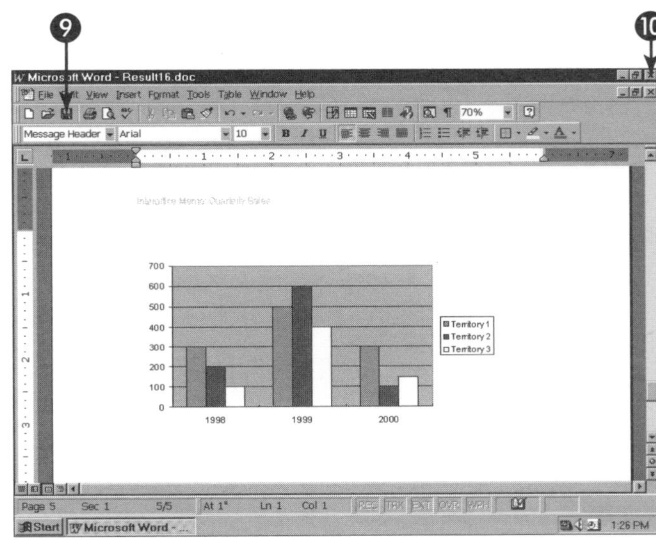

Opening Word files in Outlook

You can open any Office document in Outlook. For the purposes of this lesson, we'll open a Word file in Outlook. Outlook's Journal keeps track of your documents whether you open them in Outlook or in Word. First let's set up Microsoft Outlook so that Journal can track your documents by the date and time they were created or modified. Then we'll open the Word file.

1. From the Windows desktop, double-click the Microsoft Outlook shortcut icon. Or click the Start button on the Windows taskbar and select Programs ➢ Microsoft Outlook.

   This starts Microsoft Outlook.

2. If prompted, choose your profile.

   A user profile contains a group of settings that specify how you are set up to work with Outlook. If you don't know what your user profile is, you can ask your network administrator.

3. Click the Maximize button in the upper right corner of the Outlook window.
4. Select the Tools menu.
5. Click Options.

   The Options dialog box appears.

Opening Word files in Outlook

6 Click the Journal tab.

You see the Journal options.

If this is the first time you're using Outlook, you will see only your own name in the For These Contacts list. Also, if you have the complete Office suite installed, you will also see PowerPoint and Access in the Also Record Files From section.

7 In the Also Record Files From section, click the Microsoft Word checkbox.

This enables Microsoft Outlook to record and track any Microsoft Word documents that you open in Outlook.

8 Click OK.

Now you can open any Office document that is listed in Outlook's Journal. Let's try it.

9 Click Journal in the Outlook Bar.

If this is the first time you choose the Journal component, Outlook might take several minutes to build the journal record. Also, you might get a dialog box asking if you want to AutoArchive. If you do, choose No.

10 Click the + (plus sign) next to Entry Type: Microsoft Word.

11 Double-click any Word file.

The Journal Entry dialog box appears, showing the Word document's shortcut icon at the bottom of the dialog box.

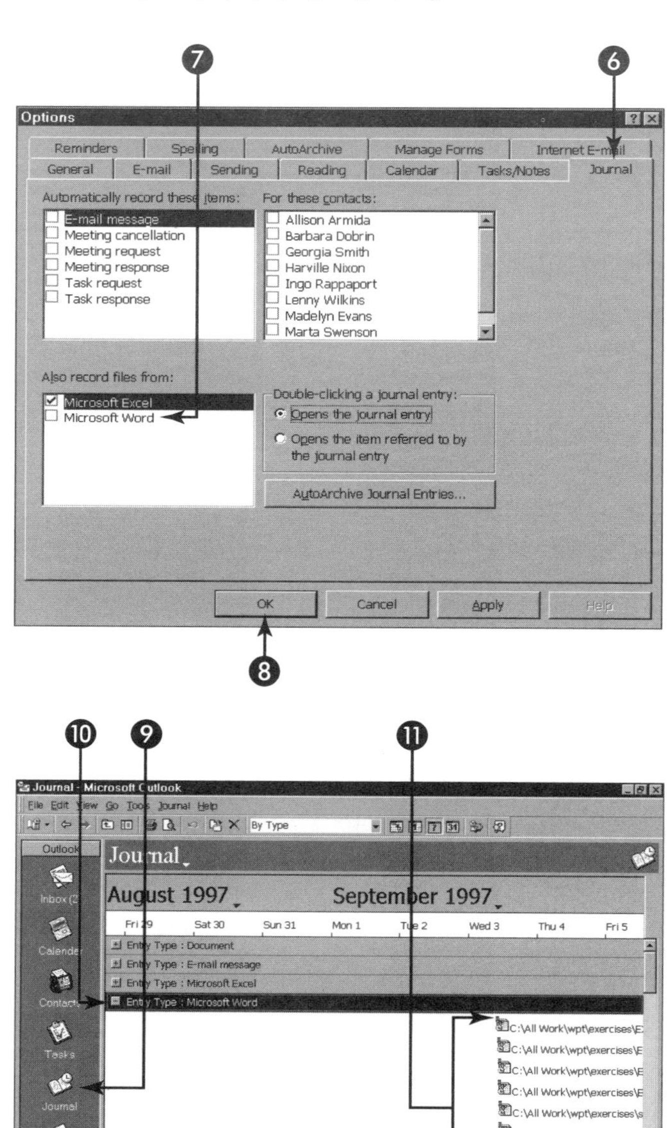

⓬ You can start the timer by clicking the Start Timer button to record any activity you perform on the Word document. Recording the activity is good for keeping track of the amount of time you spend working on a document.

⓭ Double-click the Word document shortcut icon.

Word opens and you see the Word document. At this point, you can make any necessary changes to the Word document.

⓮ Close the document, and then close Word.

⓯ If necessary, click the Pause Timer button to stop the recording process. Then close the Journal Entry dialog box and close Outlook.

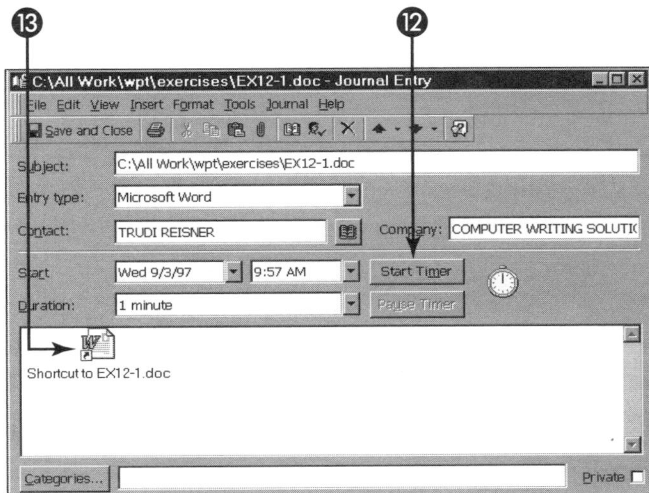

SKILLS CHALLENGE: SHARING INFORMATION IN OFFICE DOCUMENTS

In this final skills challenge exercise, you recap the skills you've learned in this lesson. You integrate an Excel worksheet with a Word document in various ways, insert a new Excel worksheet and chart, and open a Word file in Outlook. EX16-2.DOC contains a Word memo. Answer the bonus questions to review the skills and help you determine your understanding of the topics covered. The answers to the bonus questions are in Appendix C.

❶ Open the file EX16-2.DOC.

❷ Create a hyperlink to move to the Excel worksheet in your Personal Trainer folder named EX16-4.XLS.

❸ Use the hyperlink to move to the Excel worksheet.

❹ Copy the Excel worksheet.

❺ Paste the worksheet to the end of your Word memo.

❻ Insert a page break.

Skills challenge

7. Link the Excel worksheet to the Word memo.

Name the two documents involved in linking or embedding Office documents.

8. Insert another page break.
9. Embed the Excel worksheet as an object in the Word memo.

What is the difference between linking and embedding Office documents?

10. Insert a page break.
11. Insert a new Excel worksheet into your Word memo.
12. At the end of the last page in your memo, insert an Excel column chart using the data in the worksheet you just inserted at the top of the page.

When you insert an Excel chart as an object in an Office document, what are the two items you see onscreen?

13. Switch to Outlook.
14. Open a Word file in Outlook.

Which Outlook component tracks your Office documents?

15. Close the document.
16. Exit Microsoft Outlook.
17. Exit Microsoft Excel.
18. Save the changes in the Word document.
19. Close the files.
20. Exit Microsoft Word.

TROUBLESHOOTING

You've finished this lesson and learned about integrating Office documents. This table offers solutions to several problems you might have encountered when learning these skills.

Problem	Solution
I copied and pasted data from an Excel worksheet into my Word document, and then I made changes to the worksheet in Excel. But the worksheet in Word didn't change to reflect the new data.	Instead of copying and pasting, you need to link the Excel worksheet to the Word document in order to update the worksheet automatically. To do so, select the Edit ➢ Paste Special command and the Paste Link option in the Paste Special dialog box. In the As list box, make sure that Microsoft Excel Worksheet Object is selected.
After inserting a new Excel worksheet in Word and entering data in the worksheet, the Excel toolbars remain onscreen and I can't get the Word toolbars to appear.	Click outside the worksheet area to display the Word toolbars.
I embedded the wrong worksheet from the workbook in my Word document.	When you embed a worksheet object, the entire workbook is inserted. To display the correct worksheet in Word, double-click the worksheet area in the Word document, click the sheet tab you want, and then click outside of the worksheet area in Word.
Outlook's Journal doesn't record any of my Word documents.	You need to tell Outlook to track your Word documents. In Outlook, select Tools ➢ Options and click the Journal tab. In the Also Record Files From section, click the Microsoft Word checkbox. Then click OK.

Wrap up

WRAP UP

In this lesson, you practiced the following skills:

- Creating a hyperlink to move between Office documents
- Copying and pasting between Office documents
- Linking Office documents
- Embedding Office documents
- Inserting an Excel worksheet into a Word document
- Inserting an Excel chart into a Word document
- Opening Word files in Outlook

If you want more practice with these skills, embed an Excel worksheet into a Word annual report.

In the appendixes that follow, you are shown how to install Word 97 in Appendix A; you are given practice projects to do in Appendix B; you are given the answers to the bonus questions in Appendix C; and you are shown how to install the CD-ROM that accompanies this book in Appendix D. Following the appendices is a glossary that defines the Word 97 terms you might want to familiarize yourself with.

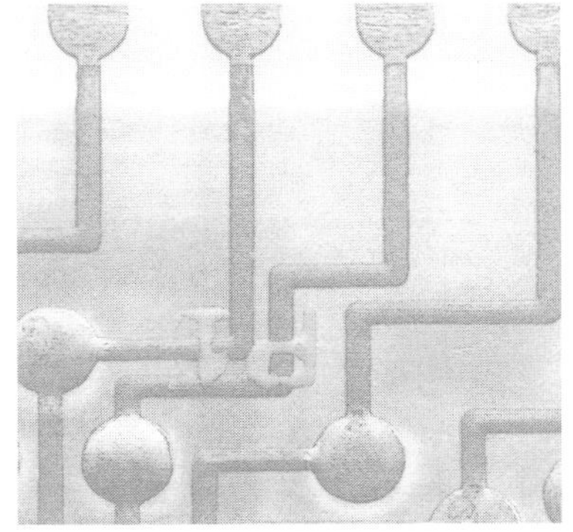

Installing Microsoft Word 97

Installing Microsoft Word 97 on your computer is a relatively simple and straightforward procedure. You can use the installation instructions in this appendix to install the stand-alone version of Microsoft Word or the Microsoft Office version. The instructions also include information on upgrading Microsoft Word from earlier versions of the program, such as Word for Windows 95.

GET READY

These instructions assume that you are loading Word 97 from a CD-ROM, that your CD-ROM drive is labeled (D:), and that you have sufficient space to support a typical installation (about 46MB). It is also assumed that you are running Windows 95.

Whether you have Microsoft Office 97 or Word 97, here's how you install Word on your computer's hard disk:

1. Turn on your computer and load Windows.
2. Insert the Word CD in your computer CD-ROM drive (usually referred to as the (D:) drive).

Word is equipped with an AutoRun feature. Under certain circumstances (such as, the CD-ROM disc is in your CD-ROM drive when you boot up your computer), you do not have to do Steps 3 through 7. The Microsoft Word 97 dialog box appears on your screen automatically. Click Install Microsoft Word. The Welcome dialog box mentioned in Step 7 appears. Go directly to Step 8.

3. Open the Start menu.
4. Select Settings.
5. Select Control Panel.
6. When the Control Panel window opens, double-click the Add/Remove Programs icon.
7. From the Install/Uninstall tab, click the Install button.

   The Install A Program from a Floppy or CD-ROM dialog box appears.
8. Choose Next to proceed.

   The Run Installation Program dialog box appears, confirming the location of the Word setup file (D:\Setup.exe).
9. Choose Finish to begin the installation.

   After a moment, the Microsoft Word 97 Setup screen appears, as shown in the accompanying illustration.

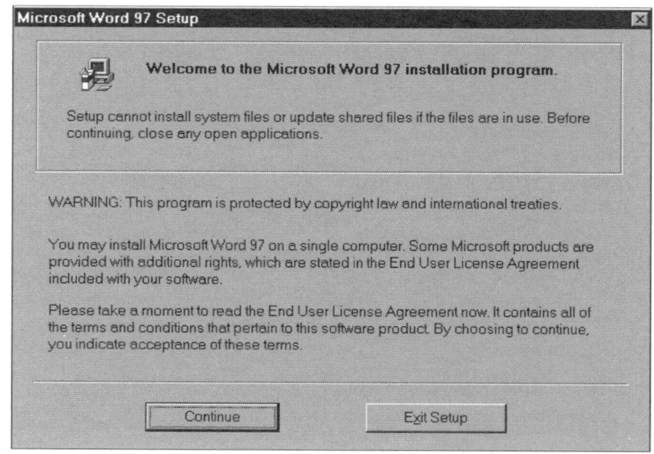

⑩ Choose Continue.

The Name and Organization Information dialog box appears, as shown in the accompanying illustration.

⑪ Type your name and, if appropriate, your organization.

⑫ Then, click OK.

Word asks you to confirm the name and organization you entered.

⑬ Click OK.

Word asks you to enter your CD-KEY which is the Product ID number. You'll find the CD-KEY on a label placed on the back of your CD-ROM jewel case.

⑭ Type **CD-KEY**.

⑮ Click OK.

Your Product ID number appears onscreen. Make a note of this number; you need to provide it if you call Microsoft technical support.

⑯ Click OK to proceed.

The dialog box in the accompanying illustration appears.

This dialog box gives you the option of changing the folder where Microsoft Word is installed. Unless you have a previous version of this program that you want to keep, you should accept the default folder name. If you want to have the program installed to a different folder, choose Change Folder and enter a new folder name. Then click OK.

⑰ Click OK to accept the default folder name.

Another dialog box opens, offering you a choice of three types of installation (if you're installing Word for the first time).

- **Typical** installs all of Word's features, as well as the most commonly used templates. This is the recommended installation for a less experienced user.

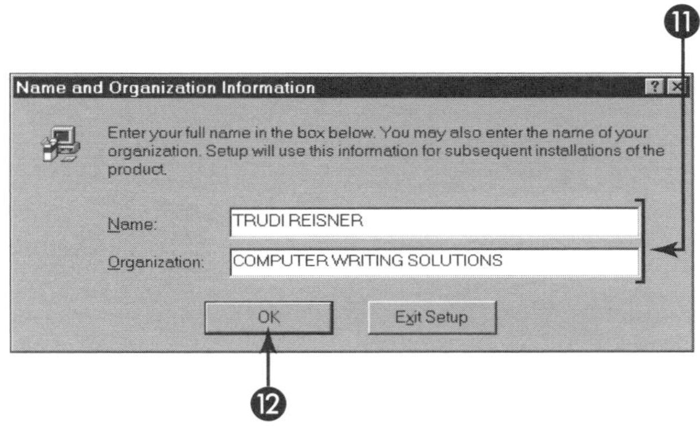

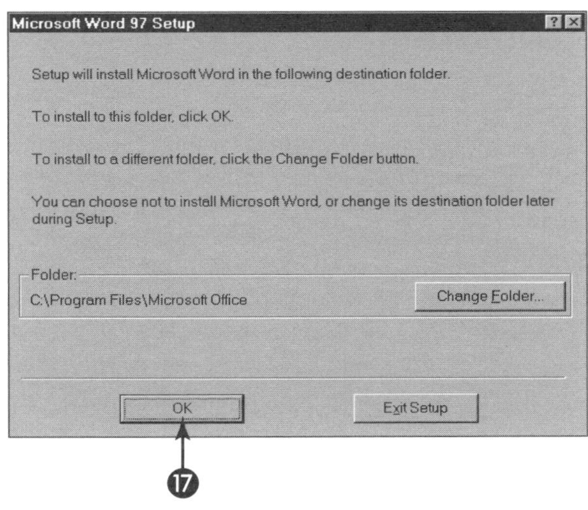

- **Custom** installs only the Word features you choose. It gives you an opportunity to pick and choose what you want to install. This is an option if you don't have enough memory for the entire program, or if you don't need certain components. If you make this choice, you see a Custom dialog box, like that in the accompanying illustration. You can deselect anything you don't want to install.
- **Run from CD-ROM** enables you to run most of Word from your CD-ROM drive. However, this makes running the software slow and much less efficient. This choice appears only if you're installing Word for the first time.

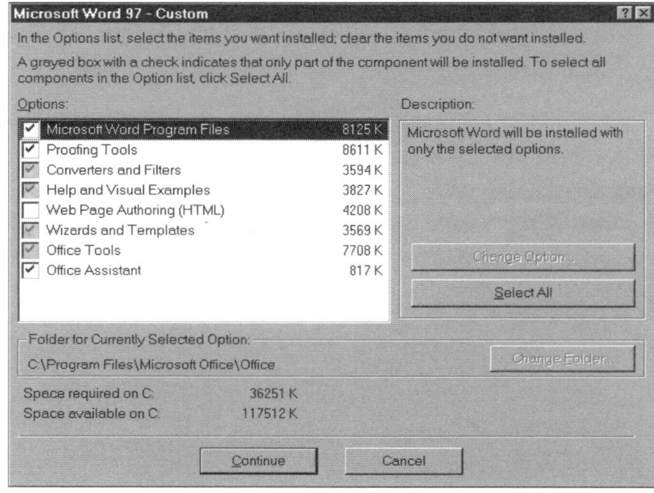

18 Click Typical.

The Typical dialog box appears, as shown in the accompanying illustration.

Check the Space required and Space available information at the bottom of the dialog box and be sure you have enough room on your hard drive to install Word. The components that are not selected in the list of Options in this dialog box can always be installed later by running this installation program again. For now, it's best to accept the default typical installation options.

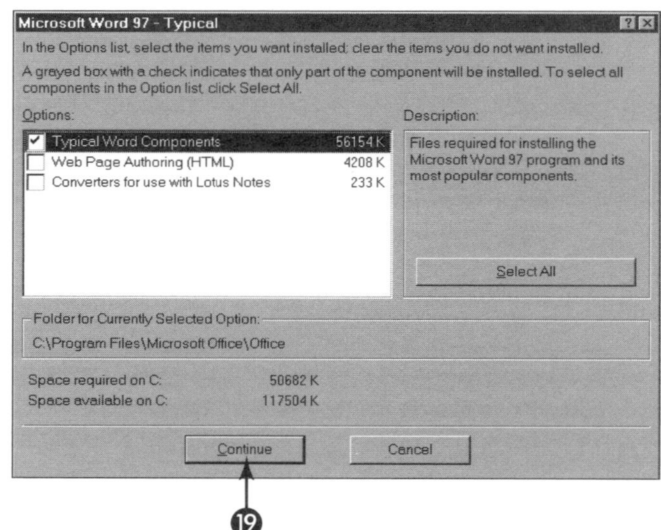

19 Choose Continue.

If you have a previous version of Word installed on your computer, you may see an Upgrade message at this point. This gives you the option of overwriting old versions or keeping them on your computer. Be aware that double versions of Word are likely to use large amounts of space on your hard drive, and choosing to retain older versions may make it impossible to install the new Word. If you don't think you need the older versions, it's best to remove old components when the Upgrade Wizard appears.

The screen in the accompanying illustration appears, tracking the installation with a percentage complete bar. (If you install Word from disks instead of a CD-ROM, you are asked to insert the disks in sequence during this procedure.) It may take several minutes for the installation to complete; it varies, depending on the speed and configuration of your computer.

Some information about Word features appears at the top of this screen. You may want to read this information to begin to familiarize yourself with the new features of Word 97. When the installation is complete, you see the accompanying screen. If you are installing Word for the first time, you will see the Restart Windows button. If you are upgrading Word, you will see the OK button. If you have a modem installed and want to register your software online, you can select Online Registration at this time.

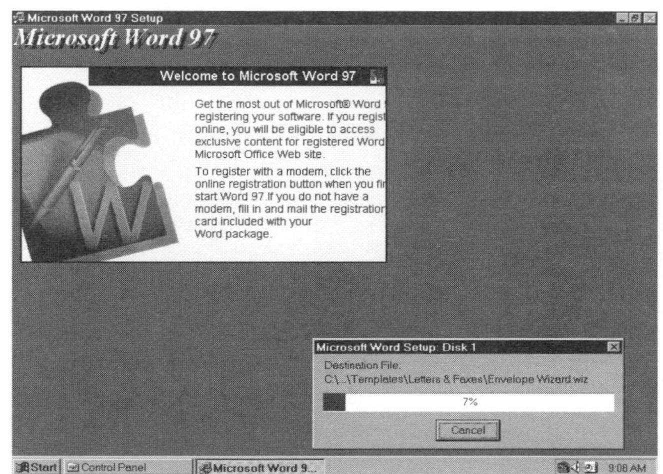

⑳ Choose Restart Windows or OK to complete the installation.

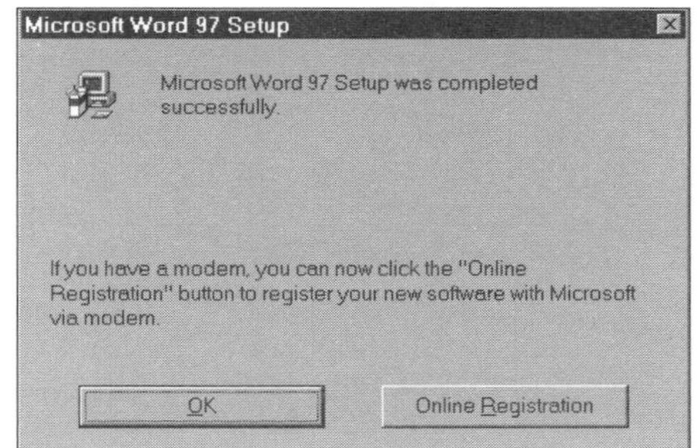

Windows has installed the Word program files on your computer, creating a program group icon called Microsoft Word on the Programs menu in Windows (if that's the program group you chose during setup).

Practice Projects

You did a great job getting through this book and picking up all the basic skills you need to become productive with Word 97. However, as with any achievement, you have to stay in practice or you lose all you've gained. Now that you've completed *Word 97 One Step at a Time,* it's important that you set yourself a regular exercise regime so your Word muscles don't get flabby.

The first few days and weeks after learning new skills are the most important. If you can spend 20 minutes each day practicing with the Word product over the next week or two, you'll not only reinforce your learning, but you'll also discover other, more advanced Word features and devise your own shortcuts for getting things done.

Appendix B suggests some projects you might use for follow-up practice. We've included projects that are useful in your daily life, such as creating a letter and updating your résumé.

PROJECT 1

Type a letter to your local mayor suggesting an idea you have to improve a policy (such as recycling) in your town. Include a letterhead with your name and address. Use a bulleted list to state the reasons why the improvement would benefit the residents of your town. Consider publishing the letter as a Web page on the Internet. A sample letter appears in the accompanying figure.

Review Lessons 2 and 8 for details about creating a letter and a bulleted list. Look at Lesson 15 for assistance with creating a Web page in Word.

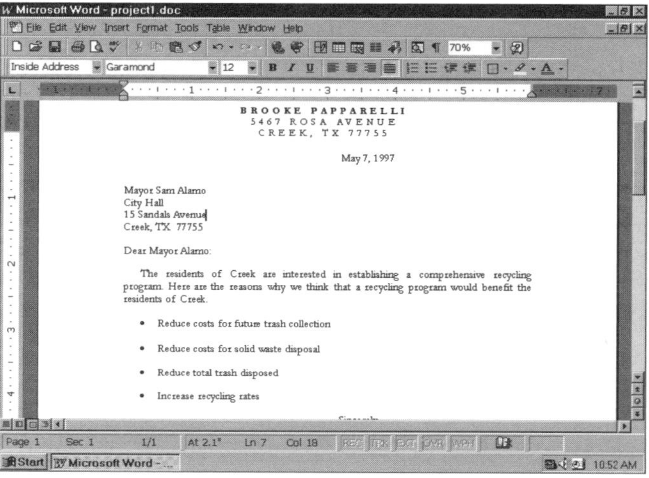

PROJECT 2

Type a memo to your coworkers informing them about your Internet address at work and home. A sample memo appears in the accompanying figure.

Need assistance with creating a memo heading? Go back to Lesson 5.

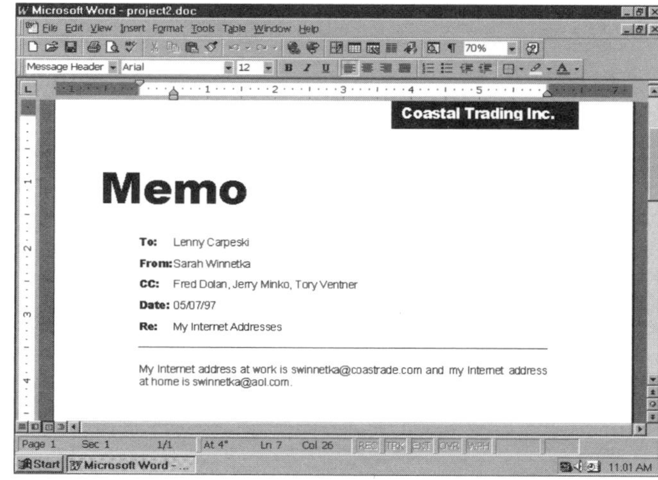

PROJECT 3

Create a table for the inventory of valuables in your home for insurance purposes. Add the following column headings: Item, Description, Replacement Value, Receipt (to indicate whether you have a receipt on file for the item). Enter information for each heading. When you've finished, print a copy and put it in a safe place. A sample inventory table appears in the accompanying figure.

Lesson 12 can help you prepare the table. Lesson 13 can help you with the printing.

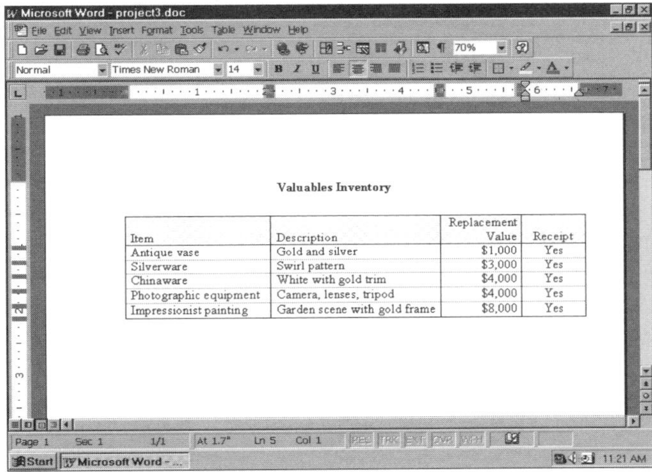

PROJECT 4

Update your résumé. Use borders, clip art, WordArt, and indentation tools to give your résumé a more polished look. Use the Word column or table feature to create side-by-side information, such as the dates of a job and its description. A sample résumé appears in the accompanying figure.

Lesson 10 can help you with graphic elements for this project.

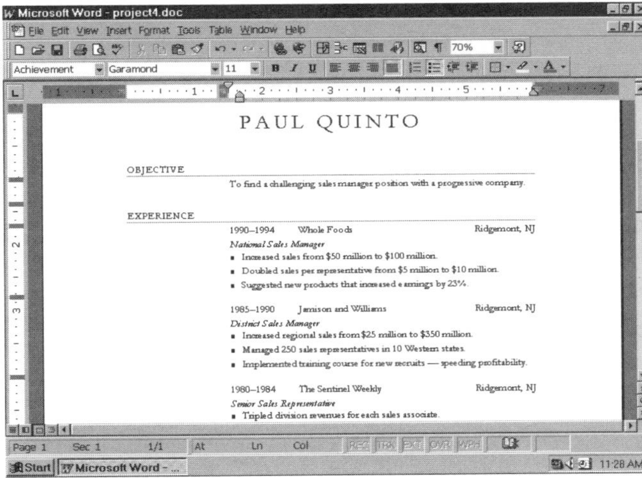

PROJECT 5

Create an itinerary for your next vacation. Include the destination, method of travel, activities, and costs. Create a table for the activities and costs. A sample itinerary appears in the accompanying figure

Word's table feature is covered in Lesson 12.

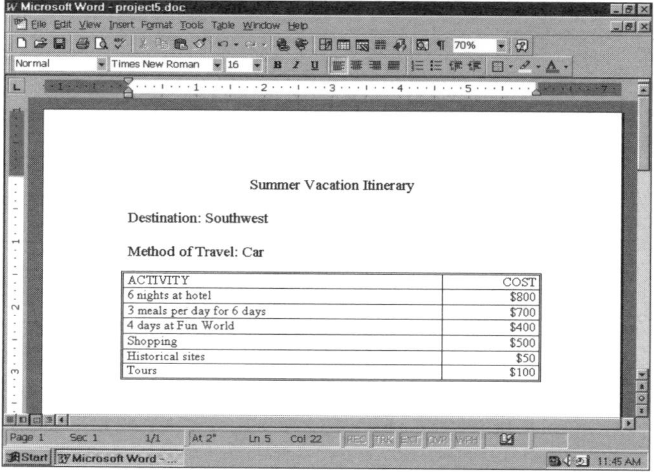

PROJECT 6

Write a two-column family newsletter in Word. Include a section on genealogy, family traditions, favorite family recipes, and amusing anecdotes. Get the family involved in thinking of content and save this one for your grandchildren to enjoy! A sample family newsletter appears in the accompanying figure.

The skills you learned in Lesson 11 come in handy for this project.

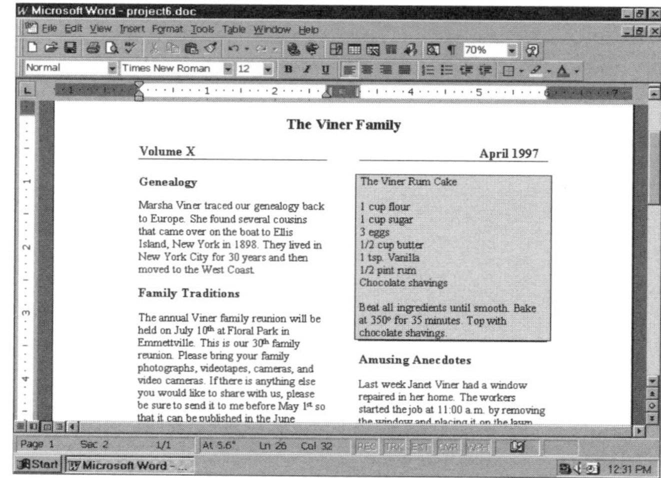

PROJECT 7

Create a mail merge form letter for your holiday greeting to friends. Personalize fields for your friends' first and last names and addresses. Put a line in the letter mentioning the amount of time since you last got together with your friend, and create a field to personalize that information in the merge. A sample mail merge form letter appears in the accompanying figure.

Lesson 14 can refresh your memory about the steps involved in creating a mail merge form letter.

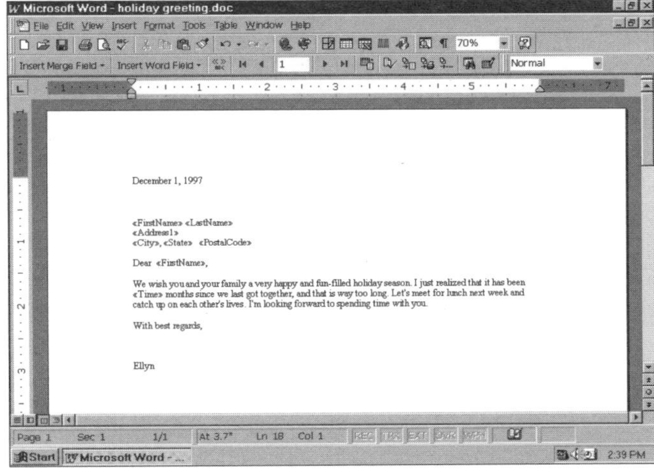

PROJECT 8

Put together a contract for selling a high-ticket item such as your car. Compile a set of three standard paragraphs that contain lines for filling in the form. Number each paragraph. The first paragraph defines who the seller and buyer are. The second paragraph discusses what the buyer agrees to. And the last paragraph mentions what the seller agrees to. A sample contract appears in the accompanying figure.

In Lesson 8, you can get help on creating a numbered list.

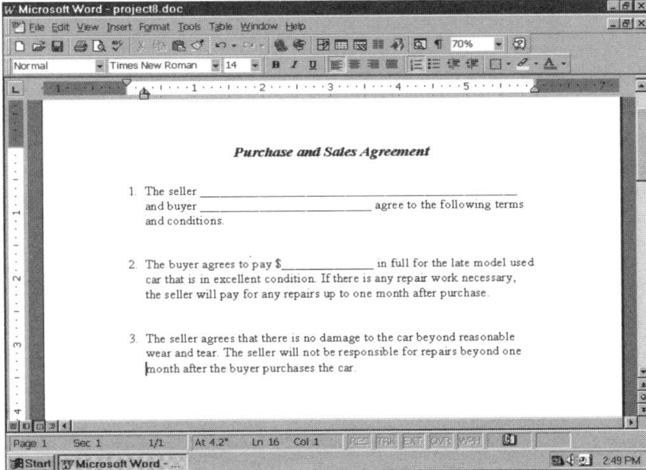

PROJECT 9

Create a multiple-page report that contains information about your neighborhood crime watch program. List neighbors involved in the program, their responsibilities, and a crime activities log for the police. Save your special formatting in a style. Use the proofreading tools to check your work. A sample report appears in the accompanying figure.

Lesson 3 provides some details about navigating documents and creating page breaks. Lesson 9 can help you with creating a style. Review Lesson 6 for tips on proofreading your report.

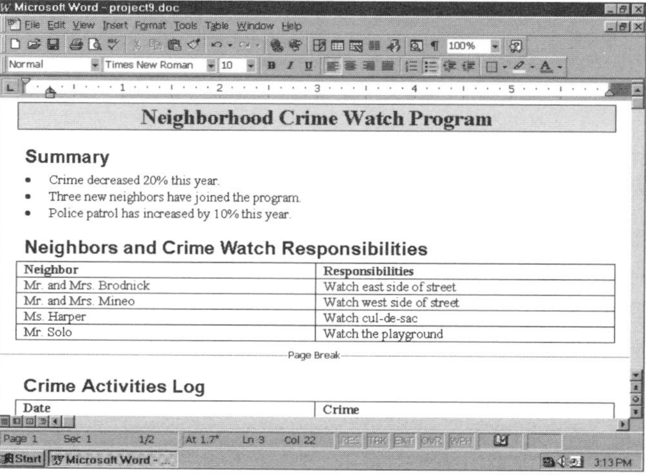

PROJECT 10

Create coupons that you can use for birthday and holiday gifts. They can include house chores, favors, and just nice things you would like to do for your family members and friends. Use clip art and borders to spruce up the coupons. A sample coupon appears in the accompanying figure.

Go to Lesson 10 for valuable information about adding borders to your coupons.

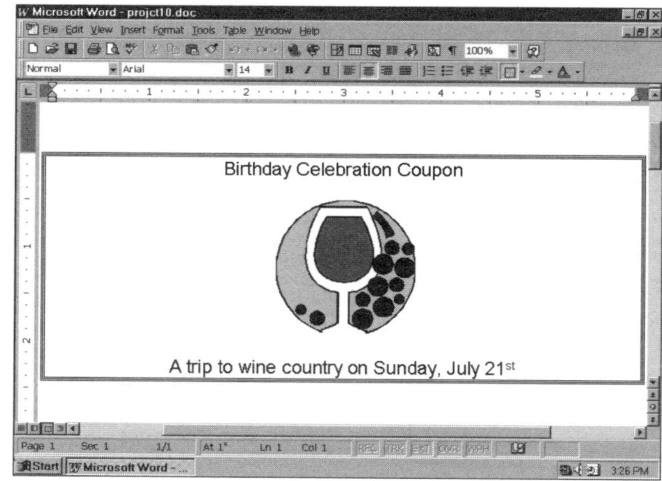

PROJECT 11

Create a menu to add flair to your dinner parties. Impress your guests with a full-course menu to read while they're eating the hors d'oeuvres. Use a script font and center every line to give a fancy look to your menu. A sample menu appears in the accompanying figure.

Need help with fonts and centered text? Take a look at Lesson 7.

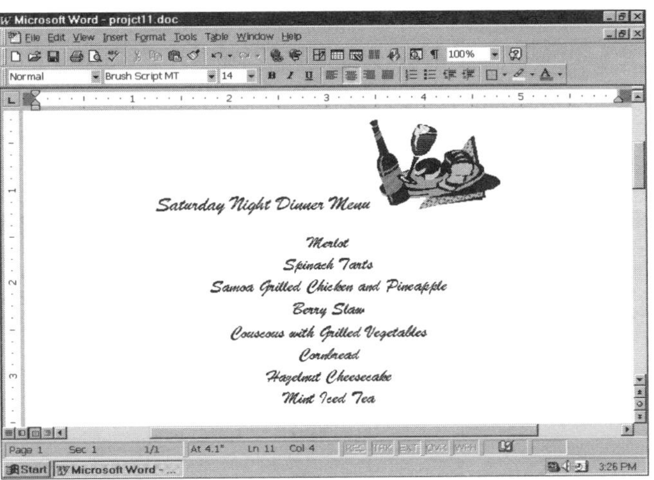

PROJECT 12

Create a fax cover sheet for your faxes. Use a 16-point bold font for the title of the cover sheet. Add borders and boxes to create a comments area. Draw small squares to use as checkboxes so you can indicate how quickly you want your recipients to respond. A sample fax cover sheet appears in the accompanying figure.

Review Lesson 7 for information on changing fonts. Go to Lesson 10 for help with drawing squares.

Feel free to put on your thinking cap and come up with other projects. The important thing is to keep at it, and take advantage of all your hard work with *Word 97 One Step at a Time*.

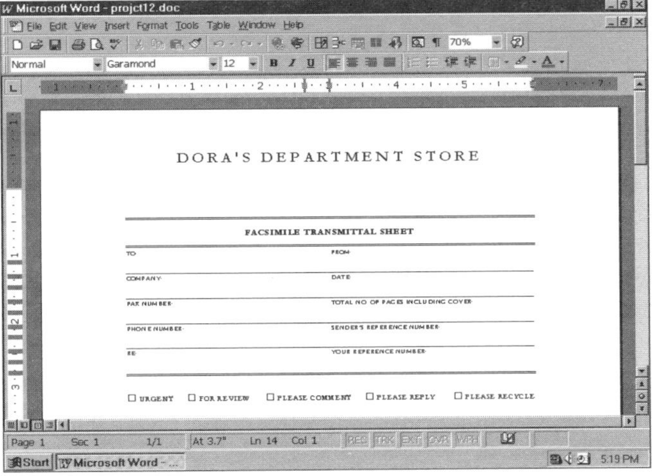

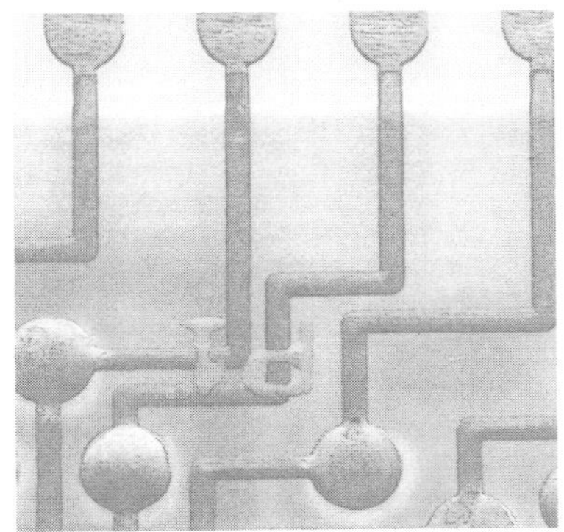

Answers to Bonus Questions

LESSON 1: MEET MICROSOFT WORD

The Minimize button has a minus sign, the Maximize button contains a window, and the Close button has an X. These buttons are located in the upper right corner of a document window.

An ellipsis next to a menu command indicates that a dialog box appears when you select the command.

To find out what a toolbar button does, leave the mouse pointer on the button for several seconds to display the button's name.

To exit Word, you can double-click the Word Control menu icon, press Ctrl+F4, or click the Close (X) button.

LESSON 2: CREATING AND SAVING DOCUMENTS

The difference between the Backspace key and the Delete key is that the Backspace key deletes characters to the left of the insertion point, and the Delete key deletes characters to the right of the insertion point.

To display or hide paragraph marks in your document, click the Show/Hide ¶ button on the Standard toolbar.

To save a file as a Word 6.0 document, select File ➢ Save As, enter a name in the File Name box, choose Word 6.0/95 (*.doc) in the Save as Type list box, and click OK.

The fastest way to close a document is to click the Close button in the upper right corner of the document window.

To view file details in the Open dialog box, click the Details button on the Open toolbar.

When Overtype mode is turned on, the OVR indicator appears in black on the Status bar at the bottom of the Word window.

LESSON 3: MOVING AROUND A DOCUMENT

To scroll to the far right side of the document, click and drag the scroll box on the horizontal scroll bar to the far right.

The key combination for moving to the bottom of the document is Ctrl+End.

A manual page break contains a dotted line and the words *Page Break*.

To remove the Find and Replace dialog box from the screen, click the Close button in the Find and Replace dialog box.

LESSON 4: CHANGING VIEWS

The default view for a document is Normal view.

Page Layout view can help you when you have a lot of formatting changes and want to see the results as you make each change.

When you want to get a closer look at your document, select a higher magnification percentage.

The view that shows you what a document roughly looks like as a Web page on the Internet is called the Online Layout view.

LESSON 5: REVISING TEXT

When you delete text, the text isn't stored on the Clipboard. When you cut or copy text, the text is stored on the Clipboard.

When you copy or cut text, it remains on the Clipboard until you copy or cut text again.

You can undo more than one action by clicking the Undo drop-down arrow in the Standard toolbar. You'll see a list of your actions, in order from the most recent to the least recent. You can undo them in this order only. Select the action(s) you want to undo, and Word reverses your action(s).

You can replace text selectively by clicking the Find Next button, and then clicking Replace to replace the occurrence or clicking the Find Next button again to skip it.

LESSON 6: PROOFREADING TEXT

If spelling checker flags a proper noun, you can choose Ignore to ignore this single occurrence, Ignore All to ignore all occurrences of the word, or Add to add the word to the dictionary.

The easiest method for correcting grammar errors is to right-click the wavy green-underlined phrase and choose an option from the Grammar shortcut menu.

The three methods for selecting a word you want to look up in the thesaurus are: 1) click before the word, 2) click within the word, and 3) double-click the word.

LESSON 7: FORMATTING FONTS AND PARAGRAPHS

The two fonts used in the document are Times New Roman and Courier New. Each font was applied with the Font box on the Formatting toolbar.

The quickest way to indent paragraphs based on the default 1/2" tab stops is to use the Increase Indent button on the Formatting toolbar.

Besides using the Center button on the Formatting toolbar, you can select Format➢Paragraph, and choose the Center alignment option in the Paragraph dialog box.

To change line spacing using the menu command, select Format➢Paragraph.

LESSON 8: CREATING LISTS, HEADERS, AND FOOTERS

The three ways to create a bulleted list are: 1) let Word create the bulleted list as you type, 2) use the Format Bullets and Numbering command, and 3) use the Bullets button on the Formatting toolbar.

When you add page numbers to a document, Word offers five alignment types: Left, Center, Right, Inside, and Outside.

After you insert page numbers, the document is in Page Layout view.

To move back and forth between the header and footer areas, click the Switch Between Header and Footer button on the Header and Footer toolbar or use the up and down arrows.

LESSON 9: TAKING SHORTCUTS

The name of the default template attached to every new document you create is NORMAL.DOT.

In addition to the style description, you can preview the paragraph and character formatting in the Style dialog box.

You can click the Format button in the New Style dialog box to add more formatting elements to a style.

The mouse pointer shape that you see when you perform the Format Painter operation is a paintbrush.

To create an AutoText entry, select Insert ➢ AutoText, and select New.

LESSON 10: SHAPING UP WITH GRAPHICS

A selected object has squares called selection handles on its sides and corners.

The purpose of the WordArt toolbar is to help you edit and format your WordArt text.

To move an object, select it. Then move the mouse pointer over the object and when you see the mouse pointer arrow and four-headed arrow, drag the object to the new location.

A quick way to resize an object is to drag its selection handles in the direction you want.

To display the patterns palette, select the Fill Effect command on the Fill Color menu and click the Patterns tab.

LESSON 11: CREATING COLUMNS

The maximum number of columns you can create using the Columns button on the Standard toolbar is four.

The Width and Spacing feature in the Columns dialog box lets you change the size of columns.

To remove an unwanted border, click the No Border button in the Border toolbar.

LESSON 12: ORGANIZING INFORMATION WITH TABLES AND OUTLINES

The mouse pointer symbol looks like a pen when you're in Draw mode.

You can press Shift+Tab to move backward from one cell to another.

When you want to insert new rows, place the insertion point where you want the first new row to appear.

The mouse pointer that appears when you move to the top of a column to select an entire column is a thick down arrow.

The mouse pointer that appears when you move to a column border to adjust column width is a double vertical bar with a left and right arrow.

LESSON 13: PRINTING YOUR WORD DOCUMENT

The File ➢ Page Setup command lets you change the layout options.

To print specific separate pages 1 and 3, you would enter 1,3 in the Page text box.

To print envelopes and labels, select Tools ➢ Envelopes and Labels.

LESSON 14: WORKING WITH MAIL MERGE

The three major functions of the Mail Merge Helper dialog box are creating a main document, creating a data source, and merging these two files.

If you already have a data source to which you want to add records, click the Edit Data Source button in the Mail Merge Helper dialog box.

To see the first record, click the First Record button at the bottom of the Data Form dialog box.

To delete a record, display the record in the Data Form dialog box, and click the Delete button.

LESSON 15: USING WORD TO CREATE A WEB PAGE

When text is displayed in Online Layout view, it is larger, and it wraps to the View window.

You can add an FTP location by selecting File ➢ Save As, clicking the Save In drop-down arrow, and choosing Add/Modify FTP Locations in the Save In list. In the Add/Modify FTP Locations dialog box, type the FTP site name, choose a Log On As option, and click OK.

To reload and update the current Web page, click the Refresh Current Page button on the Web toolbar.

The two documents are called the source document and the target document.

Linking documents allows you to display a source document in a target document, but it does not allow you to change source document data from within the target document. To update data in a target document, you must go to the source document and make your changes there. Embedding an Office document as an object allows you to make your changes to the source document's data directly in the target document.

You see a chart and a chart toolbar.

Journal tracks your Office documents.

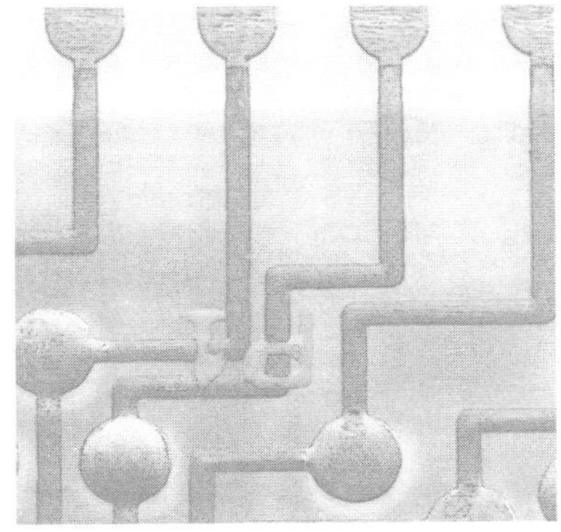

What's on the CD-ROM

The CD-ROM in the back of the book includes the exclusive *One Step at a Time On-Demand* software. This interactive software coaches you through the exercises in the book's lessons while you work on a computer at your own pace.

USING THE ONE STEP AT A TIME ON-DEMAND INTERACTIVE SOFTWARE

One Step at a Time On-Demand interactive software includes the exercises in the book so that you can search for information about how to perform a function or complete a task. You can run the software alone or in combination with the book. The software consists of three modes: Demo, Teacher, and Concurrent. In addition, the Concept option provides an overview of each exercise.

- **Demo** mode provides a movie-style demonstration of the same steps that are presented in the book's exercises, and works with the sample exercise files that are included on the CD-ROM in the One Step folder.
- **Teacher** mode simulates the software environment and permits you to interactively follow the exercises in the book's lessons.
- **Concurrent** mode enables you to use the *One Step at a Time-On Demand* features while you work within the actual Word 97 environment. This unique interactive mode provides audio instructions, and directs you to take the correct actions as you work through the exercises. (Concurrent mode may not be available to all exercises.)

Installing the software

The *One Step at a Time* software can be installed on Windows 95 and Windows NT 4.0. To install the interactive software on your computer, follow these steps:

1. Place the *Word 97 One Step at a Time* CD-ROM in your CD-ROM drive.
2. Launch Windows (if you haven't already).
3. Click the Start menu.
4. Select Run. The Run dialog box appears.
5. Type **D:\Setup.exe** (where D is your CD-ROM drive) in the Run dialog box.

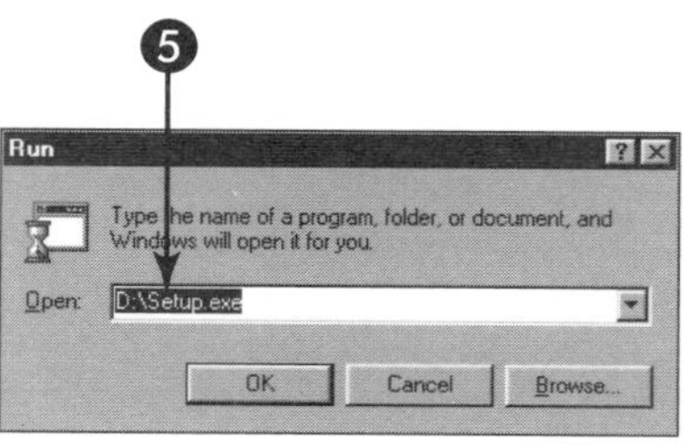

6. Click OK to run the setup procedure. The On-Demand Installation dialog box appears.
7. Click Continue. The On-Demand Installation Options dialog box appears.
8. Click the Full/Network radio button (if this option is not already selected).

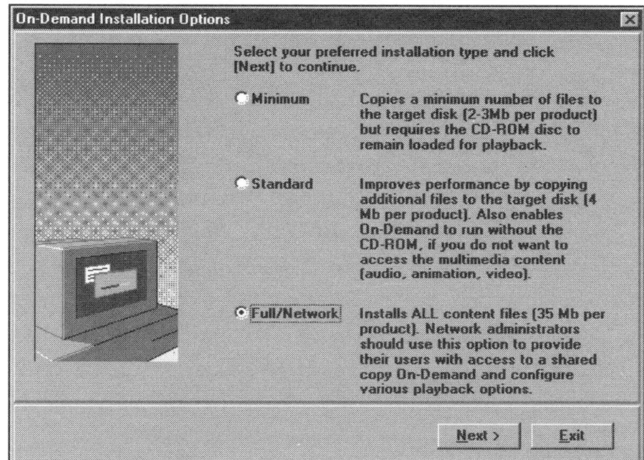

Full/Network installation requires approximately 150MB of hard disk space. If you don't have enough hard disk space, click the Standard radio button to choose Standard installation. If you choose standard installation, you should always insert the CD-ROM when you start the software to hear sound.

9. Click Next. The Determine Installation Drive and Directory dialog box appears.
10. Choose the default drive and directory that appears, or click Change to choose a different drive and directory.
11. Click Next. The Product Selection dialog box appears, which enables you to verify the software you want to install.
12. Click Finish to complete the installation. The On-Demand Installation dialog box displays the progress of the installation. After the installation, the Multiuser Pack Registration dialog box appears.
13. Enter information in the Multiuser Pack Registration dialog box.
14. Click OK. The On-Demand Installation dialog box appears.
15. Click OK to confirm the installation has been successfully completed.

■ Running Demo, Teacher or Concurrent mode

If you run the One Step at a Time-On Demand software in Windows 98, we recommend you don't work in Teacher or Concurrent modes unless you turn off the Active Desktop feature. However, Teacher mode and Concurrent mode may not work properly at all in Windows 98. At the time of the writing of this book, the final release of Windows 98 wasn't available and we couldn't test all the topics in Teacher mode and Concurrent mode.

Once you've installed the software, you can view the text of the book and follow interactively the steps in each exercise. To run Demo mode, Teacher mode, or Concurrent mode, follow these steps:

1. From the Windows desktop, click the Start menu.
2. Select Programs ➢ IDG Books Worldwide ➢ Word 97 One Step at a Time. A small On-Demand toolbar appears in the upper-right corner of your screen.
3. Launch Word 97.
4. The On-Demand Reminder dialog box appears, telling you that the On-Demand software is active. If you don't want to display the dialog box, deselect the Show Reminder check box. Then, click OK.
5. Click the icon of the professor. The Interactive Training — Lesson Selection dialog box appears.
6. Select the Contents tab, if it isn't selected already. The contents appear, divided into four parts.

   Please select the Module option, and follow the software using that option (rather than All Topics).
7. Click the plus icon next to the part you want to explore. Lessons appear. The list of lessons corresponds to the lessons in the book.
8. Click the plus icon next to the lesson you want to explore. Topics appear.

   If you wish to work in Concurrent mode, start with the first topic of the lesson, because the software will direct you to open a specific file which you will use to complete the steps in that lesson.
9. Double-click a topic of your choice. A menu appears.
10. Select Concept, Demo, Concurrent (if available), or Teacher.
11. Follow the onscreen prompts to use the interactive software and work through the steps.

In Demo mode, you only need to perform actions that appear in red. Otherwise, the software automatically demonstrates the actions for you. All you need to do is read the information that appears onscreen. (Holding down the Shift key pauses the program; releasing the Shift key activates the program.) In Teacher mode, you need to follow the directions and perform the actions that appear on screen.

GETTING THE MOST OUT OF USING THE ONE STEP AT A TIME SOFTWARE

We strongly recommend that your read the topics in the book while using the software (especially while working in Concurrent mode). In those instances where the onscreen instructions don't match the book's instructions exactly, or when the software appears to stop before completing a task, the book will provide the instructions necessary for you to continue.

STOPPING THE PROGRAM

To stop running the program at any time, press Esc to return to the Interactive Training — Lesson Selection dialog box. (To restart the software, click the Professor icon in this toolbar).

EXITING THE PROGRAM

To exit the program, press Esc when the Interactive Training — Lesson Selection dialog box appears. The On-Demand toolbar appears in the upper right corner of your screen. Click the icon that displays the lightning bolt image. A menu appears. Choose Exit. The On-Demand — Exit dialog box appears. Click Yes to exit On-Demand.

INSTALLING THE EXERCISE FILES

To access the exercise files for the lessons in this book, you'll need to set up a folder for the exercise files on your hard drive (also covered in Lesson 1). Follow these steps:

1. Double-click the My Computer icon on your desktop.
2. In the My Computer window, double-click the hard drive (C:).
3. Select the File menu.
4. Click New.
5. Choose Folder from the submenu.

   A new folder appears at the end of the list, with the name New Folder.
6. Type **One Step** to name the folder.
7. Press Enter.
8. Place the *Word 97 One Step at a Time* CD-ROM into the CD-ROM drive.
9. In the My Computer window, double-click the CD-ROM icon to open the drive where you inserted the disc.
10. In the CD-ROM window, copy the folder named Exercise by selecting it and pressing Ctrl-C. Then, close the CD-ROM window and all other open windows.
11. Double-click My Computer.
12. Double-click the hard drive (C:).
13. Double-click the One Step folder.
14. Paste the Exercise folder into the One Step folder by pressing Ctrl-V. All of the exercise files are now located within the Exercise folder, inside the One Step folder.

USING THE EXERCISE FILES

You need to make sure that you have removed the Read Only attribute from the file(s) you copied to your hard drive before you start using those files. Otherwise, when you attempt to save your work, your screen will display an error message. To remove the attribute, open the Exercise folder (inside the One Step folder) on your hard drive. Select the files by opening the Edit menu and choosing the Select All command. Open the File menu and choose Properties. The Properties dialog box appears. Click the Read Only attribute to remove the check from the checkbox.

RUNNING THE DEMO PROGRAM

You may install additional modules of On-Demand Interactive Learning and find out more about PTS Learning Systems, the company behind the software, by using a file on the CD-ROM included with this book. Follow these steps:

1. Start your browser.
2. Select File from the menu.

3. Select Open.
4. Type **D:\info\welcome.htm**, where D is your CD-ROM drive.
5. Click OK to view the contents.

A

alignment How the right and left edges of text line up with the text immediately above and below—either left, center, right, or justified. Also refers to the type of tab stops—left, centered, right, or decimal.

anonymous FTP Scheme by which users can retrieve or upload files over the Internet without having an account on the remote system. Usually, the user logs in as anonymous and leaves his or her e-mail address as the password.

B

border Line that may appear above, below, and/or next to a paragraph or a table cell.

box Border that surrounds all four sides of one or more paragraphs or table cells.

browser Software program such as Internet Explorer, Netscape, CompuServe or America Online that can read and navigate HTML documents online.

C

cell Rectangular area in a table that can hold data and represents the intersection of one row and one column. A specific cell may be identified by its row and column number, counting from the upper left corner (for example, row 4, column 6).

Clipboard Temporary memory storage area that holds selections of text or graphics after a Cut or Copy command.

column Vertical arrangement of text on a page or a vertical set of adjacent cells in a table.

context-sensitive help Help feature that presents information relevant to a selected command or option.

D

data source Source document of personalized information to be inserted into a main document when producing a mail merge form letter.

document Organized set of text and/or graphic elements that is identified by a single name. The electronic form of a document stored on disk is also called a file.

F

field Designated and named area consisting of a set of alphanumeric codes that may be inserted into a document to hold a single piece of data, such as a name for a mail merge, or information from the computer or document, such as the current date or page number.

field character Double arrow braces that designate the beginning and end of a field.

field codes Elements of a field that include the field characters and the instructions.

file Electronic form of a document that is identified by a single name.

font General shape and attributes of characters. Depending on the printer capabilities, several font families are available, such as Courier, Helvetica, and Times Roman.

footer Special block of text that appears at the bottom of every page in a document.

format Appearance of characters, lines, or paragraphs in a document. The format of any text selection or an entire document can easily be modified in Word. Also used as a verb, as in "Format the selected text as right-aligned."

FTP (File Transfer Protocol) The way files are sent and received over the Internet. Typically, a user needs an account on the remote system unless it allows anonymous FTP access (see *anonymous FTP*).

H

hanging indent A paragraph indent in which the first line begins to the left of succeeding lines.

hard page break Marker within a document that forces the following text to start on a new page.

header Special block of text that appears at the top of every page in a document.

hyperlink Codes inserted in a document that allow you to jump from that location to another place in that document, another document, or another location on your network or on the Internet.

HTML HyperText Markup Language. The language that is used to define and describe the page layout of documents displayed in a World Wide Web browser.

I

Internet The global network of networks that enables some or all of the following: exchange of e-mail messages, files, Usenet newsgroups, and World Wide Web pages. Also known as the Net.

icon Graphic symbol or shape that can be clicked to activate an operation or program.

indent Horizontal distance between a paragraph's text boundary and the document's margin. Indents can be independently set for the left side, right side, and first line of a paragraph.

insertion point Blinking vertical bar in a document display that indicates where typed-in characters will appear. The insertion point's location can be reset to the mouse pointer's position with a single click.

L

list box Scrollable list (often, drop-down) of options from which a choice may be made. List boxes appear in the Standard and Formatting toolbars and many dialog boxes.

M

mail merge Process of combining a main document (such as a standard form letter) with personalized data (such as names and addresses) to create multiple, personalized form letters.

main document Basic document in a mail merge operation that contains the common text and graphics that appear in all final documents.

menu List of related commands. Each name in the menu bar represents a different menu that drops down when its name is clicked.

menu bar Horizontal bar near the top of a window, just below the title bar, that contains one or more menu names.

merge field In the main document, the reference to the related field in the data source document.

N

the Net Another term for the Internet.

Normal Name of the global template in Word. Also the name of a default style for body text.

P

points Measure of type size based on the height of capital letters. One inch equals 72 points. Abbreviation is pt or pts.

R

record Group of information (fields) about one thing or person, for instance, a record might include a person's name, address, city, state, and zip code.

row Horizontal set of adjacent cells in a table.

S

selection Designated portion of text, from a single character to an entire document, that is to be modified by a subsequent operation. Generally, a selection is displayed in highlighted or reverse color.

selection handle One of eight small black squares around the edge of a graphic. Resizing is done by dragging any of these handles.

snaking columns Page arrangement in which text continues from the bottom of one column to the top of the adjacent one.

soft page break Marker inserted into a document by the program to indicate where a full page ends and a new page begins. The locations of the soft page breaks are automatically adjusted when text and/or graphics are added to or deleted from a document.

Status bar Row of miscellaneous information along the bottom edge of the program window. This information includes the location of the insertion point and the status of certain operations such as Extend Selection or Overtype, which appear only during the operations.

style Defined and named set of character and paragraph formatting attributes that can be applied to any block of text in one step. Each style must be given a unique name.

T

table Arrangement of alphabetic and/or numeric information, organized into rows, columns, and cells.

template Generic, model document that may consist of basic formatting, styles, text, and/or graphics. Each newly-created document must be based on a template. When a new document is created, Word bases it on the default template called NORMAL.DOT.

text box Dialog box area where a user types input.

title bar Horizontal band along the top row of a window, containing the window's title. Dragging the title bar moves the entire window.

toolbar Usually located near the top, bottom, or side of a program window. This band of icons allows quick access to Word operations.

U

URL (Uniform Resource Locator) Standardized way in which any resource is identified within a Web document or to a Web browser. Most URLs consist of the service, host name, and directory path. An example of a URL is `http://www.idgbooks.com`

W

window Rectangular area that includes a variety of controls and informational displays for a program or document.

word wrap Function of a word processor that continues text entry to the next line automatically as you type.

World Wide Web Massive, distributed hypermedia environment that is part of the Internet. Consisting of millions of documents, thousands of sites, and dozens of indexes, the Web is a fluid and often surprising collection of information and activity.

3-D Settings toolbar, 161
3-D Shapes, creating and modifying, 161-162

A

Add/Modify FTP Locations dialog box, 251-252
Align Right button (Formatting toolbar), 114, 189
alignment of text, 113-114
  in tables, 189
  vertical, 214, 215
alternate still image, for video, 249
Anonymous users, FTP access, 252, 259
antonyms, 93-95
Arrow tool (Drawing toolbar), 158-159
audio, adding to Web page, 246-247
AutoArchive, for Journal, 274
AutoCorrect spelling checker, 88, 90-92
  turning off, 91
automatic formatting
  for borders, 177
  for bulleted or numbered lists, 122, 123
  for tables, 195-196
automatic page breaks, 50, 54
AutoRun, for installing Word, 280
AutoShapes tool (Drawing toolbar), 158
AutoText feature, 128
  applying, 145-146
  creating entries, 144-145
  and templates, 142-143
  troubleshooting, 149

B

Background Sound dialog box, 246-247
Backspace key, 3
backup files, automatic, 34
beginning of document, moving to, 50
beginning of line, moving to, 48
blank document, when starting Word, 27
blinking bar, 12. *See also* insertion point
block of text
  indenting, 111, 113
  printing, 220
  replacing, 33
  Shift-clicking to select, 75
body text, in outlines, 197
bold type, 4, 101-102
borders
  automatic formatting, 177
  line length, 182
  for paragraphs, 177-178
  for tables, 194
Borders and Shading dialog box, 178
  Shading tab, 179
Borders toolbar, 179
bottom margin, default settings, 109
Break dialog box, 51-52, 175

B–D

browsing, hard drives, 39
browsing the Web
using hyperlinks, 257
from Word, 254
bulleted lists, 122
automatic creation, 133
creating, 122-123
Bullets button (Formatting toolbar), 123

C

canceling, printing, 221
capitalization, automatic, 88
Caps Lock key, 88
CD-KEY, for Word, 281
CD-ROM
contents for enclosed, 304-307
copying files to hard disk from, 10-11
installing Word from, 280-283
cells in tables, text entry, 188-189
Center button (Formatting toolbar), 114
centering, 111, 114
centering text on page vertically, 214, 215
character formatting, basics, 100-101
Check for Errors button (Mail Merge toolbar), 236
Checking and Reporting Errors dialog box, 236-237
circles, creating, 169
clip art gallery, 154
clip art, inserting, 155-156
closing
document window, 37-38
documents, 13, 34
menus, 14
windows, 11
Collapse button (Outline toolbar), 201
collating printed copies, 221
color
of font, 101
of object, 166
columns, 172-173
creating, 173
editing, 174
troubleshooting, 182
Columns dialog box, 174, 176
columns in tables
inserting and deleting, 191-193
width adjustment, 194
combining paragraphs, 31
commands
help for, 18-19
mouse to execute, 22
computer clock, 28
Concurrent mode, for CD-ROM interactive software, 305, 306
context-sensitive help, 18
Continuous option, for section break, 175
Convert Text to Table dialog box, 187
copy and paste, 77-78
between Office documents, 264-265
vs. linking Excel worksheet, 277
copy of document, creating by saving with different name, 37
copying
files from CD-ROM, 10-11
formatting, 142
Cover Sheet dialog box (Fax Wizard), 42
Create AutoText dialog box, 145
Create Data Source dialog box, 231
Create New Folder dialog box, 35-36
Current Page print option, 220
Custom install, 282
cut and paste, 76-77
merge fields, 241

D

Data Form dialog box, 232
data source file for mail merge, 228, 236
creating, 230-232
entering names and addresses, 232-233
Date and Time dialog box, 27-28
{DATE} field, in header or footer, 133

dates
automatic updates, 44
entering, 27
default settings
for fonts, 100, 118
for labels, 223
for margins, 106
for tabs, 106
for Word window, 13
deleting
page break, 52-53, 56
paragraph marks, 31
records in data source file, 233
rows and columns in tables, 191-193
section breaks, 175
styles, 141, 148
text, 3, 75-76
words, 4
Demo mode, for CD-ROM interactive software, 304, 306
Demote button (Outline toolbar), 200
demoting outline headings, 65, 197
dialog boxes, 4
closing, 22
ellipsis (...) to indicate, 13
dictionary, adding word to, 92
Document buttons, 12-13
Document Map, in Online Layout view, 61-62, 251
Document to Fax dialog box, 41, 42
document window, 12
closing, 13, 34, 38
minimizing and maximizing, 12-13
documents
closing, 34
creating, 26
discarding changes to, 38
locating, 44
moving through, 49-50
saving, 5-6, 34, 35-36
selecting entire, 75
drag and drop
to move text, 79-80
troubleshooting, 84
Draw Table feature, 187
Drawing button (Standard toolbar), 158
Drawing toolbar, 160
3-D button, 161
Arrow tool, 158
AutoShapes tool, 158
Fill Color tool, 166
Line Style tool, 166
Rectangle tool, 158
Text Box tool, 159

E

Edit menu
Go To, 52
Paste Special, 266, 268
Replace, 80
editing
columns, 174
text, 3-4
troubleshooting, 84
ellipsis (...), menu commands with, 13
embedding
Excel worksheet in Word document, 270
Office documents, 262, 267-269
end of document, moving to, 50
end of line, moving to, 48
Envelopes and Labels dialog box
Envelopes tab, 222-223
Labels tab, 223-224
envelopes, printing, 222-223
Eraser button (Tables and Borders toolbar), 209
Even Page option, for section break, 175
even pages, header or footer for, 128
Excel chart, inserting in Word document, 272-273
Excel worksheet
inserting in Word document, 271-272
linking or embedding, 270
exiting Microsoft Word, 20

F

fast formatting, 141-142
fax, in printer list, 220
fax cover sheet
template to create, 143-144
wizard to create, 40-42

F–H

Fax Software dialog box, 42
fields in data source file, 229
file list, viewing, 39
File menu
Close, 34, 37-38
New, 26, 40-41
Open, 14, 38-40
Page Setup, 109, 215
Print, 5, 218-221
File menu *(continued)*
Save, 5-6, 34, 37, 248
Save As HTML, 245
file types, 36
filenames, 6, 36
files. *See also* **documents**
printing to, 221
Fill Color tool (Drawing toolbar), 166
Find and Replace dialog box, 52, 80-82
First Line Indent Marker, 112
floppy disks, file backups on, 34
folders
changing in Open dialog box, 39
creating, 10-11, 35-36
Font dialog box, 4, 103, 105
advantages, 100-101
fonts, 100, 101
changing, 102-103
changing default, 118
minimum size for HTML document, 250
size of, 104-105
for text in tables, 190
footers
creating, 127-128
formatting, 129-130
Page Layout view for, 128
Format menu
Borders and Shading, 178
Bullets and Numbering, 123, 124, 202
Columns, 172, 174
Font, 4, 103
Paragraph, 111, 114-115
Tabs, 106
Text Direction, 190
Format Painter, Undo command for, 149
formatting. *See also* **styles**
character, 100-101
copying, 142
fast, 141-142
headers and footers, 129-130
for page numbers, 127
sections, 176
tables, 194-196
text, 4-5
troubleshooting, 118, 133
troubleshooting shortcuts, 148-149
Formatting toolbar, 15, 16-17, 100
Align Right button, 114, 189
Alignment choices, 111
Bold button, 102
Borders drop-down, 179
Bullets button, 123
Center button, 114
Font Size, 104
Indent tools, 113
Italic button, 102
Style drop-down list, 138, 139
Underline button, 102
FTP addresses, 251, 259
FTP site, sending Web page to, 251-253
function keys
F1 for help, 18
F4 for Repeat, 142, 149
F5 for Go To, 52

G

Go To command, 51
grammar checker, 89, 92-93
Grammar dialog box, 92
Grammar shortcut menu, 95
graphics. *See also* **objects**
adding objects, 154
alternate still image for video, 249
selecting objects, 162
shapes and lines, 157-159
troubleshooting, 169
WordArt, 156-157

H

Hanging Indent Marker, 112
hard drives, 10
browsing, 39
hard page break, 51
hard return, inserting, 30

Header and Footer toolbar, 128, 129
headers
creating, 127-128
formatting, 129-130
Page Layout view for, 128
headings in outlines, 197
viewing, 201
help, 18-19
hiding toolbars, 18
horizontal print orientation, 225
horizontal scroll bar, 53
HTML (HyperText Markup Language), 244
See also **Web pages**
hyperlinks, 255-256
browsing through files containing, 257
creating to move between Office documents, 263-264
hyphenation, 110

I

I-beam, 12
icons
file list as, 39
restoring document window from, 22
indenting, 112-113
block of text, 111, 113
Paragraph dialog box measurements, 115
paragraphs, 106
Insert Hyperlink dialog box, 256, 263-264
Insert key, 33
Insert menu
Background Sound, 246-247
Break, 51-52, 175
Date and Time, 27
Hyperlink, 256
Object, 203, 272
Page Numbers, 126
Picture, 155
Picture, WordArt, 156
Video, 248
Insert mode, 3, 31-32
Insert Object dialog box, 272
for organization chart, 203
Insert Rows button (Standard toolbar), 191
Insert Table tool (Standard toolbar), 186, 187
inserting
clip art, 155-156
Excel chart in Word document, 272-273
Excel worksheet in Word document, 271-272
hard return, 30
page break, 51-52
rows and columns in tables, 191-193
tables, 186-187
text, 31-32
insertion point, 3, 12
clicking mouse to place, 3
and scrolling, 49, 55
temporary for drag and drop, 79-80
installing Word from CD-ROM, 280-283
Internet
document as viewed on, 58
publishing Web page to, 245
Web browser to access, 259
ISP (Internet service provider), 244
italics type, 101-102

J

Journal (Outlook)
document tracking in, 273
options for, 274
justified alignment, 111
Justified vertical alignment, 215

K

keyboard shortcuts
for copy and paste (Ctrl+C; Ctrl+V), 78
for cut and paste (Ctrl+X; Ctrl+V), 77
for date (Alt+Shift+D), 27
for hanging indent (Ctrl+T), 113
for indenting paragraphs (Ctrl+M), 113
for line spacing (Ctrl+1; Ctrl+5), 115

(continued)

Index

keyboard shortcuts *(continued)*
for page break (Ctrl+Enter), 52
for selecting all text (Ctrl+A), 115
for selecting text (Shift-clicking), 73
for text effects, 105
for time (Alt+Shift+T), 27

L

labels, printing, 223-224
landscape orientation, 225
laser printer, margins for, 226
leader character, for tab stops, 108
left alignment, 111
Left Indent symbol, 112
left margin, default settings, 109
line styles
changing for objects, 165-166
for organization chart, 205
lines
between columns, 174
inserting, 157-159
lines of text
hard return to end, 30
selecting, 74
spacing, 111-112, 114-115
linking
Excel worksheet to Word document, 270
Office documents, 262, 265-267
vs. copying and pasting, 277
lists, 122
bulleted, 122-123, 133
numbered, 124-125
Loop option for sound, 247

M

mail merge
data source file creation, 230-232
main document creation, 229-230
to printer, 237-238
process, 236-238
setting up, 228-229
troubleshooting, 240-241
viewing and checking, 236-237
what it is, 228
Mail Merge Helper dialog box, 229-230
Mail Merge toolbar, 235
Check for Errors button, 236
Edit Data Source button, 241
Insert Merge Field button, 234
Merge to Printer button, 237
main document for mail merge, 228, 235
creating, 229-230
placing merge fields in, 234
manual page break, 51, 54
margins, 106, 109
troubleshooting, 226
and vertical alignment, 215
maximizing document window, 13
menu bar, 14
menus, 13
closing, 14, 22
merge fields, adding to main merge document, 234
Merge to Printer button (Mail Merge toolbar), 237
Microsoft Clip Gallery dialog box, 155
Microsoft Office applications
Publish to the Web wizard, 253
sharing, 262-263
Microsoft Office documents
copying and pasting between, 264-265
embedding, 267-269
hyperlinks to move between, 263-264
linking, 265-267
troubleshooting integration, 277
Microsoft Outlook, 230-231, 263
Microsoft Word
blank document when starting, 27
exiting, 20
installing from CD-ROM, 280-283
opening, 2, 11-12
troubleshooting basics, 22
Microsoft Word 97 Setup screen, 280
Microsoft Word document
closing, 37-38
linking Excel worksheet to, 270
opening in Outlook, 273-275
tracking in Outlook, 277
Microsoft Word window, 12
default settings for, 13

minimizing, document window, 12-13
mistakes, correcting, 3
mouse, to execute command, 22
mouse pointer, 12. *See also* insertion point
moving. *See* navigating
  objects, 163-164
  organization chart, 206
moving text. *See also* cut and paste
  drag and drop for, 79-80
MSOrganization Chart 2.0 program, 203-205
multiple actions,, undoing, 79
My Computer window, for folder creation, 10

N

navigating, 48-50
  troubleshooting, 55-56
New button (Standard toolbar), 26
New dialog box, 40-41
New Style dialog box, 140
newspaper-style columns, 172
Next Page option, for section break, 175
Normal view, 58
  switching to, 13
NORMAL.DOT template, 27, 142
  default font, 100
numbered lists, 122
  creating, 124-125
numbering outlines, 202
numbering pages, 126-127

O

objects
  adding, 154
  changing line styles, 165-166
  colors and patterns, 166
  moving, 163-164
  resizing, 164-165
  selecting, 162
Odd Page option, for section break, 175
odd pages, header or footer for, 128
Office Assistant, 19-20
Online Layout view, 58, 61-62, 244, 250-251
Open dialog box, 14, 39
opening
  documents, 38-40
  Microsoft Word, 2, 11-12
Options dialog box
  Edit tab, 33
  View tab, 62
organization chart
  changing, 205-206
  creating, 203-205
  moving and resizing, 206
orphans, 140
outline headings, promoting or demoting, 65
Outline toolbar, 64, 198, 199
  Collapse button, 201
  Demote button, 200
  Promote button, 200
Outline view, 59, 62-63
Outline View button (Status bar), 198
outlines
  creating, 196-199
  modifying, 65, 200-201
  viewing headings, 201
Outlook, opening Word document in, 273-275
ovals, creating, 169
overwriting text, 32-33
OVR indicator, on Status bar, 32-33

P

page breaks, 54
  deleting, 52-53, 56
  hard, 51
  inserting, 51-52, 126
  soft, 50
page indicator, on Status bar, 52
Page Layout view, 59
  for columns, 173
  header and footer display in, 128
  switching to, 59-60
page numbers
  removing from title page, 133
  ScreenTip feature to display, 50
Page Numbers dialog box, 126

P–S

Page Setup dialog box, 214
  Layout tab, 128, 215
  Margins tab, 109
  troubleshooting, 225
{PAGE} field, in header or footer, 133
pages
  moving to specific, 52
  numbering, 126-127
  selecting for printing, 220
Paragraph dialog box, 115
paragraph marks
  deleting, 31
  displaying, 30
paragraphs
  applying style to single, 138
  borders for, 177-178
  combining, 31
  indenting, 106
  selecting, 74
  separating, 30-31
  shading for, 179-180
Paste button (Standard toolbar), 77
Paste Special dialog box, 266, 268
pasting. *See* **copy and paste; cut and paste**
patterns, for objects, 166
point, 100
portrait orientation, 225
practice projects, 285-291
preview
  in dialog boxes, 4
  in Style dialog box, 138
Print dialog box, 5, 218-221
  Properties button, 219
Print Preview, 214-215, 216-217
Print Preview toolbar, Zoom box, 216, 217
printer
  mail merge to, 237-238
  selecting, 220
printing, 5, 214-215
  canceling, 221
  collating when, 221
  envelopes, 222-223
  labels, 223-224
  troubleshooting, 225-226
Product ID, for Word, 281
Promote button (Outline toolbar), 200
promoting outline headings, 65, 197
proofreading
  grammar checker, 92-93
  spelling check, 90-92
  thesaurus, 93-95
  troubleshooting, 97
Publish to the Web wizard, 253
publishing Web page to Internet, 245

R

ragged right text, 111
records in data source file, 229
  adding, 232-233, 241
  deleting, 233
Rectangle tool (Drawing toolbar), 158
Repeat key (F4), 142, 149
repeated words, speller check alert for, 89
resizing
  objects, 164-165
  organization chart, 206
right-aligned text, 111
right margin, default settings, 109
rotating text in tables, 190-191
rows in tables
  changing height, 194
  inserting and deleting, 191-193
ruler, 110
  displaying, 13
  removing tab stop from, 107
Run from CD-ROM, as install option, 282

S

Save As dialog box, 6, 35-36, 251
Save As HTML dialog box, 245
saving documents, 5-6, 34, 35-36
Schedule+, as data source, 231
screens, moving between, 48
ScreenTip feature, 17
  displaying, 22
  for page number, 50
scroll bars, 49-50, 53
section breaks, 172, 174-176
sections, 172
  formatting, 176

selecting
- objects, 162
- pages for printing, 220

selecting text, 73-75
- keyboard shortcuts for, 73, 115
- in tables, 189
- troubleshooting, 84

selection handles, 267
- for graphic, 156

Selection print option, 220
sentence, selecting, 74
separating paragraphs, 30-31
shading, for paragraphs, 179-180
shapes
- creating and modifying 3-D, 161-162
- inserting, 157-159

sharing Microsoft Office applications, 262-263
shortcut menus, 13-15
Show/Hide (¶) button (Standard toolbar), 30
sizing handles, of object, 164
small capitals, 104-105
snaking columns, 172
soft page break, 50
source document, for linking, 265
Spelling and Grammar dialog box, 91
spelling check, 90-92
Spelling shortcut menu, 91, 94
squares, drawing, 158
Standard toolbar, 15, 16
- Columns button, 173
- Cut button, 77
- displaying, 13
- Drawing button, 158
- editing and undo tools, 82
- Insert Columns button, 192
- Insert Microsoft Excel Worksheet button, 271
- Insert Rows button, 191
- Insert Table tool, 186, 187
- New button, 17, 26
- Paste button, 77
- Print button, 218
- Print Preview, 216-217
- Save button, 35, 37
- Show/Hide (¶) button, 30
- Spelling and Grammar button, 91
- Undo, 76
- Web Toolbar button, 254
- Zoom control, 58, 60-61

Start menu, Programs, 12
Start option for video, 249
starting Microsoft Word, 2, 11-12
Status bar, 12, 15, 17
- Outline View button, 198
- OVR indicator, 32-33
- page indicator, 52

Style dialog box, 138
styles, 136-137
- applying, 137-138
- creating, 139-141
- deleting, 141, 148
- locating, 148
- viewing contents, 138

subheadings
- collapsing, 201
- in outlines, 197

symbols, fonts for, 118
synonyms, 93-95

T

Tab key, 106
tab stops, 106
- clearing all, 108, 118
- setting, 106-108

Table AutoFormat dialog box, 209
Table menu
- AutoFormat, 195-196
- Convert Table to Text, 189
- Convert Text to Table, 187
- Delete Columns, 193
- Delete Rows, 191, 193
- dimmed commands on, 209
- Insert Columns, 193
- Insert Rows, 191, 193
- Show/Hide Gridlines, 194-195

tables
- column width adjustment, 194
- creating, 186
- fonts for text, 190
- formatting, 194-196
- inserting, 186-187
- inserting and deleting rows and columns, 191-193

(continued)

T–V

tables *(continued)*
- rotating text, 190-191
- selecting and aligning text, 189
- text entry in cell, 188-189
- troubleshooting, 209

Tables and Borders toolbar
- dimmed commands on, 209
- Eraser button, 209

target document, for linking, 265
Teacher mode, for CD-ROM interactive software, 304, 306
templates, 26
- and AutoText, 142-143
- and styles, 136-137

temporary insertion point, for drag and drop, 79-80
text
- changes to, 72-73
- deleting, 3, 75-76
- editing, 3-4
- entering, 3, 28-29
- formatting, 4-5
- inserting, 31-32
- overwriting, 32-33

Text Box tool (Drawing toolbar), 159
Text Direction Table Cell dialog box, 190-191
thesaurus, 89, 93-95
Thesaurus dialog box, 94, 95
thickness, of object lines, 165-166
time, entering, 27-28
{TIME} field, in header or footer, 133
title bar, 12
title page, removing page numbers from, 133
Toolbar shortcut menu, 13
toolbars, 15-18
- hiding, 18
- restoring for Word, 277

Tools menu
- AutoCorrect, 90
- Envelopes and Labels, 222-224
- Language, 93
- Language, Hyphenation, 110
- Mail Merge, 229-230
- Options, 33

top margin, default settings, 109
troubleshooting
- columns, 182
- document navigation, 55-56
- document operation basics, 44-45
- document views, 66
- editing, 84
- formatting, 118, 133
- formatting shortcuts, 148-149
- graphics, 169
- Mail Merge, 240-241
- Microsoft Word basics, 22
- Office document integration, 277
- printing, 225-226
- printing and headers and footers, 130
- proofreading, 97
- tables, 209
- Web pages, 259-260

type size, 4
Typical install, 281

U

underline, 101-102
- green wavy, 89
- red wavy, 30, 88

Underline button (Formatting toolbar), 102
Undo/Redo command, 76, 78-79
for Format Painter, 149
URL, 253
user profile, in Outlook, 273

V

vertical alignment, 214, 215
vertical printing orientation, 225
vertical scroll bar, 53
video, adding to Web page, 248-250
Video Clip dialog box, 248
View menu
- Document Map, 251
- Header and Footer, 129
- Normal view, 13, 61
- Ruler, 13

View toolbar, 12, 15, 58, 63
- Online Layout view button, 250

views, 58
troubleshooting, 66

W

Web browser, 244
to access Internet, 259
Web pages, 244
adding audio, 246-247
adding video, 248-250
hyperlinks, 255-256
minimum font size for, 250
Online Layout view for, 250-251
publishing to Internet, 245
sending to FTP site, 251-253
troubleshooting, 259-260
Web toolbar, 253, 254
white, as line color, 169
Widow/Orphan control, 140
Window menu, to switch between open documents, 40
windows, closing, 11
Windows Taskbar, Printer icon, 221
wizards, 26
for document creation, 40-42
WMF file extension, 154
Word. *See* **Microsoft Word**
word wrap, 28, 29, 44
WordArt, 156-157
words
adding to dictionary, 92
deleting, 4
hyphenating, 110
moving between, 48
selecting, 74-75
World Wide Web, browsing from Word, 254

Z

Zoom box (Print Preview toolbar), 216, 217
Zoom control (Standard toolbar), 58, 60-61
zoom features, 59, 60-61, 66

Now it's easy to remember what you just learned and more...

With *On-Demand*, you'll never rely on the help function again – or your money back.

Introducing *On-Demand Interactive Learning*™ — the remarkable software that actually makes corrections to your documents for you. Unlike the standard help function that merely provides "canned" responses to your requests for help or makes you write down a list of complicated instructions, *On-Demand* lets you learn while you work.

Concurrent Mode — makes the ***changes for you*** right in your document.

Teacher Mode — ***guides you*** step-by-step to make changes safely outside your document.

Demo Mode — ***shows you*** how the changes are made safely outside your document.

Let *On-Demand* take care of the software commands for you. Just follow the on-screen pointer and fill in the information, and you'll learn in the fastest and easiest way possible — without ever leaving your document.

In fact, *On-Demand* makes your work so easy, it's *guaranteed* to help you finish complicated documents neatly and on time. With over eleven years in software education and a development staff that's logged more than 5,000 hours of classroom teaching time, it's no wonder that Fortune 500 corporations around the world use *On-Demand* to make learning for their employees quicker and more effective.

"On-Demand Interactive Learning for Word 97. The best training title of this group..."
—PC World

The Concurrent Mode Difference

Concurrent Mode guides you through learning new functions without having to stop for directions. Right before your eyes, a moving pointer clicks on the right buttons and icons for you and then lets you fill in the information.

"On-Demand lets me get my work done and learn without slowing me down." —Rosemarie Hasson, Quad Micro

TITLES AVAILABLE FOR: Windows® 3.1, 95, NT, Microsoft® Word, Microsoft Excel, Microsoft PowerPoint, Microsoft Access, Microsoft Internet Explorer, Lotus® SmartSuite, Lotus Notes, and more! Call for additional titles.

30 DAY GUARANTEE:
Try *On-Demand* at the introductory price of **$32.95** (U.S. dollars) for one title or pay **$29.95** (U.S. dollars) each for two titles. That's a savings of almost 10%. Use *On-Demand* for 30 days. If you don't learn more in a shorter period of time, simply return the software to PTS Learning Systems with your receipt for a full refund (this guarantee is good only for purchases made directly from PTS).

Call PTS at 800-387-8878 ext. 3053 or 610-337-8878 ext. 3053 outside the U.S.

(Do not call PTS for technical support. Refer to the IDG Books Worldwide consumer customer service toll-free phone number in the front of this book.)

IDG103197

IDG BOOKS WORLDWIDE, INC.
END-USER LICENSE AGREEMENT

Read This. You should carefully read these terms and conditions before opening the software packet(s) included with this book ("Book"). This is a license agreement ("Agreement") between you and IDG Books Worldwide, Inc. ("IDGB"). By opening the accompanying software packet(s), you acknowledge that you have read and accept the following terms and conditions. If you do not agree and do not want to be bound by such terms and conditions, promptly return the Book and the unopened software packet(s) to the place you obtained them for a full refund.

1. **License Grant.** IDGB grants to you (either an individual or entity) a nonexclusive license to use one copy of the enclosed software program(s) (collectively, the "Software") solely for your own personal or business purposes on a single computer (whether a standard computer or a workstation component of a multiuser network). The Software is in use on a computer when it is loaded into temporary memory (i.e., RAM) or installed into permanent memory (e.g., hard disk, CD-ROM, or other storage device). IDGB reserves all rights not expressly granted herein.

2. **Ownership.** IDGB is the owner of all right, title, and interest, including copyright, in and to the compilation of the Software recorded on the disk(s)/CD-ROM. Copyright to the individual programs on the disk(s)/CD-ROM is owned by the author or other authorized copyright owner of each program. Ownership of the Software and all proprietary rights relating thereto remain with IDGB and its licensors.

3. **Restrictions on Use and Transfer.**

   (a) You may only (i) make one copy of the Software for backup or archival purposes, or (ii) transfer the Software to a single hard disk, provided that you keep the original for backup or archival purposes. You may not (i) rent or lease the Software, (ii) copy or reproduce the Software through a LAN or other network system or through any computer subscriber system or bulletin-board system, or (iii) modify, adapt, or create derivative works based on the Software.

   (b) You may not reverse engineer, decompile, or disassemble the Software. You may transfer the Software and user documentation on a permanent basis, provided that the transferee agrees to accept the terms and conditions of this Agreement and you retain no copies. If the Software is an update or has been updated, any transfer must include the most recent update and all prior versions.

4. **Restrictions on Use of Individual Programs.** You must follow the individual requirements and restrictions detailed for each individual program in Appendix D, "What's on the CD-ROM." These limitations are contained in the individual license agreements recorded on the disk(s)/CD-ROM. These restrictions may include a requirement that after using the program for the period of time specified in its text, the user must pay a registration fee or discontinue use. By opening the Software packet(s), you will be agreeing to abide by the licenses and restrictions for these individual programs. None of the material on this disk(s) or listed in this Book may ever be distributed, in original or modified form, for commercial purposes.

5. **Limited Warranty.**

(a) IDGB warrants that the Software and disk(s)/CD-ROM are free from defects in materials and workmanship under normal use for a period of sixty (60) days from the date of purchase of this Book. If IDGB receives notification within the warranty period of defects in materials or workmanship, IDGB will replace the defective disk(s)/CD-ROM.

(b) IDGB AND THE AUTHOR OF THE BOOK DISCLAIM ALL OTHER WARRANTIES, EXPRESS OR IMPLIED, INCLUDING WITHOUT LIMITATION IMPLIED WARRANTIES OF MERCHANTABILITY AND FITNESS FOR A PARTICULAR PURPOSE, WITH RESPECT TO THE SOFTWARE, THE PROGRAMS, THE SOURCE CODE CONTAINED THEREIN, AND/OR THE TECHNIQUES DESCRIBED IN THIS BOOK. IDGB DOES NOT WARRANT THAT THE FUNCTIONS CONTAINED IN THE SOFTWARE WILL MEET YOUR REQUIREMENTS OR THAT THE OPERATION OF THE SOFTWARE WILL BE ERROR FREE.

(c) This limited warranty gives you specific legal rights, and you may have other rights which vary from jurisdiction to jurisdiction.

6. **Remedies.**

(a) IDGB's entire liability and your exclusive remedy for defects in materials and workmanship shall be limited to replacement of the Software, which may be returned to IDGB with a copy of your receipt at the following address: Disk Fulfillment Department, Attn: *Word 97 One Step at a Time*, IDG Books Worldwide, Inc., 7260 Shadeland Station, Ste. 100, Indianapolis, IN 46256, or call 1-800-762-2974. Please allow 3-4 weeks for delivery. This Limited Warranty is void if failure of the Software has resulted from accident, abuse, or misapplication. Any replacement Software will be warranted for the remainder of the original warranty period or thirty (30) days, whichever is longer.

(b) In no event shall IDGB or the author be liable for any damages whatsoever (including without limitation damages for loss of business profits, business interruption, loss of business information, or any other pecuniary loss) arising from the use of or inability to use the Book or the Software, even if IDGB has been advised of the possibility of such damages.

(c) Because some jurisdictions do not allow the exclusion or limitation of liability for consequential or incidental damages, the above limitation or exclusion may not apply to you.

7. **U.S. Government Restricted Rights.** Use, duplication, or disclosure of the Software by the U.S. Government is subject to restrictions stated in paragraph (c) (1) (ii) of the Rights in Technical Data and Computer Software clause of DFARS 252.227-7013, and in subparagraphs (a) through (d) of the Commercial Computer—Restricted Rights clause at FAR 52.227-19, and in similar clauses in the NASA FAR supplement, when applicable.

8. **General.** This Agreement constitutes the entire understanding of the parties and revokes and supersedes all prior agreements, oral or written, between them and may not be modified or amended except in a writing signed by both parties hereto which specifically refers to this Agreement. This Agreement shall take precedence over any other documents that may be in conflict herewith. If any one or more provisions contained in this Agreement are held by any court or tribunal to be invalid, illegal, or otherwise unenforceable, each and every other provision shall remain in full force and effect.

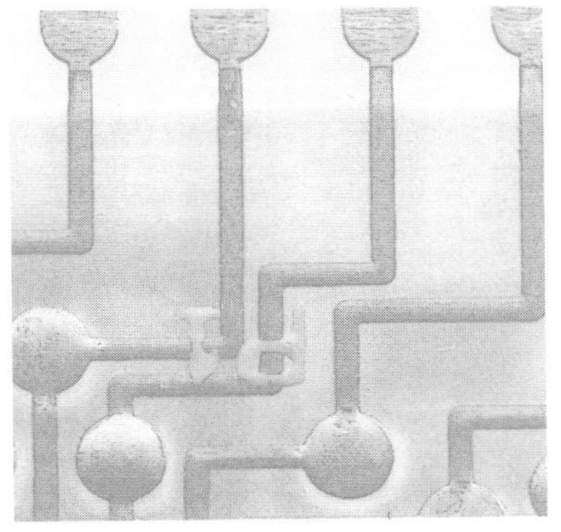

CD-ROM Installation Instructions

The CD-ROM includes the interactive *One Step at a Time On-Demand* software. This software coaches you through the exercises in the book while you work on a computer at your own pace.

INSTALLING THE ONE STEP AT A TIME ON-DEMAND INTERACTIVE SOFTWARE

The *One Step at a Time On-Demand* software can be installed on Windows 95, and Windows NT 4.0. To install the interactive software on your computer, follow these steps:

1. Launch Windows (if you haven't already).
2. Place the *Word 97 One Step at a Time* CD-ROM in your CD-ROM drive.
3. Click the Start menu.
4. Select Run. The Run dialog box appears.
5. Type **D:\Setup.exe** (where D is your CD-ROM drive) in the Run dialog box.

For Windows 3.1 users, go to Program Manager, choose File, and select Run. The Run dialog box appears. Type **D:\Setup.exe** *(where D is your CD-ROM drive) in the Run dialog box to begin installing the software.*

6. Click OK to run the setup procedure. The On-Demand Installation dialog box appears.
7. Click Continue. The On-Demand Installation Options dialog box appears.

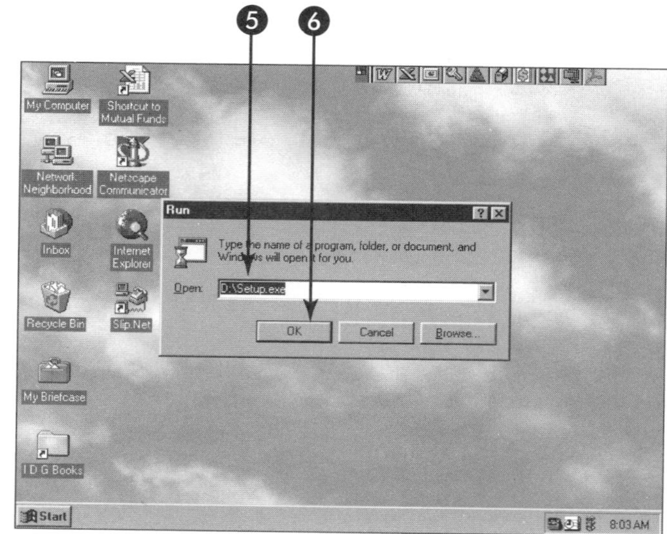

8. Click the Full/Network radio button (if this option is not already selected).

Full/Network installation requires approximately 150MB of hard disk space. If you don't have enough hard disk space, click the Standard radio button to choose Standard installation. If you choose standard installation, you should always insert the CD-ROM when you start the software to hear sound.

9. Click Next. The Determine Installation Drive and Directory dialog box appears.
10. Choose the default drive and directory that appears, or click Change to choose a different drive and directory.
11. Click Next. The Product Selection dialog box appears, which enables you to verify the software you want to install.
12. Click Finish to complete the installation. The On-Demand Installation dialog box displays the progress of the installation. After the installation, the Multiuser Pack Registration dialog box appears.
13. Enter information in the Multiuser Pack Registration dialog box.
14. Click OK. The On-Demand Installation dialog box appears.
15. Click OK to confirm the installation has been successfully completed.

Please see Appendix D, "What's on the CD-ROM," for information about running the *One Step at a Time On-Demand* interactive software.

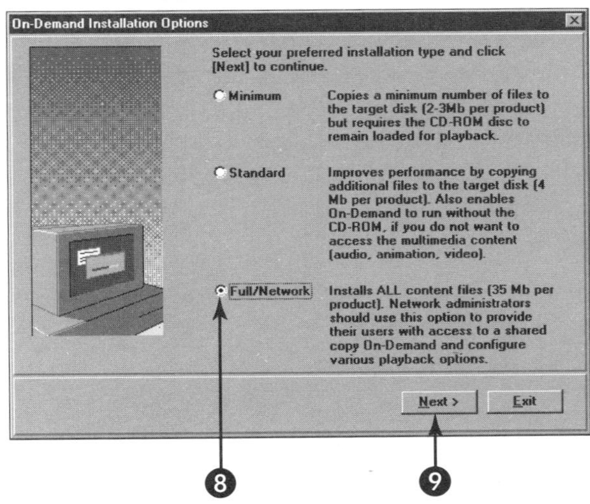

INSTALLING THE EXERCISE FILES

To access the exercise files for the lessons in this book, you'll need to set up a folder for the exercise files on your hard drive (also covered in Lesson 1). Follow these steps:

1. Double-click the My Computer icon on your desktop.

2. In the My Computer window, double-click the hard drive (C:).
3. Select the File menu.
4. Click New.
5. Choose Folder from the submenu.

   A new folder appears at the end of the list, with the name New Folder.
6. Type **One Step** to name the folder.
7. Press Enter.
8. Place the *Word 97 One Step at a Time* CD-ROM that accompanies this book into the CD-ROM drive.
9. In the My Computer window, double-click the CD-ROM icon to open the drive where you inserted the disc.
10. In the CD-ROM window, copy the folder named Exercise by selecting it and pressing Ctrl-C. Then, close the CD-ROM window and all other open windows.
11. Double-click My Computer.
12. Double-click the hard drive (C:).
13. Double-click the One Step folder.
14. Paste the Exercise folder into the One Step folder by pressing Ctrl-V. All of the exercise files are now located within the Exercise folder, inside the One Step folder.

USING THE EXERCISE FILES

You need to make sure that you have removed the Read Only attribute from the file(s) you copied to your hard drive before you start using those files. Otherwise, when you attempt to save your work, your screen will display an error message. To remove the attribute, open the Exercise folder (inside the One Step folder) on your hard drive. Select the files by opening the Edit menu and choosing the Select All command. Open the File menu and choose Properties. The Properties dialog box appears. Click the Read Only attribute to remove the check from the checkbox.